D1431999

The Decline of Natural Law

The Decline of Natural Law

How American Lawyers Once Used Natural Law and Why They Stopped

STUART BANNER

OXFORD
UNIVERSITY PRESS

OXFORD
UNIVERSITY PRESS

Oxford University Press is a department of the University of Oxford. It furthers
the University's objective of excellence in research, scholarship, and education
by publishing worldwide. Oxford is a registered trade mark of Oxford University
Press in the UK and certain other countries.

Published in the United States of America by Oxford University Press
198 Madison Avenue, New York, NY 10016, United States of America.

© Oxford University Press 2021

Library of Congress Cataloging-in-Publication Data
Names: Banner, Stuart, 1963– author.
Title: The decline of natural law : how American lawyers once used natural law
and why they stopped / Stuart Banner, UCLA School of Law.
Description: New York, NY : Oxford University Press, 2021. |
Includes bibliographical references and index.
Identifiers: LCCN 2020043255 (print) | LCCN 2020043256 (ebook) |
ISBN 9780197556498 (hardback) | ISBN 9780197556511 (epub)
Subjects: LCSH: Natural law. | Common law. | Religion and law.
Classification: LCC K450 .B36 2021 (print) | LCC K450 (ebook) | DDC 340/.112—dc23
LC record available at https://lccn.loc.gov/2020043255
LC ebook record available at https://lccn.loc.gov/2020043256

DOI: 10.1093/oso/9780197556498.001.0001

CONTENTS

Acknowledgments   vii

INTRODUCTION   1

PART I: BEFORE THE TRANSITION

1. THE LAW OF NATURE   11
2. THE COMMON LAW   46

PART II: CAUSES OF THE TRANSITION

3. THE ADOPTION OF WRITTEN CONSTITUTIONS   71
4. THE SEPARATION OF LAW AND RELIGION   96
5. THE EXPLOSION IN LAW PUBLISHING   119
6. THE TWO-SIDEDNESS OF NATURAL LAW   137

PART III: THE TRANSITION AND AFTER

7. THE DECLINE OF NATURAL LAW AND CUSTOM   167
8. SUBSTITUTES FOR NATURAL LAW   188
9. ECHOES OF NATURAL LAW   222

Index   251

ACKNOWLEDGMENTS

I'd like to thank Mark Greenberg, Dick Helmholz, Maximo Langer, Seana Shiffrin, participants in colloquia at UCLA and SUNY Buffalo, and the readers for Oxford University Press, who all offered extraordinarily helpful suggestions.

Introduction

This book is about a fundamental change in American legal thought that took place in the late 19th and early 20th centuries. Before the change, natural law played an important role in our legal system. Lawyers believed that human affairs were governed in significant part by laws of nature, laws that could be discovered in much the same way as the natural laws governing the nonhuman realm. These laws were understood to have an existence independent of human volition. They were not human creations. Before the change described in this book, for example, the law forbidding murder was understood to be a natural principle that regulated the behavior of human beings. It was a law that we *found*, not one that we *made*. To be sure, nations might enact legislation forbidding murder, but American lawyers before 1870 or so would have said, with virtual unanimity, that murder would still be illegal even in a nation that had not enacted any such legislation. It would be illegal because murder was contrary to the law of nature. The law forbidding murder was like the law of gravity or the laws of optics. It was a law that existed in nature, waiting to be discovered—not made—by humans.

This understanding of law almost completely disappeared from the legal system in the late 19th and early 20th centuries. After the change, lawyers believed that natural law plays no role in our legal system. Today, lawyers still consider murder to be wrong, of course, and they would deplore as grossly deficient the legal system of any nation that fails to prohibit murder. But they would say that murder is not illegal in that nation. Lawyers once believed that some of the rules of our legal system were not created by humans. They now believe that all the rules of the legal system are created by humans. In 1850, when a lawyer spoke in court, it would have been entirely normal for the lawyer to discuss the law of nature alongside statutes and court decisions as acknowledged sources of law. Today, if a lawyer tries to discuss natural law in court, the judge will look puzzled, and opposing counsel will start planning the victory party. Natural law is no longer a part of a lawyer's toolkit.

The Decline of Natural Law. Stuart Banner, Oxford University Press (2021). © Oxford University Press.
DOI: 10.1093/oso/9780197556498.003.0001

The decline of natural law was a fundamental change, because it caused lawyers to think differently about whether, in difficult cases, law is something judges *find* or *make*. When natural law provided a reservoir of principles for judges to draw upon in deciding cases that existing human-made law did not easily resolve, judges were understood to be finding the law. But when natural law was no longer available to judges, the process of judging looked very different. Now, when existing human-made law did not supply a ready answer, judges had nothing else to draw upon. Now judges were understood to be making the law, not merely finding it.

The routine use of natural law in the legal system seems so strange to a modern American lawyer that it raises some obvious questions. I began working on this book because I wanted to figure out the answers.

The first group of questions concerns the "before" picture. How did natural law work in practice? How did people ascertain its content? How did it relate to the law made by humans? In what contexts was it frequently invoked? Why did lawyers believe in it?

The second group of questions concerns the transition. When did lawyers cease using natural law? Why did they stop believing that it should play a role in the legal system?

The final group of questions concerns the "after" picture. When natural law dropped out of the legal system, what took its place? That is, how did lawyers adjust to the absence of natural law? What served the functions that natural law had once served? To what extent did natural law survive within the legal system, either explicitly or implicitly? To what extent did the change in the *sources* of law produce a change in the *content* of the law?

These are the questions this book tries to answer.[1] The book is divided into three parts, corresponding to these three sets of questions.

---

[1] The history of the use and decline of natural law in the American legal system has received very little scholarly attention. The last two chapters of R. H. Helmholz, *Natural Law in Court: A History of Legal Theory in Practice* (Cambridge: Harvard Univ. Press, 2015), discuss the status of natural law in early American legal education and litigation. (Most of Helmholz's book is about continental Europe and England.) The first two chapters of the present book expand upon Helmholz's indispensable account, and the final seven chapters pick up where Helmholz left off, by charting the causes and effects of natural law's decline. Andrew Forsyth, *Common Law and Natural Law in America: From the Puritans to the Legal Realists* (Cambridge: Cambridge Univ. Press, 2019), is a valuable study of how natural law figured in early university curricula and in the thought of writers such as William Blackstone and Joseph Story, but it says little about the use of natural law in the working legal system. The topic received more attention in the early 20th century, when the use of natural law in the legal system was still within living memory. See, e.g., Charles Grove Haines, *The Revival of Natural Law Concepts* (Cambridge: Harvard Univ. Press, 1930); Benjamin Fletcher Wright Jr., *American Interpretations of Natural Law: A Study in the History of Political Thought* (Cambridge: Harvard Univ. Press, 1931); Edward S. Corwin, "The 'Higher Law' Background of American Constitutional Law," *Harvard Law Review* 42 (1928): 149–85, and 42 (1929): 365–409. In recent times the history of

Part I is about American legal thought before the late 19th century, when natural law was an important part of the legal system and when lawyers believed that judges were finders, not makers, of law. This part demonstrates that natural law was not as strange a concept as it may sound. When judges used natural law, they were usually engaging in what today we call policymaking—the explanation of why one rule makes the most sense, in situations where alternative rules are possible. In any judicial system there will be cases for which the existing rules do not provide a clear answer. Judges today use a different vocabulary to describe what they do in such cases, but the process itself is similar in many respects.

It is not exactly the same, however. One key difference is that in 1800, a judge elaborating a new rule for the very first time could sincerely believe that he was *finding* the law, not making it. This belief seems clearly mistaken to us today. We wonder how the lawyers and judges of the past could have been so obtuse as not to see the reality of what they were doing. But that is because we have a different understanding of the grounding of our legal system. The task of chapters 1 and 2 is to reanimate this now-defunct conception of the legal system—to explore how it worked and to explain why it seemed like common sense to the lawyers of the time.

Among lawyers of the 18th and 19th centuries, the term "natural law" had a meaning different from two conceptions of natural law that are widely held today. We need to clarify this difference at the outset, or else this book will be hard to understand.

First, many people today, both lawyers and nonlawyers, think of natural law as a set of Christian doctrines with origins in the Bible. Natural law in this sense tends to yield conservative outcomes, such as the unlawfulness of abortion and same-sex marriage. For this reason, today natural law is often viewed with favor on the right and with suspicion on the left. But there was nothing conservative about the natural law practiced by the lawyers of the 18th and 19th centuries. Natural law had no political valence one way or the other. It was just one more source of law, like statutes or court decisions, that all lawyers employed. Lawyers used natural law to argue on all sides of an issue. To employ natural law did not brand a lawyer as conservative; it merely branded him as a lawyer.

Indeed, much of the time there was not even anything particularly religious about natural law. Natural law rested on a Christian foundation, but lawyers did not believe that the Bible offered answers to most of the litigated questions that arose in a complex commercial society like that of the United States. To the

natural law has received more attention from historians of philosophy than from legal historians. See, e.g., Knud Haakonssen, *Natural Law and Moral Philosophy: From Grotius to the Scottish Enlightenment* (Cambridge: Cambridge Univ. Press, 1996); Brian Tierney, *Liberty and Law: The Idea of Permissive Natural Law, 1100–1800* (Washington, DC: Catholic Univ. of America Press, 2014).

extent that religious belief was involved in the elaboration of natural law, it was often nothing more than the belief that God had created humans with a power of reason that enabled them to work out answers to difficult legal questions. The version of natural law advanced by its religious proponents today scarcely resembles the natural law that pervaded the legal system in the 18th and 19th centuries.

The other widely held conception of natural law today is held by philosophers and law professors. On this view, "natural law" means a view of law in which what the law *is* depends at least in part on what it *ought to be*. It is conventionally contrasted with "positivism," the view that what the law is and what it ought to be are two separate questions. As we will see, this use of the term "natural law" arose only in the mid-20th century. It captures one feature of natural law as it was understood by lawyers of the 18th and 19th centuries, but it lacks several of the other features that lawyers would have recognized as essential to natural law. The natural law discussed by a present-day philosopher of law would not have been called by that name in the 19th century. Nor would 19th-century lawyers have drawn a distinction between natural *law* and natural *rights*, as some philosophers of law do today. Rather, 19th-century lawyers would simply have said that a natural right is one protected by natural law, as distinct from a right protected by some other kind of law such as a constitutional provision or a statute.

"Natural law" today thus often has a meaning different from the one it had to lawyers in the 18th and 19th centuries. I urge readers who are familiar with natural law in either of these two present-day senses of the phrase to put that knowledge aside for the moment. Do not suppose that the lawyers of 1800 shared your understanding of the term. It is likely that they did not.

Part I of the book presents the "before" picture. It includes two chapters.

Chapter 1, "The Law of Nature," explores how natural law worked in the legal system of the 18th and 19th centuries. It discusses how lawyers believed natural law could be discerned, how natural law related to positive law, why natural law seemed so plausible, and how natural law was used in practice.

Chapter 2, "The Common Law," discusses 18th- and 19th-century lawyers' understanding of common law, the law found in court opinions. Today lawyers think of the common law as consisting of the opinions themselves, and they think of judges as making the law when they write the opinions. Before the late 19th century, by contrast, lawyers believed that the common law had an existence independent of court opinions, and that the opinions were merely *evidence of* the law rather than the law itself. Common law was understood in large part as natural law applied to specific situations. It was considered to be something found, not made, by judges.

Part II of this book is about the long-term causes of the transition from this older way of thinking to the way lawyers think today. Why did lawyers reconsider the status of natural law within the legal system?

I had two expectations about this question when I began working on this book, both of which, I am now persuaded, were wrong. I will explain them briefly because I suspect some readers may share them.

One expectation was that the decline of natural law within the legal system would be a product of lawyers' declining belief in natural law more generally. I expected to find that lawyers would have rejected the use of natural law in litigation because they came to doubt there was any such thing. The more I read, however, the more I realized that the primary change was not in how lawyers thought about natural law. It was in how they thought about the legal system. Some lawyers did indeed reject natural law in all domains of life, but most seem to have made a smaller move: they merely came to conceive of natural law as a matter of personal conscience rather than a tool to be used in litigation. They still believed or at least recognized the possibility that natural law existed, but they came to think that the courtroom was just not an appropriate venue for discussing it. One could invoke natural law in political debate, or in conversations within a religious congregation, or in thoughtful discussions among friends, but in court, human-made sources of law were the lawyer's only tools.

My second expectation was that the causes of the change would be something outside the legal system—perhaps a big event like the Civil War or the Industrial Revolution, or perhaps a big intellectual rupture like Darwin's account of evolution. Most legal history these days tends to be written this way, by attributing outcomes within the legal system to causes external to the system. I have followed this practice in my own prior writing, and I assumed I would do so here as well. Indeed, historians sometimes consider the opposite strategy, finding causes *within* the legal system, as a mark of unsophistication, because it has often been done very poorly by lawyers with a myopic focus on court opinions and an apparent lack of interest in the relationship between law and the wider world. I certainly did not set out to write an "internalist" account of the decline of natural law.

But that is what I ended up with, in large measure. The more I read, the less I was able to tell a credible story in which some set of events or intellectual trends outside the legal system caused lawyers to stop using natural law in litigation. Rather, the shift was caused by a few changes in how lawyers thought about the legal system itself. This dashed expectation, my second, is related to my first. The thing I am trying to explain is not why lawyers stopped *believing* in natural law, because it is not clear that most of them stopped believing in it. The thing I am trying to explain is why they stopped *using* natural law in their work.

It is a question about a change in lawyers' argument style, a question about professional technique. It is the kind of question most amenable to an internalist explanation.

Part II consists of four chapters, each of which focuses on one reason American lawyers of the 19th century began to doubt whether natural law should play any role in the legal system.

Chapter 3, "The Adoption of Written Constitutions," traces the effect of 19th-century constitutional thought on the decline of natural law. Written constitutions were an American innovation with no direct parallel in the English legal tradition. Natural law had long been understood as a constraint on legislation, but constitutions served the same function, which raised the question whether American judges had the authority to invalidate legislation that conflicted with natural principles rather than written constitutional text. In the course of this debate, American lawyers voiced their first sustained critiques of the use of natural law within the legal system. The adoption of written constitutions in the late 18th century thus lay the groundwork for the eventual disappearance of natural law from the legal system.

Chapter 4, "The Separation of Law and Religion," discusses an important change in lawyers' understanding of the relationship between the spheres of law and religion during the 19th century. In the early Republic these spheres substantially overlapped. Natural law was understood to have been created by God. Christianity was considered to be part of the common law. Americans may not have become any less religious in the 19th century, but they increasingly came to think of religion as part of one's private, personal life, separate from the public sphere of law. As law and religion separated, the notion that natural law should play a role in the legal system came to seem more and more anomalous.

Chapter 5, "The Explosion in Law Publishing," considers a more practical development—the rapid proliferation of case reporting that took place in the 19th century. There were few published court opinions available to lawyers in the early part of the century. Lawyers necessarily grounded their arguments on broad principles, including principles of natural law. But by the century's end, lawyers complained that they were drowning in reported cases. It was a common observation in the second half of the century that the glut of published opinions had changed the nature of law practice. Precedents had pushed principles aside.

Chapter 6, "The Two-Sidedness of Natural Law," examines several divisive issues of the 19th century in which arguments based on natural law were prominent—capital punishment, property rights, the role of women, and slavery. These were highly salient political debates, and they were also issues that often arose in litigation. Participants on both sides framed their arguments in terms of natural law. By the later part of the century, lawyers began to wonder whether, if natural law could be invoked to support both sides of such hotly contested questions, it was too indeterminate to be used in court.

Because of these four developments, American lawyers of the late 19th century were ready, to an extent they never had been before, to drop natural law from the legal system. There had been arguments against the use of natural law all through the 19th century, but they fell on deaf ears until near the century's end, when they became persuasive for the first time.

Part III of the book is about the transition itself and its aftermath.

Chapter 7, "The Decline of Natural Law and Custom," takes a close look at how natural law and custom disappeared from the legal system in the late 19th and early 20th centuries.

Chapter 8, "Substitutes for Natural Law," offers a fresh perspective on some familiar aspects of the legal thought of the late 19th and early 20th centuries, by connecting them to the decline of natural law. Much of what we now call classical legal thought can be understood as the profession's attempt to replace natural principles with principles located somewhere other than nature. At the same time, the decline of natural law led to the emergence of the view that judges are makers, not finders, of law.

Chapter 9, "Echoes of Natural Law," examines the status of natural law in the legal system over the past century. In law schools, natural law never ceased to be a topic of study. This academic interest in natural law has had almost no effect on the working legal system, where natural law has been relied upon by only the most idiosyncratic of judges and lawyers. The history of our use of natural law has nevertheless continued to exert influence on the legal system, which still contains doctrines and practices that were once based on the law of nature.

There are a few points I should make at the outset, to avoid misunderstanding.

First, this book is about the role of natural law specifically in the American legal system, not in political discourse. Natural law has always figured prominently in American politics, from the Declaration of Independence, which relies on "the Laws of Nature and of Nature's God," right up through our own era. Martin Luther King famously cited natural law to explain why it was permissible to violate southern segregation statutes. "There are just laws, and there are unjust laws," King explained in his 1963 *Letter from Birmingham Jail.* "A just law is a man-made code that squares with the moral law, or the law of God. An unjust law is a code that is out of harmony with the moral law."[2] More recently, the 2016 Republican Party Platform declared that "man-made laws must be

---

[2] King's *Letter from Birmingham Jail* is widely available on the internet, including at https://www.africa.upenn.edu/Articles_Gen/Letter_Birmingham.html.

consistent with God-given, natural laws."[3] In 2018, after a gunman killed seventeen people at a high school in Florida, the chief executive officer of the National Rifle Association insisted that the right to use firearms "is not bestowed by man, but granted by God."[4] An interesting book could be written about how natural law has been used in political argument throughout American history, but this is not it.

Second, because this book is about natural law's use and decline within the legal system, it focuses primarily on lawyers, judges, and law professors. Most of these people were not thinking about natural law in a systematic way. Most were practitioners, not theorists, and even the theorists were often writing for practitioners rather than fellow intellectuals. It may be helpful to think of this book as an exercise in the history of thought at a middling level. It is about neither the thoughts of intellectuals nor those of "the people" broadly conceived, but rather those of the members of a distinct professional culture, a set of people who were more educated and literate than average but who, with a few exceptions, were not self-consciously engaged in intellectual work. One could write a worthy book closely analyzing the work of a small number of philosophical writers who had the time and the inclination to think more thoroughly about natural law, but, again, this is not it. I do consider the work of such people where there is evidence that it had some influence on conventional thought within the legal profession, but the focus of this book is on practicing lawyers and judges.

Finally, this book is not about whether the use of natural law was good or bad, or about whether natural law should or should not be reintroduced to the working legal system. Today some wish for the revival of natural law, while others consider natural law a superstition we have happily outgrown. Both sides of this debate tend to misunderstand the way natural law was used in the legal system in the 18th and 19th centuries. Both sides are mistaken, moreover, in assuming that reviving natural law would cause the substance of the law to revert to what it was when lawyers used natural law. One of the lessons of this book is that the content of the law does not depend on whether natural law is part of the legal system, because the same results can be obtained with or without it. If we could somehow flip a switch and once again treat nature as an accepted source of law for purposes of litigation, I do not think the content of the law would change much, if at all. Lawyers would use different words in their arguments, but the substance of their arguments would remain largely the same.

---

[3] *Republican Platform 2016*, at 9, https://prod-cdn-static.gop.com/media/documents/DRAFT_12_FINAL[1]-ben_1468872234.pdf.

[4] http://transcripts.cnn.com/TRANSCRIPTS/1802/22/cnr.04.html.

PART I

BEFORE THE TRANSITION

1

The Law of Nature

American lawyers of the late 18th and early 19th centuries had no doubt that natural law played an important role in the legal system. "The law of nature," Supreme Court justice Joseph Story explained, "is that system of principles, which human reason has discovered to regulate the conduct of man in all his various relations." Story was summarizing the fundamentals of American law for the first American encyclopedia, the *Encyclopedia Americana*. "We call those rights *natural*," he continued, "which belong to all mankind, and result from our very nature and condition; such are a man's right to his life, limbs and liberty."[1] Lawyers and judges often made arguments based on natural law.[2] "The law of nature forms part of the municipal law," noted the Supreme Court justice Henry Baldwin. "There are certain great and fundamental principles of justice which, in the constitution of nature, lie at the foundation and make part of all civil law, independently of express adoption or enactment."[3] Law students read treatises and heard lectures on natural law.[4] American lawyers had to be familiar with natural law, observed the Maryland law professor David Hoffman, because "in the decisions of courts" they would find "perpetual references to the elementary principles of that science."[5]

But what exactly *was* natural law? Where did it come from? What was its content, and how was it discerned? How did it relate to human-made law? And why was it so firmly a part of early American legal thought? Why were lawyers so certain that natural law was a basic part of the legal system?

---

[1] Valerie L. Horowitz, ed., *The Unsigned Essays of Supreme Court Justice Joseph Story* (Clark, NJ: Talbot Publishing, 2015), 259, 261.

[2] R. H. Helmholz, *Natural Law in Court: A History of Legal Theory in Practice* (Cambridge: Harvard Univ. Press, 2015), 142–72.

[3] *United States v. Holmes*, 26 F. Cas. 360, 368 (C.C.E.D. Pa. 1842).

[4] Helmholz, *Natural Law in Court*, 127–42.

[5] David Hoffman, *A Lecture Being the Second of a Series of Lectures, Introductory to a Course of Lectures Now Delivering in the University of Maryland* (Baltimore: John D. Toy, 1825), 15.

The Decline of Natural Law. Stuart Banner, Oxford University Press (2021). © Oxford University Press.
DOI: 10.1093/oso/9780197556498.003.0002

The Sources of Natural Law

If an American lawyer were asked, circa 1800, "Where does the law come from?" his response would likely have begun with a distinction between *positive* or *municipal* law, the law made by humans, and *natural* law, the law made by God. Both were understood to govern human affairs. "The natural or moral law," lectured the Pennsylvania judge Jacob Rush in 1796, is "that law which is founded upon the *eternal reason and fitness of things,* and enjoins those duties, which, as dependent creatures, we owe to our Creator, and to each other." Rush, like many writers, cited murder as an example of an act contrary to natural law, in that murder was "universally evil, in every age and nation." Positive law, by contrast, was a matter of human preferences. "By a positive law," Rush continued, "is understood a law, which does not necessarily flow from the nature of things, but is founded solely on the *will* of the law-giver." He gave as an example "the *human* law, which forbids the obstructing our high-ways, or navigable waters."[6] Different jurisdictions might have different positive laws because the acts those laws prohibited, such as obstructing a highway, were not wrong in themselves. They were wrong simply because they had been made illegal by human legislation.

In understanding the law this way, Americans were following a long English and continental European tradition.[7] Early American legal thought in this respect scarcely differed from contemporary thought across the Atlantic. Much of what American lawyers wrote about natural law was remembered, or even copied directly, from English and European books that circulated in the United States. Because of this tradition, a few basic ideas quickly became accepted principles of American legal thought.

One of these ideas was that the source of natural law was God. "The only sure foundation of all right, is the will of the great Creator," declared the Boston lawyer Benjamin Oliver.[8] Such had long been the conventional view among English lawyers. Edward Coke, the most prominent English judge of the 17th century, explained, in a case well known among American lawyers, that "the law of nature is that which God at the time of creation of the nature of man infused into his heart, for his preservation and direction."[9] William Blackstone, the

---

[6] Jacob Rush, *Charges, and Extracts of Charges, on Moral and Religious Subjects* (New York: Jonathan Weeden, 1804), 12–13.

[7] Richard Tuck, *Natural Rights Theories: Their Origin and Development* (Cambridge: Cambridge Univ. Press, 1979); Knud Haakonssen, *Natural Law and Moral Philosophy: From Grotius to the Scottish Enlightenment* (Cambridge: Cambridge Univ. Press, 1996); Tamar Herzog, *A Short History of European Law: The Last Two and a Half Millennia* (Cambridge: Harvard Univ. Press, 2018), 152–64.

[8] Benjamin L. Oliver, *The Rights of an American Citizen* (Boston: Marsh, Capen & Lyon, 1832), 9.

[9] *Calvin's Case,* 77 Eng. Rep. 377, 392 (1608).

18th-century English judge and law professor whose four-volume *Commentaries* was the standard reference work for American lawyers for a century, provided a similar account of the source of natural law. "As god, when he created matter, and endued it with a principle of mobility, established certain rules for the perpetual direction of that motion," Blackstone observed, "so, when he created man, and endued him with freewill to conduct himself in all parts of life, he laid down certain immutable laws of human nature."[10] In an era when belief that God influenced human affairs was nearly universal, it was not a controversial proposition that the law of nature had been created by God.

Natural law was understood to be based on the nature of human beings (or the nature of "man," as writers of the period put it). Natural law was not a set of arbitrary rules, but was rather, as Francis Lieber explained, "the body of rights, which we deduce from the essential nature of man."[11] For example, people needed food to survive, noted the lawyer-poet William Hosmer, so the law of nature "evidently points to some exertion to procure food," and people naturally enjoyed the company of others, which suggested "that man was made for society." Such examples indicated that "at least in some things we are bound by conditions—that is, laws—which we must abide, because it is not in our power to set them aside. That is to say, physical existence acknowledges a higher law."[12]

Because natural law was created by God and was based on human nature, it followed that natural law, unlike positive law, was the same everywhere and at all times. The Ohio lawyer John Goodenow published his 1819 treatise on American jurisprudence to show how American law differed from the law of England, but Goodenow began by acknowledging that "the law of nature is common to all rational beings."[13] This too was a staple of transatlantic thought. The Swiss philosopher Jean-Jacques Burlamaqui, whose *Principles of Natural and Politic Law* was published in a few American editions, considered it an "essential characteristic of the laws of nature . . . that they be universal." As Burlamaqui explained, "This is what distinguishes natural from positive laws; for a positive law relates only to particular persons or societies."[14] The French Baron de Montesquieu, whose *Spirit of Laws* was also widely known in the early United States, likewise emphasized the universality of natural law, which regulated

[10] William Blackstone, *Commentaries on the Laws of England* (Oxford: Clarendon Press, 1765–69), 1:39–40.

[11] Francis Lieber, *Manual of Political Ethics* (Boston: Charles C. Little and James Brown, 1838–39), 1:65.

[12] William Hosmer, *The Higher Law, in its Relations to Civil Government* (Auburn: Derby & Miller, 1852), 19–20.

[13] John M. Goodenow, *Historical Sketches of the Principles and Maxims of American Jurisprudence* (Steubenville, OH: James Wilson, 1819), 7.

[14] J. J. Burlamaqui, *The Principles of Natural and Politic Law* (Boston: John Boyle, 1792), 1:116.

human affairs even before any group of humans had established positive laws to govern their communities. "To say that there is nothing just or unjust but what is commanded or forbidden by positive laws," Montesquieu insisted, "is the same as saying, that before the describing of a circle, all the radii were not equal."[15]

American lawyers were still making the same point more than a century later: Natural law did not vary across cultures or through time. "Of course, it will be expected that the peculiar genius of a people will find expression in their laws," observed the Supreme Court justice Joseph Bradley in a lecture to law students at the University of Pennsylvania, "but human nature and the great mass of human actions are essentially the same amongst all peoples." For that reason, he concluded, at bottom the law "is not an arbitrary and empirical set of rules; but is founded upon immutable and eternal principles."[16] Senator Thomas Bayard, who had been a practicing lawyer before entering politics, spoke at Yale Law School's graduation in 1883. "The nature of mankind has not changed since the lark first sang," he declared. "There is a law of nature founded on the general nature of human beings and not on the temporary and accidental situations in which they may be placed."[17]

How were these principles of natural law to be discerned? Lawyers answered this question in two very different ways. On one hand, many cautioned that determining the content of natural law was no easy matter. It required considerable study, because natural law, unlike positive law, was not written down in any authoritative source. "In natural law, the principles upon which the science is founded are not made known with that clearness and firmness, with which the principles of positive law are promulgated; neither are its sources so obvious or accessible," lamented one reviewer in the *American Jurist*. "Its principles must consequently be ascertained, by a laborious and painful investigation, which the systems of positive law do not demand; and the results of this investigation must necessarily be attended with a corresponding degree of uncertainty, which can only be removed by further and more profound investigations."[18] James Richardson, the president of the bar of Norfolk County, Massachusetts, in the 1830s, agreed that the law of nature could not be worked out "exclusively by the unguided reflections of the individual." Discerning the principles of natural law instead required "the critical investigation of all questions of right, that have

[15] Baron de Montesquieu, *Spirit of Laws* (Worcester, MA: Isaiah Thomas, 1802), 1:18.

[16] *Miscellaneous Writings of the Late Hon. Joseph P. Bradley* (Newark, NJ: L.J. Hardham, 1901), 246–47.

[17] Thomas F. Bayard, *The Responsibilities of the Legal Profession in a Republic* (New Haven: Yale College, 1883), 29.

[18] "Jouffroy on Natural Law," *American Jurist and Law Magazine* 18 (1837): 12.

arisen in all states of society, in all stages of civilization and refinement."[19] The New York judge James Kent, whose four-volume *Commentaries on American Law* became the leading domestic legal reference work after its initial publication in the 1820s, emphasized the importance of comparing legal systems in different countries in determining whether a principle was truly part of natural law. "The universality of the sense of a rule or obligation," Kent observed, "is pretty good evidence that it has its foundation in natural law."[20] Indeed, the very existence of learned European treatises delineating the principles of natural law suggested that it was no pursuit for amateurs.

On the other hand, it was often said—including in some of those very same learned treatises—that the law of nature was something instinctual that could be determined by anyone, simply by attending to one's innate sense of justice. Burlamaqui insisted that all people had a "natural bent or inclination which prompts us to approve of certain things as good and commendable, and to condemn others as bad or blameable, independent of reflection." Even "a child, or untutored peasant, is sensible that ingratitude is a vice, and exclaims against perfidy, as a black and unjust action, which highly shocks him, and is absolutely repugnant to his nature."[21] The Scottish jurist Lord Kames agreed that "we are so constituted, as to perceive a right and wrong in actions." Human beings had "a peculiar sense of approbation or disapprobation, to point out to us what we ought to do, and what we ought not to do."[22] Adam Smith likewise noted that "the greatest part of what are called natural rights" could readily be discerned by ordinary people. "That a man has received an injury when he is wounded or hurt any way is evident to reason, without any explanation," Smith observed, "and the same may be said of the injury done one when his liberty is in any way restrain'd; any one will at first perceive that there is an injury done in this case."[23]

In the United States, perhaps the most widely read discussion of an innate human ability to discern natural law came from Blackstone. If understanding the law of nature "could not otherwise be attained than by a chain of metaphysical disquisitions," Blackstone reckoned, then few would make the effort, "and the greater part of the world would have rested content in mental indolence, and ignorance its inseparable companion." Fortunately, no metaphysical disquisitions were required. God "has been pleased so to contrive the constitution and frame

---

[19] James Richardson, *An Address Delivered Before the Members of the Norfolk Bar* (Boston: Torrey & Blair, 1837), 9.

[20] James Kent, *Commentaries on American Law* (New York: O. Halsted, 1826–30), 2:263.

[21] Burlamaqui, *Principles*, 89–90.

[22] Henry Home (Lord Kames), *Essays on the Principles of Morality and Natural Religion* (London: C. Hitch et al., 1758), 37.

[23] Adam Smith, *Lectures on Jurisprudence*, ed. R. L. Meek et al. (Oxford: Clarendon Press, 1978), 13.

of humanity, that we should want no other prompter to enquire after and pursue the rule of right, but only our own self-love." That was because "he has so intimately connected, so inseparably interwoven the laws of eternal justice with the happiness of each individual, that the latter cannot be attained but by observing the former; and, if the former be punctually obeyed, it cannot but induce the latter."[24] Natural law was what felt right to ordinary people.

Thomas Rutherforth, the Cambridge divinity professor whose *Institutes of Natural Law* was one of the standard works on the topic in the early United States, provided an even clearer account of how people were naturally inclined toward the law of nature. "Whatever rules therefore are, by our own nature and the constitution of things, made necessary for us to observe, in order to be happy," Rutherforth explained, "these rules are the law of our nature." He did not mean a selfish sort of happiness unconnected with the happiness of others. From the perspective of any single individual, Rutherforth concluded, "Although his own particular happiness be the end, which the first principles of his nature teach him to pursue; yet reason, which is likewise a principle of his nature, informs him, that he cannot effectually obtain this end without endeavouring to advance the common good of mankind."[25] Happiness in this sense—collective well-being rather than individual enjoyment—was the incentive that drove the instinctive ability to follow the law of nature.

Ordinary people discerned natural law, on this view, by using the same common sense they used to identify what was reasonable, what was fair, and what was best for all concerned. Indeed, some suggested, natural law was nothing more than what was reasonable and conducive to overall happiness. "There is no general law of nature which opposes the happiness of man," declared the New York lawyer E. P. Hurlbut.[26] David Hoffman borrowed the word *utility* from Hume and Bentham to describe this relationship between natural law and the collective good. "Natural rights consist in the liberty of doing and possessing every thing not forbidden by rules drawn from general utility," he lectured. "Our individual rights are ascertained, in all states of society, by an appeal to the general utility."[27] As another lawyer put it, the law of nature was simply "the doctrine of intrinsic reasonableness."[28]

[24] Blackstone, *Commentaries*, 1:40.

[25] Thomas Rutherforth, *Institutes of Natural Law*, 3rd ed. (Philadelphia: William Young, 1799), 1:24–25.

[26] E. P. Hurlbut, *Essays on Human Rights and Their Political Guaranties* (New York: Greeley & McElrath, 1845), 16.

[27] David Hoffman, *Legal Outlines* (New York: s.n., 1848), 107.

[28] Le Baron Bradford Colt, *Addresses* (Boston: Little, Brown, 1906), 103.

American lawyers and judges often repeated that natural law was apprehended intuitively. "It is implanted in us by nature itself," affirmed the Philadelphia lawyer William Rawle. "It is felt, not learned."[29] A South Carolina judge lauded the "natural law that resides in the breast of the citizen."[30] A Missouri law professor explained that principles of natural law "are so called because they are approved by the instinct of justice, or the moral sense which is part of our being."[31] A New Jersey lawyer insisted that the law of nature was simply "common consciousness."[32] As late as 1905, when the Georgia Supreme Court became one of the first courts to recognize a right of privacy, the court declared that "the right of privacy has its foundation in the instincts of nature. It is recognized intuitively."[33] Natural law was the subject of a learned tradition, but it was also commonly said to be a subject for which no learning was necessary.

These contrasting methods of discerning natural law were analogous to one of the primary contrasting features of Catholicism and Protestantism, in that the former tradition placed a greater emphasis than the latter on expertise as a path to determining correct doctrine. American lawyers of the 19th century were overwhelmingly Protestant, particularly among the judiciary, so perhaps it is not surprising that they tended to think of natural law as a field well within the competence of ordinary people. Pointing in the same direction was the circumstance that the United States had not yet developed an academic legal culture along European lines. Europe had law professors who devoted much of their time to writing learned treatises, but the 19th-century United States did not.

The human instinct toward reasonableness provided one path to knowledge of the law of nature; revelation provided the other. Some principles of natural law *were* written down, in the Bible. "The doctrines thus delivered we call the revealed or divine law, and they are found only in the holy scriptures," Blackstone explained. These precepts were "really a part of the original law of nature."[34] As the New York lawyer Joseph Moulton put it, "The Bible, containing these revelations is, therefore, the first law-book."[35] Interpreting the modern relevance of the Bible was not always simple, because not every command in it was intended to endure for all time. Much of the law stated in the Bible was specific to the ancient

---

[29] William Rawle, *A View of the Constitution of the United States of America* (Philadelphia: H.C. Carey & I. Lea, 1825), 252.

[30] *State v. Bailey*, 1 S.C. 1, 6 (1868).

[31] Philemon Bliss, "The Right to Disinherit Without Cause," *Southern Law Review* 3 (1874): 444; see also Philemon Bliss, *Of Sovereignty* (Boston: Little, Brown, 1885), 84.

[32] E. L. Campbell, *The Science of Law* (Jersey City, NJ: Frederick D. Linn, 1887), 96.

[33] *Pavesich v. New England Life Insurance Co.*, 50 S.E. 68, 69 (Ga. 1905).

[34] Blackstone, *Commentaries*, 1:42.

[35] Josephy W. Moulton, *Analysis of American Law* (New York: John S. Voorhies, 1859), 11–12.

Hebrews, and there could be difficult questions as to which parts were which.[36] But whether natural law was discerned through instinct or by reading scripture, it was within the power of ordinary people to comprehend, without engaging in too much intellectual effort.

Natural law was thus sometimes characterized as hard and sometimes as easy to grasp. These seemingly contradictory views were reconcilable in practice, because some propositions of natural law were simply more intuitive than others. No reflection was needed to determine that murder, for example, was wrong. "Every human being endowed with reason, knows that to take the life of a human being is against the law of nature," declared a New York judge.[37] But other principles of natural law were not so easily ascertained. It took some knowledge of the commercial practices of disparate peoples before one could plausibly argue, as one lawyer did, that "trade, or an exchange of values . . . is a part of the great volume of natural law, which God has published for the inspection and government of his creatures."[38] Was keeping the Sabbath required by the law of nature? Some thought it was, based on the evident need of humans to rest every so often, but it took some reasoning to arrive at this conclusion.[39] Natural law could be understood to encompass a wide range of doctrines. Some (like the prohibition of murder) were universally accepted and thus amenable to discovery through intuition, but others were more contestable and thus had to be supported by logical argument from a premise about human nature.

The Relationship between Natural Law and Positive Law

Natural law stood in a complex relation with the positive law made by humans. To begin with, it was often said that human law was void if contrary to natural law. Blackstone again provided the canonical statement: "This law of nature, being co-eval with mankind and dictated by God himself, is of course superior in obligation to any other. It is binding over all the globe, in all countries, and at all times: no human laws are of any validity, if contrary to this." Blackstone gave

---

[36] Parsons Cooke, *The Marriage Question* (Boston: Samuel N. Dickinson, 1842), 4–5. On this problem in England, see Richard J. Ross, "Distinguishing Eternal from Transient Law: Natural Law and the Judicial Laws of Moses," *Past & Present* 217 (2012): 79–115.

[37] *People v. Montgomery*, 13 Abb. Pr. N.S. 207, 217 (N.Y. Sup. Ct. 1872).

[38] "Commercial Legislation," *Hunt's Merchants' Magazine* 7 (1842): 429.

[39] A. Barnes, "The Sabbath is the Law of Nature," *Christian Register*, 20 Oct. 1849, 1; Wilbur F. Crafts, *Addresses on the Civil Sabbath* (New York: Authors' Publishing, 1890), 48; *State v. Baum*, 33 La. Ann. 981, 990 (1881) (Todd, J., dissenting).

the example of murder. If any human law were to allow or require murder, "We are bound to transgress that human law, or else we must offend both the natural and the divine."[40] The axiom was repeated by American lawyers all through the 18th and 19th centuries. Statutes "contrary to natural right and justice, are, in our laws, and must be in the nature of things, considered as void," George Mason argued in Virginia's General Court. "The laws of nature are the laws of God; whose authority can be superseded by no power on earth."[41] An oft-reprinted textbook on American government instructed: "Men have no right to make a law that is contrary to the law of God; and we are not bound to obey it."[42] When a legal journal published a collection of maxims, one was "If ever the laws of God and man are at variance, the former are to be obeyed instead of the latter."[43] The point was made over and over again: If natural law and positive law were in conflict, it was natural law that would prevail.[44]

Stated this way, the relationship between natural and positive law may sound like the present-day relationship between constitutions and statutes, in that statutes are deemed void if they are contrary to constitutional provisions. And indeed, 19th-century American courts did sometimes refuse to enforce statutes they found contrary to natural law. (These cases will be discussed in chapter 3, which considers natural law and constitutional law in the 19th century.) But the relation between natural and positive law had several other facets that cannot be comparably analogized to the modern relation between constitutions and statutes.

To begin with, natural law was used much more often to *interpret* statutes than to strike them down. Natural law formed a backdrop against which legislation was enacted, a set of background principles from which the legislature was presumed not to wish to deviate. A Missouri statute made it a crime to "embezzle" property from another. Was it embezzlement if the defendant mistakenly believed the property was his own? The statute did not say. The court interpreted the statute in light of "the universality of the natural law which deems no one to merit punishment unless he intended evil," and thus held that a person committed embezzlement only when he knew the property was not his own.[45] A Texas statute made it unlawful to carry a pistol on Election Day within

---

[40] Blackstone, *Commentaries*, 1:41, 43.

[41] *Robin v. Hardaway*, Jeff. 109, 114 (Va. 1772).

[42] Andrew W. Young, *First Lessons in Civil Government*, 10th ed. (Auburn, NY: H. and J.C. Ivison, 1843), 16–17.

[43] "Legal Maxims," *Western Law Monthly* 5 (1863): 222.

[44] See, e.g., *Page v. Pendleton*, Wythe 211, 215 n.3 (Va. Ct. of Chancery 1793); *Memorial of the Agents of the New England Mississippi Land Company* (Washington, DC, 1804), 54; *Le Roy v. Marshall*, 8 How. Pr. 373, 376 (N.Y. Sup. Ct. 1853); Overton Howard, *The Life of the Law* (Richmond, VA: J.W. Randolph & English, 1889), 7.

[45] *State v. Reilly*, 4 Mo. App. 392, 397 (1877).

a half mile of a polling place. A man grabbed a pistol from his store and ran into the street, near a polling place, to defend his brother, who was being attacked by a crowd armed with bludgeons. Did he violate the statute? "We cannot conceive that it was the legislative intent . . . to deprive a person of the right of using arms to protect himself, or even another, from death or serious bodily injury," the court held. "Such intent would be unreasonable, and in conflict with natural law."[46] As one law professor summed up such cases, "Both judges and lawyers have to *interpret* the law. In so doing they refer to that inward standard of justice we call Natural Law. They assume rightly that the lawgiver could not possibly mean to prescribe what is wrong in itself or injurious to the common weal; and thus, in carrying out positive law, they always bear in mind, perhaps unconsciously, the universal truths from which positive law has sprung."[47]

To further complicate the picture, in some clashes between natural law and positive law, courts enforced positive law rather than natural law. In cases involving slaves, courts often observed that slavery was contrary to natural law but that courts nevertheless had to set aside the natural law and enforce the positive law establishing property rights in slaves. (The application of natural law to slavery will be considered in much more detail in chapter 6, because disputes about slavery played a role in natural law's decline as part of the working legal system.) Judges also sometimes privileged positive law over natural law in cases involving the rights of Indians. "We will not enter into the controversy, whether agriculturists, merchants, and manufacturers, have a right, on abstract principles, to expel hunters from the territory they possess," Chief Justice John Marshall explained in *Johnson v. M'Intosh*, the case denying full property rights to Indians. "Conquest gives a title which the Courts of the conqueror cannot deny, whatever the private and speculative opinions of individuals may be, respecting the original justice of the claim which has been successfully asserted."[48] Sometimes positive law was said to give way when it conflicted with natural law, but sometimes it was the reverse.

The relationship between natural and positive law was even more complex than that. It was often said that in enacting statutes, legislatures were *enforcing* the law of nature. Connecticut, for example, had a statute that required children to support their parents when the parents could not support themselves. Did the statute require a son-in-law to support his wife's parents? A Connecticut court held that it did not, because the legislature's intent was "merely to enforce the law of nature," which established a "mutual obligation of support between parent and child" in their "natural relation to each other."[49] A Tennessee statute

---

[46] *Barkley v. State*, 12 S.W. 495, 496 (Tex. Ct. App. 1889).
[47] "Teleology," *Washington Law Exchange* 2 (1890): 25.
[48] *Johnson v. M'Intosh*, 21 U.S. 543, 588 (1823).
[49] *Mack v. Parsons*, 1 Kirby 155, 156 (Conn. Super. Ct. 1786).

enacted in 1799 newly authorized courts to grant divorces for adultery. Did the statute authorize divorces where the adultery had been committed *before* 1799? Yes, the state's supreme court decided, because "adultery by the law of nature is an offence. It was so before the passage of this act," which only put the natural principle into statutory form.[50] Where a statute regulated rights, one early 19th-century pamphleteer insisted, it would be error to suppose "that the *law creates the right*; and that *the right would cease if the law was repealed*. This is an unfortunate mistake, for the *right* is self existent, and the *law* is intended only to specify it, or paint it on paper."[51] When a legislature classified acts as crimes, William Rawle agreed, "The legislature is employed, not in the discovery that these acts are unlawful, but in the application of punishments to prevent them." If the legislature failed to enact statutes criminalizing theft, robbery, or murder, Rawle pointedly asked, "Are theft, robbery, murder, no crimes? Opinions so monstrous can be entertained by none."[52]

This conception of positive law as expressing preexisting doctrines of natural law was at its strongest with respect to the rights included in constitutions. Such rights were not *created* by being listed in constitutions, Joseph Story explained. Rather, declarations of rights were "a solemn recognition and admission of those rights, arising from the law of nature."[53] The Fifth Amendment's Takings Clause, which bars the government from taking private property without compensating the owner, "does not create or declare any *new principle of restriction*," a Georgia court reasoned, but rather recognized a "principle, founded in natural justice, especially applicable to all republican governments, and which derived no additional force, as a *principle*, from being incorporated into the Constitution."[54] A New Jersey judge agreed that "the familiar principle, that private property shall not be taken for public use without just compensation, is a dictate of natural justice. It is founded in natural law."[55] The New Hampshire Supreme Court observed that although the state's constitution was unusual in containing no double-jeopardy clause, the clause's absence made no difference, because the prohibition of double jeopardy "is recognized, independently of any constitutional or statutory provision, as lying at the very foundation of human rights and privileges—a law of nature, and of obvious common sense and common justice."[56]

---

[50] *Jones v. Jones*, 2 Tenn. 2, 5 (1804).

[51] *Sampson Against the Philistines, or the Reformation of Lawsuits* (Philadelphia: W. Duane, 1805), 89.

[52] Rawle, *View of the Constitution*, 251–52.

[53] Joseph Story, *Commentaries on the Constitution of the United States* (Boston: Hilliard, Gray, 1833), 1:309.

[54] *Young v. McKenzie*, 3 Ga. 31, 44 (1847).

[55] *In re Public Highway*, 22 N.J.L. 293, 302 (1849).

[56] *Fay v. Parker*, 53 N.H. 342, 389 (1872).

Lemuel Shaw, who served thirty years as the chief justice of the Massachusetts Supreme Court, reflected that constitutional provisions were better understood as reminders than as enactments. "Many of them are so obviously dictated by natural justice and common sense, and would be so plainly obligatory upon the consciences of legislators and judges," Shaw recalled, "that some of the framers of state constitutions, and even the convention which formed the Constitution of the United States, did not originally prefix a declaration of rights."[57]

But this understanding of positive law was not limited to constitutional rights. It was also frequently applied to statutes, which were also said to be declaratory of preexisting natural law. "Legislation is not the law, but the expression of the law antecedently existing," declared the South Carolina lawyer James Walker. "The thought was already in the mind and the heart of the people."[58] The long-serving federal judge Ashur Ware affirmed that "the municipal law of the country is founded upon and enforces the precepts of natural law."[59] "With the exception of those comparatively few regulations, which are in their nature positive and directory, the law of the land is, in general, but another name for the law of nature," Francis Hilliard observed in his 1835 treatise on American law. "Municipal rules are founded upon the basis of equity, reason, and right."[60] On this view, the job of a legislator was not to make new laws, but rather to create mechanisms for enforcing old ones that already existed as principles of natural law. "The true mission of the legislator is to discover the natural laws incident to every condition and relation which can exist in society," argued the New York lawyer Joel Tiffany, "and to devise means by which such laws can have just sway without interruption. For every individual being, as well as every atom of matter, is the subject of natural law."[61] Indeed, another lawyer suggested, "If the principles of natural justice were everywhere well understood, . . . positive laws would be wholly unnecessary."[62]

This view of positive law as often declaratory of natural law can help explain a few aspects of early American legal thought that would otherwise be puzzling. Most obviously, it suggests one reason judges tended to use natural law to interpret statutes rather than to invalidate them. Although in theory a statute contrary to natural law was void, in practice, because statutes were understood as legislative efforts to enforce natural law, a statute could be contrary to natural

---

[57] *Jones v. Robbins*, 74 Mass. 329, 340 (1857).

[58] James M. Walker, *A Theory of the Common Law* (Boston: Little, Brown, 1852), 8.

[59] *The Etna*, 8 F. Cas. 803, 806 (D. Me. 1838).

[60] Francis Hilliard, *The Elements of Law* (Boston: Hilliard, Gray, 1835), vi.

[61] Joel Tiffany, *A Treatise on Government, and Constitutional Law* (Albany, NY: W.C. Little, 1867), 156.

[62] William O. Bateman, *Political and Constitutional Law of the United States of America* (St. Louis: G.I. Jones, 1876), 2.

law only if legislators were seriously mistaken in ascertaining the law of nature. For this reason, the Philadelphia law teacher William Porter could not think of "a settled law of nature which the municipal law contravenes." As Porter told his students, "A good lawyer can show to be law what any other man can prove to be right."[63] Because judges understood statutes as attempts to enforce natural law, they were far more likely to use natural law as a guide to what the statute meant than as a measuring stick for determining the statute's validity. "When it is said in the books," James Kent explained, "that a statute contrary to natural equity and reason . . . is void, the cases are understood to mean, that the courts are to give the statute a reasonable construction. They will not readily presume, out of respect and duty to the lawgiver, that any very unjust or absurd consequence was within the contemplation of the law."[64]

This declaratory view of positive law also helps explain why statutory interpretation was much less literal in the 19th century than it is today. When a statute is understood to express the will of the legislature, the precise words used by the legislature assume paramount importance. But if the legislature is only trying to enforce a preexisting natural right, the words of the statute matter less than the nature of the right itself. "All the great lawyers, divines, and judges look beyond the written laws and precedents before them for something above these," explained the Baltimore lawyer Philip Friese. "With this view they appeal in their arguments, to reason, to the law of nature," because "there is an unwritten law superior to all written law, and its original and exemplar; and of which the written law is only a partial and imperfect expression."[65] The Massachusetts senator Rufus Choate expressed this view in a well-known address at Harvard Law School in 1845. He declared that "the law is not the transient and arbitrary creation of the major will, nor of any will. It is not the offspring of will at all."[66] This passage is scarcely comprehensible today, when we understand the law as embodying the will of a majority of the public, or the will of our elected representatives. But it made perfect sense in the first half of the 19th century, when statutory interpretation was a matter not of parsing statutory text but of reasoning back to the natural principles the text was supposed to enforce.

This declaratory view also offers insight into an aspect of early American trial practice that has largely vanished today—the use of juries to decide questions of law as well as questions of fact. Today, judges generally determine the law, while juries are generally confined to finding the facts. This division of labor makes

---

[63] William A. Porter, *The Introductory Address Delivered Before the Law Academy of Philadelphia* (Philadelphia: Edmond Barrington & Geo. D. Haswell, 1849), 10.

[64] Kent, *Commentaries*, 1:447.

[65] Philip C. Friese, *The Unconstitutionality of Congressional Action* (Baltimore: Murphy, 1867), 11.

[66] *The Works of Rufus Choate* (Boston: Little Brown, 1862), 430.

sense in a world in which statutes are interpreted literally as statements of the law, because legally trained judges are better able to understand statutes than untrained jurors. But in a world where the statutes are often said to be declaratory of natural law, and where ordinary people can use their intuition to perceive the natural law, the gap in qualifications between judges and jurors shrinks dramatically.

Of course, no one would have said that *all* statutes were declarations of pre-existing natural law. Lawyers frequently spoke of natural law as governing only the most fundamental aspects of life, with human law filling in the details. Blackstone, for example, contrasted murder, which was forbidden by natural law, with the "exporting of wool into foreign countries." Natural law neither required nor prohibited the export of wool. The law of nature simply had nothing to say on the matter, so Parliament, which makes human laws, "has scope and opportunity to impose, and to make that action unlawful which before was not so."[67] The Ohio judge John Wilson Campbell drew the same contrast between crimes that were "offenses against the law of nature" and "certain other acts, which for reasons of State, are made criminal, not being so intrinsically; such, for instance, as vending goods without license."[68] The California Supreme Court provided a similar (although more politically freighted) contrast during the Civil War, in affirming the validity of a state statute requiring attorneys, as a condition of practice, to swear their allegiance to the United States. Property rights, which were fundamental, "are founded in the law of nature," the court acknowledged. But "the right to practice law is not an absolute right, derived from the law of nature. It is the mere creature of the statute, and when the license is issued and the official oath taken, which authorizes the attorney to exercise the right, it confers but a statutory privilege, subject to the control of the Legislature."[69]

This contrast between fundamentals and details was often noted regarding issues that were said to be governed by both natural and positive law. Natural law provided the general principles, while positive law supplied the specific rules delineating how the natural principles would be implemented. Incestuous marriage was contrary to natural law, noted Joseph Story, but positive law differed from one jurisdiction to the next as to precisely how close the relationship had to be before it would classified as an unlawful marriage.[70] "The right to

---

[67] Blackstone, *Commentaries*, 1:42–43. This was a distinction that went back to Aristotle. *See* Richard McKeon, ed., *The Basic Works of Aristotle* (New York: Random House, 1941), 1014 (*Nicomachean Ethics* V:7).

[68] *Biographical Sketches; With Other Literary Remains of the Late John W. Campbell* (Columbus, OH: Scott & Gallagher, 1838), 143–44.

[69] *Cohen v. Wright*, 22 Cal. 293, 325, 319 (1863).

[70] Joseph Story, *Commentaries on the Conflict of Laws* (Boston: Hilliard, Gray, 1834), 104–7.

transmit property by descent, to one's own offspring, is dictated by the voice of nature," James Kent reasoned, because "it is in accordance with the sympathies and reason of all mankind, that the children of the owner of property, which he acquired and improved by his skill and industry, and by their association and labour, should have a better title to it at his death, than the passing stranger." But this general principle left many open questions about how exactly property could be transferred to descendants, questions to which natural law did not speak. Kent concluded that "the particular distribution among the heirs of the blood, and the regulation and extent of the degrees of consanguinity to which the right of succession should be attached, do undoubtedly depend essentially upon positive institution."[71] The Texas Supreme Court drew the same contrast. "The statutes of descents and distributions in all countries are mere arbitrary rules," the court explained, rules that were "established by society, or civil government, for its own peace and tranquility, and not because any particular person or class of persons possess any natural right to the inheritance." But while the details of such rules varied, "It will be found that all governments or legislatures, in prescribing determinate methods for the transmission of property, have uniformly availed themselves of a law of physics, which is unerring in its operations, and not fickle and capricious, like the passions and sentiments of mankind, to render that transmission fixed and certain, and easily traceable by the natural law." This natural "law of physics" was "the law of consanguinity, or of blood," which provided that blood relatives should be the heirs.[72] Natural law painted with a broad brush, while positive law filled in the details.

Judges and commentators found this contrast pervasive. "It would be a false and unreasonable conclusion, to infer, that natural reason is sufficient to furnish a rule, in every particular case," Lemuel Shaw observed. For instance, although "it is an obvious dictate of natural justice, that an infant, of tender years, cannot be bound by a contract," natural law did not establish a precise age at which a person became old enough to be bound by contracts. That was a matter for positive law. Likewise, natural law required a limitations period for the enforcement of contracts, because "such is the loss of life, and memory, and other sources of evidence, that it is obviously quite fit, that simple contracts, if enforced at all, should be enforced within some limited time." But natural law did not say exactly how long that time should be, which was a question for positive law to answer. Natural law required some form of established government, "But no natural principle requires that there should be a President, a Senate, or House of Representatives, or Supreme Court." In all these examples, "Natural justice

[71] Kent, *Commentaries*, 2:263–64.
[72] *Jones' Heirs v. Barnett's Heirs*, 30 Tex. 637, 639–40 (1868).

furnishes the general principle, positive or conventional law the exact rule."[73] As Shaw put it on another occasion, "Universal law and natural obligation, on the one hand, and municipal law on the other, are not antagonistic to each other. On the contrary, municipal law assumes the existence of moral duty, arising from natural law, and regulates it, so that it may form a plain and practical rule, adapted to the exigencies of a civilized community."[74] This was another sense in which positive law could be said to "enforce" natural law—not just by restating it, but by furnishing detailed provisions for its implementation.

This sense of positive law as regulating details not covered by natural law provides additional insight into why it was so rare for judges to find legislation inconsistent with natural law. Where a statute governed an area in which natural law had no reign, as with statutes regulating imports or business licenses, there could be no inconsistency between positive and natural law. Where a statute governed an area to which natural law *did* apply, a judge who understood the statute as an effort to enforce natural law or to supply detailed content to natural principles would be motivated to use natural law to interpret the statute rather than to strike it down. "It is clear, that statutes passed, against the plain and obvious principles of common right, and common reason, are absolutely null and void," a South Carolina court explained. "In the present instance, we have an act before us, which, were the strict letter of it applied to the case of the present claimants, would be *evidently* against *common reason*." But that was a reason, not for finding the statute void, but rather for supposing that the legislature did not intend the statute to apply to the case at hand. The court continued: "We are therefore bound to give such a construction" to the statute "as will be consistent with justice, and the dictates of natural reason, though contrary to the strict letter of the law."[75] As Pennsylvania's chief judge John Bannister Gibson put it, "Where a court has to deal with a question of construction," in close cases the law of nature "must always turn the scale."[76] A judge in Maine explained that this interpretive strategy was useful whenever a statute regulated a matter as to which natural law had some bearing. Where a law "is calculated merely to enforce the law of nature, and contains words of ambiguous or indefinite import, which require interpretation," he explained, "we recur to the laws of nature, to the rules and precepts of natural equity to explain them." But resort to natural law was not available to interpret a statute that "is purely arbitrary, if it does not command or

[73] Lemuel Shaw, "Profession of the Law in the United States," *American Jurist & Law Magazine* 7 (1832): 68–69.

[74] *May v. Breed*, 61 Mass. 15, 32 (1851).

[75] *Ham v. McClaws*, 1 S.C.L. 93, 95–96 (1789).

[76] *City of Philadelphia v. Commissioners of Spring Garden*, 7 Pa. 348, 363–64 (1847).

prohibit what is right or wrong, in itself, intrinsically." In such cases, "We look to the will of the legislature itself."[77]

Positive law was in this sense understood to fill gaps left unregulated by natural law, but there was also a sense in which the opposite was true—in which natural law was understood to fill gaps left unregulated by the positive law. When judges used natural law to decide a case, it was often because they reported finding no positive law that was helpful. "We are placed in a singular situation, in this state," despaired New York's Chancery Court, "since we have no statute regulating marriage." The court had to decide the validity of a marriage in which one spouse had been insane at the time of the marriage, but New York had no positive law addressing the question. The court accordingly turned to natural law and held the marriage void.[78] In North Carolina, the state supreme court had to decide whether a person who received a counterfeit banknote could undo a transaction where the party who gave him the note had been unaware that it was counterfeit. "There are but few cases to be found on this subject, in the books to which we usually resort, and these are by no means decisive of the question," the court noted. But there was a solution. "Where the positive laws are silent," the court explained, "all Courts must determine on maxims of natural justice, dictated by reason; that is, according to the law of nature." The court cautioned that this resort to natural law would be improper where positive law supplied the governing rule. "We cannot recur to primary principles of right and wrong, where the municipal institutions are express," the court explained, "for it is then presumed that they are founded on the laws of nature, or contain nothing repugnant to it."[79] In this sense, the law of nature did not supersede positive law, but was rather available as a guide where positive law ran out.

There are abundant examples of judges using natural law in this way. Did a state governor have the right to imprison a defendant alleged to have committed a crime in Canada? "As the legislature have not determined that the interest of the state required them to pass any law on this subject, and have not passed any," the Vermont Supreme Court observed, "we must look elsewhere than to our code of municipal laws for any regulation authorizing the governor to make the order in question." The court accordingly embarked on a lengthy survey of treatises discussing natural law.[80] Who was entitled to unclaimed bales of cotton that washed up on the Florida coast after a shipwreck, the finder or the government? Because the court could find "no final disposition of the question by the judicial decisions or the legislative enactments of our country," the court

[77] *United States v. The William Arthur*, 28 F. Cas. 624, 627 (D. Me. 1861).

[78] *Wightman v. Wightman*, 4 Johns. Ch. 343, 347–51 (N.Y. Ch. 1820).

[79] *Hargrave v. Dusenberry*, 9 N.C. 326, 326–27, 328 (1823).

[80] Ex parte *Holmes*, 12 Vt. 631, 637–42 (1840).

resorted to natural law.[81] If a father kicked his daughter out of the house, was he still entitled to her services, as he would have been under the law of the era had the family remained intact? "No authority in point has been stated, and perhaps the like of this case cannot be found," the court explained. But "the law of nature teaches, that the father is neither to leave his own offspring to perish, nor by abandoning it, is he to cast the burden of it upon others." The father was thus not entitled to his daughter's services.[82] There was always "a large class of cases which are inevitably left unprovided for by every system of human legislation," observed the Boston lawyer Luther Cushing, "and it becomes an interesting inquiry to determine, what are the rules of conduct, and what is the measure of justice, in reference to such cases." The answer was that "the laws, applicable to such cases, are those precepts of natural right, which have not been superseded by express legislation. If a case is left wholly unprovided for by the positive law, it is governed solely by the natural law."[83] As the Louisiana Supreme Court put it, "When positive law is silent, an appeal must be made to natural law."[84]

Such cases were common because life presented all kinds of unanticipated questions for which positive law provided no answer. When a father was missing and hadn't been heard from in many years, could the mother make employment arrangements for her minor children? "The right is not regulated by statute," the New Jersey Supreme Court found. The court accordingly turned to "the clear principle of natural law," that "a mother is not only authorized, but bound," to exercise authority over her children in this situation.[85] Was a man born in Peru, to an American father and a Chilean mother, a citizen of the United States? "The case does not come within the provisions of any of the statutes of the United States on the subject," the court observed. The court thus resorted to what it termed the natural law principle that "children, if legitimate, follow, in regard to their political rights and duties, the condition of their fathers," and deemed the man an American citizen.[86] Was it a crime to sell "unwholesome beef"? "Can any case be found in the books, in which the exact question arose?" asked the judge. "I have not found one; and in the absence of precedent, we must resort to general principles." The judge found it a "plain dictate of reason, or natural law,"

[81] *Russell v. Forty Bales Cotton*, 21 F. Cas. 42, 43–44, 46–48 (S.D. Fla. 1872). For a similar case, also involving unclaimed cotton and a resort to natural law, see *Peabody v. Proceeds of Twenty-Eight Bags of Cotton*, 19 F. Cas. 39, 45–48 (D. Mass. 1829).

[82] *Gary v. James*, 4 S.C. Eq. 185, 195–96 (1811).

[83] Luther S. Cushing, *An Introduction to the Study of the Roman Law* (Boston: Little, Brown, 1854), 17.

[84] *State ex rel. Kneeland v. City of Shreveport*, 29 La. Ann. 658, 661 (1877).

[85] *Osborn v. Allen*, 26 N.J.L. 388, 391, 393–94 (1857).

[86] *Ludlam v. Ludlam*, 26 N.Y. 356, 360, 368 (1863).

that the knowing commission of an act that would cause injury was a crime.[87] Positive law did not cover everything, so natural law was an indispensable backstop. "When the statutes are silent," the Massachusetts Supreme Court declared, judges should consult "the law of nature as generally recognized by all civilized peoples."[88]

In fact, one of the best-known cases of the 19th century is of this sort. In *Pierson v. Post*, an early New York case studied by generations of law students, while one hunter pursued a fox with hounds, a second hunter killed the fox. To which hunter did the fox belong? New York had no positive law that could answer the question. As Judge Henry Brockholst Livingston lamented, "We are without any municipal regulations of our own." The lawyers on both sides accordingly based their arguments on natural law. The judges did the same. The majority determined that chasing a fox was not enough to claim ownership of it, because natural law conferred ownership of the fox on the hunter who first physically possessed it.[89]

In using natural law to decide such cases, courts often referred to principles of morality and religion. For example, in 1834 the Vermont Supreme Court considered a case in which a debtor had concealed his property from his creditors and falsely claimed to be unable to pay his debts in full, to induce his creditors to settle the debts for less than their true value. When the creditors found out, they tried to recover the difference. The Vermont Supreme Court could not find any positive law that governed this situation. "This application presents, it must be confessed, a new case," the court explained, "and we are not furnished with any precedent of a decree such as the bill seeks, made under circumstances precisely like the present." The court accordingly determined to "resort to first principles," and in particular "the rule, which requires good faith and an adherence to truth in human affairs." That rule, the court reasoned, "is a part of the moral and municipal code of every civilized people; and in every christian community is universally acknowledged as resting upon higher and more sacred authority than mere human enactment." The court used this principle of natural law to decide in favor of the creditors.[90]

But natural law was not synonymous with morality, with religion, or even with justice. There were many moral and religious obligations that were not legal obligations, and natural law could produce unjust outcomes in individual cases. In one early case, for example, the US Supreme Court decided a fundamental commercial question: was it unlawful for a party with superior information to

---

[87] *People v. Parker*, 38 N.Y. 85, 86 (1868).
[88] *Commonwealth v. Lane*, 113 Mass. 458, 463 (1873).
[89] *Pierson v. Post*, 3 Cai. R. 175, 182 (N.Y. Sup. Ct. 1805).
[90] *Richards, Truesdale & Co. v. Hunt*, 6 Vt. 251, 253 (1834).

exploit his knowledge by buying or selling at a price different from the price that would have been agreed to if the parties had the same knowledge? Such exploitation might well be immoral, the better-informed party's lawyer argued, but that it did not make it illegal. "Human laws are imperfect in this respect," he suggested, "and the sphere of morality is more extensive than the limits of civil jurisdiction." The Supreme Court agreed.[91] The law often diverged from morality or good manners. Was a father obliged to pay his son's debts? Yes in a moral sense, the Massachusetts Supreme Court held, but not in a legal sense.[92] Did people always have to keep their promises? Keeping promises was "a moral obligation," observed a treatise on the law of contracts, but not necessarily a legal one. "Moral duties and legal obligations are not made coextensive," the treatise explained. The law "gives effect only to contracts that are founded on the mutual exigencies of men, and does not compel the performance of any merely gratuitous engagements."[93]

As many lawyers noted, one important difference between moral obligations and obligations of natural law was that morality could be assessed case by case, but natural law had to take the form of practical rules governing whole categories of cases. It might be immoral in a particular case to exploit superior information to get a better price, but commerce would grind to a halt if every contract had to be preceded with a complete recitation of everything both parties knew. It was immoral for an individual father to refuse to pay his son's debts, but if every father had to pay in these circumstances, improvident children might rack up debts everywhere they went. The legal system needed general rules, one judge explained, and "It is no objection to such general rules, that in some few instances they will operate injustice."[94] Even equity jurisprudence, which was supposed to temper the stricter rules of the common law, "left many matters of natural justice wholly unprovided for," Joseph Story acknowledged. It was simply not practical "to give a legal sanction to duties of imperfect obligation, such as charity, gratitude, and kindness."[95]

Positive and natural law were thus each understood to fill gaps in the other. On one hand, natural law provided broad principles to govern certain matters, while positive law supplied the finer-grained rules needed to put those principles into practice, as well as rules to govern the matters as to which natural law was indifferent. On the other hand, where there was no positive law that applied to a particular question, natural law provided a reservoir of first principles that

[91] *Laidlaw v. Organ*, 15 U.S. 178, 193, 194 (1817).

[92] *Angel v. McLellan*, 16 Mass. 28, 31–32 (1819).

[93] Theron Metcalf, *Principles of the Law of Contracts* (New York: Hurd and Houghton, 1867), 161.

[94] *Stout v. Jackson*, 23 Va. 132, 150 (1823).

[95] Joseph Story, *Commentaries on Equity Jurisprudence* (Boston: Hilliard, Gray, 1836), 1:2.

could help decide a case. From today's perspective, it may sound strange that two bodies of law could each serve to fill gaps in the other. But there is no indication that the lawyers who worked within this system found it strange. The gap-filling was done in different ways and in different cases. Moreover, much of the actual content of natural law (as we will see shortly) consisted of principles so broad that they could plausibly relate to just about any litigated dispute for which positive law provided no answer.

Why the Use of Natural Law Made Sense to 19th-Century Lawyers

Why did this view of the law make sense? Today, we recognize the importance of natural laws in the nonhuman realm, such as the laws of motion or of optics, but natural law plays no role in the human realm governed by our legal system. Why did Americans think differently in the 18th and 19th centuries?

Discussions of natural law often began with the observation that because humans were part of nature just like other animals, they were governed by the laws of nature as other animals were. "Looking around," Kames remarked, "we find creatures of very different kinds, both as to their external and internal constitutions. Each species having a peculiar nature, ought to have a peculiar rule of action resulting from its nature." Kames observed "how accurately the laws of each species are adjusted to the external frame of the individuals which compose it, and to the circumstances in which they are placed, so as to procure the conveniences of life in the best manner, and to produce regularity and consistency of conduct." For example, "A lion is made to purchase the means of life by his claws. Why? because such is his nature and constitution. A man is made to purchase the means of life by the help of others, in society. Why? because, from the constitution both of his body and mind, he cannot live comfortably but in society."[96] Indeed, noted Montesquieu, all physical objects were governed by natural laws. "Man, as a physical being, is like other bodies, governed by invariable laws," he argued. "All beings have their laws."[97]

American commentators often made the same point. Henry St. George Tucker, a law professor at the University of Virginia, began his introductory lecture with the natural laws governing the crystallization of chemicals, before proceeding to the growth of sunflowers and the law of gravity. Only then did he turn to the laws governing human affairs. "If there be a law for all other created

[96] Home, *Essays*, 27–28.
[97] Montesquieu, *Spirit*, 19, 17.

things," Tucker exclaimed, "*why not for man!*"[98] The law of nature encompassed everything from the revolution of planets to the effect of solar heat on vegetation to "the conduct of man in society," one writer affirmed.[99] James Wilson, one of the initial justices of the US Supreme Court, agreed that "when we view the in-animate and irrational creation around and above us, and contemplate the beautiful order observed in all its motions and appearances," it hardly seemed likely that humans could be the only part of nature not governed by regular laws. "Is not the supposition unnatural and improbable," Wilson asked, "that the rational and moral world should be abandoned to the frolicks of chance, or to the ravage of disorder?"[100]

Indeed, over the preceding two centuries, Europeans and their descendants had acquired what they considered an unprecedented ability to discover the natural laws governing human affairs. They had learned an enormous amount of new information about peoples all over the world, in Africa, Asia, and the Americas. Although societies enjoyed widely varying ways of life and levels of technological development, people everywhere seemed to have a core of common beliefs and practices, a finding that reinforced the idea that natural laws governed human life. Over the last century, James Mackintosh marveled in 1799, "Vast additions have been made to the stock of our knowledge of human nature." Mackintosh was an English lawyer whose lectures on natural law were read widely in the United States. "Many hitherto unknown regions of the globe have been visited and described by travelers," he noted. "We may be said to stand at the confluence of the greatest number of streams of knowledge flowing from the most distant sources, that ever met at one point." Beneath all the "useful and beautiful variety of governments and institutions, and under all the fantastic multitude of usages and rites which have prevailed among men," lay "the same fundamental, comprehensive truths, the sacred master-principles which are the guardians of human society, recognized and revered (with few and slight exceptions) by every nation on earth."[101] Burlamaqui agreed that even "the most savage people . . . have laws and rules among themselves" that resembled European laws in some basic respects. "Sincerity and plain dealing are esteemed there as in other places, and a grateful heart meets with as much commendation among them as with us."[102]

[98] Henry St. George Tucker, *A Few Lectures on Natural Law* (Charlottesville, VA: James Alexander, 1844), 4–5.

[99] "The Law of Nature," *Western Examiner* 2 (1835): 137.

[100] *The Works of the Honourable James Wilson, L.L.D.* (Philadelphia: Bronson and Chauncey, 1804), 1:113.

[101] James Mackintosh, *A Discourse on the Study of the Law of Nature and Nations* (London: T. Cadell and W. Davies, 1799), 25, 27.

[102] Burlamaqui, *Principles*, 91–92.

All this new information about disparate peoples suggested that advances would soon be made in understanding the natural law that governed human affairs.

Optimism on this score was also prompted by the great recent progress that had been made in discovering the natural laws regulating the nonhuman world. "The astronomer has discovered the agency of gravitation in effecting the revolution of the heavenly bodies," observed the Connecticut judge Zephaniah Swift. "The philosopher has investigated the laws of motion, the mechanical powers, the laws of optics, fluids, and electricity. The chemist has demonstrated that the composition and decomposition of material substances, are caused by the power of attraction, of cohesion, and repulsion." Perhaps similar progress would soon be made in discovering the natural laws that governed human affairs. After all, Swift reasoned, "Man, who is the subject of these enquiries, is a compound being, consisting of matter and mind."[103] The South Carolina lawyer Thomas Grimké likewise looked with envy upon scientific advances. "The moral world, so much more important to the best interests of man[,] has been comparatively neglected," he lamented. "If the minuteness of research, the profound investigation, the variety of talent, and the inexhaustible stores of learning, which have been lavished on the natural world, had been dedicated to the improvement of man, in all the diversified relations of his moral being, we had now beheld him centuries in advance of his actual condition." Fortunately, he concluded, "The day of neglect has passed away; for the practical science and philosophical common sense, now at work, in the civilized world, will never rest; till the moral relations of man, religious, political and civil, social and domestic, are brought to the test of principles, to the standard of experimental wisdom."[104] If one looked back on the progress that had been made in understanding the laws of nature, one could only be optimistic about what we might learn about how those laws regulated human life. "Where the arts and sciences flourish, political and moral improvements will likewise be made," James Wilson predicted. "Our progress in virtue should certainly bear a just proportion to our progress in knowledge."[105]

As comments like these suggested, the natural laws governing human affairs were often thought of as similar to the laws governing the natural world, discoverable by the same methods. In England, John Locke had voiced a conventional view when he suggested that scientific inquiry would "place morality amongst the sciences capable of demonstration: wherein . . . the measures of right and wrong might be made out, to anyone that will apply

---

[103] Zephaniah Swift, *A System of the Laws of the State of Connecticut* (Windham, CT: John Byrne, 1795), 7.

[104] Thomas Grimké, *An Oration, on the Practicability and Expediency of Reducing the Whole Body of the Law to the Simplicity and Order of a Code* (Charleston, SC: A.E. Miller, 1827), 4–5.

[105] Wilson, *Works of Honourable James Wilson*, 1:142–43.

himself with the same indifferency and attention to the one, as he does to the other of these sciences."[106] American lawyers described a similar parallel between the natural laws that reigned in the human and nonhuman worlds. "Is there any real connection between a physical law, such as gravitation, and a human positive law, such as a law forbidding theft?" asked the San Francisco lawyer John Proffatt. "I claim there is, and that jurisprudence, so treated, may take its place as one of those inductive sciences in which, by the observation of facts and the use of reason, systems of doctrine are established which are universally received as truths among thoughtful men."[107] Just as the natural law of gravity could be identified from the repeated observation of falling bodies, the natural law against theft could be identified from the repeated observation of human instinct, which seemed to consistently proscribe theft. "The laws of nature are only the ways in which nature works," explained the Yale law professor George Kellogg. "We describe these *ways*, formulate them and call them 'laws,' as in the laws of heat and light. So too the real laws of society are the *ways* by which communities live and thrive."[108] The Utah lawyer J. H. Murphy suggested that natural laws were like hydraulics or mechanics, in that "human beings can do nothing to change, impair or improve nature's ordinances."[109]

One similarity between the natural laws governing the physical and human worlds was that both preexisted human choice; they were discovered, not made. "The principles of law have always existed," declared one law professor. "It is the business of the lawyer to discover and apply them." He provided a helpful analogy. "The law of gravitation was not created by Newton. Apples had been falling for centuries before he was born. He simply stated the law in scientific terms. Who created the law that if A hires B at $1.00 per day to work for him and B performs the work satisfactorily, A must pay B $1.00? Where is the statute that enacts any such law? These are illustrations of natural law and human law, the one as fixed and immutable as the other."[110]

To modern sensibilities, there seems to be one obvious difference between the natural laws that were said to govern the human realm and those that govern the nonhuman realm. Falling bodies cannot disobey the law

---

[106] Quoted in Roger Woolhouse, *Locke: A Biography* (New York: Cambridge Univ. Press, 2007), 340.

[107] John Proffatt, *Law as a Science and an Art* (San Francisco: A.L. Bancroft, 1878), 9.

[108] George Kellogg, "The Dignity of Litigation," *Yale Law Review* 1 (1892): 115.

[109] J. H. Murphy, *A Treatise on the Application of Law* (Terre Haute, IN: Moore & Langen, 1894), 21–22.

[110] Paul Howland, "The Case Method," *Western Reserve Law Journal* 4 (1898): 31.

of gravity, but humans can disobey the law prohibiting murder or the law requiring contracting parties to keep their commitments. From today's perspective, this seems like an important distinction. Physical laws are empirical regularities, not normative injunctions.[111] The law of gravity is that apples always *do* fall at a particular rate, not that they *should* fall at that rate. The natural law said to govern human affairs, by contrast, seems today to consist of normative injunctions, not empirical regularities. The law governing murder is that people *should* avoid killing others, not that they always *do* avoid killing others. As we will see, when the prevailing conception of natural law came to be questioned in the late 19th century, critics began to raise this objection. Today, this distinction between empirical natural laws and normative human laws may seem an insuperable obstacle to accepting the view that the laws governing human affairs are usefully understood as similar to the laws governing the natural world.

When natural law was a working part of the legal system, however, lawyers did not make such a sharp distinction between the empirical and the normative. In this respect the lawyers were emblematic of their broader culture, which, as Isaiah Berlin has observed, had long treated nature not just as a source of information but also as a guide to what ought to be done.[112] Americans in the 18th and 19th centuries inherited a long tradition, going back centuries, of understanding natural laws in the nonhuman realm as the commands of God, just like natural laws in the human realm.[113] Thus Boyle, for example, referred to "the laws of motion and rest, that God has established among other things corporeal."[114] Today we typically think of science and religion as separate ways

---

[111] Philosophically minded readers will recognize that this sentence ignores the question of whether natural laws in the present-day scientific sense are best understood as empirical regularities or as something else. See D. M. Armstrong, *What Is a Law of Nature?* (Cambridge: Cambridge Univ. Press, 1983); Marc Lange, *Natural Laws in Scientific Practice* (Oxford: Oxford Univ. Press, 2000). For our purposes there is no need to settle on any specific understanding. The relevant point is only that today we are likely to perceive an important difference between natural laws in the physical world, which are today the domain of "science," and natural laws that might govern human beings within the legal system.

[112] Isaiah Berlin, *Political Ideas in the Romantic Age*, 2nd ed. (Princeton: Princeton Univ. Press, 2014), 80–87.

[113] Bas C. van Fraassen, *Laws and Symmetry* (Oxford: Oxford Univ. Press, 1989), 1–10; Jane E. Ruby, "The Origins of Scientific 'Law,'" *Journal of the History of Ideas* 47 (1986): 341–59; Edgar Zilsel, "The Genesis of the Concept of Physical Law," *Philosophical Review* 51 (1942): 245–79.

[114] Quoted in Steven Shapin, *A Social History of Truth: Civility and Science in Seventeenth-Century England* (Chicago: Univ. of Chicago Press, 1994), 330.

of understanding the world, but that boundary was much less sharp during the 18th and most of the 19th centuries.[115]

Even when lawyers distinguished between the empirical and the normative, they did not consider the distinction as important as we would today. Nathaniel Chipman, who taught law at Middlebury College after serving as Vermont's chief justice, discussed this point at some length in his 1833 treatise on American law and government. "In speaking of the laws of nature," Chipman explained, "we include as well the laws which are supposed to govern action, attending matter animate, or inanimate, and which are sometimes called physical laws, as those laws which govern the actions and conduct of man, as a moral intelligence, and which are the subject of our present inquiry." He acknowledged that there was "a very important distinction" between the two kinds of natural law. A physical law was "a law, not of obligation, but necessity. The subjects are mere passive means or instruments, without will, intention, or power of resistance. No moral consequences are attached to the action." By contrast, the natural law governing human beings was "a law of obligation, not of necessity." A person, unlike mere physical matter, was "furnished with intelligence, with a faculty by which he attains the perception of moral relations and their result in duty." A rock obeyed the law of gravity without perceiving the law or feeling any obligation to obey it, while a person obeyed natural law because he was conscious of it and felt an obligation to obey. But after describing this difference, Chipman proceeded to a thoroughly conventional discussion of natural law and its status in the legal system. The distinction between the two kinds of natural law had no effect on his belief that natural law governed human affairs, that it was the source of much positive law, and that positive law lacked any force if it was contrary to the law of nature.[116]

In the 18th and early 19th centuries it was thus plausible, indeed compelling, to believe that natural law governed human affairs in much the same way it governed the nonhuman world. Nature had its laws and humans were part of nature. If we knew more about the natural laws of physics than the natural laws of crime or contracts, that said more about the meager state of our own knowledge than it said about nature. With continued progress, lawyers hoped, our understanding of the human realm would catch up.

[115] Matthew Stanley, *Huxley's Church and Maxwell's Demon: From Theistic Science to Naturalistic Science* (Chicago: Univ. of Chicago Press, 2015); Peter Harrison, *The Territories of Science and Religion* (Chicago: Univ. of Chicago Press, 2015), 145–82.

[116] Nathaniel Chipman, *Principles of Government* (Burlington, VT: Edward Smith, 1833), 159 (for the quoted material), 160–70 (for the conventional discussion of natural law). For a similar view, see Miles Sanford, "Volney's Theory of the Law of Nature Disproved by an Appeal to Matter of Fact," *Western Christian Advocate* 4 (1837): 81.

The Role of Natural Law in Legal Education

One indication of the importance of natural law to early American lawyers is the place it occupied in legal education. In the 18th century and through much of the 19th, aspiring lawyers were consistently advised to study natural law.

Most would-be lawyers of the era did not go to law school. They served as apprentices. While working for a lawyer, they read what they could. John Adams, who was an apprentice in the 1750s, was told by the Boston lawyer Jeremiah Gridley to "study common Law and civil Law, and natural Law."[117] As an older man, Adams gave the same advice to his grandson. Adams was glad "that you are reading Burlamaqui," he told his grandson. "My early patron Mr. Gridley of whom who have so often heard me speak with veneration, who educated more young gentlemen to the Bar than any other lawyer, had so high an opinion of Burlamaqui, that he reduced the whole Book into questions and obliged his pupils to answer them in writing." But Adams instructed his grandson not to stop with Burlamaqui. "From Burlamaqui, I presume you will proceed to Vattel," he continued, "and I advise you to give particular attention to Heineceius on the law of Nature and Nations—Nor must you be fright'ned by the sight of Grotius or Puffendorf or Bynkershoek."[118] This was a daunting syllabus of treatises on the law of nature.

Thomas Jefferson likewise advised a young apprentice to read works of natural law.[119] So did the well-known English judge Lord Mansfield, in a letter published in a Philadelphia magazine in the 1790s.[120] So did the author of *Advice on the Study of the Law*, a book published in Baltimore in 1811. "To become learned in the law," the book suggested, "a clerk should not commence his studies by perusing volumes written on the laws of his own country; if he does, he will find he has begun with works he cannot clearly understand, and has been endeavouring to acquire from the rivulets, what is only to be gained from the fountain of jurisprudence." Rather, the first task was to obtain "a knowledge of the law of nature."[121]

---

[117] L. H. Butterfield, ed., *Diary and Autobiography of John Adams* (Cambridge: Belknap Press, 1961), 1:55.

[118] John Adams to George Washington Adams, 13 Jan. 1822, *Founders Online*, National Archives (founders.archives.gov/documents/Adams/99-03-02-3995). George Washington Adams, the oldest son of John Quincy Adams, was briefly a lawyer before committing suicide at the age of twenty-eight.

[119] Thomas Jefferson to John Minor, 30 Aug. 1814, including Thomas Jefferson to Bernard Moore (ca. 1773), *Founders Online*, National Archives (founders.archives.gov/documents/Jefferson/03-07-02-0455).

[120] "Course of Study in Law; Recommended by Lord Mansfield to Mr. Drummond—1774," *Universal Asylum and Columbian Magazine*, Aug. 1791, 82.

[121] *Advice on the Study of the Law* (Baltimore: Edward J. Coale, 1811), 31.

As law came to be taught in universities, natural law assumed an even more prominent place in the curriculum, because the universities aimed to teach law in a more systematic manner than was possible in an apprenticeship. David Hoffman began teaching law at the University of Maryland in the 1820s. His syllabus laid out an ambitious program of 301 lectures, of which the first 8 concerned natural law. Only then would students learn anything about the positive law.[122] "I have commenced the course with the metaphysicks and ethicks of the law," he explained, "from a profound conviction of their particular serviceableness to the lawyer." Positive law "was not a system of merely positive and arbitrary rules. It has its deep foundations in the universal laws of our moral nature, and, all its positive enactments, proceeding on these, must receive their just interpretation with a reference to them." Hoffman provided several examples of what he meant. "Would it be possible," he asked, "to interpret justly a law, or explain a contract, without knowledge of the general principles on which they are promulgated or entered into? Whence proceeds the rule that laws should not be retrospective, but from the principle of natural law, or ethicks, that associations are bound only by rules to which they may be supposed to have consented? What are the rules of evidence, but metaphysical and ethical modes of investigating truth on the one hand, and limiting our deductions by a regard to human rights and feelings, and to our moral constitution, on the other?" When such issues arose, "There can be no just design on the part of legislators, nor correct interpretation on those who administer their provisions, without knowledge of the true principles of moral and political philosophy." Lawyers needed to know the laws of nature just as engineers did, Hoffman insisted, because they too were responsible for building edifices that rested on natural laws. "As in the construction of the most elaborate machine, no law of nature can possibly be transgressed, so in the great scheme of government, provisions seemingly the most arbitrary, and the most connected with an artificial state of society, cannot violate, with impunity, the great moral law," he told his students, "and therefore, whether as legislators or expounders of legislative institutions, you must be sure that you understand justly their principles."[123]

When Joseph Story began teaching at Harvard in 1829, he too announced that his lectures would cover "first, the Law of Nature." Natural law "lies at the foundation of all other laws," Story explained, "and constitutes the first step in the science of jurisprudence."[124] He had the support of Harvard's president,

---

[122] David Hoffman, *Syllabus of a Course of Lectures on Law; Proposed to be Delivered in the University of Maryland* (Baltimore: Edward J. Coale, 1821), 9–16.

[123] David Hoffman, *A Lecture, Introductory to a Course of Lectures, Now Delivering in the University of Maryland* (Baltimore: John D. Toy, 1823), 44–46.

[124] Joseph Story, *A Discourse Pronounced Upon the Inauguration of the Author, as Dane Professor of Law in Harvard University* (Boston: Hilliard, Gray, Little, and Wilkins, 1829), 42.

Josiah Quincy, who was also a lawyer. Law was not merely a set of rules, Quincy explained, but was rather, quoting Montesquieu, "the necessary relations resulting from the nature of things." Indeed, he argued, it was law's foundation in nature that made it a suitable subject for a university to teach. "The law, considered as a science, has so intimate a connexion with the sciences in general," Quincy declared, "that, at first view, we are ready to wonder, why it was not made earlier a branch of education in Universities."[125]

As organized legal education spread, it became conventional to teach natural law at, or at least very near, the beginning. At the short-lived law school founded in Connecticut by Sylvester Gilbert, the first lecture was on the law of nature.[126] At South Carolina College (now the University of South Carolina), Thomas Cooper's introductory lecture covered natural law.[127] At the University of Virginia, Henry St. George Tucker began his law course with natural law because, as he told his students, it was "the source from which all human laws derive their validity," and for that reason "nothing could be more interesting or salutary than to mark out to the student the correspondences and connexions between natural law, and positive or municipal institutions."[128] At the University of Pennsylvania, George Sharswood lectured on natural law because lawyers had to learn "the general and immutable principles of right and wrong, which apply to those matters which fall within the legitimate province of human laws."[129]

Starting off legal education with the law of nature was such a convention that when teachers departed from the norm, they felt obliged to explain why. Benjamin Butler, who was attorney general under Andrew Jackson, was one of the founders of New York University. For the law department, he proposed a course of instruction that he acknowledged was "an important departure from the ordinary scientific course." Law students "usually commence with the Law of Nature, as the foundation of all Legal Science," he recognized. That plan, Butler conceded, was "undoubtedly the philosophical order in which the Law, as a general science, ought to be unfolded." At NYU, however, Butler expected that the students "will all have taken their places in Law offices" while they were enrolled in school—that is, the students would be

---

[125] Josiah Quincy, *An Address Delivered at the Dedication of Dane Law College in Harvard University* (Cambridge: E.W. Metcalf, 1832), 6.

[126] Elizabeth Forgeus, "An Early Connecticut Law School: Sylvester Gilbert's School at Hebron," *Law Library Journal* 35 (1942): 201.

[127] Thomas Cooper, *An Introductory Lecture to a Course of Law* (Columbia, SC: Telescope Office, 1834), 28.

[128] Henry St. George Tucker, *Introductory Lecture Delivered by the Professor of Law in the University of Virginia* (Charlottesville, VA: Magruder & Noel, 1841), 9–10.

[129] George Sharswood, *Lectures Introductory to the Study of the Law* (Philadelphia: T. & J.W. Johnson, 1870), 114.

working as apprentices alongside their legal training. They would be immediately thrown into "legal proceedings, which, it must be confessed, are not
very intelligible to a tyro." The student needed practical knowledge right away.
"Nothing can be more inappropriate," Butler argued, "and if custom had not
made it common, nothing would strike us as more absurd, than to place in his
hands, at the very commencement of these labors, and as his chief objects of
study, books treating of the Law of Nature." To get the students up to speed as
apprentices as quickly as possible, "Strict philosophical method must therefore give way to the necessities of the case; and what might otherwise be left
to a later period, should, under the circumstances and for the reasons just
stated, be taken up at the beginning." Butler accordingly proposed to "invert
the present order of study," and to teach natural law only after introducing the
students to "Practice and Pleading," the rules governing lawsuits in New York's
courts.[130] At Columbia, for the same reason, Theodore Dwight likewise began
with practical details, after acknowledging that this was an unusual way to in-
troduce students to law. Most introductions to the topic, he recognized, begin
with "a general disquisition upon law in the abstract—upon the divine law as
revealed in the Bible, upon the law of nature and of reason."[131]

The fundamentality of natural law was also a staple of law school graduation speeches. "To obtain a thorough knowledge of our Municipal law, we must
trace it to its sources, and examine the foundation upon which it rests," declared
the New York judge Alonzo Paige at the graduation ceremony of the State and
National Law School in Saratoga County, New York. "These foundations are
the Law of Nature and the Law of Revelation."[132] Columbia students may have
learned natural law later than students elsewhere, but at their graduation they
were reminded that "there are certain moral obligations, springing from the
reason and nature of things, evidently imposed upon by his Creator; just as certain rules of order, modes of operation, or laws (so called) have been imposed
by the Creator upon His material works."[133] At the University of Wisconsin,
Edward Ryan, soon to be appointed to the Wisconsin Supreme Court, spoke to
graduating law students about the importance of the "the law of nature," which

[130] Benjamin F. Butler, *Plan for the Organization of a Law Faculty and for a System of Instruction in Legal Science, in the University of the City of New-York* (New York: University Press, 1835), 16–17.

[131] Theodore W. Dwight, *An Introductory Lecture Delivered Before the Law Class of Columbia College* (New York: Wynkoop, Hallenbeck & Thomas, 1859), 1.

[132] Alonzo C. Paige, *Address to the Graduating Class of the State and National Law School* (Albany: Little, 1852), 11.

[133] Horatio Potter, *A Sermon Preached Before the Graduating Class of the Law School of Columbia College* (New York: Trustees of Columbia College, 1872), 10.

he called "the foundation of all civil law."[134] At the beginning of a course of law study and at the end, students were taught the centrality of natural law.

The Content of Natural Law

Natural law was understood as fundamental, but how was it actually used in the legal system? In examining the cases in which natural law played a role, there is a risk of overlooking the much larger group of cases in which natural law did not figure. One can read volumes of case reports without encountering any mention of natural law. Many litigated cases involved factual disputes, not disputes about the law. Where the parties did disagree about the law, many cases could be resolved entirely by reference to positive law. There were nevertheless a few contexts in which natural law was regularly invoked, and there were a few topics on which natural law was often said to offer guidance.

Natural law was especially prominent in the field of international law, which governs the relationships among nations. "The law of nature when applied to states or political societies, receives a new name, that of the law of nations," James Wilson explained. "The law of nations is the law of states and sovereigns. On states and sovereigns it is obligatory in the same manner and for the same reasons, as the law of nature is obligatory upon individuals."[135] Because there was no international legislature, there was no international positive law comparable to domestic positive law, so natural law had a much larger role to play.[136] Natural law was not the only source of international law. Nations could agree to treaties, and international law could also arise from customary practice. Sovereigns were "capable of binding themselves by that tacit convention which is fairly to be implied from the approved usage and practice of nations, and by their general acquiescence in certain positive rules," observed the international lawyer Henry Wheaton.[137] Such unwritten conventions were "binding rules of conduct," agreed Henry Halleck, the lawyer and Civil War general, "where not contrary to the law of nature."[138] But natural law was nevertheless understood to loom larger in the international sphere than in the domestic, due to the relative weakness of international institutions capable of generating positive law.

---

[134] Edward G. Ryan, *An Address Delivered Before the Law Class of the University of Wisconsin* (Madison, WI: Democrat Company Book and Job Printers, 1873), 10.

[135] *Henfield's Case*, 11 F. Cas. 1099 (C.C.D. Pa. 1793).

[136] Timothy Walker, *Introduction to American Law* (Cincinnati: Derby, Bradley, 1846), 623.

[137] Henry Wheaton, *Elements of International Law* (Philadelphia: Lea and Blanchard, 1846), 38.

[138] H. W. Halleck, *International Law* (San Francisco: H.H. Bancroft, 1861), 46.

In domestic law, judges often invoked natural law as part of what we would today call the discussion of policy, the effort to figure out the rule that makes the most sense. In an 1854 case, for example, the Pennsylvania Supreme Court considered the rationale for the fellow servant doctrine, a common law rule stating that an employer was not liable for an employee's workplace injury caused by the carelessness of another employee. The court listed the standard arguments in favor of the doctrine: employees were adults who needed no special protection from the law, it would be unfair to hold employers liable when they were not personally at fault, and the injured employee could always bring suit against the careless coworker who was responsible for the injury. The court concluded that subjecting the employer to liability "would violate a law of nature" because it would insulate the injured employee "against the ordinary dangers of his business, and it would be treating him as incapable of taking care of himself."[139] The court used natural law not as a constraint on policy reasoning but as a synonym for it—as embodying what the court considered plain common sense.

The West Virginia Supreme Court invoked natural law in much the same way in an 1885 case involving the doctrine of partnership law that people holding themselves out as partners would be liable as partners to third parties who, believing them to be partners, lent them money. "This doctrine results from principles of natural law and justice," the court explained. "For wherever one of two innocent parties must suffer from false confidence reposed in a third person, he who has misled the other to his loss, . . . ought to suffer the loss, and not the person who, trusting to his representations, has been misled by them." Again, natural law was a synonym for sound policy.

The actual content of natural law—the specific set of doctrines that natural law comprised—was thus highly context dependent. American courts classified a wide range of propositions as rules of natural law in the 19th century. It was a principle of natural law that a litigant could not prove he owned a parcel of land merely by showing the weakness in his opponent's title; he had to prove the strength of his own.[140] Natural law required a wrongdoer to compensate a victim for injuries.[141] Natural law allowed a city to knock down houses to prevent the spread of a fire.[142] Natural law required a train engineer to give a proper warning to pedestrians walking on the track, but not to stop the train.[143] If the pedestrian was a child, however, natural law held the railroad responsible for the child's

---

[139] *Ryan v. Cumberland Valley Railroad Company*, 23 Pa. 384, 387–88 (1854).

[140] *Patterson's Devisees v. Bradford*, 3 Ky. 101, 111 (1807).

[141] *Kerwhaker v. Cleveland, Columbus and Cincinnati Rail Road Company*, 3 Ohio St. 172, 188 (1854).

[142] *American Print Works v. Lawrence*, 21 N.J.L. 248, 257–58 (1847).

[143] *Sinclair v. Chicago, Burlington & Kansas City Railway Company*, 34 S.W. 76, 77 (Mo. 1896).

injuries.[144] Natural law, as reasonableness or sound policy, could be invoked in just about any situation.

That said, there were certain propositions that were often said to be doctrines of natural law. One was the permissibility of self-defense when attacked.[145] "The right of self-defence," an Ohio lawyer observed in a typical remark, "is founded upon an eternal law of nature; it is absolutely necessary for the preservation of the individual and the species."[146] Natural law was often said to bar separating children from their mothers,[147] and to require parents to support their children.[148] Marriage was an especially favored topic for discussions of natural law. As a Georgia judge explained, "Marriage is founded in the law of nature, and is anterior to all human law."[149] Was consummation required for a marriage to be complete? No, said a Kentucky court; the law of nature included no such requirement.[150] Where a couple lived together as married for many years, without being formally married, were they in fact married? Yes, several courts held, because marriage was a relationship defined by natural law.[151] Could a man marry his mother's sister? Massachusetts law prohibited such a marriage, but the law of England did not, so when Samuel and Ann Sutton moved from England to Massachusetts, a difficult question arose. Marriages contracted elsewhere were valid in Massachusetts unless they were contrary to the law of nature. The state's supreme court determined that natural law did not bar the marriage, so the Suttons would be recognized as married.[152]

Indeed, marriage was so strongly understood as governed by natural law that in the mid-19th century, when some states began loosening the requirements for obtaining a divorce, the change set off a controversy as to whether divorce was permissible under natural law.[153] The Ohio lawyer Henry Folsom Page insisted

[144] *Anderson v. Union Terminal Railroad Company*, 81 Mo. App. 116, 120 (1899).

[145] Nathan Dane, *A General Abridgment and Digest of American Law* (Boston: Cummings, Hilliard, 1823–29), 7:123; *Gray v. Combs*, 30 Ky. 478, 481 (1832); *Russell v. Barrow*, 7 Port. 106, 109 (Ala. 1838); *McPherson v. State*, 29 Ark. 225, 233–34 (1874); *Parrish v. Commonwealth*, 81 Va. 1, 12 (1884).

[146] Elias E. Ellmaker, *The Revelation of Rights* (Columbus: Wright & Legg, 1841), 118.

[147] *Directors of the Poor of Bucks County v. Guardians of the Poor of Philadelphia*, 1 Serg. & Rawle 387, 389 (Pa. 1815); *Foster v. Alston*, 7 Miss. 406, 427–35 (1842); *State ex rel. Stephen Ball v. Hand*, 1 Ohio Dec. Reprint 238, 242 (Ohio Super. Ct. 1848).

[148] *Stanton v. Willson*, 3 Day 37, 41, 51 (Conn. 1808); G. W. Field, *The Legal Relations of Infants, Parent and Child, and Guardian and Ward* (Rochester, NY: Williamson & Higbie, 1888), 57.

[149] *Askew v. Dupree*, 30 Ga. 173, 189 (1860).

[150] *Dumaresly v. Fishly*, 10 Ky. 368, 372 (Ky. Ct. App. 1820).

[151] *Johnson v. Johnson's Administrator*, 30 Mo. 72, 86–89 (1860); *Carmichael v. State*, 12 Ohio St. 553, 558–59 (1861); *Buchanan v. Harvey*, 35 Mo. 276, 281 (1864).

[152] *Sutton v. Warren*, 51 Mass. 451, 453–54 (1845).

[153] See, for example, the majority and dissenting opinions in *Lanier v. Lanier*, 52 Tenn. 462 (1871).

that natural law required marriages to be perpetual, at least in the absence of egregious misconduct by one of the spouses.[154] "Marriage was before human law, and exists by higher and holier authority," agreed a Wisconsin judge. "The natural tie of marriage is beyond the jurisdiction of divorce."[155] A New York lawyer writing under the name "Agonistes" took the opposite view. "By the law of nature," he reasoned, "there is no reason why the union should not be dissolved."[156] The mere existence of this debate demonstrated the pervasiveness of the belief that, as the Boston lawyer James Schouler put it, the obligations of marriage "are fixed by society in accordance with principles of natural law."[157]

Natural law also loomed large in discussions of property. Lawyers often spoke of "property as a natural right—as a right derived from the law of nature."[158] But agreement on that general proposition was of little help in answering the specific questions that were the daily life of law practice. Some lawyers and judges asserted that natural law denied American Indians ownership of the land they occupied,[159] while others argued that under the law of nature such occupancy was what *created* property rights in land.[160] Some claimed that copyrights were part of natural law,[161] others that they were not.[162] Some argued that natural law required allowing people to leave property to their descendants,[163] while others insisted that natural law only required control over property to last for the owner's lifetime.[164] When an economy became as complex as that of the United

[154] Henry Folsom Page, *A View of the Law Relative to the Subject of Divorce, in Ohio, Indiana and Michigan* (Columbus: J.H. Riley, 1850), 39–42.

[155] *Campbell v. Campbell*, 37 Wis. 206, 214 (1875).

[156] "Agonistes," *Doctrine of Divorce* (Albany: s.n., 1857), 27.

[157] James Schouler, *A Treatise on the Law of Husband and Wife* (Boston: Little, Brown, 1882), 19.

[158] "Property and Its Origin," *United States Jurist* 2 (1872): 324.

[159] *Thompson v. Johnston*, 6 Binn. 68, 76 (Pa. 1813); Francis Lieber, *Essays on Property and Labour as Connected with Natural Law and the Constitution of Society* (New York: Harper & Brothers, 1841), 73–76.

[160] Joseph K. Angell, *An Inquiry Into the Rule of Law Which Creates a Right to an Incorporeal Hereditament, by an Adverse Enjoyment of Twenty Years* (Boston: Hilliard, Gray, Little and Wilkins, 1827), 12; Timothy Walker, *Introduction to American Law* (Philadelphia: P.H. Nicklin & T. Johnson, 1837), 319.

[161] George Ticknor Curtis, *A Treatise on the Law of Copyright* (Boston: Charles C. Little and James Brown, 1847), 1–25; John Appleton Morgan, *The Law of Literature* (New York: James Cockroft, 1875), 1:1.

[162] "International Copy-Right," *American Law Journal* 8 (1848): 50–55.

[163] Franklin G. Comstock, *A Digest of the Law of Executors and Administrators* (Hartford, CT: H.F. Sumner, 1832), 13.

[164] O. A. Brownson, *Defence of the Article on the Laboring Classes* (Boston: Benjamin H. Greene, 1840), 65; Daniel Raymond, "Law Reform in Regard to Real Estate," *Western Law Journal* 3 (1846): 386–87.

States, noted the Vermont lawyer Daniel Chipman, "Difficult and doubtful questions will arise, not easily decided on the principles of the natural law."[165]

The content of natural law was thus often sharply contested, especially as one descended from general to specific propositions. Natural law was reasonableness, and people often differed over what was reasonable. But these were debates over which particular doctrines were part of natural law, not over whether natural law existed or what its role in the legal system should be. Such debates would come in time. For much of the 19th century, however, there was little controversy about whether natural law governed human affairs. Within the American legal system, as one court put it in the 1840s, the laws of nature, "being taught by nature and reason, have of themselves justice and authority, which oblige the people to obey them."[166]

---

[165] Daniel Chipman, *An Essay on the Law of Contracts, for the Payment of Specifick Articles* (Middlebury, VT: J.W. Copeland, 1822), v.

[166] *McLeish v. Burch*, 22 S.C. Eq. 225, 241 (1847).

2

The Common Law

The *common law* is the law found in court opinions. Today, lawyers think of common law as consisting of the opinions themselves: the texts the judges write *are* the common law. In the 18th and 19th centuries, by contrast, the prevailing view was that court opinions were merely *evidence of* the common law, which had an existence independent of what judges wrote. Today, lawyers think of the common law as something *made* by judges. In the 18th and 19th centuries, the prevailing view was very different. Lawyers believed that the common law was something *found* by judges. The common law existed before judges ever declared what it was.

This is a conception of the common law so different from the one that prevails today that it raises all sorts of questions. If the common law was not made by judges, how did it come into existence? What were its sources—that is, where exactly did it come from? How were judges supposed to go about finding it?

The Unwritten Law

As with so much of the legal system, the early American conception of common law was inherited from England, where the common law had long been understood to be based largely on custom.[1] "Ancient Customes" constituted one major part of the law, declared John Cowell in the mid-17th century.[2] Writing in the early 18th century, Thomas Wood agreed that English

---

[1] Michael Lobban, "Custom, Nature and Authority: The Roots of English Legal Positivism," in David Lemmings, ed., *The British and Their Laws in the Eighteenth Century* (Woodbridge, UK: Boydell Press, 2005), 27–58. On 18th-century English common law thought, see David Lieberman, *The Province of Legislation Determined: Legal Theory in Eighteenth-Century Britain* (Cambridge: Cambridge Univ. Press, 1989).

[2] John Cowell, *The Institutes of the Lawes of England* (London: Joseph Ridley, 1651), 5.

The Decline of Natural Law. Stuart Banner, Oxford University Press (2021). © Oxford University Press.
DOI: 10.1093/oso/9780197556498.003.0003

law was in large part "*General Customs*; these Customs are properly called the *Common Law*."[3]

In the early United States, the canonical discussion of common law's basis in custom was found in William Blackstone's ubiquitous *Commentaries*. "The municipal law of England," Blackstone explained, "may with sufficient propriety be divided into two kinds; the *lex non scripta*, the unwritten, or common law; and the *lex scripta*, the written, or statute law." Blackstone hastened to clarify that by calling the common law *unwritten*, he did not mean to say the common law was "merely *oral*, or communicated from the former ages to the present solely by word of mouth." The principles of the common law were unwritten in the sense that "their original institution and authority are not set down in writing, as acts of parliament are, but they receive their binding power, and the force of laws, by long and immemorial usage." When a custom had been observed for long enough, it became law.[4]

To become part of the common law, Blackstone observed, a custom had to be "of higher antiquity than memory or history can reach." It had to be so old that its origin had been forgotten. As he explained, "In our law the goodness of a custom depends on its having been used time out of mind; or, in the solemnity of our legal phrase, time whereof the memory of man runneth not to the contrary." It was extreme age that gave a custom its "weight and authority; and of this nature are the maxims and customs which compose the common law, or *lex non scripta*, of this kingdom."[5]

Blackstone then turned to two practical questions: "How are these customs or maxims to be known, and by whom is their validity to be determined?" He answered his second question first. Judges were the ones who decided which customs qualified as common law. "They are the depositary of the laws," Blackstone declared, "the living oracles, who must decide in all cases of doubt." Judges were able to classify customs as either in or out of the common law because "their knowledge of that law is derived from experience and study ... and from being long personally accustomed to the judicial decisions of their predecessors." Blackstone then turned to his first question. *How* did the judges make this determination? By reading earlier judicial decisions. "These judicial decisions are the principal and most authoritative evidence, that can be given, of the existence of such a custom as shall form a part of the common law," he observed. Past court decisions were "carefully registered and preserved," so that they could be found whenever "former precedents may give light or assistance." Judges were expected "to abide by former precedents, when the same points come again in

[3] Thomas Wood, *An Institute of the Laws of England* (London: Richard Sare, 1720), 1:6.

[4] Blackstone, *Commentaries*, 1:63–64.

[5] *Id.* at 1:67.

litigation," a self-restraint that would "keep the scale of justice even and steady, and not liable to waver with every new judge's opinion." Once a question had been decided, the decision "is now become a permanent rule, which it is not in the breast of any subsequent judge to alter or vary from, according to his own private sentiments."[6]

An apparent tension between theory and practice lurked in Blackstone's account of the common law, one that permeated English legal writing and would pop up repeatedly in the United States as well. In theory, the content of the common law was determined by custom. If one took this statement literally, when a judge determined whether a particular doctrine was part of the common law, the judge should act something like an anthropologist, surveying the actual life of the community or the nation to determine whether the doctrine was in fact a custom, and if so, whether it was old enough to qualify. On Blackstone's account, however, judges did not perform this task in practice. Rather than looking to custom to determine whether a doctrine was part of the common law, they looked only to prior cases.

This tension was resolvable by supposing that judges of the distant past actually did look to custom to determine the content of the common law, and that once the legal system built up a large enough set of doctrines, judges of the present no longer needed to survey custom in an anthropological sense but could rely instead on the decisions of their predecessors. On this view, the common law *originated* in custom, but custom had long ago ceased to generate the common law.[7] The requirement that a custom be ancient before it could qualify as part of the common law also helped to resolve the tension between theory and judicial practice. How could a present-day judge ascertain the age of a custom? Customs did not come stamped with birthdates. The best evidence of a custom's antiquity was that sometime in the past a judge had recognized the custom as part of the common law. Prior decisions were the most sensible place to look for evidence of which customs were old enough. The conventional view was thus that the common law consisted of ancient customs, and that the evidence of such customs could be found in reports of prior cases.

Earlier court decisions were not sacrosanct, Blackstone continued. A judge could reach a different result if the earlier decision was "most evidently contrary to reason." But when that happened, he explained, "The subsequent judges do not pretend to make a new law, but to vindicate the old one from misrepresentation." That is, "If it be found that the former decision is manifestly absurd or

---

[6] *Id.* at 1:69.

[7] This may be what actually happened in England and parts of the continent. James Q. Whitman, "Why Did the Revolutionary Lawyers Confuse Custom and Reason?," *University of Chicago Law Review* 58 (1991): 1321–68.

unjust, it is declared, not that such a sentence was *bad law*, but that it was *not law*; that is, that it is not the established custom of the realm, as has been erroneously determined." When judges overruled a prior case, they were understood to be disagreeing with the prior judge's empirical conclusion that a particular doctrine was a long-established custom. They were not saying that the law was once A and would henceforth be B, but rather that A was in fact not the ancient custom that the prior judge believed it to be, and thus that A had never actually been the law. "Hence it is that our lawyers are with justice so copious in their encomiums on the reason of the common law," Blackstone declared, "that they tell us, that the law is the perfection of reason, that it always intends to conform thereto, and that what is not reason is not law."[8]

Here Blackstone described what present-day readers may perceive as another kind of tension, again one that would recur in the United States. After taking care to show that the common law is based on custom, Blackstone here suggests that the common law is also based on reason, and that when the two clash, it is reason that prevails. The idea that the common law is grounded on reason was also familiar to English lawyers of the era. Coke had famously written that "the common law itselfe is nothing else but reason"—not the kind of plain reason available to anyone, but "an artificiall perfection of reason, gotten by long study, observation, and experience."[9] Thomas Wood, writing in the early 18th century, had likewise declared that "the Common Law is the Absolute Perfection of Reason."[10] In theory, there could be inconsistency between these two foundations of the common law. A doctrine that is reasonable might not be customary, if, for example, the doctrine governs a situation that has not previously arisen frequently enough or for a long enough time. A doctrine that is customary might not be reasonable, if, for instance, better information has recently become available or prevailing attitudes have changed. In practice, however, custom and reason virtually always pointed in the same direction, because an unreasonable doctrine was very unlikely to have become customary. If a practice was followed by everyone, or virtually everyone, for a very long period of time, the practice would almost certainly seem reasonable.

Each of the newly independent American states followed English common law as the background set of principles governing its legal system. Some states enacted statutes or constitutional provisions explicitly adopting the common

---

[8] Blackstone, *Commentaries*, 1:69–70.

[9] Edward Coke, *The First Part of the Institutes of the Laws of England* (1628), 18th ed. (London: J. & W.T. Clarke, 1823), § 138 [Co. Litt. 97b]. On the tension between custom and reason in Coke's writing, see Allen D. Boyer, *Sir Edward Coke and the Elizabethan Age* (Stanford: Stanford Univ. Press, 2003), 83–88.

[10] Wood, *Institute*, 1:7.

law, but the common law lingered on in all states, even those without such provisions, because it filled an obvious need and it had no competitors. "Though the common law of England hath not, as such, nor ever had, any force here," explained the Connecticut Supreme Court, "yet, in the progress of our affairs, whatever was imagined at the beginning, it long since became necessary, in order to avoid arbitrary decisions, and for the sake of rules, which habit had rendered familiar, as well as the wisdom of ages matured, to make that law our own, by practical adoption."[11] The common law was simply too useful, and too familiar to lawyers, to do without. "To a very great extent," Lemuel Shaw acknowledged, "the unwritten law constitutes the basis of our jurisprudence, and furnishes the rules by which public and private rights are established and secured, the social relations of all persons regulated, their rights, duties, and obligations determined, and all violations of duty redressed and punished." Common law was needed to serve all these purposes because it was not possible to write statutes that could govern every conceivable situation that might arise. Without the aid of the common law, Shaw noted, "The written law, embracing the constitution and statute laws, would constitute but a lame, partial, and impracticable system." Even where a statute regulated a particular issue, the common law was often needed to fill in details the legislature had left unarticulated. For example, "In cases of murder and manslaughter, the statute declares the punishment, but what acts shall constitute murder, what manslaughter, or what justifiable or excusable homicide, are left to be decided by the rules and principles of the common law."[12] The common law would play as important a role in the American legal system as it had in the English.

The prominence of the common law in the early United States can be seen perhaps most clearly in criminal cases. Today, crimes are defined in statutes. The prevailing view today is that a person cannot be criminally punished for doing something that is not proscribed by statute, on the theory that it would be unfair to punish people for conduct that has not previously been publicly declared to be a crime, and that the publication of the statutes is what gives people notice of precisely which actions are forbidden. In the early 19th century, by contrast, crimes were often defined by the common law rather than by statute. For instance, in 1815 a group of men in Philadelphia charged customers a fee to enter a house where they could view "a certain lewd, wicked, scandalous, infamous and obscene painting, representing a man in an obscene, impudent and indecent posture with a woman." Was that a crime? "There is no act [that is, no statute] punishing the offence charged against the defendants," the Pennsylvania

---

[11] *Fitch v. Brainerd*, 2 Day 163, 189 (Conn. 1805).

[12] *Commonwealth v. Chapman*, 54 Mass. 68, 69 (1847).

Supreme Court noted, "and therefore, the case must be decided upon the principles of the common law." The court accordingly examined English cases, along with Blackstone's *Commentaries*, and determined that the defendants had committed a crime. The court concluded that "although every immoral act, such as lying, etc., is not indictable, yet where the offence charged is destructive of morality in general; where it does or may affect every member of the community, it is punishable at common law."[13]

American lawyers thus worked within the English common law tradition, even after independence. They inherited not just the use of common law but the entire constellation of thought that surrounded it. Like their English predecessors, American lawyers conceived of the common law as based on both custom and reason. As James Kent put it, the "rules of the common law" are "founded in the common reason and acknowledged duty of mankind, sanctioned by immemorial usage."[14]

The Common Law as Custom

As in England, lawyers in the United States often cited custom as a source of the common law. "The whole common law is founded on custom," insisted the Virginia lawyer George Wythe, the first university-based law professor in the United States.[15] The Pennsylvania Supreme Court likewise observed that the "common law . . . is founded on popular custom, and when the judges declare it, they merely discover and declare what they find existing in the life of the people as the rule of their relations."[16] Indeed, one lawyer supposed, "All laws relating to property and contracts . . . must have originated, in the natural order of things, in the customs of individuals acquiring the force of law."[17] In the early stages of any society, people would naturally enter into various recurring relationships, such as buyer and seller of property, before there were any statutes governing those relationships. When disputes arose, the most sensible way to resolve them would be in accordance with what was customarily done. In the long run, another lawyer reasoned, all law "is and can be nothing but custom," because any rule contrary to the custom would eventually be discarded.[18]

---

[13] *Commonwealth v. Sharpless*, 2 Serg. & Rawle 91, 101, 103 (Pa. 1815).

[14] *Wightman v. Wightman*, 4 Johns. Ch. 343, 350 (N.Y. Ch. 1820).

[15] *Blackwell v. Wilkinson*, Jeff 73, 82 (Va. 1768).

[16] *Effinger v. Lewis*, 32 Pa. 367, 369 (1859).

[17] "Customs and Origin of Customary Law," *American Jurist* 4 (1830): 42.

[18] Sidney George Fisher, *The Trial of the Constitution* (Philadelphia: J.B. Lippincott, 1862), 18.

Joseph Story provided a lengthy description of the process by which custom became common law in his article "Law" for the *Encyclopedia Americana.* "The legislation of no country, probably, ever gave origin to its whole body of laws," Story suggested. "In the very formation of society, the principles of natural justice, and the obligations of good faith, must have been recognized before any common legislature was acknowledged. Debts were contracted, obligations created, property, especially personal property, acquired, and lands cultivated, before any positive rules were fixed." Because human activity almost certainly preceded the enactment of rules to regulate that activity, Story supposed that "the first rudiments of jurisprudence resulted from general consent or acquiescence." Thus formed the common law. Story declared that he knew of no nation "in which a positive system of laws for the exigencies of the whole society was coëval with its origin; and it would be astonishing if such a nation could be found." Rather, at the origin of any nation, "A few positive rules suffice, for the present, to govern them in their most pressing concerns; and the rest are left to be disposed of according to the habits and manners of the people. Habits soon become customs; customs soon become rules; and rules soon fasten themselves as firmly upon the existing institutions, as if they were positive ordinances." It was this process that yielded England's common law, Story concluded, just like it yielded customary law in every society.[19]

Because they understood the common law as based on custom, American lawyers often said that judicial opinions were merely evidence of the common law, not the common law itself. Judicial opinions were the "written monuments" of the common law, James Wilson lectured, "and its written monuments are accurate and authentick. But though, in many cases, its *evidence* rests, yet, in all cases, its *authority* rests not, on those written monuments. Its authority rests on reception, approbation, custom, long and established."[20] A proposition in a court opinion was part of the common law because it was an established custom, not because it appeared in a court opinion. "The *decision* of a court is but *evidence* of what the law is," agreed the Pennsylvania judge Hugh Henry Brackenridge."[21] As James Kent cautioned, "Even a series of decisions are not always conclusive evidence of what is law." Because judges could make mistakes like anyone, "The records of many of the courts in this country are replete with hasty and crude decisions."[22] The writings of judges were understood as "opinions" in the most

[19] Joseph Story, "Law, Legislation, Codes," *Encyclopedia Americana,* ed. Francis Lieber (Philadelphia: Carey & Lea, 1831), 7:585–86.

[20] Wilson, *Works of Honourable James Wilson,* 2:38.

[21] Hugh Henry Brackenridge, *Law Miscellanies* (Philadelphia: P. Byrne, 1814), 91.

[22] Kent, *Commentaries on American Law,* 1:444.

literal sense; they were not the law itself, but rather the judges' opinions of what the law was.

A common law based on custom—on the daily practices of ordinary people—was not just a specialized body of knowledge accessible to trained lawyers. It was part of the fabric of everyday life. "We live in the midst of the common law," declared the Philadelphia lawyer Peter Du Ponceau. "We inhale it at every breath, imbibe it at every pore; we meet it when we wake and when we lay down to sleep, when we travel and when we stay at home; it is interwoven with the very idiom that we speak."[23] Du Ponceau was giving a graduation speech at the Law Academy of Philadelphia, but it would be wrong to take his words as a mere flight of fancy for a ceremonial occasion. Early American lawyers could genuinely believe that the common law was found everywhere, because customs could be found everywhere. The New York lawyer John Anthon described the common law in much the same way in his treatise for beginning law students. "Like the common atmosphere," Anthon exclaimed, the common law "embraces prince and peasant, and adapts itself to all the changes and vicissitudes of individual or national conditions, expanding or contracting as exigencies require."[24] Like their English predecessors, early American lawyers understood the common law as consisting of judges' efforts to use customary practices as a guide to resolving disputes.

As in England, however, American judges virtually always found the common law in prior judicial opinions rather than by actually looking to contemporary customs. In principle, it was possible for a litigant to testify about the existence of a custom. "Indeed," the Massachusetts Supreme Court observed, if one wished to insert a custom into the common law for the first time rather than resting on one already recognized in a court decision, "there is no other way of proving such law."[25] But cases in which courts actually looked to custom rather than to prior court opinions were few and far between. Such a case arose in New York, where a man born as Myron Maynard began calling himself Maurice Mansfield when he was twenty-two years old and continued to call himself Maurice Mansfield for the rest of his life. New York had a statutory procedure for name changes, but Mansfield had not used it; he had simply changed his name on his own. When he died in a hunting accident, his life insurance company refused to pay, on the ground that he had falsely called himself Maurice Mansfield when he purchased the insurance. Both sides agreed that the insurance company had to pay if the man's real name was Maurice Mansfield, but that the company did not have to

---

[23] Peter Du Ponceau, *A Dissertation on the Nature and Extent of the Jurisdiction of the Courts of the United States* (Philadelphia: Abraham Small, 1824), 91.

[24] John Anthon, *The Law Student* (New York: D. Appleton, 1850), 68.

[25] *Raynham v. Canton*, 20 Mass. 293, 296 (1825).

pay if his real name was Myron Maynard. "The question presented by this appeal, therefore, is whether at common law a man can change his name in good
faith and for an honest purpose by adopting a new one," the court reasoned.
"As the common law rests so largely upon the customs of the people, it is often
necessary to search the history of remote periods, both in England and in this
country, in order to learn its full scope and reasoning." The Court proceeded to
survey the history of Anglo-American customs regarding name changes, from
the origins of English surnames to some recent famous Americans who had
changed their names, such as Ulysses Grant (who had been born as Hiram) and
Grover Cleveland (who had been born as Stephen). The court concluded that
the common law allowed a person to change his name at will.[26]

From time to time, courts had similar opportunities to incorporate custom
into the common law. In the early years of the automobile, before the enactment of detailed traffic statutes, the California Supreme Court had to ascertain
the common law of the road. "So long continued and universal is the custom in
California for approaching vehicles or pedestrians to pass to the right," the court
held, "that it may be said to be a part of our common law."[27] In Arizona, a man
convicted of sexually assaulting a teenage girl appealed on the ground that at
his trial all the spectators had been banished from the courtroom. The Arizona
Supreme Court found that "there has ever been a common understanding that
the general good demands less notoriety or publicity be given to a trial involving
sexual offenses—such as rape, abortion, seduction, and criminal conversation—
than to other trials, especially so when the morals and chastity of children are
involved." For this reason, the trial court had done nothing wrong, the supreme
court concluded. "Through a sense of propriety and decency, universal consent,
we may say, has in this country ripened this custom into a part of our common
law."[28] Every so often, judges would observe a custom in society and incorporate
it into the common law.

But such cases were unusual. Although the common law was understood to
be based on custom, judges typically found the common law in earlier court
opinions rather than in the customs themselves. "It may well be questioned,"
the South Carolina Supreme Court suggested, "whether any modern custom
becomes incorporated in the common law" simply because it was a custom,
without having already "been established as a matter of fact by judicial authority" as a doctrine of the common law.[29] Indeed, there was something troubling about giving judges the power to convert their own observations of custom

[26] *Smith v. United States Casualty Co.*, 90 N.E. 947, 948–49 (N.Y. 1910).
[27] *Raymond v. Hill*, 143 P. 743, 746–47 (Cal. 1914).
[28] *Keddington v. State*, 172 P. 273, 274 (Ariz. 1918).
[29] *Bonham v. C.C. & A. Railroad Co.*, 13 S.C. 267, 276 (1880).

into law. As one early Vermont judge worried, "Where are the Courts to look for this common law of Vermont?" If the law depended on the beliefs of judges and lawyers as to what constituted customary practice, "We must resort for the most part to the fallible memory of the Judges, or members of the bar," in identifying the actual content of the common law. The result would be "a crude undigested mass, or rather farrago of opinions, adopted through indolence or want of present information." Far better to stick with "the authority of decided cases" and "the writings of the ancient sages of the law, approved through a succession of ages."[30] The Pennsylvania Supreme Court agreed that "there cannot perhaps be a greater calamity than a disposition in the judges to dispense with or modify the law according to their notions of the exigencies of times and circumstances. It destroys, at once, all confidence in the security of person or property."[31] No legal principle would be certain if it could be overturned due to a judge's opinion that contemporary custom warranted the change. Lawyers often described the common law as founded on custom, but to the extent any actual customs were involved, they were far more often customs of the misty English past, which had long ago made their way into the common law, than American customs of the present day.

Early American lawyers accepted that the common law, founded in custom, would play an important role in the legal system, but certain aspects of conventional English thought regarding the common law were hard to reconcile with the belief that the United States was a democracy in which political authority was vested in the people themselves. It did not take long for Americans to begin thinking of the common law a bit differently than their predecessors had in England.

Why, for instance, should the antiquity of a custom be a point in its favor? In England, to be part of the common law, a custom had to be so old that its origin had been forgotten. Antiquity was what gave a custom sufficient weight. In the United States, by contrast, the extreme old age of a custom or a doctrine was as likely to be viewed as a reason for discarding it as for obeying it. As the Boston pamphleteer Benjamin Austin wondered, "Why should a young Republic be ruled by laws framed for the particular purpose of a monarchical government?"[32] To some it seemed absurd to treat only the oldest customs as worthy of common law status. For example, one advocate of press freedom pointed out that in England "the common law knows nothing of printing or the liberty of the press," as "the art of printing was not discovered, until toward the close of the 14th

---

[30] *State v. Parker*, 1 D. Chip. 298, 301 (Vt. 1814).

[31] *Green v. Hern*, 2 Pen. & W. 167, 169 (Pa. 1830).

[32] "Honestus" [Benjamin Austin], *Observations on the Pernicious Practice of the Law* (Boston: Adams and Nourse, 1786), 12.

century." English printers had no freedom from government censorship, because "There can be no common law, no immemorial usage or custom concerning a thing of so modern a date."[33] England hardly seemed the right model to follow.

This disdain for the antiquity of a custom was often expressed in a more technical way. No custom in the United States could *ever* exist longer than human memory ran, lawyers argued, because the country had been settled by Europeans so recently. Customs thus should not have to be old in order to be incorporated into the common law. "There is no reason why custom in this country should not in time grow into common law, the same as in England," argued the prolific treatise-writer Joel Bishop. "True indeed we may not be able to show immemorial usage, in precisely the English technical sense; but, because our country is recently settled, we may well claim modifications of the technical rule applicable to the establishment of a custom, so as to bring us within its meaning, when our circumstances exclude us from the letter."[34] John Lawson, a law professor at the University of Missouri, agreed that "it is obvious that the English rule" requiring antiquity "could never have any application here."[35]

But that was not the only conclusion to be drawn from the fact that the United States had been settled by Europeans relatively recently. Some lawyers drew the opposite conclusion—that an American custom could never become part of the common law. In New Jersey, for example, when a litigant argued that he had a common law right to store timber on his neighbor's land because that was the custom, the court rejected the claim on this ground. The court observed that according to Blackstone, to be part of the common law a custom had to date at least to the reign of Richard I, who ruled in the 12th century. "This is sufficient to destroy all common law customs in New Jersey," the court concluded, "for the country was not discovered by civilized inhabitants, and civil rights could not consequently have been in use, till more than three hundred years after the beginning of the reign of Richard the first."[36] In Virginia, a court had the same reaction when an agricultural tenant claimed a common law right, founded in custom, to harvest crops after his lease expired. "Any practice or usage, however general, introduced into this country since its settlement," the court held, "can have no force on the ground of custom; because it lacks the essential ingredient of a good custom—it is not immemorial."[37] As one South Carolina lawyer put it, "No custom is old in this country," so no custom could be added to the common law.[38]

[33] "Hortensius," *An Essay on the Liberty of the Press* (Richmond: Samuel Pleasants, Jr., 1803), 30.

[34] Joel Prentiss Bishop, *The First Book of the Law* (Boston: Little, Brown, 1868), 38.

[35] John D. Lawson, *The Law of Usages and Customs* (St. Louis: F.H. Thomas, 1881), 27.

[36] *Ackerman v. Shelp*, 8 N.J.L. 125, 130 (1825).

[37] *Harris v. Carson*, 34 Va. 632, 638–39 (1836).

[38] *Singleton v. Hilliard*, 32 S.C.L. 203, 211 (S.C. Ct. App. 1847).

The fact that a custom could never grow old enough by English standards could thus lead either to the view that American judges should recognize customs of recent origin as legally binding or the view that in the United States custom had completely ceased to be a source of the common law. This debate never got resolved. There were never many cases in which litigants claimed common law status for an American custom, and eventually the legal system would all but abandon the notion that the common law rested on custom.

There was also a more fundamental sense in which the English idea of a common law based on custom was difficult to square with the ideology of American democracy. If power to make the law was vested in the people, why should the people be bound by rules on which they had never voted? "This may be necessary in arbitrary governments," admitted the Connecticut judge Jesse Root, but not "in a free government like ours."[39] Why, having fought a war to be free from English rule, would Americans submit themselves to a system of law based on the customs of their former rulers? James Sullivan, the attorney general of Massachusetts, acknowledged that "there have been strong prejudices against what is called the Common Law, from an idea, that it is a system imposed upon us, by a power now foreign to our national existence."[40] American lawyers faced a problem their English predecessors had not: how could a custom-based common law be reconciled with democracy?

The answer they developed in the late 18th and early 19th centuries was that custom was nothing more than popular will.[41] Root argued that for this reason the common law was just as democratic as any statute. "As statutes are positive laws enacted by the legislature, which consists of the representatives of the people," he suggested, "so these unwritten customs and regulations" with "the sanction of universal consent and adoption in practice, amongst the citizens at large or particular classes of them, have the force of laws under the authority of the people."[42] Statutes were the voice of the people filtered through legislators; the common law, precisely *because* it was based on custom, was the voice of the people filtered through judges. "When we reflect one moment upon what it is that constitutes a law," Sullivan reasoned, there could be no objection to the common law on the ground that it was antidemocratic. Just like statutes, the common law comprised "the will of the community."[43] When the community's

---

[39] Jesse Root, *Reports of Cases Adjudged in the Superior Court and Supreme Court of Errors* (Hartford: Hudson and Goodwin, 1798), xii.

[40] James Sullivan, *The History of Land Titles in Massachusetts* (Boston: I. Thomas and E.T. Andrews, 1801), 13.

[41] Ellen Holmes Pearson, *Remaking Custom: Law and Identity in the Early American Republic* (Charlottesville: Univ. of Virginia Press, 2011); Kunal M. Parker, *Common Law, History, and Democracy in America, 1790–1900* (New York: Cambridge Univ. Press, 2013), 67–116.

[42] Root, *Reports of Cases*, xii.

[43] Sullivan, *History of Land Titles*, 17.

norms changed, so would the common law. As the Pennsylvania judge John Bannister Gibson exclaimed, "It is one of the noblest properties of this common law, that instead of moulding the habits, the manners and the transactions of mankind, to inflexible rules, it adapts itself to the business and circumstances of the times, and keeps pace with the improvements of the age."[44]

James Wilson provided an appropriately democratic account of how customs originated. "How was a custom introduced?" he asked. "By voluntary adoption. How did it become general? By the instances of voluntary adoption being increased. How did it become lasting? By voluntary and satisfactory experience." In a custom-based common law, therefore, "We find the operations of consent universally predominant."[45] The way a practice became a custom in the first place was by "being known and assented to by every individual," as an article in the *American Jurist* put it.[46] The common law was "a species of legislation by the people themselves," Gibson declared, because it was "general custom obtaining by common consent."[47] The idea of a custom-based common law was thus reconceived by early American lawyers as a democratic institution. Custom was not the dead hand of ancient English practices. It was the living embodiment of the will of the people.

The Common Law as Reason

But custom was not the only source of the common law in the early United States. Like their English predecessors, American lawyers also conceived of the common law as founded in reason.

The common law is "nothing else but common reason," James Wilson declared.[48] When the Philadelphia lawyer Joseph Hopkinson defended the common law against a critic who emphasized its Englishness, Hopkinson likewise argued that the common law was pure reason. "It is not because it is *English* law that we would have it received and obeyed," he insisted, "but because it is the law of *reason* and *justice*. It should bind us, not as subjects of England, but as *men*; as reasonable creatures perceiving and pursuing our happiness; discerning and adopting that system of policy, best calculated to secure our individual rights,

---

[44] *Lyle v. Richards*, 9 Serg. & Rawle 322, 351 (Pa. 1823).

[45] Wilson, *Works of Honourable James Wilson*, 1:99–100.

[46] J. Louis Telkampf, "On Codification, or, the Systematizing of the Law," *American Jurist & Law Magazine* 26 (1841): 132.

[47] *Lyle*, 9 Serg. & Rawle at 338.

[48] Wilson, *Works of Honourable James Wilson*, 2:4.

and preserve the general peace and safety of society."[49] Although the common law was very old, explained the Pennsylvania judge John Ross, "It is nevertheless not entitled to our veneration on account of its antiquity." It was entitled to respect because it was "moulded by the wisdom of the ablest statesmen, and a succession of learned and liberal minded judges, into a flexible system, expanding and contracting its provisions, so to correspond to the changes that are continually taking place in society."[50]

Some lawyers saw no inconsistency in thinking of the common law as based on both custom and reason, because a practice could scarcely become customary without being reasonable. "*Usages* and *customs* are nothing more than natural truths, founded on the nature and reason of things, arising from their fitness to answer great and beneficial ends and purposes," one lawyer suggested. "And hence it follows, that what has been long in *use*, and what has been *observed for a long time*, is in itself useful and just."[51] A custom that was not reasonable "can never grow up," explained the South Carolina judge Langdon Cheves. "The free course of trade will not permit it, as well might a plant vegetate under a great incumbent weight. That it is a usage is itself a proof, of its reasonableness, so irrefragable, that no abstract reasoning can explain it away."[52] On this view, custom and reason pointed in the same direction. At the very least, John Lawson concluded in his treatise on customs, "Proof that a custom is general and established raises a presumption that it is reasonable."[53]

Custom and reason repeatedly clashed, however, in one very common situation. American judges did not adopt all of the English common law. Whether by constitutional provision, by statute, or by their own decision, the judges' task was to adopt only so much of the common law as was not inconsistent with local conditions. In one sense this was a simple housekeeping matter. English common law was full of doctrines that obviously had no relevance to the United States, such as the law governing the prerogatives of the royal family, and the complex rules regulating English forms of property that had no American counterparts. The Vermont judge Nathaniel Chipman explained that American lawyers could safely disregard "many of the rules and maxims, full of absurdity and oppression," that made up such areas of English common law.[54]

[49] Joseph Hopkinson, *Considerations on the Abolition of the Common Law in the United States* (Philadelphia: William P. Farrand, 1809), 19.

[50] *Snowden v. Warder*, 3 Rawle 101, 103–4 (1831).

[51] *Lindsay v. Commissioners*, 2 S.C.L. 38, 50 (1796).

[52] *Barksdale v. Brown & Tunis*, 10 S.C.L. 517, 525 (1819).

[53] Lawson, *Law of Usages*, 68.

[54] Nathaniel Chipman, *Reports and Dissertations* (Rutland, VT: Anthony Haswell, 1793), 122.

But there was much more to adapting common law to local conditions than simply discarding the irrelevant parts. In any matter that might come before a judge, the party who would lose under an English common law precedent had every incentive to argue that the precedent should not be followed because it was unsuitable for the American legal system. Each case thus required the judge to decide whether or not to follow English common law. The common law was "not imported in parcels and packages from England," one lawyer explained. It had to be examined, one doctrine at a time, so it could be "modified and altered by circumstances and made suitable to the people."[55] As another lawyer insisted, "This country has been settled long enough to have a common law of our own, and we have such upon many subjects, different from the common law of England, and adapted to our condition."[56] Case by case, American judges were thus charged with pruning the common law, by ridding it of doctrines incompatible with conditions in the United States.

How were the judges to decide which parts of the common law to retain and which to reject? "There is no general rule to ascertain what part of the English common law is valid and binding," Zephaniah Swift admitted. "To run the line of distinction, is a subject of embarrassment to the courts, and the want of it great perplexity to the student."[57] When John Adams asked his youngest son Thomas "to enquire, ascertain and establish all those points of the Common law, which are now in force in the United States," Thomas Adams responded that the task was impossible. It "would swell to a volume in the hands of any one," he explained, and would require knowledge of every state's statutes, customs, and norms of law practice.[58] The Kentucky lawyer Charles Humphries noted that while Blackstone's summary of English law was useful for English lawyers, an American lawyer "has at present no means of knowing with tolerable certainty, whilst passing over Blackstone, what is or is not law, and is therefore constrained to labour much to imprint on his mind a collection of principles which he does not discover to be of little use, until long afterwards, when he has become acquainted with the statutes of his own country and the practice of the courts."[59] Humphries did his best to solve the problem, but he could tackle only a tiny corner of it. His 1822 book took nearly six hundred pages to specify which parts

[55] *Vidal v. Philadelphia*, 43 U.S. 127, 166 (1844).

[56] *Lord v. Wormwood*, 29 Me. 282, 283–84 (1849).

[57] Zephaniah Swift, *A System of the Laws of the State of Connecticut* (Windham, CT: John Byrne, 1795), 42.

[58] Thomas Boylston Adams to John Adams, 3 Mar. 1802, Founders Online, National Archives (founders.archives.gov/documents/Adams/99-03-02-1061).

[59] Charles Humphries, *A Compendium of the Common Law in Force in Kentucky* (Lexington, KY: William Gibbes Hunt, 1822), vii.

of the common law were in effect, and that was just for Kentucky. A contemporaneous effort for South Carolina was even longer.[60]

From the judge's point of view, as one lawyer lamented, deciding a case required "selecting from the inexhaustible magazines of the mother country, what might be adapted to our circumstances and wants."[61] It was not enough to identify the relevant English precedents. "The American lawyer has gone through but half his task when he has informed himself of what the common law is," complained Richard Rush, the attorney general under Presidents Madison and Monroe. "The remaining and perhaps most difficult branch of inquiry is, whether it does or does not apply to his case."[62]

As a practical matter, there was only one way a judge could decide whether an English common law decision or doctrine should be part of American law. If it was reasonable, given local conditions, it would be followed; if not, it would be rejected. "Our courts must exercise their judgment on the subject," Zephaniah Swift observed, "and if they find the decision to be unsupported by principle, they will consider it of no weight."[63] The only common law principles in force in New Hampshire, one of its judges affirmed, were those "applicable to our state of society and of jurisprudence, and founded on axioms of intelligent reason."[64] The Virginia judge Spencer Roane voiced the conventional view when he declared that "while I consider myself bound to *pare down* . . . the common law of *England* to the standard of our free republican constitution," he would adhere to well-reasoned English opinions on aspects of the common law that were the same in both countries. "I do not see that we may not avail ourselves of the testimony of the eminent and able judiciary of *England*," Roane explained. "I am not willing that an appeal to my *pride*, as a citizen of *independent America*, should prevail over the best convictions of my understanding."[65] American judges thus gradually grew into the habit of assessing the reasonableness of common law doctrines.

One good example is the case of *Van Ness v. Pacard*, decided by the US Supreme Court in 1829. In England, the common law rule was that where a tenant built a house on rented land, he could not take the house with him when the lease expired. The house belonged to the landlord. Was that also the common law in the United States? The Court held that it was not, because conditions in the United States were so different that the rule was not a reasonable one. "The

---

[60] Benjamin James, *A Digest of the Laws of South-Carolina* (Columbia, SC: Telescope Press, 1822).

[61] "Dane's Abridgment," *American Jurist and Law Magazine* 4 (1830): 64.

[62] Richard Rush, *American Jurisprudence* (Washington, DC: s.n., 1815), 16.

[63] Zephaniah Swift, *A Digest of the Law of Evidence* (Hartford: Oliver D. Cooke, 1810), ix.

[64] *Houghton v. Page*, 2 N.H. 42, 44 (1819).

[65] *Baring v. Reeder*, 11 Va. 154, 161–62 (1806).

common law of England is not to be taken in all respects to be that of America," Justice Story cautioned. "Our ancestors brought with them its general principles, and claimed it as their birthright; but they brought with them and adopted only that portion which was applicable to their situation." In the United States, he suggested, the English rule would lead to unpalatable consequences. "The country was a wilderness," he noted, "and the universal policy was to procure its cultivation and improvement. The owner of the soil as well as the public, had every motive to encourage the tenant to devote himself to agriculture, and to favour any erections which should aid this result; yet, in the comparative poverty of the country, what tenant could afford to erect fixtures of much expense or value, if he was to lose his whole interest therein by the very act of erection?" Even if the English doctrine suited a country that was already thickly settled, in the United States the doctrine would only deter settlers from bringing new land into cultivation, because the settler's "cabin or log-hut, however necessary for any improvement of the soil, would cease to be his the moment it was finished." The Court accordingly rejected the English common law rule.[66]

Lowber v. Wells, a case decided in the 1850s by the New York judge James Roosevelt (Theodore's great-uncle), provides another example. The disputing parties owned adjacent sawmills on the Hudson River. The downstream owner complained that obstructions placed in the river by the upstream owner were blocking logs from reaching his mill. Had the dispute arisen under the common law of England, Roosevelt noted, the upstream owner would win. But he refused to follow the common law of England. "One thing appears perfectly clear," he declared. "The common law of England on this subject is not the common law of America. Rules which reason and convenience may have dictated in reference to such streams as the Thames and the Avon, and to an island like Great Britain, may be wholly inapplicable to the Mississippi, the Ohio and the Hudson, and to a continent like America." A rule that constituted "reason and convenience" in England, where the waterways were "petty creeks and untimbered streamlets," made no sense for "such a river as the Hudson, in this state, running through immense primeval forests." Roosevelt ordered the upstream owner to stop blocking the downstream owner's logs.[67]

These two cases are typical of those in which American judges found English common law unsuited to local conditions, in that both decisions encouraged the development of land—by agriculture in one case, and by logging in the other. Land development was an uncontroversial goal in the United States in the first half of the 19th century. There was no parallel in England, where there

[66] *Van Ness v. Pacard*, 27 U.S. 137, 144–45 (1829).
[67] *Lowber v. Wells*, 13 How. Pr. 454, 455–56 (N.Y. Sup. Ct. 1856).

were no comparably vast tracts of undeveloped land. American judges discarded several English common law property doctrines on the ground that they would discourage the development of land. In England, under the doctrine of ancient lights, it was unlawful to construct a building that would block sunlight from reaching a neighbor's window, if the neighbor had enjoyed sunlight for twenty years. American judges found this doctrine unreasonable in the United States, because it would allow the early settlers in any given place to block the growth of cities around them. In England, a tenant could not chop down trees to clear land for agriculture without the landlord's permission. American judges rejected this doctrine as unreasonable too, because it would deter land development.[68] The common law of property regulated factual circumstances that were very different in the two countries, so it was an area in which judges did not hesitate to discard English common law.[69]

American judges thus routinely had to decide whether common law doctrines were reasonable, and American lawyers invoking common law doctrines routinely had to defend their reasonableness. They sometimes had to consider custom as well, but not nearly as often. One might expect that this habit of evaluating the reasonableness of the common law much more often than its customariness would have encouraged American judges and lawyers to think of reason more than custom as a source of the common law. To put it more precisely, one might expect that the balance between custom and reason characteristic of 18th-century English lawyers would have tipped more toward reason in the 19th-century United States. But it is hard to find evidence that this was so. American judges and lawyers certainly did not stop *saying* that the common law was based on custom as well as reason. Even if they had many fewer opportunities to put custom into practice, so to speak, than to put reason into practice, they continued to believe that custom and reason were both sources of the common law.

The Common Law as Applied Natural Law

To the extent the common law was understood as based on custom, it followed that the common law was found, not made, by judges. Judges did not invent

---

[68] Stuart Banner, *American Property: A History of How, Why, and What We Own* (Cambridge: Harvard Univ. Press, 2011), 16–19.

[69] Morton Horwitz has argued that American judges became more instrumental and less tradition-bound after the Revolution. Morton Horwitz, *The Transformation of American Law, 1790–1860* (Cambridge: Harvard Univ. Press, 1977). If so, the judges' need to assess the reasonableness of each common law doctrine sheds some light on why this change took place.

customs. The customs existed in the world before the judges ever had any occasion to use them. "There is hardly such a thing as judge-made law, only judge-
spoken law," Francis Lieber explained. "The doctrine pronounced to-day from a
bench, may, indeed, not be found in any law book; but the judge has ascertained
and declared the sense of the community, as already evinced in its usages and
habits of business."[70] When a judge decided a case by invoking the common law
as found in the case reports, the judge was understood to be applying a doctrine
that some prior judge, perhaps long ago, had determined to be customary. The
prior judge discovered the common law in custom; the present judge discovered the common law in the case reports. Neither judge was understood to be
making law.

But what about when the common law was understood as based on reason?
Today, the prevailing view is that a judge is *making* law when the judge decides
which rule would be the most reasonable. We are especially likely to see judges
as lawmakers when they overrule an old case on the ground that it is unreasonable, because today we understand the judges to be *changing* the common law.
In the 18th century and for much of the 19th, by contrast, lawyers would have
been far more likely to say that the judge was not making law. Even where judges
overruled an old case, they would not have seen the common law as changing.
"Look into the law books from the earliest times, and see how that which has
been supposed to be the common law in a great variety of points, has undergone
successive changes by subsequent determinations founded, as mankind have
admitted by their acquiescence, upon better reasons," one lawyer observed.
"Yet it would be improper to say the common law is altered—it is only better
ascertained as mankind have gradually acquired greater lights, more freedom
for discussion, and a wider space for the exercise of the mental powers, in proportion as the tyranny of superstition and of government have worn away, and
opened to the discovery of mankind the way to truth."[71] The judges were not
using their reason to *change* the common law, but rather to discern the common
law more accurately. The prevailing view was thus that even when a judge used
reason, not custom, to determine the common law, the judge was nevertheless
finding the law.[72]

This view made sense in a world in which the law of nature was understood
to fill gaps in the positive law, and in which natural law was discoverable through
the use of reason. The use of reason to determine the common law was simply
one more example of this process of finding law. The common law, to the extent

---

[70] Lieber, *Manual of Political Ethics*, 1:265.

[71] *Young v. Erwin*, 2 N.C. 323, 327 (1796).

[72] The same was true in England before the late 19th century. J. H. Baker, *An Introduction to English Legal History*, 4th ed. (Oxford: Oxford Univ. Press, 2002), 195.

it was a product of reason, was simply natural law applied to human affairs—"the application of the dictates of natural justice, and of cultivated reason, to particular cases," as James Kent described it.[73] "What is common law?" asked Jesse Root. "Common law is the perfection of reason, arising from the nature of God, of man, and of things."[74] The Maine lawyer Jeremiah Hill was not troubled by the absence of a bill of rights in the Constitution, he told a friend, because "a Bill of Rights was no more than a Collection of Sentences from the Common Law, which sprang from the Law of nature."[75] "The Maxims and Principles, which form the ground-work of the Common law," concluded another lawyer, "are Rules, deduced from Reason, Natural Law, and Justice."[76]

The absence of precedents thus did not leave a judge bereft of common law. "In such a case," one lawyer advised, "although there be no precedent, the Common Law will judge according to the Law of Nature."[77] Another lawyer suggested that in such novel cases a judge would draw upon "the general principles of the common law, or rather perhaps the sources from which it is drawn." These were "the law of nature; the revealed law of God; christianity, morality, and religion; common sense, legal reason, justice, natural equity, humanity." The result was "a system" that left "the law in the breast of the judge, till the occasion arose on which it should be declared," at which point the judge would "apply the principles of morality, religion, and humanity, to the solution of the problem."[78] In such cases, where the statutes and the common law precedent did not compel an outcome, the law of nature would fill in the gaps just as it always did. Despite "our multiplied books of commentaries and reports," remarked one New York judge, much "must be left to the wisdom and discretion of judges, and of jurors; and to that moral sense of right and wrong, which, like the senses of tasting and feeling, in every man, makes a part of his nature."[79]

Natural law was the same everywhere, but different jurisdictions could develop different common law as they applied natural principles to their own unique circumstances. The Ohio judge Benjamin Tappan instructed a jury that "although the common law, in all countries, hath its foundation in reason and the laws of nature, and therefore is similar, in its general principles; yet in its application, it hath been modified and adapted to various forms of government." He analogized the common law to architecture, which likewise varied from place to

---

[73] Kent, *Commentaries*, 1:439.

[74] Root, *Reports of Cases*, ix.

[75] Jeremiah Hill to George Thatcher, 9 Jan. 1788, *Historical Magazine* 6 (1869): 264.

[76] William Barton, *Observations on the Trial by Jury* (Strasburg, PA: Brown & Bowman, 1803), 37.

[77] Edwin T. Freedley, *The Legal Adviser* (Philadelphia: J.B. Lippincott, 1857), 45.

[78] E. L. C., "Kent's Commentaries on American Law," *American Jurist & Law Magazine* 25 (1841): 102–3.

[79] *Rensselaer Glass Factory v. Reid*, 5 Cow. 587, 597 (N.Y. 1825).

place despite being based on a single set of natural principles. The common law of Ohio thus differed somewhat from that of England, Tappan concluded, in light of "our more free and happy habits of government."[80] Common law was *applied* natural law, "the application of natural law to the state and condition of society," as one New York lawyer put it."[81] Each society had its own particular character-istics, so each might have its own common law. In the early years of American independence, the most obvious differences were those between England and the United States. As time went on, and some aspects of the common law began to develop differently in different states, differences among states would become more salient. Toward the end of the 19th century, as we will see, these differences among jurisdictions would eventually play a part in the turn away from thinking of the common law as something found rather than made. Before then, however, differences among jurisdictions in the content of the common law did not cause lawyers to doubt that the common law was founded in the law of nature. Such differences were only to be expected, because while natural principles regulated all jurisdictions equally, no two jurisdictions were exactly alike.

Just as the common law could differ across space, it could differ across time, because different eras gave rise to different circumstances. "I admire that prin-ciple of flexibility in the common law, which enables it to be adapted to the ever-varying condition of human society," one New York judge noted. "But I understand that flexibility to consist, not in the change of great and essential principles, but in the application of old principles to new cases, and in the mod-ification of the rules flowing from them, to such cases as they arise."[82] Natural principles were eternal, but the facts to which those principles applied were con-stantly changing, so the common law—the output of applying the principles to the facts—could change as well.

Because the common law was understood to be based on natural law, it shared natural law's affinity with the scientific laws that governed the nonhuman realm. As James Wilson noted, the common law consisted of doctrines built up from the study of individual cases. In that sense, he argued, "Common law, like nat-ural philosophy, when properly studied, is a science founded on experiment." Each new case, decided by each new judge, provided one more point of infor-mation that would guide the development of the common law, just as each new experiment by each new scientist improved our knowledge of the natural world. "Indeed," Wilson concluded, "what we call human reason, in general, is not

---

[80] John M. Goodenow, *A Review of the Question Whether the Common Law of England, Respecting Crimes and Punishments, is in Force in the State of Ohio* (Pittsburgh: Butler & Lambin's Letter Press Printing Office, 1817), 5.

[81] *People v. Croswell*, 3 Johns. Cas. 337, 358 (N.Y. Sup. Ct. 1804).

[82] *Rensselaer Glass Factory*, 5 Cow. at 628.

so much the knowledge, or experience, or information of any one man, as the knowledge, and experience, and information of many, arising from lights mutually and successively communicated and improved." The common law was the collective reason of generations of judges, the cumulative wisdom gained from successive inquiries into the law of nature.[83]

In this way of thinking, the common law was found, not made, by judges. Such was certainly the view of the judges themselves, who were adamant that they were not lawmakers. In Georgia, for instance, Henry Brawner sued Winston Oliver for seducing his daughter. Oliver promptly died. Did the suit survive his death? The common law rule was that such a suit was personal to the defendant and died along with him. Joseph Henry Lumpkin, the chief justice of the Georgia Supreme Court, sympathized with Brawner. "We have struggled hard to maintain this proceeding," he explained. But the court would not depart from the traditional rule. "We must not, in this or any other case, permit our sympathy, or anything else, to draw us off from the position so early taken, and so firmly and uniformly adhered to by this Court," Lumpkin insisted, "namely: that what is or is not sound policy is a question for the Legislature, and not for the Judiciary. The line between the legislative and judicial power, should be kept constantly in view by both these departments, and never invaded or transcended by either. It is *our province* to expound and apply, and not make or change the law. We protest alike against *judge-made* law, and the exercise of judicial power by the Legislature."[84] Judges often made similar declarations of the limits of their role. Would Ohio modify the common law rule denying an action for slander where one man had accused another of bestiality? No, said an Ohio judge, because "a court [was] created to *declare the law*," not to "make law."[85] "Judge-made law," agreed an Indiana judge, would "be the law of a tyrant."[86] Judges believed they were finding law, not making it.

Today, in the context of our own beliefs about how the common law changes, such claims may sound insincere. These same judges regularly assessed the reasonableness of common law doctrines and adapted them to local conditions. How, we might ask, could they believe they were always law-finders and never lawmakers? But the judges were working within an intellectual climate very different from our own, in which they could sincerely believe they were finding the law. When they determined whether a common law doctrine was reasonable, they understood themselves to be discerning the law of nature and applying it to local conditions. To the extent that common law was based on reason,

---

[83] Wilson, *Works of Honourable James Wilson*, 2:44, 46.

[84] *Brawner v. Sterdevant*, 9 Ga. 69, 69–70 (1850).

[85] *McKean v. Folden*, 2 Ohio Dec. Reprint 248, 249 (Ohio Ct. Comm. Pl. 1859).

[86] *Marvin v. State*, 19 Ind. 181, 184 (1862).

therefore, it was law that was found, not made, by judges, just as much as when it was based on custom. "The common law is grounded upon the general customs of the realm, and comprehends the law of nature," asserted the highest court of Maryland.[87] As George Wythe described it, it was "the law of nature, called common law."[88] This conception of the common law of course rested on the then-prevailing understanding of natural law as something judges *found*. Toward the end of the 19th century, when lawyers began to doubt the relevance and the existence of natural law, they would begin to think of the common law as something that judges *made*.

---

[87] *Griffith v. Griffith's Executors*, 4 H. & McH. 101, 115 (Md. 1798).
[88] *Page v. Pendleton*, Wythe 211, 214 note e (Va. Ch. 1793).

PART II

CAUSES OF THE TRANSITION

3

The Adoption
of Written Constitutions

Over the course of the 19th century, American lawyers and judges would very gradually begin to debate the status of natural law within the legal system. They first expressed doubts about the use of natural law while engaging in constitutional interpretation. This chapter will accordingly examine the relationship between natural law and constitutional law from the late 18th to the late 19th century, because this is where we find the beginning of the decline of natural law as a working part of the American legal system.

One of the most difficult constitutional questions that early American courts faced was whether natural law provided constraints on legislatures in addition to those contained in written constitutions. This question arose again and again, in a wide variety of contexts. Were the constitutional limits on legislative power the *only* limits that could be enforced by judges? Or did judges also have the authority to invalidate legislation on the ground that it was inconsistent with natural law? Were there judicially enforceable rights other than the ones expressly mentioned in constitutions?[1]

---

[1] This debate has not received much recent attention. When it has, scholars have primarily been interested in the implications for present-day constitutional interpretation. See, e.g., Suzanna Sherry, "Natural Law in the States," *Cincinnati Law Review* 61 (1992): 171–222; John F. Hart, "Human Law, Higher Law, and Property Rights: Judicial Review in the Federal Courts, 1789–1835," *San Diego Law Review* 45 (2008): 823–62. A still-useful older discussion is Charles Grove Haines, "The Law of Nature in State and Federal Judicial Decisions," *Yale Law Journal* 25 (1916): 617–57, which was later reworked as Charles Grove Haines, *The Revival of Natural Law Concepts* (Cambridge: Harvard Univ. Press, 1930), 77–103. The position of natural law in constitutional thought *before* the ratification of the Constitution has received more attention because of the topic's relevance to present-day originalist arguments. See, e.g., Thomas C. Grey, "Origins of the Unwritten Constitution: Fundamental Law in American Revolutionary Thought," *Stanford Law Review* 30 (1978): 843–93; Helen K. Michael, "The Role of Natural Law in Early American Constitutionalism: Did the Founders Contemplate the Judicial Enforcement of 'Unwritten' Individual Rights?," *North Carolina Law Review* 69

The Decline of Natural Law. Stuart Banner, Oxford University Press (2021). © Oxford University Press.
DOI: 10.1093/oso/9780197556498.003.0004

This debate would never be definitively resolved. The relevant thing for our purposes is that in the 19th century the debate was the occasion for the first sustained critiques of natural law in the American legal system. In case after case, judges had to reflect on the role natural law should play. Some of them reaffirmed natural law's importance. But others began to question whether judges had the authority to base their decisions on natural law.

The Relation between Natural Law and Written Constitutions

England had no written constitution, but most of the American states adopted written constitutions in 1776 or shortly thereafter, and of course the United States adopted one in 1788. Most of the state constitutions included guarantees of individual rights, as did the federal Constitution once the Bill of Rights was ratified in 1791. It did not take long for courts to begin exercising the power of judicial review—that is, the authority to deny validity to statutes inconsistent with these new constitutional provisions.[2] In only a decade or two, the American legal system acquired a domain of constitutional law and a practice of judicial review with no English counterparts.[3]

In England, the absence of a written constitution meant that natural law was the only theoretical constraint on the power of Parliament. But the absence of judicial review in England meant that this constraint was not understood to be enforceable by judges, or indeed by anyone else.[4] "I know it is generally laid down more largely, that acts of parliament contrary to reason are void," Blackstone acknowledged. "But if the Parliament will positively enact a thing to be done which is unreasonable, I know of no power that can control it." In England, judges could use natural law to interpret a statute, not to invalidate one. "Thus if an act of parliament gives a man power to try all causes, that arise within his manor of Dale," Blackstone explained, "yet, if a cause should arise in which he himself is

---

(1991): 421–90; Philip A. Hamburger, "Natural Rights, Natural Law, and American Constitutions," *Yale Law Journal* 102 (1993): 907–60; Jud Campbell, "Judicial Review and the Enumeration of Rights," *Georgetown Journal of Law & Public Policy* 15 (2017): 569–92.

[2] William Michael Treanor, "Judicial Review before *Marbury*," *Stanford Law Review* 58 (2005): 455–562.

[3] On the early development of American constitutional interpretation, see Jonathan Gienapp, *The Second Creation: Fixing the American Constitution in the Founding Era* (Cambridge: Harvard Univ. Press, 2018).

[4] R. H. Helmholz, "Bonham's Case, Judicial Review, and the Law of Nature," *Journal of Legal Analysis* 1 (2009): 325–54.

party, the act is construed not to extend to that; because it is unreasonable that any man should determine his own quarrel. But, if we could conceive it possible for the parliament to enact, that he should try as well his own causes as that of other persons, there is no court that has power to defeat the intent of the legislature."[5] In the United States, by contrast, courts *did* have the power to defeat the legislature's intent by finding a statute unconstitutional. Could they also use this power to find a statute void according to natural law? That was a question English precedent could not answer, because American judges had a power that English judges did not.

As we saw in chapter 1, the new American constitutions were often understood to recognize preexisting natural rights rather than to create new rights. Some state constitutional provisions were explicitly worded in this way. The New Hampshire Constitution of 1784, for example, provided that "all men have certain natural, essential, and inherent rights," including "the enjoying and defending life and liberty," "acquiring, possessing and protecting property," and "a natural and unalienable right to worship God according to the dictates of his own conscience."[6] The Virginia Constitution of 1776 likewise declared that "all men are by nature equally free and independent, and have certain inherent rights" such as the rights to life, liberty, and property.[7] Some of the state constitutions did not label rights as "natural" or "inherent," but this omission is unlikely to have been intended to suggest that the rights involved were any less natural. For instance, the Maryland Constitution of 1776 listed several individual rights, including the freedom of speech, the right to petition the legislature, and the right not to be deprived of life, liberty, or property other than by the law of the land, without specifying that these were natural rights.[8] But the drafters of Maryland's constitution almost certainly did not mean to imply that these rights did not exist in Maryland before the adoption of the state's constitution, or that constitutional rights had a different status in Maryland than in states where the constitution expressly called them natural. In light of the role natural law played in the legal system, it is far more likely that these rights were generally understood as natural, even without being explicitly labeled as such.

The federal Constitution's Bill of Rights did not explicitly characterize the rights it included as natural rights, but, as we have seen, some of them, at least, were understood that way.[9] Other parts of the Bill of Rights were understood as declarations of preexisting rights under the common law. For example, Joseph

---

[5] Blackstone, *Commentaries*, 1:91.

[6] N.H. Const. 1784, Part I, arts. II, V.

[7] Va. Const. 1776, Bill of Rights, § 1.

[8] Md. Const. 1776, Declaration of Rights, §§ VIII, XI, XXI.

[9] Jud Campbell, "Natural Rights and the First Amendment," *Yale Law Journal* 127 (2017): 246–321.

Story described the Double Jeopardy Clause as "but a constitutional recognition of an old and well established maxim of the common law," and Francis Wharton called it "nothing more than a solemn asseveration of the common law maxim."[10]

When the original Constitution was sent to the states for ratification, one of the primary objections was the absence of a bill of rights. One of the principal responses to this objection was that a bill of rights was unnecessary and even dangerous—unnecessary in part because whatever rights would be included in a bill of rights were already guaranteed by natural law, and dangerous because a list of specific rights might be construed to deny the existence of others not mentioned.[11] The solution to the latter problem was the Ninth Amendment, which provides: "The enumeration in the Constitution of certain rights shall not be construed to deny or disparage others retained by the people." The Ninth Amendment does not say where these other rights come from, but one obvious source was the law of nature.[12] The Ninth Amendment nevertheless played virtually no role in the 19th-century debate over whether courts could use natural law to invalidate statutes. One reason was that the debate took place mostly in state courts, in cases involving state constitutions. The Bill of Rights was not yet interpreted as a constraint on state governments, and during this period state governments interacted with individuals much more than the federal government did, so most challenges to government action were filed in state courts and were based on state constitutions. But the Ninth Amendment played little part in the debate even when the Constitution was at issue. The Ninth Amendment confirmed the existence of rights beyond those enumerated in the Constitution, but the debate was not over whether natural rights *existed*. On that question there was as yet scarcely any disagreement. The debate was over the role that natural rights should play in the legal system—whether judges had the power to invalidate statutes contrary to natural rights. That was a question the Ninth Amendment did not address.

Could judges invalidate legislation contrary to natural law? The two competing positions were laid out clearly in *Calder v. Bull*, a case decided by the US Supreme Court in 1798 that remains to this day the best-known example of the debate. After a Connecticut court found a will invalid, the state legislature enacted a statute setting aside the court's decision. The question for the Supreme Court was whether the state statute violated the Ex Post Facto Clause of the

---

[10] *United States v. Gibert*, 25 F. Cas. 1287, 1294 (C.C.D. Mass. 1834); Francis Wharton, *A Treatise on the Criminal Law of the United States* (Philadelphia: James Kay, Jr., 1846).

[11] Michael J. Klarman, *The Framers' Coup: The Making of the United States Constitution* (New York: Oxford Univ. Press, 2016), 548–54.

[12] Kurt T. Lash, *The Lost History of the Ninth Amendment* (New York: Oxford Univ. Press, 2009), 46–48.

Constitution. The Court unanimously determined that it did not, on the ground that the established meaning of an "ex post facto" law was one that attached *criminal* penalties to an act after the act had already been committed. Because the Connecticut statute merely reopened a civil case, it did not violate the Ex Post Facto Clause. The justices delivered their opinions seriatim, as was still the norm. Only four of the six justices participated: Oliver Ellsworth was absent due to illness, while James Wilson was hiding from his creditors and would die of a stroke within a couple of weeks.[13]

Calder v. Bull did not raise the question whether courts could enforce rights in addition to those listed in constitutions. As Justice Samuel Chase explained, this was "a question of very great importance, and not necessary NOW to be determined." Chase nevertheless provided a lengthy argument that statutes contrary to natural law were void. "I cannot subscribe to the omnipotence of a State Legislature, or that it is absolute and without control; although its authority should not be expressly restrained by the Constitution," Chase began. "There are certain vital principles in our free Republican governments, which will determine and over-rule an apparent and flagrant abuse of legislative power." In particular, "an ACT of the Legislature (for I cannot call it a law) contrary to the great first principles of the social compact, cannot be considered a rightful exercise of legislative authority."[14]

Chase then provided some examples of legislative acts that would be void for this reason. "A law that punished a citizen for an innocent action, or, in other words, for an act, which, when done, was in violation of no existing law; a law that destroys, or impairs, the lawful private contracts of citizens; a law that makes a man a Judge in his own cause; or a law that takes property from A. and gives it to B.: It is against all reason and justice, for a people to entrust a legislature with SUCH powers; and, therefore, it cannot be presumed that they have done it." Some of the legislative acts on this list (such as punishment for an action that was not illegal when done, and the impairment of contracts) were prohibited by clauses in the Constitution, while others (such as making a man a judge in his own cause) were not, at least not in explicit terms. But Chase's point was that such legislative acts would be outside the legislature's power even in the absence of express constitutional provisions prohibiting them. "The genius, the nature, and the spirit, of our State Governments, amount to a prohibition of such acts of the legislation," he continued, "and the general principles of law and reason forbid them. The Legislature may enjoin, permit, forbid, and punish, and they may declare new crimes; and establish rules of conduct for all its citizens

---

[13] Maeva Marcus, ed., *The Documentary History of the Supreme Court of the United States, 1789–1800* (New York: Columbia Univ. Press, 1985–2007), 8:93 nn. 33–34.

[14] *Calder v. Bull*, 3 U.S. 386, 387–88 (1798).

in future cases; they may command what is right, and prohibit what is wrong; but they cannot change innocence into guilt; or punish innocence as a crime; or violate the right of an antecedent lawful private contract; or the right of private property." Chase did not use the term "natural law," but this was easily recognizable as a natural law argument, one based on "general principles of law and reason" rather than on written constitutions. As Chase saw it, constitutions were not the only limits on legislative power. He concluded: "To maintain that our Federal, or State, Legislature possess such powers, if they had not been expressly constrained, would, in my opinion, be a political heresy, altogether inadmissible in our free republican governments."[15]

Why, if *Calder v. Bull* did not raise the question, did Chase feel the need to bring it up? He may have been responding to his colleague James Iredell, who had expressed the contrary view two months earlier in a different case. Supreme Court justices rode circuit as trial judges, and in that capacity, Iredell presided at the trial of *Minge v. Gilmour*, a property dispute in which one of the issues was the constitutionality of a North Carolina statute. After finding the statute constitutional, Iredell noted that it was "further urged by the counsel for the plaintiff that this act is contrary to natural justice, and therefore void." This claim required Iredell to consider whether natural law could invalidate a statute. "Some respectable authorities do, indeed, countenance such a doctrine—that an act against natural justice is void," he observed. "Others maintain a different one, with at least an equal claim to respect. Under these circumstances, I can only consult my own reason; and I confess I think no court is authorized to say that an act is absolutely void merely because, in the opinion of the court, it is contrary to natural justice."[16]

Iredell spelled out his reasoning, in what appears to have been the first substantial expression by an American judge of doubts about the role natural law should play in the legal system. "Two principles appear to me to be clear," he explained. "If an act be unconstitutional, it is void. If it be constitutional, it is valid. In the latter case it must be admitted that the legislature have exercised a trust confided to them by the people. In doing so they necessarily are left to their own discretion, and it is to be presumed they will have a due regard to justice in all their conduct." Thus far, Iredell's remarks were consistent with the general view among English and American lawyers, that the legislature must be assumed to have acted consistently with the law of nature, and that statutes should accordingly be interpreted in that light. "If they"—that is, the legislature—"abuse their trust in the execution of an acknowledged power," he continued, "they are

---

[15] *Id.* at 388–89.
[16] *Minge v. Gilmour*, 17 F. Cas. 440, 443–44 (C.C.D.N.C. 1798).

indeed responsible, in the only way in which a legislature can be responsible, for not exercising their authority properly." Iredell presumably meant that the legislature would be responsible to the voters, who, if they were unsatisfied, would choose different representatives at the next election.[17]

Iredell then turned to natural law itself. "The words 'against natural justice' are very loose terms, upon which very wise and upright members of the legislature and judges might differ in opinion," he remarked. "If they did, whose opinion is properly to be regarded—those to whom the authority of passing such an act is given, or a court to whom no authority, in this respect, naturally results?" As Iredell saw it, the inherent ambiguity of natural law was a good reason judges should not be authorized to use it to supersede legislation. He drew the conclusion that constitutional limits on the legislature were the only limits. "It may surely be inferred," he added, "that if, in addition to other restrictions on the legislative power, such a restriction as that in question was intended, so as to leave it to the courts, in all instances, to say whether an act was agreeable to natural justice or not, this restriction would have been inserted." But no constitution expressly gave courts this power. Iredell concluded that "no court has the authority to say the act is void because in their opinion it is not agreeable to the principles of natural justice."[18]

In *Minge*, Iredell argued, in effect, that American courts' assumption of the power of judicial review did not warrant any departure from English practice, under which courts could not invalidate legislation for being contrary to natural law. In *Calder v. Bull*, Samuel Chase may have seen an opportunity to respond to Iredell's opinion in *Minge*. Iredell then replied to Chase in his own opinion in *Calder*, with an even clearer statement of his position.[19] If a constitution "imposed no limits on the legislative power," Iredell argued, "the consequence would inevitably be, that whatever the legislative power chose to enact, would be lawfully enacted, and the judicial power could never interpose to pronounce it void. It is true, that some speculative jurists have held, that a legislative act against natural justice must, in itself, be void; but I cannot think that . . . any Court of Justice would possess a power to declare it so."[20] Iredell was making the

---

[17] *Id.* at 444.

[18] *Id.*

[19] In the report of the justices' seriatim oral opinions, Chase's opinion comes before Iredell's, so I am assuming that Iredell was able to hear Chase deliver his opinion before he delivered his own. It is also possible that the reporter changed the order of the opinions, and that Iredell was the one who first brought the issue up in *Calder*, in which case Chase was responding to Iredell's *Calder* opinion rather than his *Minge* opinion. The normal practice at the time was to deliver opinions orally rather than in print. Indeed, in *Calder*, Iredell says, "I will endeavour to state the general principles, which influence me, on this point, succinctly and clearly, though I have not had an opportunity to reduce my opinion to writing." *Calder*, 3 U.S. at 398.

[20] *Id.*

same point Blackstone had made with respect to English courts a few decades earlier: Whatever theoretical constraints natural law placed on legislative power, as a practical matter courts had no authority to refuse to enforce statutes contrary to natural law.

Iredell repeated his point about the ambiguity of natural law, in even stronger terms than in *Minge*. "The ideas of natural justice are regulated by no fixed standard," he argued. "The ablest and purest men have differed upon the subject; and all that the Court could properly say, in such an event, would be, that the Legislature (possessed of an equal right of opinion) had passed an act which, in the opinion of the judges, was inconsistent with the abstract principles of natural justice."[21] The result would be a stalemate, in which the court's interpretation of natural law would be entitled to no greater credence than the legislature's interpretation.

Iredell's argument that the content of natural law was too uncertain and subjective for judges to enforce would, many years later, be one of the principal critiques of the use of natural law within the legal system. Among American lawyers in the 1790s, the argument was well before its time. It is possible, although there is no direct evidence for it, that Iredell was influenced by Jeremy Bentham, one of the earliest English critics of natural law. Bentham's *Fragment on Government*, published in 1776, was a thorough attack on Blackstone's *Commentaries*, in which Bentham mocked natural law as an excuse for a person "to rise up in arms against any law whatever that he happens not to like."[22] Bentham returned to the subjectivity of natural law in his *Introduction to the Principles of Morals and Legislation*, published a few years before Iredell wrote. "A great multitude of people are continually talking of the Law of Nature," Bentham sneered, "and then they go on giving you their sentiments about what is right and what is wrong; and these sentiments, you are to understand, are so many chapters and sections of the Law of Nature."[23] Bentham would later famously declare that "there are no such things as natural rights" and that "*natural rights* is simple nonsense; natural and imprescriptible rights, rhetorical nonsense,—nonsense upon stilts."[24] Bentham's work had not yet been published in the United States, but books published in London often crossed the Atlantic, and early American lawyers were avid purchasers of English books, so perhaps Iredell had read Bentham.

---

[21] *Id.* at 399.

[22] Jeremy Bentham, *A Fragment on Government* (London: T. Payne, 1776), 149.

[23] Jeremy Bentham, *An Introduction to the Principles of Morals and Legislation* (London: T. Payne, 1789), xiv.

[24] John Bowring, ed., *The Works of Jeremy Bentham* (Edinburgh: William Tait, 1838–43), 2:500–501.

None of Iredell's colleagues on the Supreme Court shared his certainty that judges should not review statutes for consistency with natural law. Three years before *Calder v. Bull*, Justice William Paterson had given a jury charge that suggested that he, like Samuel Chase, believed that courts could invalidate statutes that infringed natural rights. "The right of acquiring and possessing property, and having it protected, is one of the natural, inherent, and unalienable rights of man," Paterson instructed the jury. "Men have a sense of property: Property is necessary to their subsistence, and correspondence to their natural wants and desires." This assertion of a natural right of property would hardly have been controversial at the time. The harder question was whether a court had the power to invalidate a statute that conflicted with the natural right of property, by, for example, forcing a person "to surrender or sacrifice his whole property" without compensation. Paterson suggested that a court did have this power. "Such an act would be a monster in legislation, and shock all mankind," he argued. "The legislature, therefore, had no authority to make an act divesting one citizen of his freehold, and vesting it in another, without a just compensation. It is inconsistent with the principles of reason, justice, and moral rectitude; it is incompatible with the comfort, peace, and happiness of mankind; it is contrary to the principles of social alliance in every free government; and lastly, it is contrary both to the letter and spirit of the Constitution."[25] Paterson's mention of the Constitution at the very end of this passage introduces a bit of ambiguity, because it is not completely clear whether he would also have considered himself authorized to invalidate a statute that was contrary merely to reason and justice but not the letter of the Constitution. Nevertheless, it seems more likely that Paterson would have sided with Chase than with Iredell.

The Court returned to the issue in 1810 in *Fletcher v. Peck*, in which a Georgia statute revoking a prior land grant was challenged as contrary to natural law and to the Constitution's Contracts Clause. In the Court's majority opinion, Chief Justice John Marshall tentatively suggested that courts could invalidate statutes contrary to natural law, but he acknowledged that the question was a difficult one. "It may well be doubted," Marshall began, "whether the nature of society and of government does not prescribe some limits to the legislative power." The extent of the constraints on what a legislature could do, "in cases where the constitution is silent, never has been, and perhaps never can be, definitely stated." Marshall found no need to decide the question, because in his view the Georgia statute violated the Contracts Clause, and that was enough to decide the case. Justice William Johnson, writing separately, explained that he would have invalidated the statute on natural law grounds instead, because he did not think

---

[25] *Vanhorne's Lessee v. Dorrance*, 2 U.S. 304, 310 (C.C.D. Pa. 1795).

the statute was contrary to the Contracts Clause. As Johnson saw it, the statute was void based "on a general principle, on the reason and nature of things; a principle which will impose laws even on the deity."[26]

A few years later, in *Terrett v. Taylor*, Justice Joseph Story implied that he too believed that it was possible for judges to review statutes for consistency with natural law, although, as in *Fletcher*, there was no need to do so in *Terrett*. Before the Revolution, Virginia had granted land in Alexandria to an Episcopal congregation, at a time when the Episcopal Church was the established church of the colony. After the Revolution, when Virginia disestablished the Episcopal Church, who owned the land—the congregation or the state? The unanimous Court concluded, in an opinion written by Story, that the congregation still owned the land, based on the principle that a government could not revoke land grants once made, even after a change as big as the Revolution. It was "a principle of the common law that the division of an empire creates no forfeiture of previously vested rights of property," Story explained. He continued: "And this principle is equally consonant with the common sense of mankind and the maxims of eternal justice." In the end, the Court decided the case on statutory grounds, so it was not "necessary to rest this cause upon the general doctrines already asserted." Nevertheless, Story understood natural law as at least potentially relevant. He did not take Iredell's view that natural law had no place in assessing the validity of statutes.[27]

The members of the early Supreme Court thus expressed the full range of views on what would be a persistent question of constitutional law throughout the 19th century. On one side, Samuel Chase, William Johnson, and perhaps Joseph Story thought that written constitutions were not the only constraints on legislative power. They believed that American courts' power of judicial review also included the authority to determine whether statutes were consistent with natural law. On the other side, James Iredell took the view that written constitutions were the only limits on legislative power, and that judges had no authority to use natural law to invalidate statutes. In the middle, John Marshall was uncertain which side of the debate was correct. He thought that perhaps judges did have the power to strike down statutes contrary to natural law, although he was not sure under what circumstances, and he seemed happy not to have to decide.

It bears emphasizing that in the early 19th century this was a genuinely hard question. Both sides of the debate were plausible. It was generally accepted that natural law existed and that it played an important role in the legal system. It was

[26] *Fletcher v. Peck*, 10 U.S. 87, 135–36, 143 (1810).
[27] *Terrett v. Taylor*, 13 U.S. 43, 50 (1815).

likewise common ground that many of the rights listed in written constitutions were preexisting natural rights, which the constitutions were not creating but restating. But what did that mean when courts exercised their power of judicial review? Could they strike down a statute that was contrary to natural law but not to a written constitutional provision? A constitution was an expression of popular sovereignty, a declaration of fundamental law that authorized judges to disregard legislation, but were the constitution's enumerated grounds for doing so meant to be exclusive? Was a constitution the *only* fundamental law? This question would be a subject of controversy for the rest of the century.

A Century of Debate

In the early 1820s, William Tipton sued William Harris in a Tennessee court and won a judgment of approximately $1,200. The trial was conducted by a judge sitting without a jury, because the statute under which Tipton sued did not require a jury, and the state constitution did not require a jury in such cases either. When Harris appealed, claiming that he had nevertheless been entitled to a jury as a matter of general principle, the Tennessee Supreme Court faced what it called "a question of the greatest moment": Could the right to a jury trial be located in a source other than the written constitution? Or to put the question more generally, were there extraconstitutional limits on the power of the legislature? The court decided there were not. "The sovereign legislative power of Tennessee, like the sovereign power of all other States, of whatsoever character they may be, may do all things, not naturally impossible, which it deems promotive of the public welfare, except in such instances where, by the fundamental law of the nation, written by the mighty hand of the people, it is forbidden," the court declared. The Tennessee legislature could do anything not expressly prohibited in the constitution.[28]

But the court reached precisely the opposite conclusion a few years later. Charles Cooper, a clerk at Tennessee's short-lived state bank, stole money from the bank. He was tried by a special court the legislature had established to hear cases involving the bank, a court that sat without a jury. Cooper stole the money before the legislature established the special court. He argued that the statute establishing the court was impermissibly retroactive—that a statute could not govern conduct that took place before the statute's enactment. The state constitution did not prohibit the legislature from enacting retroactive statutes. The Tennessee Supreme Court nevertheless held that the statute was void. Justice

[28] *Tipton v. Harris*, 7 Tenn. 414, 418 (1824).

Nathan Green, a newly appointed member of the court, noted that in Tipton's case the court had stated that the legislature could do whatever the constitution did not explicitly forbid. "To this proposition," Green explained, "I cannot give my assent." In the court's new view, "Certain limits to the exercise of legislative power have been recognized from the earliest times. It is a principle of the English common law, as old as the law itself, that a statute, even of the omnipotent Parliament of Great Britain, is not to have a retrospective effect." The source of this principle, Green noted, was the law of nature. "It was so considered because there are eternal principles of justice which no government has a right to disregard. It does not follow, therefore, because there may be no restriction in the constitution prohibiting a particular act of the legislature, that such act is therefore constitutional. Some acts, although not expressly forbidden, may be against the plain and obvious dictates of reason."[29] Within a few years, the Tennessee Supreme Court had taken both sides of the debate.

The court's change of heart was emblematic of the trouble judges had in deciding whether the constitution's limits on legislative power were the only ones, or whether statutes could also be invalidated as contrary to natural law. The California Supreme Court revealed the same division of opinion when it considered the state's "Settler Law" of 1856, which required a landowner who successfully brought suit ejecting a trespasser to compensate the trespasser for improvements the trespasser had made to the land. The Settler Law, as its name suggested, favored settlers over absentee landowners by changing preexisting law, under which trespassers who improved land were not entitled to the value of the improvements. The court acknowledged that the Settler Law was not contrary to any provision of the constitution. But that did not end the inquiry, Chief Justice Hugh Murray reasoned in his majority opinion. Murray explained that "it has been erroneously supposed, by many, that the Legislature of a State might do any Act, except what was expressly prohibited by the Constitution." This view, Murray noted, would mean that "if laws are passed which are immoral, or violate the principles of natural justice, the subject is bound to obey them." But "in this country," he declared, "the spirit of free institutions is at war with such a principle." Regardless of what the constitution said, "The Legislature cannot pass a law divesting vested rights," and in Murray's view the Settler Act had done just that, in newly requiring landowners to pay for improvements they had not authorized. He recognized that the legislature meant well. The act was intended "to encourage settlement in good faith upon vacant lands as a means of developing agricultural interests" at a time when settlers were pouring into the state. But "however desirable such a policy may be, and however necessary to the interest

[29] *Bank of the State v. Cooper*, 10 Tenn. 599, 603 (1831).

of the state," Murray cautioned, "it ought not to be encouraged or maintained when founded in wrong and injustice to her citizens. It is a law as immutable as those of nature, that States and nations, like individuals, are bound to obey the principles of natural justice in all their dealings with their subjects and others." Because the Settler Act was contrary to these natural principles, it could not be enforced.[30]

Justice David Terry dissented, in an opinion that spelled out the other side of the debate at considerable length. "The doctrine, that judges have power to annul a law, because, in their opinion, its provisions are in violation of natural justice, is one of dangerous consequences," Terry warned. "The question whether a particular law is in violation of natural justice, may be one of difficult solution. Its determination is governed by no fixed rules, and often depends on considerations of policy and public advantage, which are more properly the subjects of legislative than judicial exposition." Terry worried that judges were arrogating legislative power by claiming a right to invalidate statutes contrary to natural law. "If it is once admitted that there exists in this Court a power to declare a State law void, which conflicts with no constitutional provision—if we assume the right to annul it for its supposed injustice or oppressive operation, we become the makers and not the expounders of the Constitution," he insisted. "Our opinions would not be a judgment on what was the preexisting law of the case; but upon what it is, after we have so amended or modified it, as to meet our ideas of justice, policy, and wise legislation, by a direct usurpation of legislative power."[31]

As these cases suggest, there was no clear answer to whether courts had the authority to evaluate statutes for consistency with natural law. The question "is undetermined," confessed Stephen Hosmer, the chief justice of Connecticut's Supreme Court in the 1820s, after reviewing the opinions of Chase and Iredell in *Calder v. Bull*. "Men of profound learning and exalted talents, have greatly differed on the subject." Hosmer could conclude only that "it is an enquiry beset with difficulty."[32] By mid-century the answer was even less clear, because there were ample precedents on both sides. In the 1850s, the *American Law Register* summarized many cases "sufficient to show the tendency of some courts and some judges to hold that there are certain great principles of right justice or government, which it is the duty of the judiciary to apply as restraints on legislative action, independently of constitutional provisions." On the other hand, the *Law Register* observed, "There are numerous and weighty authorities to the

---

[30] *Billings v. Hall*, 7 Cal. 1, 10–15 (1857).

[31] *Id.* at 19–21.

[32] *Town of Goshen v. Town of Stonington*, 4 Conn. 209, 225 (1822).

contrary."[33] Theodore Sedgwick reviewed many of the same authorities in his 1857 treatise on constitutional and statutory interpretation, and he reached the same nonconclusion. The question "has been frequently examined in various points of view, and by writers of great authority," Sedgwick reported, "some contending for the absolute supremacy of the legislature, others for the superior authority of the courts as competent to declare and enforce the doctrines of natural justice."[34] After half a century of debate, this fundamental question was no closer to being resolved. So long as natural law played an explicit role in the legal system, it never would be.

On one side of the debate, courts throughout the century invalidated statutes for violating principles of justice that were not written into constitutions. These cases did not arise often, but there were enough to constitute a firm base from which to argue that judicial review encompassed natural law as well as written constitutional provisions. One group of these cases that deserves special attention, as the precursor to the substantive due process cases of later in the century, are those in which courts invoked natural law to strike down statutes that granted special privileges to individuals or small groups of people. In Massachusetts, for example, when Moses Holden missed the deadline for filing a suit to recover money he was owed, he persuaded the state legislature to pass a statute extending the statute of limitations just for him. No provision of the state constitution prohibited the legislature from helping Holden in this way, but the state supreme court found it unseemly that an otherwise generally applicable rule should be suspended for the benefit of a single person. "It is manifestly contrary to the first principles of civil liberty and natural justice, and to the spirit of our constitution and laws, that any one citizen should enjoy privileges and advantages which are denied to all others in like circumstances," the court insisted. The court concluded that the statute enacted for Holden's benefit would have no effect, and that his suit was accordingly filed too late.[35]

Likewise, when the Wisconsin legislature enacted a statute exempting the city of Janesville, but no other party, from the requirement that the loser of a suit pay the winner's filing fees, the Wisconsin Supreme Court held that "fundamental principles of law and justice" barred the legislature from granting such special favors. Normally the court would base such a decision on some specific clause of the constitution, Chief Justice Luther Dixon acknowledged, "but the rule is

---

[33] W.W.B., "The Right of a Legislature (Without Reference to the Law of Eminent Domain) to Change the Legal Character of Estates, or the Title to Property, by General or Special Enactments," *American Law Register* 7 (1859): 458.

[34] Theodore Sedgwick, *A Treatise on the Rules Which Govern the Interpretation and Application of Statutory and Constitutional Law* (New York: John S. Voorhies, 1857), 148.

[35] *Holden v. James*, 11 Mass. 396, 405–6 (1814).

not without its exceptions." He relied on the US Supreme Court's cases invoking natural law, especially Justice Chase's opinion in *Calder v. Bull*, to conclude that "the grant of legislative powers, though without prohibition or restraint that the legislature shall not discriminate and do gross and palpable injustice between man and man by the passage of unequal and partial laws, does not carry with it the power to pass such laws."[36] The Georgia Supreme Court agreed that this sort of "class legislation" was contrary to "the great fundamental principles of human rights."[37] As we will see in chapter 8, toward the end of the century, as natural law became a less important part of the legal system, the basis for such holdings would shift to the Due Process Clause of the Constitution, a shift that would help give rise to the doctrine of substantive due process.

Courts also sometimes invoked natural law to invalidate a statute that seemed to trample upon property rights, but in a way not forbidden by any clause of the state constitution.[38] (This too was a function that would shift to the Due Process Clause toward the end of the century.) In 1845, for instance, the New York legislature enacted a statute to straighten the road between Somers and Peekskill. The statute provided compensation for affected landowners. Landowners duly removed fences from the parts of their property where the road would go, but before the road was improved and before the landowners could receive any compensation, the legislature repealed the statute. The landowners were left with the expense of rebuilding their fences. No statute or constitutional provision required compensation, but Judge Seward Barculo nevertheless held that the legislature had to pay. "It can hardly be said that under this general power of legislation it is omnipotent: that it can pass acts against natural right and justice," Barculo declared. "Such power is the prerogative of despotism—not of free government." Just because the constitution did not prohibit a particular kind of legislation did not mean that the legislature was free to enact it. "Suppose it should prescribe a uniformity of dress, or the quantity and quality of food for each person, or regulate the hours which every citizen should devote to labor and to sleep," Barculo worried. "Would such laws be valid? Could any court be found to enforce them?"[39]

One recurring situation in which courts used natural law to strike down statutes involved local government efforts to encourage the construction of railroads. At mid-century many towns issued bonds to obtain money to subsidize or buy stock in railroad companies, as an inducement for the railroad to

[36] *Durkee v. City of Janesville*, 28 Wis. 464, 467, 469 (1871).

[37] *Bethune v. Hughes*, 28 Ga. 560, 565 (1859).

[38] J. A. C. Grant, "The 'Higher Law' Background of the Law of Eminent Domain," *Wisconsin Law Review* 6 (1931): 67–85.

[39] *People ex rel. Fountain v. Board of Supervisors*, 4 Barb. 64, 71 (N.Y. Sup. Ct. 1848).

run through the town, which, it was hoped, would spur local economic development. When these investments went sour, towns were left with the unappealing prospect of having to raise taxes on local residents to pay off the bondholders, who were often investors in far-off places. If the constitution did not bar towns from investing in railroads, were the bondholders entitled to be paid? Some courts held that they were not, because natural law prohibited the use of public money for this purpose. If governments could do anything not barred by the constitution, one court insisted, "Popular will when thus exercised, could legalize the execution of the citizen; could take A's property and give it to B. These propositions would be regarded as monstrous." But how was it different to force people to pay taxes "for a purpose entirely foreign to the support of government? I see no difference in principle, and there is none certainly when viewed in reference to these fundamental rights which are secured to us by the natural law, and which no legislation can take from us."[40] In a similar case, another court declared that the state legislature, which had purported to authorize towns to issue bonds to subsidize railroads, lacked the "authority to make laws inconsistent with natural right. If conceded that outside of constitutional restrictions, the legislature possesses the sovereign power of the state, it is only the power the people possessed; and they did not possess the power to destroy the natural rights of a citizen, to declare innocence a crime, or, on their own volition, to take the property of one and give it to another. Inhibition against such acts was unnecessary, because they were inhibited by the higher law of natural right."[41]

A similar case—better known because it was decided by the Supreme Court—involved not a railroad but the King Wrought-Iron Bridge Manufacturing and Iron-Works Company. To encourage the company to build a factory in Topeka, Kansas, the city issued $100,000 in bonds and used the money to subsidize the factory. Two years later, when a bank in Cleveland tried to compel the city to pay the interest promised by the bonds, the Court held that the city did not have to pay, because the state legislature had lacked the power to authorize the city to

[40] *Stokes v. Scott County*, 10 Iowa 166, 172 (1859). *Stokes* came toward the end of a series of Iowa cases culminating in *Gelpcke v. City of Dubuque*, 68 U.S. 175 (1863), in which the Supreme Court required towns to pay off the bondholders. The reasoning of *Gelpcke* is famously murky, but the Court seemed to rely on the natural rights of the bondholders, by basing its decision on "truth, justice, and the law," *id.* at 206, despite its failure to identify any federal law requiring payment, and despite the Iowa Supreme Court's conclusion that under state law no payment was required.

[41] *Sweet v. Hulbert*, 51 Barb. 313, 318 (N.Y. Sup. Ct. 1868). See also *Cincinnati, Wilmington and Zanesville Railroad Co. v. Commissioners of Clinton County*, 1 Ohio St. 77, 84 (1852) ("the authority of the General Assembly is much too broadly stated, when it is claimed that all their acts must be regarded as valid, which are not expressly prohibited by the constitution. A moment's attention to principles, which must be regarded as fundamental, in all the American systems of government, will demonstrate the unsoundness of such a conclusion").

issue the bonds in the first place. "There are limitations on such power which grow out of the essential nature of all free governments," the Court explained. "No court, for instance, would hesitate to declare void a statute which enacted that A. and B. who were husband and wife to each other should be so no longer, but that A. should thereafter be the husband of C., and B. the wife of D. Or which should enact that the homestead now owned by A. should no longer be his, but should henceforth be the property of B." The Court determined that one of these natural limits on legislative power was the principle that tax revenue could not be handed over to a private business. "To lay with one hand the power of the government on the property of the citizen, and with the other to bestow it upon favored individuals and private enterprises and build up private fortunes, is none the less a robbery because it done under the forms of law and is called taxation," the Court declared. "This is not legislation. It is a decree under legislative forms." Justice Nathan Clifford dissented on the ground that the constitutional limits on legislative power were the only limits. "Courts cannot nullify an act of the State legislature on the vague ground that they think it opposed to a general latent spirit supposed to pervade or underlie the constitution where neither the terms nor the implications of the instrument disclose any such restriction," Clifford protested. "Such a power is denied to the courts, because to concede it would be to make the courts sovereign over both the constitution and the people, and convert the government into a judicial despotism."[42]

There was a wide variety of contexts in which natural law might override a statute. During the Civil War, West Virginia confiscated the property of residents who were absent from the state because they were fighting for the Confederacy. Near the war's end, the state enacted a statute establishing a procedure for returning residents to recover property that had been wrongly confiscated. Such residents had to swear that they had never fought for the Confederacy. The West Virginia Supreme Court evaluated this procedure for consistency with natural law as well as with the constitution. The court explained: "Not only is the exercise of legislative power limited and constrained by the organic law which the people, the source of all power, have ordained in the form of the constitution; but civil power is itself limited by its own nature to the objects of the civil compact." The court cited Thomas Rutherforth's *Institutes of Natural Law*, along with Samuel Chase's opinion in *Calder v. Bull*, to establish that judicial review was not limited to the written constitution. "Should, therefore, the legislature assume to exercise a power, though not prohibited by the express limitations of the constitution, yet should be no part of the civil power springing from the social compact, but an unwarrantable usurpation of arbitrary power, it would be a solemn

[42] *Loan Association v. Topeka*, 87 U.S. 655, 663–64, 669 (1874).

duty of the judiciary to interpose in the exercise of its judicial functions, and pronounce the pretended law a nullity," the court held. "Nor could the courts shrink from this high duty any more in such a case, than in the case of a plain and palpable violation of the express prohibition of the constitution."[43]

The US Supreme Court made a similar observation about the ability of states to keep out corporations from other states. As a condition of doing business, a state could require out-of-state corporations to consent to be sued within the state, the Court noted. The Court cautioned: "Such condition must not, however, encroach upon that principle of natural justice which requires notice of a suit to a party before he can be bound by it."[44] The Court's implication was that a state law that *did* violate this natural principle could not be enforced.

There was thus a steady stream of cases, all through the 19th century, in which courts asserted the authority to strike down statutes contrary to natural law. The number of cases in which courts actually exercised that authority was smaller than the number in which they asserted it, but it was large enough for commentators to be justified in arguing that the power of judicial review was not limited to the express terms of written constitutions. The Pennsylvania lawyer H. L. Richmond had ample support when he stated that if a statute should conflict with the law of nature, the courts "would, at once, pronounce it void, on principles of Natural Law."[45] George Robeson, the attorney general of New Jersey, provided reasonable advice when he informed the state senate that it had the power to make any rules it liked concerning riparian rights—"subject, however, to the restrictions of the Federal and State constitution, and to the obligations of that natural law which lies at the foundation of all government."[46] Throughout the century, there was a sizable body of opinion that statutes contrary to natural law were void.

But there was also considerable opinion on the other side of the debate. All through the 19th century, courts repeatedly insisted that the judges could not use natural law to invalidate statutes.

One prominent proponent of this view was the Supreme Court justice Henry Baldwin. In 1830, as a circuit judge, Baldwin had two opportunities to discuss the relationship between constitutional law and the law of nature. In *Bennett v. Boggs*, a man convicted of illegal fishing in the Delaware River argued that the New Jersey statute regulating fisheries was void because the public had a natural right to fish in navigable rivers. "The enjoyment of this right is secured to the public in all civilized nations," his lawyer insisted, citing Grotius and Pufendorf,

---

[43] *Peerce v. Carskadon*, 4 W. Va. 234, 244, 247 (1870).

[44] *St. Clair v. Cox*, 106 U.S. 350, 356 (1882).

[45] H. L. Richmond, *Law and the Duties and Obligations it Imposes* (Meadville, Pa.: J.C. Hays, 1851), 16.

[46] George M. Robeson, *Opinion Concerning Riparian Rights* (Trenton: State Gazette, 1867), 5.

among others; "the sea, the shore, and the right of fishing therein, are common property, which cannot be appropriated to private use." Baldwin would have none of it. "We cannot declare a legislative act void because it conflicts with our opinions of policy, expediency or justice," he insisted. "We are not the guardians of the rights of the people of a state unless they are secured by some constitutional provision which comes within our judicial cognizance." As James Iredell had done a generation before, Baldwin worried that natural law was too ambiguous for judges to enforce. "There is no paramount and supreme law which defines the law of nature, or settles those great principles of legislation which are said to control state legislatures," he explained. Like Iredell, he thought judges would trespass on the legislature's territory if they took their views of natural law into account. "If it is once admitted that there exists in this court a power to declare a state law void, which conflicts with no constitutional provision—if we assume the right to annul them for their supposed injustice, or oppressive operation, we become the makers and not the expounders of constitutions," Baldwin declared. "Our opinion will not be a judgment on what was the pre-existing law of the case, but on what it is after we shall have so amended and modified it as to meet our ideas of justice, policy and wise legislation, by a direct usurpation of legislative powers."[47]

Baldwin returned to this theme a few months later in *Livingston v. Moore*, in which a property dispute turned on the validity of a Pennsylvania statute. One of the litigants argued that the statute was void, and once again Baldwin insisted that constitution supplied the only means of striking down a statute. "It is the constitution that must be violated, and not any man's opinions of right and wrong, or his principles of natural justice," Baldwin declared. "These are uncertain standards of legislative power, and must be referred to the discretion of those to whom the people have given that power, and to whom they must answer for an abuse of it."[48] The ambiguous realm of natural law was a matter for the legislature, not the courts.

Judges would make the same point for the rest of the century. "The duty of obeying the divine law when human law is in conflict with it, on a point of morals or religious faith, is everywhere taken for granted," explained New Hampshire chief justice Charles Doe. "But this duty does not legally require or empower a judge or other officer of the government to officially nullify a law which he is under an express official oath or implied official obligation to officially maintain." The constitution recognized the existence of God and the right of individual conscience, Doe concluded, but "it does not establish anarchy by legalizing

---

[47] *Bennett v. Boggs*, 3 F. Cas. 221, 224, 227, 228 (C.C.D.N.J. 1830).
[48] *Livingston v. Moore*, 15 F. Cas. 677, 685 (C.D.E.D. Pa. 1830).

every principle and practice that may be approved by anybody's interpretation of the higher law, nor authorize the court to destroy the constitution and laws which they are commissioned to administer."[49]

Some emphasized that courts would gain an uncomfortable degree of policymaking power if they could use natural law to invalidate statutes. "It is difficult, upon any general principles, to limit the omnipotence of the sovereign legislative power, by judicial interposition, except so far as the express words of a written constitution give that authority," reasoned Gulian Verplanck, the former congressman who sat on New York's highest court. "There are indeed many *dicta*, and some great authorities, holding that acts contrary to the first principles of right are void," he acknowledged. But Verplanck could "find no authority for a court to vacate or repeal a statute on that ground alone." In his view, "It is only in express constitutional provisions, limiting legislative power and controlling the temporary will of a majority, by a permanent and paramount law, settled by the deliberate wisdom of the nation, that I can find a safe and solid ground for the authority of courts of justice to declare void any legislative enactment. Any assumption of authority beyond this, would be to place in the hands of a judiciary, powers too great and too undefined."[50]

The content of natural law was determined by the exercise of reason, but so too was the content of legislation, which for some judges made discerning natural law feel more legislative than judicial. When Michigan prohibited the sale of alcohol, and a barkeeper claimed a natural right to sell liquor, the Michigan Supreme Court rejected the claim on the ground that determining the content of natural law was a task for the legislature. "What is the process by which that determination is made?" the court asked. "Are we nicely to compare the value of this right with the injury which the exercise of it would inflict upon the public, and strike the balance? Or are we to compare it with other individual rights, which, by the general legislation of the country, have been made subservient to the public interests?" Neither method seemed palatable. "It will not be difficult to see that it is of no importance whether the *one* rule or the *other* is adopted," the court concluded. "They both resolve themselves into the same question: a question of policy; a question very suitable and proper for the discussion and deliberation of a legislative body, but one which cannot be entertained by this court." (As if to prove the difficulty of the question, a dissenting judge wrote at length on the history of liquor consumption from the Bible up to the present, to demonstrate that selling liquor truly *was* a natural right and that Michigan's prohibition statute was accordingly void.)[51]

---

[49] *Orr v. Quimby*, 54 N.H. 590, 610–11 (1874) (Doe, J., dissenting).

[50] *Cochran v. Van Surlay*, 20 Wend. 365, 381–82 (N.Y. 1838). Verplanck was a New York state senator at the time. Until 1846, members of the state senate sat on the state's highest court.

[51] *People v. Gallagher*, 4 Mich. 244, 258, 261–65 (1856).

It could feel uncomfortably undemocratic, even for judges accustomed to exercising a learned superintendence over the legal system, to strike down statutes for being contrary to natural principles. "I admit that men have, by the laws of nature, the right of acquiring, and possessing property," Supreme Court justice Robert Trimble acknowledged. "But when men form a social compact, and organize a civil government, they necessarily surrender the regulation and control of these natural rights and obligations into the hands of the government." As a result, "The *natural* obligation of *private* contracts between individuals in society, ceases, and is converted into a *civil* obligation." Written positive law, in Trimble's view, supplanted unwritten natural principles. "If the positive law of the State declares the contract shall have no obligation it can have no obligation," he concluded, "whatever may be the principles of natural law in relation to such a contract." Otherwise, he worried, "The States can have no control over contracts."[52]

Some judges emphasized the ambiguity of natural law. If the legislature found a statute consistent with natural law, but the courts found the statute contrary to natural law, how could one tell which view was correct? "Transferring the seat of authority from the legislature to the Courts, would be putting our interests in the hands of a set of very fallible men," worried the Pennsylvania Supreme Court. Judges had no clearer view of natural law's content than legislators did. The court was accordingly "convinced that the words of the constitution furnish the only test to determine the validity of a statute, and that all arguments, based on general principles outside of the constitution, must be addressed to the people, and not to us." The court was addressing the same claim that succeeded in other states—that natural law prohibited the investment of public money in private enterprises such as railroads. "This is, beyond comparison, the most important cause that has ever been in this Court since the formation of the government," Chief Justice Jeremiah Black observed. But because nothing in the Pennsylvania Constitution prohibited the statute, the court refused to strike it down. "The constitution has given us a list of the things which the legislature may not do," Black declared. "If we extend that list, we alter the instrument, we become ourselves the aggressors, and violate both the letter and spirit of the organic law as grossly as the legislature possibly could."[53]

This same concern about the ambiguity of natural law recurred in several other cases. The judiciary "cannot run a race of opinions upon points of right, reason, and expediency with the lawmaking power," insisted the Indiana Supreme Court. Because the courts' opinion of natural law was no better than the

---

[52] *Ogden v. Saunders*, 25 U.S. 213, 319–21 (1827).
[53] *Sharpless v. Mayor of Philadelphia*, 21 Pa. 147, 162, 158, 161 (1853).

legislature's, "The legislative power in this State, where the constitution imposes no limits, must be practically absolute, whether it operate according to natural justice, or not."[54] The Nevada Supreme Court agreed that it could not invalidate laws based on "that uncertain thing called natural justice; or . . . what Judges are pleased to call the principles of eternal justice."[55] A Pennsylvania judge recalled that natural law had been cited in support of such disparate programs as Plato's Republic, the French Revolution, and "the various systems of socialism," none of which had been successfully put into practice for long. There was no reason to expect that a court's interpretation of natural law would be any better.[56]

By mid-century, commentators could cite such cases to support the assertion that judges lacked the authority to strike down statutes as contrary to natural law. The best-known mid-century treatise on constitutional law, the Michigan Supreme Court justice Thomas Cooley's *Constitutional Limitations*, took this view with some vehemence. A court cannot "declare a statute unconstitutional and void, solely on the ground of unjust and oppressive provisions, or because it supposed to violate the natural, social, or political right of the citizen, unless it can be shown that such injustice is prohibited or such rights guaranteed or protected by the constitution," Cooley argued. "The courts are not the guardians of the rights of the people of the State, unless those rights are secured by some constitutional provision which comes within the judicial cognizance. The remedy for unwise or oppressive legislation, within constitutional bounds, is by an appeal to the justice and patriotism of the representatives of the people."[57] Just as there was ample support for the proposition that statutes were unenforceable if contrary to natural law, there was also ample support for the opposite proposition—that judges could refuse to enforce statutes only where the statutes were contrary to express constitutional provisions, and that natural law provided no basis for invalidating a statute.

How Judges Could Avoid the Question

Faced with these conflicting authorities, judges avoided deciding the question when they could. One avoidance technique was to rely on natural law *and* a constitutional provision simultaneously. For instance, in upholding the rights

---

[54] *Madison and Indianapolis Railroad Co. v. Whiteneck*, 8 Ind. 217, 222 (1856).

[55] *Gibson v. Mason*, 5 Nev. 283, 294 (1869).

[56] *Commonwealth ex rel. Thomas v. Commissioners of Allegheny County*, 32 Pa. 218, 237–38 (1858) (Lowrie, C.J., concurring).

[57] Thomas M. Cooley, *A Treatise on the Constitutional Limitations Which Rest Upon the Legislative Power of the States of the American Union* (Boston: Little, Brown, 1868), 164, 168.

of New York ferry operators against a recently enacted statute that exposed the ferries to new competition, the court declared: "Their rights, in this respect, rest not merely upon the constitution, but upon the great principles of Eternal Justice, which lie at the foundation of all free governments."[58] By relying on both natural law and the written constitution, a judge could express his view about the importance of natural law without provoking criticism from his colleagues or reversal by a higher court.

Another way to avoid the question was the time-honored method of using natural law to construe a statute in a nonliteral way, on the assumption that the legislature could not have intended to violate natural law. We saw some examples in chapter 1. One of the most often cited of these cases was *Gardner v. Village of Newburgh*, decided by Chancellor James Kent of New York in 1816. A state statute authorized the village of Newburgh to divert a stream in order to ensure the village a water supply. The statute provided compensation for anyone who lost land as result of the diversion, but not for those who lost access to water. Gardner, a farmer who depended on the stream's old location for his crops and his cattle, argued that the statute unlawfully deprived him of property. In most states he could have based his argument on the takings clause of the state constitution, but New York's constitution lacked a takings clause. (The state would later adopt one when it revised its constitution in 1821.) The takings clause of the federal Constitution, like the rest of the Bill of Rights, was still interpreted to constrain only the federal government, not the states, so Gardner could not rely on that either. His argument was therefore based on natural law.[59]

Kent agreed that natural law required compensation for Gardner. He cited Grotius, Pufendorf, and Bynkershoek for the proposition that a requirement of compensation, where the government infringes property rights, "is admitted by the soundest authorities, and is adopted by all temperate and civilized governments, from a deep and universal sense of its justice." But rather than striking down the statute, Kent declared that he was "persuaded that the legislature never intended, by the act in question, to violate or interfere with this great and sacred principle of private right." He determined that unless "some provision be made for affording him compensation, it would be unjust, and contrary to the first principles of government, and"—here came the key part—"equally contrary to the intention of this statute." Having interpreted the statute nonliterally to require compensation for Gardner, Kent enjoined the diversion of the stream until Gardner had been compensated. Through this technique of statutory interpretation, a judge was able to achieve a result consistent with natural law, without

---

[58] *Benson v. City of New York*, 10 Barb. 223, 245 (N.Y. Sup. Ct. 1850).
[59] *Gardner v. Village of Newburgh*, 2 Johns. Ch. 162 (N.Y. Ch. 1816).

having to face the knotty question of whether courts had the power to invalidate statutes contrary to natural law.

The Iowa Supreme Court used the same method to interpret a statute authorizing railroads to take land involuntarily from private landowners to build track, so long as they compensated the landowners. A landowner argued that the payment had to precede the taking of land, while a railroad insisted that it could take the land first and pay later. "The plaintiff needed no constitutional declaration to protect him in the use and enjoyment of his property," the court held. "To be thus protected and secure in the possession of his property is a right inalienable, a right which a written constitution may recognize or declare, but which existed independently and before such recognition, and which no government can destroy." In light of this natural principle, the court construed the statute to require the railroad to pay the landowner first.[60]

Courts also used the natural principle forbidding "class legislation"— that is, legislation conferring special privileges—to interpret statutes. As the Pennsylvania Supreme Court explained, "Special or class legislation is so manifestly wrong that its existence should not be presumed unless the legislative intent is free from doubt or difficulty." The court therefore refused to allow the Borough of Bethlehem to impose a tax on money lent at interest, despite the clause in Bethlehem's charter that seemingly authorized it to do so, on the ground that this was a power of taxation the legislature had withheld from the other boroughs in the state.[61] "There ought to be no *class legislation* in this country," agreed the Georgia Supreme Court, which accordingly interpreted a statute exempting only mechanics and day laborers from wage garnishment to apply to all wage earners, even those not mentioned in the statute. "All who come within the spirit of the Act, should be brought within its provision," insisted Chief Justice Joseph Henry Lumpkin. "I know no reason why the employees of corporations, or even journeymen mechanics, aye, or even Irish ditchers, should have privileges, withheld from those who till the earth."[62]

Could judges use natural law to strike down statutes? The question endured as long as natural law remained a working part of the legal system. At midcentury, in a book intended for students, the Boston lawyer Joel Bishop did his best to reconcile the two competing points of view. "It is pretty plainly the better opinion, in our country, that there are limitations upon legislative power other than what are expressed in our State and national constitutions," Bishop explained. There were any number of cases in which judges had invoked these unwritten constraints on legislative power, constraints that rested not on any

---

[60] *Henry v. Dubuque & Pacific Railroad Co.*, 10 Iowa 540, 543–44 (1860).
[61] *Goepp v. Borough of Bethlehem*, 28 Pa. 249, 255 (1857).
[62] *Caraker v. Mathews*, 25 Ga. 571, 574–75 (1858).

positive law but on the law of nature. "On the other hand," Bishop continued, "it is neither the province nor the right of a judge to decide any cause on his individual, private views." Judges had to apply the law, not their own interpretations of what justice required. "We may, therefore, conclude, that courts will not usually disregard a plain and distinct legislative act, merely because the individual judges consider its provisions unjust, or contrary to natural reason, or to the law of God."[63] Bishop, struggling to find a middle ground, had to distinguish between natural law, which could invalidate a statute, and a judge's own understanding of natural law, which could not. But this was no middle ground at all. The content of natural law, like the content of any kind of law, could be identified only by human beings, so every assertion of the law was merely an assertion of the speaker's understanding of the law.

In the long run, the most significant aspect of this debate was not how it was resolved, for it would never be resolved.[64] The important thing is that the debate brought forward the first sustained critiques of the use of natural law within the American legal system. Lawyers and judges argued that natural law was too subjective, too ambiguous, too susceptible of multiple interpretations. They argued that using natural law was too close to policymaking, too close to legislation, to fall within the role of the judiciary. For most of the 19th century, these arguments were directed at the specific question whether constitutional provisions were the only limits on legislation. But the arguments had implications well beyond this specific question. If natural law was subjective and ambiguous, should it play *any* role in the legal system? If using natural law was too close to legislation, should judges use natural law in *any* context? In the later part of the century, lawyers would begin to raise these broader questions.

[63] Bishop, *First Book*, 69–71. On the relationship between Bishop's religious views and his jurisprudential views, see Stephen A. Siegel, "Joel Bishop's Orthodoxy," *Law and History Review* 13 (1995): 215–59.

[64] See, e.g., Robert P. Reeder, "Constitutional and Extra-constitutional Restraints," *University of Pennsylvania Law Review* 61 (1913): 441–57; Walter F. Dodd, "Extra-constitutional Limitations upon Legislative Power," *Yale Law Journal* 40 (1931): 1188–1218.

4

The Separation of Law and Religion

"The christian religion is part of our common law, with the very texture of which it is interwoven," the Harvard law professor Simon Greenleaf declared in 1834.[1] At the time, few lawyers would have disagreed. In the late 18th century and for much of the 19th, lawyers had little doubt that Christianity and American law were closely intertwined.

This close relationship between law and religion played a role in lawyers' acceptance of the use of natural law in court. The common law was understood to rest on a mixture of natural law and custom, both of which had religious content. The law of nature had been created by God. Christianity, the customary religion of the overwhelming majority of Americans, was nearly synonymous with morality and good order. In the early Republic there was thus a large overlap between the domains of law and religion.

This overlap gradually shrank throughout much of the 19th century. Americans may not have become any less religious, but they increasingly began to think of religion as an area of life separate from that of law and government. As the domains of law and religion slowly pulled apart, lawyers began to question whether Christianity was truly part of the common law. These doubts would eventually weaken the position of natural law within the legal system. For this reason, it is worth giving some attention to the relationship between Christianity and the common law over the course of the 19th century. What did lawyers mean when they said that Christianity was part of the common law? Why did they believe this was true? And why, as time went on, did they stop believing it?

---

[1] Simon Greenleaf, *A Discourse Pronounced at the Inauguration of the Author as Royal Professor of Law in Harvard University* (Cambridge: James Munroe, 1834), 24. On Greenleaf's views on the relationship of law and religion, see Daniel D. Blinka, "The Roots of the Modern Trial: Greenleaf's *Testimony* to the Harmony of Christianity, Science, and Law in Antebellum America," *Journal of the Early Republic* 27 (2007): 293–334.

The Decline of Natural Law. Stuart Banner, Oxford University Press (2021). © Oxford University Press.
DOI: 10.1093/oso/9780197556498.003.0005

Part and Parcel of the Common Law

"Christianity is a part of the common law," Supreme Court Justice James Wilson declared in his lectures at the College of Philadelphia in the early 1790s.[2] "*Christianity* is a part of the law of the land," agreed the chief justice of the Connecticut Supreme Court a few years later.[3] Variants of this maxim would be repeated over and over by American judges and lawyers. The Arkansas Supreme Court observed that "the christian religion . . . is recognized as constituting a part and parcel of the common law."[4] "Christianity," the Alabama Supreme Court suggested, "is justly regarded, in a certain sense, as a part of the common law of the land."[5] Legal treatises routinely made the same point.[6] In 1844, the US Supreme Court even proclaimed: "It is said, and truly, that the Christian religion is a part of the common law."[7] By the turn of the century, the New York lawyer Arthur Barber could look back on a long list of such pronouncements and conclude that "text writers have reiterated and courts have affirmed the maxim that Christianity is part and parcel of the common law."[8] The matter, suggested one Philadelphia judge, had been "decided over and over again."[9]

As with so much of early American legal thought, the maxim was an import from England. "The judges in England have often decided, that Christianity is a part of the common law," Nathan Dane explained in his comprehensive digest of American law, published in several volumes through the 1820s.[10] The first English case in which the maxim appeared was the 1676 prosecution of John Taylor "for uttering of divers blasphemous expressions, horrible to hear," including "that Jesus Christ was a whoremaster, religion was a cheat; and that he neither feared God, the devil, or man." Chief Justice Matthew Hale held that blasphemy was not just an offense against religion but a crime against the state as well because "Christianity is parcel of the laws of England."[11]

---

[2] James DeWitt Andrews, ed., *The Works of James Wilson* (Chicago: Callaghan, 1896), 2:425.

[3] *Lyman v. Wetmore*, 2 Conn. 42, 43 (1795).

[4] *Shover v. State*, 10 Ark. 259, 263 (1850).

[5] *Goree v. State*, 71 Ala. 7, 9 (1881).

[6] Joel Prentiss Bishop, *Commentaries on the Criminal Law* (Boston: Little, Brown, 1856–58), 1:325; Edward Buck, *Massachusetts Ecclesiastical Law*, rev. ed. (Boston: Congregational Publishing Society, 1865), 203; Fortunatus Dwarris, *A General Treatise on Statutes*, ed. Platt Potter (Albany, NY: William Gould & Sons, 1871), 559.

[7] *Vidal v. Philadelphia*, 43 U.S. 127, 198 (1844).

[8] Arthur William Barber, "Christianity and the Common Law," *Green Bag* 14 (1902): 267.

[9] *In re Granger*, 7 Phila. Rep. 350, 355 (1870).

[10] Nathan Dane, *A General Abridgment and Digest of American Law* (Boston: Cummings, Hilliard, 1823–29), 6:675.

[11] *Taylor's Case*, 86 Eng. Rep. 189 (K.B. 1676). For more on the case, see Elliott Visconsi, "The Invention of Criminal Blasphemy: *Rex v. Taylor* (1676)," *Representations* 103 (2008): 30–52.

Hale's phrasing of the maxim may have been new, but the substance of the maxim was not. England had an established church. Blasphemy had been prosecuted in the secular courts many times before.[12] As the legal historian William Holdsworth observed, the "maxim would, from the earliest times, have been accepted as almost self-evident by English lawyers."[13] But if the doctrine was familiar, Hale's formulation must have caught the imagination of English lawyers, because his words began popping up in subsequent opinions. When the publisher of two early 18th-century obscene books—"the one stil'd, The Nun in Her Smock; the other, The Art of Flogging"—argued that he had not committed any crime, the court rejected the argument on the ground that "religion was part of the common law; and therefore whatever is an offence against that, is evidently an offence against the common law."[14] When the Reverend Thomas Woolston of the University of Cambridge published tracts in which he maintained that the New Testament was an allegory and that Christ had not literally performed miracles, he too was convicted of blasphemy.[15] The court reasoned that "Christianity in general is a parcel of the common law of England, therefore to be protected by it; now whatever strikes at the very root of Christianity, tends manifestly to a dissolution of the civil government."[16] When the merchant Elias de Paz left in his will a fund for the teaching of Judaism, the court invalidated the bequest because it was "in contradiction to the Christian religion, which is a part of the law of the land."[17] William Blackstone's four-volume *Commentaries*, the standard reference work in the United States for a century after its publication, summed up such cases in a single sentence: "Christianity is part of the laws of England."[18]

It soon became part of American law as well. The New York judge James Kent was the first American lawyer to discuss at length the relationship between Christianity and the common law. The occasion was the blasphemy prosecution of John Ruggles. On a Sunday in the fall of 1810, in the small town of Salem, New York, near the Vermont border, Ruggles stood in public and announced, in a loud voice: "Jesus Christ was a bastard, and his mother must be a whore."[19] He was convicted in a local court of blasphemy and sentenced to three months

---

[12] G. D. Nokes, *A History of the Crime of Blasphemy* (London: Sweet & Maxwell, 1928).

[13] W. S. Holdsworth, *A History of English Law* (London: Methuen, 1922–38), 8:403 n. 5.

[14] *R. v. Curl*, 94 Eng. Rep. 20 (K.B. 1727).

[15] Leonard W. Levy, *Blasphemy: Verbal Offense against the Sacred, from Moses to Salman Rushdie* (Chapel Hill: Univ. of North Carolina Press, 1995), 308–15; Courtney Kenny, "The Evolution of the Law of Blasphemy," *Cambridge Law Journal* 1 (1922): 133–34.

[16] *R. v. Woolston*, 94 Eng. Rep. 655, 656 (K.B. 1729).

[17] *De Costa v. De Paz*, 36 Eng. Rep. 715, 716 (Ch. 1754).

[18] Blackstone, *Commentaries*, 4:59.

[19] *People v. Ruggles*, 8 Johns. 290, 291 (N.Y. Sup. Ct. 1811).

in prison and a fine of $500, an enormous amount equivalent to more than two years' wages for the average rural manufacturing worker.[20] The case was removed to New York's Supreme Court, over which Kent presided as chief justice.

Ruggles's lawyer argued that while blasphemy was punishable under the common law of England, where Christianity was part of the law, such was not the case in New York. The state had no established religion, unlike England. From the Constitution's protection of religious freedom, he contended, it could be "inferred that *christianity* did not make a part of the common law of this state." Because "the constitution allows a free toleration to all religions and all kinds of worship," Ruggles's lawyer argued, "*Judaism* and *Mahometanism* may be preached here, without any legal animadversion." Indeed, he noted, Ruggles himself "may have been a *Jew*, a *Mahometan*, or a *Socinian*; and if so, he had a right, by the constitution to declare his opinions."[21]

Kent disagreed. Before he became a judge, Kent was a law professor at Columbia, where in his lectures he discussed the importance of religion to the enforcement of the law. In allowing for the freedom of religion, Kent told his students, the United States was "setting a new, a liberal, and a just precedent to mankind. But I apprehend that we should grossly abuse it if government were to abandon all patronage of religious instruction, and all superintendance of the cultivation of public morals." In Kent's view, the freedom *of* religion did not mean the freedom *from* religion, because without religion, citizens would have insufficient incentive to follow the law. "A general conviction of the reality of moral obligation and future retribution, have always been found necessary to give due consideration and efficacy to the sanctions of the civil law," he explained. As religious belief provided support for the law, the law had to provide reciprocal support for religious belief, at least to the extent of punishing offenses "which strike at the foundations of natural rectitude, and public decorum."[22]

For Kent, *Ruggles* was a perfect example of the role Christianity played in undergirding the legal system. Kent quoted the English cases stating that "christianity was parcel of the law," and then proceeded to explain exactly why. He began by observing that blasphemy's status as a common law crime was "independent of any religious establishment or the rights of the church." It was the legal system, not the church, that needed buttressing. "We stand equally in need, now as formerly, of all that moral discipline, and of those principles of virtue,

---

[20] *Historical Statistics of the United States* (Cambridge Univ. Press online edition), table Ba4245 (using data for 1820, the closest available year).

[21] *Ruggles*, 8 Johns. at 291–92. Socinians were a sect of Christians, but in the United States "Socinian" was sometimes used as a general term for anyone with unorthodox religious views.

[22] James Kent, *Dissertations: Being the Preliminary Part of a Course of Law Lectures* (New York: George Forman, 1795), 23–24.

which help to bind society together," he reasoned. "The people of this state, in common with the people of this country, profess the general doctrines of christianity, as the rule of their faith and practice; and to scandalize the author of these doctrines is not only, in a religious point of view, extremely impious, but, even in respect to the obligations due to society, is a gross violation of decency and good order." Kent saw considerable danger if statements like the one made by Ruggles were allowed to proliferate. "Nothing could be more offensive to the virtuous part of the community, or more injurious to the tender morals of the young, than to declare such profanity lawful," he worried. "It would go to confound all distinction between things sacred and profane." Kent compared blasphemous statements to other "things which corrupt moral sentiment, as obscene actions, prints and writings," which "have, upon the same principle, been held indictable, and shall we form an exception in these particulars to the rest of the civilized world?"[23]

In *Ruggles*, as in his lectures, Kent found no inconsistency between the constitutional guarantee of the freedom of religion and Christianity's status as part of the common law. "The free, equal, and undisturbed, enjoyment of religious opinion, whatever it may be, and free and decent discussions on any religious subject, is granted and secured," he acknowledged, "but to revile, with malicious and blasphemous contempt, the religion professed by almost the whole community, is an abuse of that right." Offenses against Christianity were cognizable at common law, not because they struck at religion, but "because they strike at the root of moral obligation, and weaken the security of the social ties." The law of New York tolerated the practice of all religions, but it did not permit "licentious, wanton, and impious attacks upon christianity itself," because Christianity was essential to the maintenance of morality and order. Attacks on Christianity were therefore punishable, while comparable attacks on other religions were not. Kent saw no reason to punish "the like attacks upon the religion of *Mahomet* or of the grand *Lama*; and for this plain reason, that the case assumes that we are a christian people, and the morality of the country is deeply ingrafted upon christianity, and not upon the doctrines or worship of these impostors." Minority religions did not serve Christianity's function as the moral grounding of the community, so the common law did not protect them as it did Christianity.[24]

A decade later, at New York's 1821 constitutional convention, Kent had another opportunity to elaborate on the relationship between Christianity and the common law. Kent was one of the delegates at the convention, as was Erastus Root, a state legislator and a former member of Congress. Root was evidently

---

[23] *Ruggles*, 8 Johns. at 293–95.
[24] *Id.* at 295–96.

disturbed by Kent's opinion in the *Ruggles* case. He proposed a constitutional provision barring the judiciary from declaring any religion to be the law of the land. He "wished for freedom of conscience," Root explained. "If judges undertake to support religion by the arm of the law, it will be brought into abhorrence and contempt."[25]

Kent responded that Root had misunderstood his remarks in *Ruggles*. "The court had never declared or adjudged that christianity was a religion established by law," he explained. "They had only decided that to revile the author of christianity in a blasphemous manner, and with a malicious intent, was an offence against public morals." Attacks on Christianity "were indictable on the same principle as the act of wantonly going naked, or committing impure and indecent acts in the public streets." Christianity was "the basis of the public morals," and for that reason blasphemy would "degrade our character as a christian people." As for the Constitution's protection of religious freedom, Kent added, "the authors of our constitution never meant to extirpate christianity, more than they meant to extirpate public decency." Kent's explanation satisfied the convention. In *Ruggles*, the judges "had never undertaken to uphold, by the authority of law, any particular sect," agreed Daniel Tompkins, then serving as US vice president, who presided over the convention. "But they had interposed, and rightfully interposed, as the guardians of the public morals, to suppress those outrages on public opinion and public feeling, which would otherwise reduce the community to a state of barbarism, corrupt its purity, and debase the mind." Root's proposed provision was not included in New York's new constitution.[26]

Kent's view became one of the standard explanations of why Christianity was part of the common law, an explanation repeated by many other writers. For instance, when Joseph Story gave his inaugural address as a Harvard law professor, he likewise pronounced that Christianity and morality were inseparable. "One of the beautiful boasts of our municipal jurisprudence is, that Christianity is part of the common law," Story observed. "There has never been a period, in which the common law did not recognize Christianity as lying at its foundation." This was because the common law "repudiates every act done in violations of its [i.e., Christianity's] duties of perfect obligation."[27] A few years later, in his *Commentaries on the Constitution*, Story devoted several pages to the subject. "Piety, religion, and morality are intimately connected with the well being of the state, and indispensable to the administration of civil justice," he reasoned. "At all events, it is impossible for those, who believe in the truth of Christianity, as

---

[25] *Reports of the Proceedings and Debates of the Convention of 1821, Assembled for the Purpose of Amending the Constitution of the State of New-York* (Albany: E. and E. Hosford, 1821), 463.

[26] *Id.* at 463–64.

[27] Story, *A Discourse Pronounced*, 20–21.

a divine revelation, to doubt, that it is the especial duty of government to foster, and encourage it among all the citizens and subjects." Story was certain that he was expressing something close to a consensus. "There will probably be found few persons in this, or any other Christian country, who would deliberately contend, that it was unreasonable, or unjust to foster and encourage the Christian religion generally, as a matter of sound policy, as well as of revealed truth," he suggested. "Indeed, in a republic, there would seem to be a peculiar propriety in viewing the Christian religion, as the great basis, on which it must rest for is support and permanence."[28]

The point was often made in court opinions by judges seeking to clarify why Christianity was part of the common law. "The municipal law looks to something more than merely the protection of the lives, the liberty, and the property of the people," argued the Tennessee Supreme Court. "Regarding Christianity as part of the law of the land, it respects and protects its institutions, and assumes likewise to regulate the public morals and decency of the community."[29] In New York, when a lawyer contended that "christianity is not part either of our law or government; for to make it such would be to give it a preference over the Jewish creed, which would be inconsistent with the constitution and bill of rights," the court responded with a thorough defense of the maxim. Christianity was "intimately connected with a good government" and was "the only sure basis of sound morals," the court declared. For that reason, "Christianity is a part of the common law of this state." Without Christianity as the foundation of the common law, the judges worried, "A man may go naked through the streets, establish houses of prostitution *ad libitum* and keep a faro-bank on every corner."[30] The Missouri law professor Christopher Tiedeman summed up such cases by observing that "the fostering and encouragement of a worshipful attitude of mind, the development and gratification of the religious instinct, should be of great concern to the state. While morality is distinguishable from religion, the most important principles of morality receive their highest sanction and their greatest efficacy, as a civilizing force, in becoming the requirements of religion." Because "Christianity is essentially the religion of this country," and because religion was necessary for morality and public order, Christianity was part of the common law.[31]

Meanwhile, judges were elaborating a second explanation for why Christianity was part of the common law: There were many common law doctrines that were

[28] Story, *Commentaries on the Constitution*, 3:722–24.

[29] *Bell v. State*, 31 Tenn. 42, 44 (1851).

[30] *Lindenmuller v. People*, 33 Barb. 548, 558, 563, 560, 574 (N.Y. Sup. Ct. 1861).

[31] Christopher G. Tiedeman, *A Treatise on the Limitations of Police Power in the United States* (St. Louis: F.H. Thomas Law Book, 1886), 167.

taken directly from Christian principles. The earliest extended discussion of this view came in another early 19th-century blasphemy case, the prosecution of Abner Updegraph. Updegraph was a member of a Pittsburgh debating society. During an 1821 debate on religious matters, he declared that "the Holy Scriptures were a mere fable: that they were a contradiction, and that although they contained a number of good things, yet they contained a great many lies." Updegraph was convicted of blasphemy and sentenced to pay a small fine. On appeal to the Pennsylvania Supreme Court, Updegraph's lawyer argued that blasphemy was not a common law crime in Pennsylvania as it had been in England, because while Christianity was part of the common law of England, it was not part of the common law of Pennsylvania.[32]

The Pennsylvania Supreme Court had only derision for this argument. "The bold ground is taken, though it has often been exploded, and nothing but what is trite can be said upon it—it is a barren soil, upon which no flower ever blossomed—the assertion is once more made, that Christianity never was received as part of the common law of this Christian land," remarked an astonished Justice Thomas Duncan. "Christianity, general Christianity, is and always has been a part of the common law of Pennsylvania." If Updegraph's argument was "worth anything," Duncan continued, "all the laws which have Christianity for their object—all would be carried away at one fell swoop." These laws included "the act against cursing and swearing, and breach of the Lord's day; the act forbidding incestuous marriages, perjury by taking a false oath upon the book, fornication and adultery, *et peccatum illud horrible non nominandum inter Christianos*"—homosexuality, the sin so awful that it could not even be named among Christians. "All these are founded on Christianity," Duncan pointed out. If Christianity were not part of the common law, much of the criminal law would vanish. Duncan found it inconceivable that the law should lose its connection to Christianity. "A people wholly without religion, no traveler hath yet seen; and a city might as well be erected in the air, as a state be made to unite, where no divine worship is attended," he insisted. "No free government now exists in the world, unless where Christianity is acknowledged, and is the religion of the country."[33]

By mid-century many likewise argued that Christianity must be part of the common law because the common law embodied so much of Christianity. "Upon it rest many of the principles and usages, constantly acknowledged and enforced, in the Courts of justice!" exclaimed John Belton O'Neall, the chief

---

[32] *Updegraph v. Commonwealth*, 11 Serg. & Rawle 394, 394–95, 397 (Pa. 1824).

[33] *Id.* at 399, 406. The court nevertheless reversed Updegraph's conviction, on the ground that the indictment omitted the word "profanely" and failed to specify the precise words Updegraph had said. *Id.* at 409–10.

justice of South Carolina. For example, "Crimes are classed into *mala in se* and *mala prohibita*," he noted, referring to the familiar distinction between acts that were inherently criminal and those that were criminal merely because they had been prohibited by statute. "What gives them that character?" he asked. "The authority of these divine precepts comes to us through Christianity." O'Neall provided another example. "Our law declares all contracts *contra bonos mores* [contrary to good morals], as illegal and void. What constitutes the standard of good morals? Is it not Christianity? There certainly is none other. Say *that* cannot be appealed to, and I don't know what would be good morals." He provided a third example: "In the Courts over which we preside, we daily acknowledge Christianity as the most solemn part of our administration. A Christian witness, having no religious scruples against placing his hand upon the book, is sworn upon the holy Evangelists—the books of the New Testament, which testify of our Saviour's birth, life, death, and resurrection; this is so common a matter," O'Neall observed, "that it is little thought of as an evidence of the part which Christianity has in the common law."[34] Joseph Henry Lumpkin, chief justice of the Georgia Supreme Court, similarly pointed out that the law's treatment of marriage came straight from the book of Matthew. "By the Common Law and by the Bible, which is the foundation of the Common Law," Lumpkin noted, "the union of man and wife was a junction of persons and fortunes—'no more twain, but one flesh.' "[35]

This close congruence between legal principles and Christian doctrine was only to be expected in a world where law and religion both rested on the same natural law created by God. "Christianity constitutes a part of the common law," explained the St. Louis lawyer George Ritter, "because the teachings of Christ are said to correspond very closely with the laws of nature."[36] The Michigan judge Thomas Cooley provided a similar account in his influential 1868 treatise. "It is frequently said that Christianity is a part of the law of the land," he reflected. "The best features of the common law, and especially those which relate to the family and social relations; which compel the parent to support the child, and the husband the wife; which make the marriage tie permanent, and forbid polygamy, have either been derived from, or have been improved and strengthened by, the prevailing religion and the teachings of its sacred book."[37] Lawyers of the period thus tended to think of Christianity and the common law as overlapping bodies of doctrine, with much of the same content.

---

[34] *City Council of Charleston v. Benjamin*, 33 S.C.L. 508, 521–23 (1848).

[35] *Wylly v. S.Z. Collins & Co.*, 9 Ga. 223, 237 (1851).

[36] George A. Ritter, *An Essay on the Lawyer and the Law as a Profession* (St. Louis: L.C. Lavat, 1880), 7.

[37] Cooley, *Treatise on Constitutional Limitations*, 472.

The conception of common law as derived from custom provided another reason for believing that Christianity was part of the common law. Christianity was obviously an important part of American life, and if the common law was drawn from the norms of everyday life, it would necessarily incorporate a great deal of Christianity. Daniel Webster elaborated on this connection in one of his best-known Supreme Court arguments. Webster was representing relatives of the late Stephen Girard, who at his death was likely the wealthiest man in the United States. In Girard's will he left $2 million to establish a school for orphans at which he specified that no minister would be allowed to teach. Webster contended that this bequest was unlawful, in part because "Christianity is part of the law of the land." Webster continued:

> *Every thing declares it.* The massive cathedral of the Catholic; the Episcopalian church, with its lofty spire pointing heavenward; the plain temple of the Quaker; the log church of the hardy pioneer of the wilderness; the mementoes and memorials around and about us; the consecrated graveyards, their tombstones and epitaphs, their silent vaults, their mouldering contents; all attest it. *The dead prove it as well as the living.* The generation that are gone before speak to it, and pronounce it from the tomb. We feel it. All, all, proclaim that Christianity, general, tolerant Christianity, Christianity independent of sects and parties, that Christianity to which the sword and fagot are unknown, general, tolerant Christianity, is the law of the land.[38]

This argument was so popular that it was published as a stand-alone book, under the title *A Defence of the Christian Religion.*[39] It is an argument that would sound grossly out of place in the Supreme Court today, because it is not about any of the sources of law that are today recognized as legitimate. We do not get our law from a landscape of churches and graveyards. At the time, by contrast, Webster's words were perceived as conventional legal argument. The common law was based on custom. No custom was more widely followed in the United States than adherence to Christianity. The best evidence of that was the landscape of churches and graveyards, which proved that disparate kinds of people

[38] *The Writings and Speeches of Daniel Webster* (Boston: Little, Brown, 1903), 11:176. The Court agreed with Webster that Christianity was part of the law of the land, but the Court nevertheless held the bequest valid. *Vidal v. Philadelphia*, 43 U.S. 127, 198 (1844); see Perry Miller, *The Life of the Mind in America from the Revolution to the Civil War* (New York: Harcourt Brace Jovanovich, 1965), 198–202; Robert A. Ferguson, "The Girard Will Case: Charity and Inheritance in the City of Brotherly Love," in Jack Salzman, ed., *Philanthropy and American Society* (New York: Center for American Culture Studies, 1987), 1–16.

[39] Daniel Webster, *A Defence of the Christian Religion* (New York: Mark H. Newman, 1844).

in far-flung locations all over the country agreed on this point. Christianity was an American custom.

Many other lawyers and judges would draw the same connection between the common law and the customariness of American Christianity. "We are a Christian people," declared the Pennsylvania Supreme Court, "in so far as we have entered into the spirit of Christian institutions, and become imbued with the sentiments and principles of Christianity; and we cannot be imbued with them, and yet prevent them from entering into and influencing, more or less, all our social institutions, customs, and relations, as well as all our individual modes of thinking and acting." When Christianity was so pervasive, it had to seep into the law. "It is involved in our social nature," the court continued, to the extent that "even those among us who reject Christianity, cannot possibly get clear of its influence, or reject those sentiments, customs, and principles which it has spread among the people, so that, like the air we breathe, they have become the common stock of the whole country, and essential elements of its life." In light of this influence, the court concluded, "The declaration that Christianity is part of the law of the land, is a summary description of an existing and very ob-vious condition of our institutions."[40] The New York lawyer Theodore Sedgwick agreed that "it is often said that Christianity is part and parcel of the common law," because "though Christianity is not the religion of the State, considered as a political corporation, it is nevertheless closely interwoven into the texture of our society, and is intimately connected with all our social habits and customs."[41]

W. H. Platt, a law professor in San Francisco, taught his students the mech-anism by which this customary Christianity influenced the common law. "Law exists so long as public opinion permits it to exist," Platt lectured. "The public opinion of this country is Christian opinion; therefore, law lives or dies at the bidding of Christianity, and not Christianity at the bidding of the law. If the Legislature should enact, or the Court should enunciate as law, anything that gravely wounded the Christian sentiment of the land, thousands upon thousands of Christian pulpits, presses, books, and organizations would at once and persistently assail, if not destroy it." Platt provided some hypothetical examples. "Suppose all marriages, in any form, were deemed no longer neces-sary; or husbands and wives could divorce themselves at pleasure; or there was permitted a plurality of husbands and wives; or a promiscuous living of men and women together—how long do you suppose such a law would stand? With a Christianized public opinion, you must have Christian laws."[42] So long as custom

---

[40] *Mohney v. Cook*, 26 Pa. 342, 347 (1855).

[41] Sedgwick, *Treatise on the Rules*, 17–18.

[42] W. H. Platt, *The Unity of Law* (San Francisco: Law College, University of California, 1879), 182–83.

was a source of the law, and so long as Christianity was the customary religion of the United States, Christianity would be part of the common law.

Reliance on custom as the connection between Christianity and the common law yielded different consequences from reliance on the law of nature as the connection. If American law and the Christian religion were understood to be founded on the same law of nature, they were both true, in the sense that today we understand scientific principles to be true. It would be inconceivable that the common law would include some religion other than Christianity, or no religion at all. By contrast, if it was custom that made Christianity part of the common law, there was no reason why the common law might not include some other religion, if that other religion were to become the prevailing custom in the United States, or indeed no religion at all, if atheism were to become the prevailing custom. Several judges accordingly suggested that Christianity's status as part of the common law rested, not on anything essential in the nature of the law, but on the empirical fact that Christianity happened to be the majority religion. "Christianity is indeed recognized as the predominant religion of the country," noted John Bannister Gibson, chief justice of the Pennsylvania Supreme Court. "But further the law does not protect it."[43] The legislature could require shops to close on Sundays, the North Carolina Supreme Court held, "in the same way as the exhibition of animals, or the sale of spirituous liquor within a certain distance of a religious assembly is prohibited," to protect the peace of churchgoers, the large majority of whom observed the Sabbath on Sundays. But if the legislature were to go further, and prohibit Sunday "labor which is done in private, and which does not offend public decency or disturb the religious devotions of others, the power is exceeded, and the statute is void." Sunday laws were permissible, not for the religious reason that Sunday was a holy day, but for the practical reason that Sunday was the day most North Carolinians wanted peace and quiet.[44]

"The maxim . . . has been misunderstood," cautioned the Delaware Supreme Court, taking the same view that custom was the connection between Christianity and the common law. It meant only that the law recognized Christianity as "the prevailing religion of the people. If in Delaware the people should adopt the Jewish or Mahometan religion, as they have an unquestionable right to do if they prefer it, this court is bound to notice it as their religion, and to respect it accordingly." The court was in the midst of affirming the blasphemy conviction of a man who had proclaimed publicly that "the virgin Mary was a whore, and Jesus Christ was a bastard," but the court was careful to

---

[43] *Harvey v. Boies*, 1 Pen. & W. 12, 13 (Pa. 1829).
[44] *Melvin v. Easley*, 52 N.C. 356, 360 (1860).

note that this declaration constituted blasphemy only because most residents of Delaware were Christians and would find it offensive. "The people of Delaware have a full and perfect constitutional right to change their religion as often as they see fit," the court reasoned. "They may to-morrow, if they think it right, profess Mahometanism or Judaism, or adopt any other religious creed they please." If they did, the courts would protect offenses against that religion just like they currently protected offenses against Christianity. "Put the case, then, that they repudiate the religion of their fathers and adopt Judaism," the court imagined. "On an indictment against any man for maliciously reviling Moses in public, in the language of this defendant, and publishing the Jewish religion as a villainous imposition, are we or are we not bound to sentence him?"[45]

This empirical recognition of Christianity as the customary religion of the United States accounts for one of the Supreme Court's best-known and most often misunderstood pronouncements on religion, Justice David Brewer's 1892 declaration that "this is a Christian nation."[46] Brewer himself was a profoundly religious man whose personal view, like that of American judges reaching back to James Kent in the early part of the century, was that Christianity was an essential pillar of civic morality.[47] But in calling the United States a Christian nation, Brewer was not stating his personal view.[48] He was merely acknowledging the fact that most Americans were Christians. The Court was deciding whether, when Congress prohibited assisting foreigners to come to the United States to perform labor, Congress meant to include foreign clergymen within the prohibition. The Court concluded that although the clergy were encompassed within the literal words of the statute, Congress could not have intended to exclude them from the country, not because Christianity was true or because it had any official status, but because excluding Christian ministers would have been so unpopular that Congress would never have voted for such a measure.

The idea that Christianity was part of the common law was thus deeply ingrained in American legal culture for much of the 19th century. It was based on a few beliefs that were widely shared among American lawyers: first, that Christianity was essential to public morals and the observance of the law; second, that many legal doctrines were based on Christian principles; and third, that Christianity was empirically the customary religion in the United States.

---

[45] *State v. Chandler*, 2 Del. 553, 562–63, 567–68 (1837).

[46] *Holy Trinity Church v. United States*, 143 U.S. 457, 471 (1892).

[47] Linda Przybyszewski, "Judicial Conservatism and Protestant Faith: The Case of Justice David J. Brewer," *Journal of American History* 91 (2004): 471–96.

[48] Steven K. Green, "Justice David Josiah Brewer and the 'Christian Nation' Maxim," *Albany Law Review* 63 (1999): 427–76.

Few lawyers disagreed in the early 19th century. The most prominent and vociferous critic of the notion that Christianity was part of the common law was Thomas Jefferson, whose opposition to the maxim spanned his entire professional career. As an apprentice in the 1760s, while he was still in his early twenties, Jefferson wrote in his commonplace book a long history of the maxim, in which he argued that the maxim entered English law erroneously in the early 17th century, through a mistaken translation from French into English.[49] He returned to the topic fifty years later, in 1814, perhaps prompted by James Kent's discussion of the maxim in the *Ruggles* case a few years before. "Our judges," he complained to John Adams, "extend the coercions of municipal law to the dogmas of their religion, by declaring that these make a part of the law of the land." He repeated to Adams his theory that it had all been a big mistake, caused by the faulty translation in the 17th century of the French phrase *ancien scripture* as *holy scripture*, when a more accurate translation would have been *ancient writing*. "We find this string of authorities all hanging by one another on a single hook, a mistranslation," he groused, "and who can now question but that the whole Bible and Testament are a part of the Common law?"[50]

Jefferson's views became public knowledge in 1824, a couple of years before his death, when his letter on the subject to the English reformer John Cartwright was published in newspapers in Boston and London. Christianity could not be part of the common law, Jefferson argued, because "the common law existed while the Anglo-Saxons were yet Pagans; at a time when they had never yet heard the name of Christ pronounced, or knew that such a character existed." He retold his account of how the maxim rested on a mistranslation from French to English. "What a conspiracy this, between church and state!!!" Jefferson exclaimed. "Sing tantararara, rogues all; rogues all; sing tantararara, rogues all!"[51]

Jefferson's mistranslation theory does not seem to have persuaded many people. "Upon looking into the original authorities, I think his construction of the words untenable," Joseph Story confided to a friend. "It appears to me inconceivable how any man can doubt, that Christianity is part of the Common Law

---

[49] Jefferson to Thomas Cooper, 10 Feb. 1814, J. Jefferson Looney, ed., *The Papers of Thomas Jefferson: Retirement Series* (Princeton: Princeton Univ. Press, 2004–16), 7:190–91 (enclosing "a sample from my Commonplace book, of the pious disposition of the English judges to connive at the frauds of the clergy, a disposition which has even rendered them faithful allies in practice, when I was a student of the law, now half a century ago"). This entry from Jefferson's commonplace book would eventually be published after his death in Thomas Jefferson, *Reports of Cases Determined in the General Court of Virginia* (Charlottesville: F. Carr, 1829), 137–42.

[50] Jefferson to John Adams, 24 Jan. 1814, *Papers of Thomas Jefferson*, 7:147–48.

[51] Jefferson's letter to Cartwright was also published in Thomas Cooper, *A Treatise on the Law of Libel and the Liberty of the Press* (New York: G.F. Hopkins & Son, 1830), 175–84. The quoted material is at 182 and 184. Information about publication in Boston and London newspapers is at 175.

of England, in the true sense of this expression, which I take to be no more than that Christianity is recognized as true, and as the established religion of England. Upon what other foundation stands her whole ecclesiastical system?" Story was incredulous that Jefferson could think otherwise. "Can you believe," he asked, "that when heresy was punishable with death, and Statute Laws were made to enforce Christian rites and doctrines, it was no part of the Law of England, that to revile the established religion was a crime?" At the time of the supposed mis-translation, Story pointed out, "England was overrun with all sorts of ecclesias-tical establishments, nunneries, and monasteries, and Christianity constituted a great part of the public concern of all men. To suppose it had not the entire sanction of the State, is, with reverence be it spoken, to contradict all history."[52] After Jefferson's death, Story made his criticism public. In his inaugural lecture at Harvard in 1829, he referred only to "the specious objection of one of our dis-tinguished statesmen," although many in the audience presumably knew which statesman he meant.[53] A few years later, in an article in the *American Jurist* maga-zine, he referred to Jefferson by name.[54]

Story won this debate. It was hard to argue that Christianity had not been part of the law of England. But an argument could be made that even if Christianity was once part of the English common law, it was not part of the common law in the United States. American lawyers and judges began making this argument in the mid-19th century, and by the early 20th century it would be the conven-tional wisdom.

The Separation of Law and Religion

Over the course of the 19th century, the domains of law and religion gradually began to pull apart. Americans probably did not become less religious. Religiosity is a tricky thing to measure, but the available data suggest that Americans re-ported *more* religious adherence later in the century.[55] Rather, Americans in-creasingly began to conceive of religion as a private, personal sphere of life,

---

[52] Story to Edward Everett, 15 Sept. 1824, William W. Story, ed., *Life and Letters of Joseph Story* (Boston: Charles C. Little and James Brown, 1851), 1:430.

[53] Story, *A Discourse Pronounced*, 21.

[54] Joseph Story, "Christianity a Part of the Common Law," *American Jurist & Law Magazine* 9 (1833): 346–48. On Story's view, see James McClellan, *Joseph Story and the American Constitution: A Study in Political and Legal Thought* (Norman: Univ. of Oklahoma Press, 1971), 118–59.

[55] Roger Finke and Rodney Stark, *The Churching of America, 1776–1990: Winners and Losers in Our Religious Economy* (New Brunswick, NJ: Rutgers Univ. Press, 1992), 16; Mark A. Noll, *America's God: From Jonathan Edwards to Abraham Lincoln* (New York Oxford Univ. Press, 2002), 187–208.

separate from the public sphere of law.[56] We can see this gradual separation in a few areas.

One early example was the disestablishment of churches. At independence, most states had established churches, a varied status that could include state support of churches with tax revenue and/or land grants, state control over church doctrine and personnel, and requirements that state officeholders be church members.[57] (The Establishment Clause of the federal Constitution prohibited a federally established church and barred Congress from interfering with state establishments, but it was not originally understood to prohibit state establishments.) A few states disestablished their churches shortly after independence. The rest did so in a trickle throughout the late 18th and early 19th centuries, until the last state with an established church, Massachusetts, ceased supporting the church in the early 1830s.[58] The details and short-run causes of these disestablishments varied from place to place, but behind them all was a reconceptualization of churches as private voluntary associations, separate from the state.[59]

Another example was the withering away of prosecutions for blasphemy. Blasphemy cases were already on the decline by the early 19th century, as part of a broader decline in the prosecution of religion-based offenses.[60] The last celebrated American blasphemy case was the prosecution of Abner Kneeland in Massachusetts in the 1830s. Kneeland was an idiosyncratic minister who founded his own newspaper in which he denied the existence of Christ, miracles, the resurrection of the dead, and many of the characteristics conventionally attributed to God. He was convicted of blasphemy in a case that attracted a great deal of attention at the time.[61] Kneeland's case has continued to receive attention from historians, in part because Massachusetts chief justice Lemuel Shaw wrote a lengthy opinion defending the constitutionality of the state's blasphemy

[56] Philip Hamburger, *Separation of Church and State* (Cambridge: Harvard Univ. Press, 2002); Steven K. Green, *The Second Disestablishment: Church and State in Nineteenth-Century America* (New York: Oxford Univ. Press, 2010); John G. West Jr., *The Politics of Revelation and Reason: Religion and Civic Life in the New Nation* (Lawrence: Univ. Press of Kansas, 1996).

[57] Michael W. McConnell, "Establishment and Disestablishment at the Founding, Part I: Establishment of Religion," *William and Mary Law Review* 44 (2003): 2105–2108.

[58] Carl H. Esbeck, "Dissent and Disestablishment: The Church-State Settlement in the Early American Republic," *Brigham Young University Law Review* 2004 (2004): 1458.

[59] Mark Douglas McGarvie, *One Nation under Law: America's Early National Struggles to Separate Church and State* (DeKalb: Northern Illinois Univ. Press, 2004); Nathan O. Hatch, *The Democratization of American Christianity* (New Haven: Yale Univ. Press, 1989).

[60] William E. Nelson, *Americanization of the Common Law: The Impact of Legal Change on Massachusetts Society, 1760–1830* (Cambridge: Harvard Univ. Press, 1975), 36–40, 110–15.

[61] *Commonwealth v. Kneeland*, 37 Mass. 206 (1838).

statute.[62] Blasphemy prosecutions continued for some time—indeed, the Maine Supreme Court affirmed a blasphemy conviction as late as 1921—but their frequency seems to have dwindled considerably in the decades after the Kneeland case.[63] Blasphemous statements no longer seemed as deserving of prosecution.

In the daily work of the courts, perhaps the most frequently recurring intersection of Christianity and the law involved assessing the qualifications of witnesses, a task that had to be performed at every trial. Here too, the legal system gradually shed some of its religious content. The general rule in the early 19th century was that a witness was competent to testify only if the witness believed that God would punish him or her for testifying falsely. The rationale for this requirement was that otherwise witnesses would lack sufficient incentive to tell the truth.[64] "What if a witness should declare, that there was no God;—that he believed in no God, and worshipped none;—shall he be permitted to appeal to God, and imprecate his vengeance if he speak falsely?" asked the Connecticut Supreme Court. "This would be the first-born of absurdities! Yet belief in God lies at the foundation of all true religion. Hence, the court may, as it is universally conceded, ascertain the religious belief of a witness."[65] John Henry Hopkins, who was both a lawyer and a bishop in the Episcopal Church, voiced the conventional view when he insisted "that a belief in the essential truths of Christianity is the grand foundation of all judicial oaths, and that all moral evidence, and all confidence in human veracity, must be weakened by apostasy, and overthrown by total infidelity."[66] Witnesses had to swear upon the Bible to speak the truth, an oath that repeatedly reinforced the connection between religion and the law. "I have been taught that christianity is part of the law of the land," remarked the Tennessee judge Robert Whyte. "The four gospels upon the clerk's table admonish me it is so every time they are used in administering oaths."[67]

By the end of the century, most states had changed the rule to allow witnesses to testify regardless of their religious beliefs. Truth-telling was not completely

[62] Leonard W. Levy, ed., *Blasphemy in Massachusetts: Freedom of Conscience and the Abner Kneeland Case* (New York: Da Capo Press, 1973); Leonard W. Levy, *The Law of the Commonwealth and Chief Justice Shaw* (Cambridge: Harvard Univ. Press, 1957), 43–58; Henry Steele Commager, "The Blasphemy of Abner Kneeland," *New England Quarterly* 8 (1935): 29–41.

[63] *State v. Mockus*, 113 A. 39 (Me. 1921); Sarah Barringer Gordon, "Blasphemy and the Law of Religious Liberty in Nineteenth-Century America," *American Quarterly* 52 (2000): 682–719.

[64] Jud Campbell, "Testimonial Exclusions and Religious Freedom in Early America," *Law and History Review* 37 (2019): 431–92; Ronald P. Formisano and Stephen Pickering, "The Christian Nation Debate and Witness Competency," *Journal of the Early Republic* 29 (2009): 219–48; James S. Kabala, *Church-State Relations in the Early American Republic, 1787–1846* (London: Pickering & Chatto, 2013), 137–47.

[65] *Atwood v. Welton*, 7 Conn. 66, 77 (1828).

[66] John Henry Hopkins, *The American Citizen* (New York: Pudney & Russell, 1857), 37.

[67] *Fields v. State*, 9 Tenn. 156, 164 (1829).

disengaged from Christianity—some states still clung to the old rule well into the 20th century, while even under the new rule, a witness could, in principle, be cross-examined as to his or her nonbelief in order to persuade the jury that the witness was not credible.[68] But this sort of religious cross-examination was probably quite rare. As one New York judge suggested, a few years after the state's new constitution explicitly abolished religious requirements for witnesses, "So long as no religious test shall be required for judges and jurors, parties will be loth to cross-examine witnesses as to their opinions on matters of religious belief."[69] In this respect, Christianity gradually receded from day-to-day courtroom practice.

An otherwise unremarkable 1895 West Virginia case illustrates the extent to which Christianity and law came to be understood as separate spheres by the end of the century. In *Mayer v. Frobe*, the West Virginia Supreme Court considered whether a jury could award punitive damages. Judge Marmaduke Dent's opinion for the court discussed the many cases and treatises allowing such an award. He then devoted a long paragraph to a discussion of some passages from Exodus that likewise seemed to authorize punitive damages, which he considered evidence that punitive damages were consistent with natural law. This kind of discussion would not have raised any eyebrows in the first half of the century. By 1895, however, biblical interpretation felt incongruous in a court opinion. Three members of the court felt compelled to append a short note explaining that while they agreed with Dent's legal analysis, it was improper "to assert or deny any particular distinctive Christian creed or dogma." The court's duty, they observed, was "to expound alike for all the municipal law of the land," but not "to expound religious principles, or expressly or impliedly disparage any man's belief." They concluded: "While we, as individuals, have the highest regard and respect for Christianity generally, we do not think it proper, in an opinion of this court, to appear to espouse or enforce any particular or distinctive Christian creed."[70]

The idea that Christianity is part of the common law likewise began to come under sustained criticism in the second half of the 19th century. One could find occasional critics in the first half of the century, such as Thomas Cooper, the president of the college that would later become the University of South Carolina. "I have no respect for Sir Matthew Hale," Cooper declared of the English judge who first stated the maxim in the late 17th century; "he was a weak and bigoted man, deeply dyed with the legal servility of the times." Cooper was persuaded by Jefferson's account of how Christianity had crept into English common law

---

[68] Irving Browne, *Short Studies in Evidence* (New York: Banks & Brothers, 1897), 90–95; Thomas Raeburn White, "Oaths in Judicial Proceedings and Their Effect upon the Competency of Witnesses," *American Law Register* 51 (1903): 395.

[69] *Stanbro v. Hopkins*, 28 Barb. 265, 271 (N.Y. Sup. Ct. 1858).

[70] *Mayer v. Frobe*, 22 S.E. 58, 61, 66 (W. Va. 1895).

through a mistranslation. "This gifted oracle of the bench," Cooper said sarcastically of Hale, "asserted Christianity to be part and parcel of the common law, either through gross and culpable negligence, not consulting; or through gross and culpable ignorance, misunderstanding and mistranslating a passage in the Year Book."[71]

But such expressions of doubt were unusual before mid-century. They tended to come only from lawyers who were arguing—without success—that the maxim should not be applied to their clients. In 1846, for example, Pennsylvania charged Jacob Specht for hauling manure in violation of the state's Sunday law, which prohibited the performance of any "worldly employment or business on the *Lord's day,* commonly called *Sunday.*" Specht was a Seventh Day Baptist who observed the Sabbath on Saturday. His lawyer argued that the Sunday law was unconstitutional and could not be justified by the doctrine that Christianity was part of the common law. "That doctrine was promulgated in the worst times, and by the worst men of a government that avowedly united church and state; in times when men were sent to the block or the stake on any frivolous charge of heresy," he contended. "This convenient doctrine enabled Henry the Eighth to dispose of all whom he chose to call his enemies, whether they were learned and conscientious gentlemen, like Sir Thomas More, or were wives of whose beauty he was weary." But this was a losing argument at the time.[72]

The first American court to say that Christianity was *not* part of the common law was the Ohio Supreme Court, in an 1853 case in which one party to a real estate contract tried to avoid his obligation on the ground that the contract had been signed on a Sunday. Christianity had been part of English common law, the court noted, and perhaps English contracts signed on Sundays were not enforceable for that reason. But the court declared that "neither christianity, nor any other system of religion, is a part of the law of this state." The freedom of religion guaranteed by the state constitution meant that "we have no union of church and state, nor has our government ever been vested with authority to enforce any religious observance, simply because it is religious."[73] The Ohio Supreme Court returned to the issue two decades later and rejected the maxim even more emphatically. Those who assert that Christianity is part of the common law "can hardly be serious," the court scoffed. "If Christianity is a *law* of the state, like every other law, it must have a *sanction*. Adequate penalties must be provided to enforce obedience to all its requirements and precepts. No one seriously contends for any such doctrine." Christianity was the majority religion, the court acknowledged. But "true Christianity asks no aid from the sword of

---

[71] Cooper, *Law of Libel,* 119–20.
[72] *Specht v. Commonwealth,* 8 Pa. 312, 315–16 (1848).
[73] *Bloom v. Richards,* 2 Ohio St. 387, 390–91 (1853).

civil authority. It began without the sword, and wherever it has taken the sword it has perished by the sword. To depend on civil authority for its enforcement is to acknowledge its own weakness." In short, "*Legal* Christianity is a solecism, a contradiction of terms. When Christianity asks the aid of government beyond mere *impartial protection*, it denies itself. Its laws are divine, and not human."[74]

A half century earlier, the conventional view had been that Christianity was an essential part of the legal system, but now the highest court of a state was saying precisely the opposite—that Christianity was something separate from the realm of law. Charles Doe, the chief justice of New Hampshire and one of the most respected judges of the era, made the same point at considerable length in an 1868 case. "The principles of Christianity are no part of the principles of the common law," he explained. "If Christianity were in any sense, theoretically or practically, a part of the common law of New Hampshire, it would be the right and duty of this court to decide what Christianity is, and to enforce it as law." But the courts did nothing of the kind. "The profession and dissemination of all theological doctrines are equally lawful at common law," Doe continued. Christianity was the majority religion, "But it cannot be argued that a particular system of theology is established by law, by a mere effort to preserve peace and order through police regulations adopted to the actual condition of the people by whom that theology is, in fact, generally accepted." Religion and law were separate spheres of life. "It is no disparagement of the law to say that miraculously revealed Christianity is not a part of it," Doe concluded, "as it is no depreciation of a physical science or a mechanical art to say that miraculous revelation is no part of it. Every institution, art, and science is not ordained for the accomplishment of all the purposes of creation; some are assigned to one work, some to another." For Kent and Story, Christianity had been the foundation of the common law, but for Doe, Christianity and the common law were simply two different realms of human knowledge.[75]

Many commentators likewise disagreed with the maxim in the last quarter of the century. "It might well, at least in this country, pass into disuse among writers and judges," suggested the *Albany Law Journal.* "At the most, there is but a fragment of truth in it, and that truth is not aptly expressed."[76] The *Western Jurist* agreed that the maxim "is comparatively meaningless. In the form in which it is commonly stated it is calculated to confuse the mind and mislead

---

[74] *Board of Education of Cincinnati v. Minor,* 23 Ohio St. 211, 247–48 (1872).

[75] *Hale v. Everett,* 53 N.H. 9, 202–10 (Doe, J., dissenting). The court's majority did not address whether Christianity was part of the common law, so we do not know whether they disagreed with Doe on this point. On Doe's views, see John Phillip Reid, *Chief Justice: The Judicial World of Charles Doe* (Cambridge: Harvard Univ. Press, 1967), 238–43.

[76] "Christianity and the Common Law," *Albany Law Journal* 13 (1876): 368.

the judgment."[77] Francis Wharton, one of the leading treatise-authors of the period, concluded that "as the dogmas of Christianity are beyond the reach of statute, we must hold that they are not part of the common law of the land."[78] The *American Law Register* called the maxim "merely the rhetorical piety of the judiciary," while the *American Law Review* called it "a proposition which is demonstrably the veriest rubbish."[79] At best, acknowledged the Harvard law professor James Bradley Thayer, it was "a highly figurative expression, very likely to be misunderstood."[80]

Others expressed uncertainty about the maxim. "By some of the authorities it is held that Christianity is a part of the common law, and by others that it is not," the California Supreme Court noted in 1881.[81] "Upon this subject," one lawyer observed, "there is a diversity of opinion."[82] These doubts were at their most striking when they came from sources who, a few decades before, would likely have been among the maxim's most ardent defenders. On at least three occasions in the first half of the century, the Pennsylvania Supreme Court had declared that Christianity was part of the common law, but when the issue came up again in 1870, the court was no longer so sure. A Philadelphian named Levi Nice left in his will a bequest for the formation of an Infidel Society, to build a hall for the free discussion of religion. His relatives argued that the gift was void, in part because Christianity was part of the common law of Pennsylvania. "It is unnecessary here to discuss the question," the court decided. "Even if Christianity is no part of the law of the land," the bequest was void, because it was unlawful to leave property to an organization that did not yet exist.[83] US Supreme Court justice William Strong displayed the same agnosticism in an 1875 lecture on relation of the legal system to church governance. "Whether it be true," he ventured, "that Christianity is, in a limited sense, a part of the common law of the land, or whether it be not true," blasphemy deserved to be punished.[84] It would have been almost inconceivable for a Supreme Court justice to express such doubt about the maxim a few decades earlier.

[77] "Relations of Christianity to the Common Law," *Western Jurist* 13 (1879): 543.

[78] Francis Wharton, *Philosophy of Criminal Law* (Philadelphia: Kay & Brother, 1880), 29.

[79] A. H. Wintersteen, "Christianity and the Common Law," *American Law Register* 38 (1890): 277; "Enjoining the Sunday Opening of the World's Fair," *American Law Review* 27 (1893): 573.

[80] James Bradley Thayer, "Trial by Jury of Things Supernatural," *Atlantic Monthly* 65 (1890): 465.

[81] Ex parte *Burke*, 59 Cal. 6, 14 (1881).

[82] P. Emory Aldrich, "The Christian Religion and the Common Law," *Proceedings of the American Antiquarian Society* 6 (1889): 24.

[83] *Zeisweiss v. James*, 63 Pa. 465, 471, 468 (1870).

[84] William Strong, *Two Lectures Upon the Relations of Civil Law to Church Polity, Discipline, and Property* (New York: Dodd & Mead, 1875), 32.

The maxim was nearly defunct by the end of the 19th century. A few state courts explicitly rejected it. "It is incorrect to say that Christianity is a part of the common law of the land," the North Carolina Supreme Court insisted. Religion "must be left to the consciences of men."[85] The Louisiana Supreme Court pointedly observed that Christianity could not be part of Louisiana law, because Louisiana was unique among American states in not adopting the common law. "We have been as yet spared in this State the infliction of similar outcroppings of the spirit of Puritanism," the court remarked.[86] But rather than disclaiming the maxim, most state courts simply stopped citing it. By 1891 one commentator could report that "in America the dogma that Christianity is a part of the common law has been repudiated."[87] Another declared in 1898 that American courts "have renounced Christianity as a part of the common law in the States." The maxim had been "superseded by religious liberty—the equality of religions."[88]

Strictly speaking, these obituaries were premature. Scattered lawyers and judges would continue to assert that Christianity was part of the common law well into the 20th century. In 1927, in what appears to be the last instance of a state supreme court citing the maxim, the Pennsylvania Supreme Court held that the state could bar the Philadelphia A's, a professional baseball team, from playing games on Sundays. "Christianity is part of the common law of Pennsylvania," the court stated, "and its people are Christian people. Sunday is the holy day among Christians. No one we think would contend that professional baseball partakes in any way of the nature of holiness."[89] In one of the last published decisions to invoke the maxim, a trial judge enjoined a 1947 radio employees' strike in an opinion containing twelve numbered conclusions of law, one of which was "The Christian spirit of do unto others as you would they should do unto you, and meet your neighbor as a friend is part of the common law of the United States." At a later point in the opinion, the judge also concluded: "The Soviet power aims to turn this friendly world into a scowling world of hate."[90] But such late uses of the maxim were unusual. Christianity had been firmly a part of the common law in the early 19th century, but by the early 20th century, Christianity and the

[85] *Rodman v. Robinson*, 47 S.E. 19, 21 (N.C. 1904).

[86] *State v. Bott*, 31 La. Ann. 663, 666 (1879).

[87] William Addison Blakely, "Introduction," in William Addison Blakely, ed., *American State Papers Bearing on Sunday Legislation* (New York: National Religious Liberty Association, 1891), 16.

[88] Prentiss Webster, "The Church and State in American Law," *American Law Review* 32 (1898): 548.

[89] *Commonwealth ex rel. Woodruff v. American Baseball Club of Philadelphia*, 138 A. 497, 499 (Pa. 1927).

[90] *Scranton Broadcasters, Inc. v. American Communications Ass'n*, 48 Lackawanna Jurist 241, 245, 250 (1947).

common law were generally understood as separate spheres. Neither was part of the other.

This change required rethinking the place of natural law within the legal system. When law and religion were understood to be intertwined, constituting mutually reinforcing systems of public order, it made perfect sense for principles placed in the world by God to be enforceable by judges. But when law and religion were reconceptualized as separate domains, the use of natural law in the legal system began to seem anomalous. Law was a domain of public life, containing rules that governed everyone, simply by virtue of their presence in the jurisdiction. Religion, by contrast, had come to be understood as a domain of private life, in which each denomination had its own rules governing members but not outsiders. Legal doctrines and religious doctrines, once seen as overlapping sets, were now seen as separate.

The gradual separation of the spheres of law and religion did not weaken lawyers' belief in the *existence* of natural law so much as it weakened their belief in the *relevance* of natural law to the court system. To return to the example with which this book began, a lawyer in 1800 would have been confident that murder was illegal, even in a jurisdiction that lacked any human-made law prohibiting murder, because murder so clearly violated natural law. Murder was explicitly forbidden in the Bible. It was obviously contrary to human well-being. If any Christian principle could be said to form a part of the American legal system, this was it. In the early 20th century, a lawyer would have been likely to agree that murder was contrary to natural law, for the same reasons—it was forbidden in the Bible and it was contrary to human well-being. But the lawyer would have been much less likely to believe that murder was therefore illegal in a jurisdiction that lacked any human-made law prohibiting it. The lawyer would have said that murder was wrong and that it was condemned by religious doctrine. But the 20th-century lawyer would have stopped short of the final link in the earlier lawyer's chain of reasoning—the proposition that the American legal system incorporates religious doctrines. The murderer's violation of natural law was now a matter for his conscience and for his minister, if he had one, but not for a judge. The judge was restricted to human-made law.

5

The Explosion in Law Publishing

Thus far we have examined two intellectual developments that contributed to the decline of natural law within the American legal system—the use of written constitutions to assess the validity of legislation and the gradual separation of the spheres of law and religion. In this chapter, by contrast, we will turn to a distinctly practical development, the growth of American law publishing.

In the late 18th and early 19th centuries, law books were scarce. Lawyers and judges often had to rely on broad principles rather than closely parsing the text of judicial opinions, simply because there were not many opinions to parse. The scarcity of published court opinions was thus conducive to a culture in which natural principles could play a role.

Over the course of the century, however, the number of available case reports steadily grew. Lawyers could cite ever-more court opinions as governing precedent, and they could argue that these opinions were more directly applicable to the case at hand than any broad natural principle. As this strategy proved successful in persuading judges, the culture of lawyers began to change. By the later part of the century, it was a common observation that principle was giving way to precedent. A profession that had once privileged broad natural principles was transforming into one in which court opinions formed the primary building blocks of legal argument. In this way, the growth of American law publishing facilitated the decline of natural law.

A Mighty Sea of Books

Court opinions were hard to find in the late 18th century. "The Study of the Law was a dreary Ramble," John Adams recalled. "I suffered very much for Want of Books."[1] When James Kent became a judge in 1798, "There were no reports or

---

[1] L. H. Butterfield, ed., *Diary and Autobiography of John Adams* (Cambridge: Harvard Univ. Press, 1961), 3:273–74.

The Decline of Natural Law. Stuart Banner, Oxford University Press (2021). © Oxford University Press.
DOI: 10.1093/oso/9780197556498.003.0006

State precedents," he remembered. "The opinions from the bench were delivered *ore tenus* [orally]. We had no law of our own, and nobody knew what it was."[2] Such remarks no doubt contained some measure of self-congratulation, some pride in having succeeded under difficult conditions, but it was nevertheless true that law books were scarce by later standards. The first generation of American lawyers "had not the advantages which students now have," a Massachusetts lawyer reminded his colleagues in 1826. "Hundreds of volumes of reports were not then published every year."[3]

That began to change in the early 19th century.[4] At first, lawyers welcomed the growing number of American case reports. "Many of them are the vehicles of decisions, interesting and important in public estimation," said one satisfied customer. With their publication, "The principles of the common law are becoming every day, from such frequent application, better understood."[5] Joseph Story saw the new case reports as a sign of progress. While "we in the nineteenth century may look with some apprehension upon the accumulations" of books, he acknowledged, "in truth, the common law, as a science, must be forever in progress; and no limits can be assigned to its principles or improvements."[6] With more published cases, others agreed, the law would become clearer and more certain.[7]

It did not take long, however, for lawyers to complain that there were too *many* court opinions being published. As early as 1821, Peter Du Ponceau already lamented "that mass of decisions, which daily issue in the form of Reports from the presses of the different states." He predicted, correctly, that this "immense increase of bulky reports . . . does not seem likely to diminish."[8] David Hoffman recalled that in 1804, "the American books of Reports did not exceed

---

[2] James Kent to Thomas Washington, 6 Oct. 1828, in "Autobiographical Sketch of Chancellor Kent," *Albany Law Journal* 6 (1872): 43.

[3] George Bliss, *An Address to the Members of the Bar of the Counties of Hampshire, Franklin and Hampden, at Their Annual Meeting at Northampton, September 1826* (Springfield: Tannatt, 1827), 67–68.

[4] On early case reporting, see Craig Joyce, "The Rise of the Supreme Court Reporter: An Institutional Perspective on Marshall Court Ascendancy," *University of Michigan Law Review* 83 (1985): 1291–391; Richard A. Danner, "More Than Decisions: Reviews of American Law Reports in the Pre-West Era" (2015), Duke Law School Public Law & Legal Theory Series No. 2015-27, https://ssrn.com/abstract=2622299; Dennis P. Duffey Jr., "Genre and Authority: The Rise of Case Reporting in the Early United States," *Chicago-Kent Law Review* 74 (1998): 263–76.

[5] "Greenleaf's Reports," *North American Review* 22 (1826): 29.

[6] Story, *A Discourse Pronounced*, 32–33.

[7] Book review, *North American Review* 27 (1828): 179–81; "Recent Reports," *American Jurist & Law Magazine* 3 (1830): 314.

[8] Peter Du Ponceau, "An Address Delivered at the Opening of the Law Academy of Philadelphia," *Jurisprudence* 1 (1821): 216.

eight volumes, whereas they amount, at this time, to about *one hundred and seventy!*"[9] Even Story saw trouble ahead. "The danger indeed seems to be," he noted, "not that we shall hereafter want able Reports, but that we shall be overwhelmed with their number and variety."[10]

The numbers kept mounting. By 1836, Hoffman estimated that there were over 450 volumes of American case reports. "The increase of this portion of our legal literature within the last thirty years, has no parallel in the juridical history of any other country," he declared.[11] A year later, the Cincinnati law professor Timothy Walker counted a thousand volumes, including digests, abridgments, and commentaries along with case reports. It would "be a Herculean labor to master the content of so many volumes," he despaired.[12] In 1839, another lawyer calculated that the case reports alone had grown to 536 volumes, with 30 more being published every year.[13] "We are in a mighty sea of books," one Massachusetts lawyer grumbled to his colleagues. "We can scarce glance at one, ere another rises to our view, laying perhaps an equal claim upon our notice and attention."[14] Another lawyer agreed that "reports seem to be stretching on to the crack of doom." He wished "for those good old days," when "all the books of the common law might be carried in a wheel-barrow. Such a quantity, even if dark with black letter, we might hope to read; but who can hope to read all the volumes which now clothe the walls of our libraries!"[15]

Complaints like these seemed quaint a few decades later, when the case reports numbered in the thousands. "They crowd upon us like the pests of Egypt," said one lawyer at the American Bar Association's 1883 convention. He counted at least 3,100 volumes, with another hundred coming out annually.[16] Indeed, the rate of growth was increasing. By 1893, there were more than 4,000 volumes of reports, according to the Missouri law professor John Lawson.[17] Hiram Gilbert, a judge in Illinois, counted 6,000 in 1909, but that figure may have been too

---

[9] Hoffman, *Syllabus of a Course*, vi.

[10] Joseph Story, "An Address Delivered Before the Members of the Suffolk Bar, at Their Anniversary, on the Fourth Day of September, 1821, at Boston," *American Jurist* 1 (1829): 13.

[11] David Hoffman, *A Course of Legal Study, Addressed to Students and the Profession Generally* (Baltimore: Joseph Neal, 1836), 657.

[12] Timothy Walker, *Introductory Lecture on the Dignity of the Law as a Profession* (Cincinnati: Daily Gazette Office, 1837), 14.

[13] "American Reports and Reporters," *American Jurist & Law Magazine* 22 (1839): 141.

[14] Joseph Willard, *An Address to the Members of the Bar of Worcester County* (Lancaster, MA: Carter, Andrews, 1830), 110.

[15] "Notices of New Books," *Law Reporter* 6 (1844): 425.

[16] John M. Shirley, *The Future of Our Profession: A Paper Read Before the American Bar Association* (Philadelphia: George S. Harris & Sons, 1883), 17.

[17] John D. Lawson, *The Principles of the American Law of Contracts* (St. Louis: F.H. Thomas Law Book, 1893), 4.

low, because the following year the lawyer-historian Charles Warren tallied up 8,208.[18] An individual volume might include a hundred cases or more, so the flow of words was even more daunting when measured by cases rather than volumes. Roger Cooley, a law professor in North Dakota, estimated that from 1789 through 1896, there were 500,000 reported cases. In the single decade from 1897 through 1906, the courts had added 225,000 more.[19] "If you read fifty pages every day in the year," calculated the Arkansas judge Henry Caldwell, "including Sundays, Christmas, New Years and the Fourth of July," it would take 230 years to read all the published cases. "But during your long course of reading," Caldwell continued, "the judges have been engaged in making this kind of law at the rate of 16,000 cases a year; so that after you have read 230 years you will find the volumes of reports that have accumulated since you began to read exceed by many times the number you have read."[20] Complaints about the impossibility of keeping up with the flood of reported cases became a staple of the legal press.[21]

One indication of the pervasiveness of the perceived problem was that lawyers who published books began explaining why *their* books were necessary, despite the glut that already existed. "This is the only work of this character extant in this country," ventured the author of a treatise on the law of elections, so there was good reason for its publication, "notwithstanding the prevailing and generally well founded prejudice against the multiplication of books of law."[22] Another author insisted that "the practitioner, however able and industrious, will continue to be confronted with new inquiries," so that "though he may at times decry the rapid multiplication of books, the necessity of his calling will ever make him, though perhaps unwittingly, cry for more," particularly the author's own treatise.[23]

Some lawyers recognized the irony in having too many printed volumes of common law. "If this common law is but oral tradition," wondered the New York lawyer William Sampson, "how comes it to fall about our ears in overwhelming

---

[18] Hiram T. Gilbert, *The Administration of Justice in Illinois* (s.l.: s.n., 1909); Charles Warren, *A History of the American Bar* (Boston: Little, Brown, 1911), 557.

[19] Roger W. Cooley, "Use of Law Books," *Law Library Journal* 2 (1909): 1.

[20] Henry C. Caldwell, "A Lawyer's Address to a Lay Audience," *American Law Review* 24 (1890): 279.

[21] Edward M. Doe, "Codification," *Western Jurist* 5 (1871): 289; Emory Washburn, *Lectures on the Study and Practice of the Law* (Boston: Little, Brown, 1872), 54; "Publications Received," *Legal Gazette* 5 (1873): 377; "Current Topics," *Albany Law Journal* 23 (1881): 341.

[22] George W. McCrary, *A Treatise on the American Law of Elections*, 3rd ed. (Chicago: Callaghan, 1887), v.

[23] Abraham Clark Freeman, *A Treatise on the Law of Executions*, 3rd ed. (San Francisco: Bancroft-Whitney, 1900), 1:v.

showers of printing?"[24] Timothy Walker likewise found it absurd that an ostensibly unwritten body of law could "be ascertained only by ransacking thousands of volumes of Reports."[25] The explosion of case reporting demonstrated all too well that even if the common law had once been unwritten, it had become no less written than legislation.

Some acknowledged the long tradition of complaining about having too many books. One lawyer recounted that "an English judge, in the reign of Charles II, told the bar that the reports were at that time grown too voluminous; 'for when he was a student, he could carry a complete library of books in a wheelbarrow; but that they were so wonderfully increased in a few years, that they could not then be drawn in a wagon.' "[26] The arsonists of the ancient library of Alexandria probably felt the same way, suggested a couple of New York lawyers.[27] But if there was nothing new about feeling overwhelmed by case reports, the lack of novelty hardly made lawyers any more welcoming of the flood. "The men of the law seem to have suffered under more than their just share of this general and ancient calamity, if we may believe their lamentations over the ratio of their number of books, to that of their clients," one lawyer joked.[28] "If Coke in his day lamented the existence of so many as fifteen volumes of reported decisions," one law student asked, referring to the 17th-century English judge Edward Coke, "what is to be said of the present state of affairs, when these volumes are to be counted by tens of thousands?"[29]

Lawyers sometimes blamed the judges for writing too many unnecessary opinions. "We should not be made to read, in hundreds of new volumes, the redecisions of questions perfectly settled by the generations before us," one lawyer groused.[30] "The profession ought not to complain of the booksellers, but of the judges, when regarding the quantity of reports annually published," another agreed. "The judges could restrain their pens in many instances."[31] But would fewer opinions be a cure worse than the disease? "Lawyers who think they think that the 'multiplicity of reports' is an evil should stop to consider what the state

---

[24] William Sampson, *An Anniversary Discourse Delivered Before the Historical Society of New-York* (New York: E. Bliss and E. White, 1824), 54.

[25] Timothy Walker, *The Reform Spirit of the Day: An Oration Before the Phi Beta Kappa Society of Harvard University* (Boston: James Munroe, 1850), 11.

[26] "Law Reports," *North American Review* 18 (1824): 376.

[27] John S. Derby and Herbert L. Luques, *A Legal Monograph Upon Provisional Remedies Under the Code* (New York: S.S. Peloubet, 1886), v.

[28] "Pickering's Reports," *North American Review* 20 (1825): 181.

[29] "Reform in Law Reporting," *Harvard Law Review* 9 (1895): 347–48.

[30] "A List of the Various Reporters, Arranged in Order of Time, With Remarks, &c.," *American Law Magazine* 2 (1844): 290 n. 1.

[31] "Book Reviews," *Current Comment and Legal Miscellany* 1 (1889): 272.

of the practice would be if they were taken at their word," one lawyer responded. The plan had been tried in New York in the 1830s and 1840s, he recalled, until "the bar awoke to a realizing sense of the situation" and pleaded with the judges to resume publishing opinions.[32] For a practicing lawyer, too few opinions might be worse than too many. "The reports are burdensome, it is true," another lawyer acknowledged, "but what would be our predicament without them? Of course, the same legal questions would arise, as now, and how could a lawyer advise his clients?"[33]

Others blamed the judges, not for writing too many opinions, but for making them too long. "In these latter days," a lawyer from Kansas City chuckled, "every man who gets on the bench of an appellate court begins at once to imagine that he is an Eldon, a Mansfield, or a Marshall, and straightaway proceeds to demonstrate in the most voluminous and untiring manner, and to the thorough satisfaction of every one who has occasion to use the reports, that he is nothing of the kind."[34] A New Jersey lawyer complained of "the long, diffusive opinions of American judges which fill our overloaded reports," opinions that typically did no more than decide "a legal principle which has already been decided once and again."[35] A law journal cited the example of one of the judges of the Maryland Supreme Court, who "found it necessary to inflict upon practitioners one hundred solid pages of print, in order, as he thought, to make himself understood." As the journal saw it, "A judge who cannot be understood in fewer words than is contained in that opinion should be allowed to retire."[36]

But if judges could sometimes be faulted for their wordiness, they were scarcely responsible for the increase in the number of published volumes of case reports. In every state by the early 19th century, court opinions began to be published soon after statehood, first by private reporters and later by the government itself.[37] It was the demand from lawyers that drove publication. The judges were not to blame.

Why were lawyers so disturbed by the availability of so many published court opinions? One complaint was the cost of having to buy them. "I have heard of an American lawyer of eminence whose whole property is said to consist in a large and expensive law library," the Pennsylvania legislator Charles Ingersoll remarked in 1823, when the total output of case reports was still minuscule

[32] "Attempts to Suppress Judicial Opinions," *Law Book News* 1 (1894): 34.

[33] Harvey Henderson, "Origin and Utility of Case-Law," *Kansas Law Journal* 4 (1886): 105.

[34] "Correspondence," *Central Law Journal* 31 (1890): 352–53.

[35] "Correspondence," *Central Law Journal* 31 (1890): 293.

[36] Untitled editorial, *Central Law Journal* 31 (1890): 281.

[37] Erwin C. Surrency, *A History of American Law Publishing* (New York: Oceana Publications, 1990), 37–72.

by later standards.[38] "Such has been this increase" in reports, another lawyer explained the following year, "that very few of the profession can afford to purchase, and none can read all the books which it is thought desirable, if not necessary, to possess."[39] As the number of volumes multiplied, so did the difficulty of acquiring them. By 1840, according to one lawyer, there were already sixty volumes of cases from the federal courts alone. "When the practitioner learns that this important information is to be sought in upwards of sixty volumes, which cost over two hundred and fifty dollars," he jested, "there will be very likely to arise a 'conflict' between the 'law' of his purse and the 'law' of his mind, which will probably wait a long time for adjudication and settlement."[40]

As more and more volumes of cases were published, lawyers also began to worry about gaining access to all of them. Few, if any, complete collections of case reports could be found outside of the largest cities, one lawyer explained in the 1880s.[41] Thomas Ewing, a former Kansas judge, told the state bar that of the out-of-state cases that might be cited in his court, "not half of them are to be found in the State library, and not one-fifth of them in all the lawyers' offices of any town in Kansas."[42] A system built on precedent would not work well if the precedents grew so numerous that many were inaccessible.

Worse, if there were so many published cases that lawyers could not keep track of them all, the law itself would become less certain. James Kent was already concerned with this problem in the 1820s. "The evils resulting from an indigestible heap of laws, and legal authorities, are great and manifest," he observed. "They destroy the certainty of the law, and promote litigation."[43] A half century later, the Los Angeles lawyer George Smith had the same worry. "With the immense number of reports already in existence, reinforced every year by hundreds of volumes," he observed, "obviously it is beyond the power of the human intellect to be familiar with them, or with any considerable proportion of them. The law therefore must be different to different men, according to the decisions with which they happen to be familiar." Each lawyer would have his own unique view of the law, depending on which cases he happened to have read. "The judges themselves differ in the same way," Smith continued. "Some are acquainted with some authorities, some with others," and for that reason "the views of the law entertained by them are as widely different as their individual accumulations"

---

[38] C. J. Ingersoll, *A Discourse Concerning the Influence of America on the Mind* (Philadelphia: Abraham Small, 1823), 37.

[39] Book review, *North American Review* 19 (1824): 433.

[40] "Critical Notices," *American Jurist & Law Magazine* 23 (1840): 244.

[41] Robert T. Devlin, *A Treatise on the Law of Deeds* (San Francisco: Bancroft-Whitney, 1887), 1:iv.

[42] Thomas Ewing, "Codification," *Albany Law Journal* 41 (1890): 440.

[43] Kent, *Commentaries on American Law*, 1:442.

of knowledge. When every judge had his own personal understanding of the law, litigation was a gamble. "It is all luck," Smith despaired, "and in the plainest case no one can say, whether the court will take the view of the plaintiff, or that of the defendant, or some view that has never been suspected by either."[44] A system built on precedent would break down completely if there were too many precedents for any judge to be aware of them all.

Lawyers noticed, meanwhile, that the sheer volume of cases was forcing them to narrow their focus to a single state. Earlier in the century, a diligent lawyer could be conversant with general trends in Anglo-American jurisprudence.[45] As reading so many cases became less practical, however, a lawyer had to limit himself to the law of his home state. "The lucubrations of our courts are spread abroad throughout the magnificent extent of two thousand massive volumes," one lawyer complained in 1870. "The result is, that even our leading lawyers, as a rule, no longer attempt to keep up with the reports of other states or of England, being satisfied if they are able to possess or peruse those of their own state."[46] Robert Earl, a judge on New York's highest court, reported in the 1890s that while his court had once routinely cited cases from England and other states, such citations had become much less common, and he predicted that they would soon become very rare.[47] Distinguished antebellum state court judges like James Kent and Lemuel Shaw had national reputations, because lawyers all over the country read their opinions, but by 1875 it was already clear that there would be no nationally renowned state court judges in the second half of the century, because lawyers had largely stopped reading opinions from other states.[48] With the increase in reported cases, lawyers and judges alike had been forced to become more provincial in outlook.

The problem of too many case reports brought forth many proposed solutions, none of which was completely successful. There were recurring calls to codify the common law—that is, to replace it with statutes—either in whole or in part.[49] The legislature "would at once apply the sponge and obliterate the whole mass" of published court opinions, one proponent of codification urged in the 1830s. Codifying the common law would "consign some hundreds of

---

[44] George H. Smith, "On the Certainty of the Law and the Uncertainty of Judicial Decisions," *American Law Review* 23 (1889): 717. For a similar concern, see Edward B. Whitney, "The Doctrine of Stare Decisis," *Michigan Law Review* 3 (1904): 100–101.

[45] Daniel J. Hulsebosch, "An Empire of Law: Chancellor Kent and the Revolution in Books in the Early Republic," *Alabama Law Review* 60 (2009): 377–424.

[46] "Current Topics," *Albany Law Journal* 2 (1870): 371.

[47] "The Deluge of Decisions," *Albany Law Journal* 58 (1898): 219–20.

[48] "Summary of Events," *American Law Review* 10 (1875): 370.

[49] Charles M. Cook, *The American Codification Movement: A Study of Antebellum Legal Reform* (Westport, CT: Greenwood Press, 1981).

volumes of useless erudition and conflicting subtleties to that limbo of oblivion in which the hecatombs of the scholastic vanities of the middle ages have so long slept in undisturbed repose."[50] David Dudley Field, a prominent supporter of codification in the second half of the century, described his proposed code as "the only means of stopping the overflow of precedents, which bewilder and impoverish the lawyers of the country."[51] No state completely codified the common law, but many states did codify significant parts of it, particularly in the newer states of the West, where there were fewer lawyers who had invested their careers in mastering the common law.[52] Whatever good these partial codifications may have accomplished, they did nothing to stanch the flow of published court opinions.

Another proposed reform was to coordinate the reporting of cases. The courts in each state made their own publication decisions, without conferring with the courts of any other state. If there were a nationwide council of reporters, one lawyer suggested in the 1860s, each state could send its cases to the council, and the council could determine which ones merited publication. To ease the burden on the council and on the lawyers who had to purchase reports, cases could be divided by subject matter. There would be a single set of reports of criminal cases, for example, from all the states, and similar sets for insurance cases, real estate cases, and so on.[53] This idea was never adopted. It required concerted action by state governments, but the prime beneficiaries would have been lawyers, not state governments.

The only partial solution to the problem of too many law books was, paradoxically, more law books. The burst of case reporting gave rise to a corresponding burst of legal treatises, as lawyers spotted a market for works that imposed a rational order on the mass of published cases.[54] Later in the century, an entrepreneur named John West began publishing inexpensive collections of cases from every state, with points of law indexed by number so they could be found

[50] "Written and Unwritten Systems of Laws," *American Jurist & Law Magazine* 9 (1833): 34.

[51] David Dudley Field, *Codification: An Address Delivered Before the Law Academy of Philadelphia* (Philadelphia: Law Academy, 1886), 24.

[52] Lawrence M. Friedman, *A History of American Law*, 2nd ed. (New York: Simon & Schuster, 1985), 403–7.

[53] "An American Council of Reporters," *Western Jurist* 3 (1869): 193–97.

[54] M. H. Hoeflich, *Legal Publishing in Antebellum America* (New York: Cambridge Univ. Press, 2010); Richard A. Danner, "Oh, the Treatise!", *Michigan Law Review* 111 (2013): 821–34; A. W. B. Simpson, "The Rise and Fall of the Legal Treatise: Legal Principles and the Forms of Legal Literature," *University of Chicago Law Review* 48 (1981): 668–74; G. Blaine Baker, "Story'd Paradigms for the Nineteenth-Century Display of Anglo-American Legal Doctrine," in Angela Fernandez and Markus D. Dubber, eds., *Law Books in Action: Essays on the Anglo-American Legal Treatise* (Oxford: Hart Publishing, 2012), 82–107.

quickly.[55] Because of West's efforts, remarked one grateful lawyer, "There has never been a time, certainly for half a century, when it was so easy to find out what has been decided."[56] Such efforts at organizing the information found in all the cases would continue through the 20th century, in the form of restatements, uniform laws, and still more treatises.

But while such innovations made finding the law a little easier, more case reporters kept rolling off the presses each year, with all the associated problems that lawyers had identified since the 1820s. "Unfortunately both for the teacher and the student, our case-law is embodied in many thousands of volumes of reports," John Forrest Dillon noted in the 1890s. Dillon had been a professor at Yale and Columbia, the chief justice of Iowa, the president of the American Bar Association, and a practicing attorney in New York, so he had an unusually comprehensive view of the American legal system. The only solution to the mass of reports, he suggested, was "to cast our law into a more orderly, methodical, and scientific form." That was "a work which belongs to the future, but it is a work which I think must sooner or later be done."[57] Well-meaning lawyers had been saying much the same for nearly a century, but the goal always remained just over the horizon.

The Substitution of Precedents for Principles

The explosion of legal publishing contributed to a shift in the profession's argument style, one that took attention away from arguments based on natural law. A legal argument typically consisted of a mixture of broad principles and specific precedents. As the number of precedents grew, lawyers started emphasizing the precedents at the expense of the principles. Natural law, a body of broad principles, began to recede in prominence.

For most of the 19th century, it was a big insult to call someone a "case lawyer." A case lawyer was one who knew the decided cases but not the principles that lay behind the cases. He was a small-minded person who missed the forest for the trees. "A mere case lawyer can never be a great one," declared Jesse Bledsoe, a judge and law professor in Kentucky, "for when he finds a case, differing in a

[55] Robert M. Jarvis, "John B. West: Founder of the West Publishing Company," *American Journal of Legal History* 50 (2008–10): 1–22; Thomas A. Woxland, "'Forever Associated with the Practice of Law': The Early Years of the West Publishing Company," *Legal Reference Services Quarterly* 5 (1985): 115–24.

[56] Irving Browne, "The Lawyer's Easy Chair," *Green Bag* 6 (1894): 93.

[57] John F. Dillon, *The Laws and Jurisprudence of England and America* (Boston: Little, Brown, 1894), 87.

single particular from the one which he has read, altho' that circumstance may not vary the principle, he is at a loss for the proper decision."[58] "Put a legal question of some nicety to a mere 'case lawyer,' " sneered the New York judge Alfred Conkling, "and if he happens to remember a reported case exactly *in point*, he will tell you how it *has been decided*. If he recollects no such case he has no opinion to give." Conkling contrasted the case lawyer with "a lawyer of the opposite stamp," one who attended to legal principles rather than the cases that exemplified those principles. Such a lawyer "will give you the best possible answer, by informing you how it *ought* to be decided, and how an enlightened court may therefore be expected to decide it."[59]

A case lawyer was an inferior lawyer because the "cases"—that is, the written opinions of judges—were not understood to be the law themselves. They were merely evidence of the law, which was understood to consist of general principles. Case lawyers "collect cases and assume that they assert the law, losing sight of the fact that there can be no valid induction without an underlying general principle," advised one handbook for litigators. From a judge's perspective, the handbook noted, "The lawyers least to be depended upon are those who are in constant pursuit of cases in point to govern their judgment, and who, therefore, seldom have sufficient knowledge of principles."[60]

Lawyers analogized case lawyers to other kinds of poor workers who knew lots of details but who lacked an understanding of the basic principles underlying their craft. "Case lawyers are like pilots unskilled in the science of navigation, who succeed well enough while they hug the coast and keep the headlands in view, but are always in danger of being lost when they are driven beyond the sight of land," explained the Michigan judge Isaac Christiancy. By contrast, "He whose mind is well stored with the principles and reasons of the law—who, when a question is presented, instead of seeking first for a case, recurs at once to his own internal resources, determines what, upon principle, the law must be, and resorts to cases only for illustration and proof—such a man is ready for any emergency."[61] Joel Bishop, the author of several legal treatises, compared a case lawyer to an engineer who tried to design a suspension bridge without

---

[58] Jesse Bledsoe, *Hon. J. Bledsoe's Introductory Lecture on Law* (Nashville: Republican & Gazette, 1827), 9.

[59] Alfred Conkling, *Legal Reform: An Address to the Graduating Class of the Law School of the University of Albany* (Albany: W.C. Little, 1856), 11–12.

[60] Byron K. Elliott and William F. Elliott, *The Work of the Advocate: A Practical Treatise Containing Suggestions for Preparation and Trial* (Indianapolis: Bowen-Merrill, 1888), 611–12, 58.

[61] Isaac Christiancy, *Address of the Hon. I.P. Christiancy to the Graduating Class of the Law Department of the Michigan University* (Detroit: Barns, French & Way, 1860), 9.

understanding the scientific principles on which the bridge depended.[62] The New York lawyer Lucius Proctor provided a similar analogy. "The case lawyer," he declared, "uses legal precedent as a mason does a brick or stone, the carpenter a stick of timber, without understanding the philosophy, the logic, or lesson by which it was established."[63]

At law school graduations and in introductory lectures, speakers accordingly warned students not to become "mere 'case lawyers.'"[64] In Washington, the graduates of the new National University's law department were counseled to "be very careful not to make yourself a mere case lawyer," because "the case hunter can never be a successful practitioner."[65] In New Orleans, the dean of the law faculty at the University of Louisiana declared that "a mere *case lawyer* is like a third rate player, who repeats the words of others, without troubling himself whether he is uttering sense or nonsense." He cautioned that "we must take heed not to lose sight of principles, in following the easy and beaten track of precedent."[66] If there was one thing an aspiring attorney knew not to be, it was a case lawyer.

But the glut of case reports was turning the profession into case lawyers.[67] "The rapid accumulation of so large a mass of precedents," one lawyer complained, was causing "the substitution of precedents for principles in the practical administration of justice." With so many cases to read, "There is constant temptation to forget the underlying principle in the search for a precedent exactly in point. The tendency is to try our cases upon precedent rather than upon principle," he noted, "and it is a matter of common remark among the elder school of lawyers and judges that the younger men at the bar rely too much upon books and too little upon the elementary doctrines by which all cases should be decided." He concluded that this result, "pernicious in the extreme," was "in large measure due to the vast accumulation of reported cases."[68] As another despaired, "The principles of the law cannot be disentangled from the confused mass of conflicting reports daily showered upon us."[69]

---

[62] Joel Prentiss Bishop, "The Elements Distinguishing the Successful from the Ordinary Legal Practitioner, and What They Suggest," *American Law Review* 17 (1883): 84.

[63] L. B. Proctor, *The Bench and Bar of New-York* (New York: Diossy, 1870), 104–5.

[64] D. Bethune Duffield, *The Lawyer's Oath: An Address Delivered Before the Class of 1867, of the Law Department, University of Michigan* (Ann Arbor: Dr. Chase's Steam Printing House, 1867), 23.

[65] Richard Harrington, *Address of Richard Harrington to the Graduating Class of the Law Department of the National University* (Washington, DC: W.H. & O.H. Morrison, 1873), 7.

[66] Christian Roselius, *Introductory Lecture of Christian Roselius* (New Orleans: Daily Delta Steam Book and Job Printing House, 1854), 23.

[67] Richard A. Danner, "Cases and Case Lawyers," *Legal Reference Services Quarterly* 35 (2016): 147–78.

[68] J. L. High, "What Shall Be Done with the Reports?," *American Law Review* 16 (1882): 439.

[69] "Legal Reporting and Judicial Legislation," *Albany Law Journal* 3 (1871): 353.

The lament became a common one in the last quarter of the century: Lawyers, awash in cases, were losing sight of the principles the cases represented. Law "is a science consisting of legal principles, not bruised and crushed together arbitrarily, but fitly and scientifically joined together," insisted the Missouri lawyer J. D. Shewalter. But "the multiplicity of books, and especially the reports of decided cases, has become so vast," he despaired, that "the lawyer of the present day immediately proceeds to find some case whose facts agree with the case he has in hand, and when he has found it, he rests content."[70] In his commencement address at Cincinnati Law School, the federal judge Charles Drake warned the graduating class "against allowing yourselves to become mere *case*-lawyers. There are now more than four thousand volumes of British and American Reports, and the annual increase is largely over one hundred volumes," Drake pointed out. "In my view, this multiplication of Reports tends to diminish the discussion of cases on principle, and to control their decision by the mere club-law, so to speak, of precedents." Lawyers, Drake concluded, had become "mere hunters of cases, instead of thinkers applying the maxims and principles of law."[71] The Harvard law professor Joel Parker worried that "the immense addition of cases and arguments which the books furnish, fill the mind of the student with a mass of material," posing the danger that the student would "become merely a 'case lawyer.' "[72] It was widely believed that the precedents were crowding out the principles, and that the profession was deteriorating as a result.

Biographies of past lawyers and judges exhibited considerable nostalgia for an era with fewer published cases, in which members of the profession were not distracted from the broad principles that constituted the law itself. "In those days cases were decided on principle," recalled the grandson of Chief Justice Morrison Waite, referring to Waite's pre-judicial career as a mid-century lawyer. "The case lawyer was an impossibility. The court rode about the circuit on horseback, and the capacity of the saddlebags was limited to only one or two well-chosen text books. The lawyer had to rely on a well stocked brain."[73] James Iredell and Alfred Moore, two early Supreme Court justices, worked at a time when "there were no Encyclopedias, no Codes, no State Reports, but precious little home-made Statute Law, and no 'case lawyers,'" a North Carolina lawyer declared when their portraits were hung in the state supreme court. "Only strong men

---

[70] J. D. Shewalter, "Reform in the Practice and Administration of the Law," *American Lawyer* 6 (1898): 172.

[71] Charles D. Drake, *Address, Delivered May 8, 1878, at the Annual Commencement of the Cincinnati Law School* (Washington, DC: Thomas McGill, 1878), 13.

[72] Joel Parker, *The Law School of Harvard College* (New York: Hurd and Houghton, 1871), 22.

[73] Morrison R. Waite, "Morrison R. Waite," *Western Reserve Law Journal* 1 (1895): 95.

could succeed."[74] A leader of the Connecticut bar, when asked why the lawyers who framed the Constitution had such mastery of legal principles, responded "Why, they had so few books!"[75] When Charles Southmayd became a lawyer in New York in the early 1840s, "There were no such floods of books as those in which the law itself is now thoroughly drowned," read his eulogy seventy years later. Southmayd was thus able "to make himself master of all the important cases that would naturally be cited, and of the principles thereby established."[76] Even a more recent figure like David Davis, who served on the Supreme Court in the 1860s and 1870s, could be praised for knowing "just enough law to be a great judge, and not enough to spoil him." As an admiring Illinois lawyer explained, "The poorest lawyers I have ever known are men who know the most law. Such overcrammed men are sometimes called case lawyers."[77]

By the later part of the century, lawyers were convinced that this age of legal giants had passed, and that the explosion in legal publishing was to blame. "When the number of courts was small and their work comparatively light, and when such reports as were published were the deliberate work of some of the best men at the bar, exercising their judgment on what was worthy to be recorded, it was possible for the lawyer to master the principles of the law," the *Albany Law Journal* recalled. "Accordingly we read of a time when the learned serjeants were in the habit of resorting to some public place for the purpose of consulting with clients, and advising them off-hand." But those days were long gone. Now "the principles of the law cannot be disentangled from the confused mass of conflicting reports daily showered upon us, if indeed any such principles are in many of them involved. Hence both judges and counsel are obliged too often to appeal helplessly to the last cases on the subject, instead of relying on sound scientific knowledge and vigorous common sense." With so many cases to keep track of, the lawyers and judges of the present were lesser figures, who could no longer rest their arguments and decisions on broad principle.[78]

The only glimmer of hope seemed to rest in the possibility that the crush of cases would become so overwhelming that lawyers would be forced to disregard them and return to principles. "As the labor of examining the multitude of reports becomes more and more onerous," John Forrest Dillon predicted, the "result will be a tendency more and more to diminish the importance of the

[74] Junius Davis, *Alfred Moore and James Iredell: Revolutionary Patriots and Associate Justices of the Supreme Court of the United States* (Raleigh: Edwards & Broughton, 1899), 6.

[75] Edward J. Phelps, "Methods of Legal Education," *Yale Law Journal* 1 (1892): 142.

[76] Joseph H. Choate, *Memorial of Charles F. Southmayd* (New York: Bar Association of the City of New York, 1912), 11–12.

[77] Leonard Swift, *David Davis: Address Before the Bar Association of the State of Illinois* (Chicago: Barnard & Gunthorp, 1886), 10.

[78] "Legal Reporting and Judicial Legislation," *Albany Law Journal* 3 (1871): 353.

'case lawyer' and to make felt the importance of a knowledge of the great, living, fundamental *principles* of our law."[79] The St. Louis judge Seymour Thompson expected that "the multiplication of judicial reports will, by a natural reaction, create the same condition which visited the profession in the early stages of our jurisprudence, when they had no such reports at all. The mass will be so great that no particular thing can be found in it." As Thompson put it, "It will be not merely the case of searching for a needle in a haymow, but of hunting for some particular straw in a haymow." When that blessed day came, the glut of cases would "drive the lawyers and judges to the habit of relying less on what may have been decided, and of working out and deciding causes on lines of natural justice," as in the old days.[80] Until then, however, lawyers were hunters of precedents rather than expounders of principle.

Judges sometimes blamed the lawyers who appeared before them, for turning litigation into a case-citing contest. "Case law is fast becoming the great bane of the bench and bar," grumbled Reuben Wanamaker of the Ohio Supreme Court. "Our old-time great thinkers and profound reasoners who conspicuously honored and distinguished our jurisprudence have been succeeded very largely by an industrious, painstaking, far-searching army of sleuths, of the type of Sherlock Holmes, hunting some precedent in some case, confidently assured that if the search be long enough and far enough some apparently parallel case may be found to justify even the most absurd and ridiculous contention." In the disputes that came before Wanamaker's court, "Case after case is piled, Ossa on Pelion, and about an equal number can be found on each side; then the court is expected to strike the balance and decide according to the preponderance of cases rather than the preponderance of reason and justice."[81] The US Supreme Court justice Samuel Miller had the same grievance. "If it were not so common it would be a matter of wonder," he complained, "that counsel, in making what they call a 'brief,' or even in a printed argument, where a proposition of law is suggested as applicable to the case, should append to it from twenty to a hundred citations of adjudged cases."[82]

Lawyers, for their part, placed the blame on the judges, for deciding cases on precedent rather than principle. "The case lawyer is a necessary resultant from a case judge and a case court," charged the Alabama lawyer J. J. Willett. "How often have we seen cases full of merit, carefully and thoughtfully prepared, and backed by arguments founded upon learning and common justice, dismissed

[79] John F. Dillon, *American Institutions and Laws: Annual Address Before the American Bar Association* (Philadelphia: George S. Harrison & Sons, 1884), 33.

[80] Seymour D. Thompson, "Good and Bad Law Reporting," *Green Bag* 11 (1899): 107.

[81] *State v. Rose*, 106 N.E. 50, 52 (Ohio 1914).

[82] Samuel F. Miller, "The Use and Value of Authorities," *American Law Review* 23 (1889): 175.

without comment upon the authority of a somewhat similar case decided under different circumstances."[83] Another lawyer insisted that "the courts nowadays seem to require a great display of law-books before them. Precedent and parallelism rule the times." He complained that "a lawyer may know the principle," but the court would be skeptical "until he knows just where that book authority for his principle is to be found."[84] Lawyers had to satisfy judges, so if judges wanted precedents, lawyers had to supply them.

By the turn of the century, as lawyers perceived their argument styles shifting ever farther toward precedents and away from principles, the label "case lawyer" began to lose its critical edge. It would eventually disappear from the lexicon, because all lawyers had become case lawyers. There was no other kind. "The time was when it was supposed to be a reproach to call one a case lawyer," recalled the distinguished Arkansas lawyer Uriah Rose, "but now we are all either case lawyers, or we are not lawyers at all."[85] John Dos Passos, a leader of the New York bar (and the novelist's father), was of the same view. "The lawyers of to-day are case and code lawyers," he acknowledged. "The search for *principle* is subordinate to an investigation for a *precedent*." Under the weight of "a mass of irreconcilable decisions," lawyers had narrowed their horizons. "It requires a different kind of intellectual development to be a lawyer than it did in the days long gone by," Dos Passos suggested. "The modern advocate's nose is always to be found in a digest, 'case'-law accumulating so fast that he must have indices to search for his precedents. Poor soul! if he cannot find a precedent, he is in a terrible sweat."[86]

Reliance on precedents could be a matter of professional survival. In 1895 the American Bar Association appointed a committee to investigate the consequences of "the multiplication of the law reports." The committee concluded that lawyers had become case lawyers because case lawyers won their cases. "The term 'case lawyer' is frequently used as a term of reproach for a laborious practitioner," the committee reported, "but it is nevertheless true that principles are to be found in cases, and are frequently found applied to a similar state of facts. Hence the 'case lawyer' wins cases because he has examined the books thoroughly."[87] By 1916, when John W. Davis addressed the ABA, he called his speech "The Case for the Case Lawyer." Davis was the solicitor general of the United States and one of the most respected lawyers in the country. "So long as

[83] J. J. Willett, "The Case Lawyer," *American Lawyer* 1 (1893): 36.

[84] Percy Edwards, "A Serious Problem," *Green Bag* 5 (1893): 358, 356.

[85] U. M. Rose, "The Present State of the Law," *Virginia Law Register* 2 (1897): 656.

[86] John R. Dos Passos, *The American Lawyer: As He Was—As He Is—As He Can Be* (New York: Banks Law Publishing, 1907), 13–14.

[87] "Report of the Committee on Law Reporting," *Annual Report of the American Bar Association* 18 (1895): 344, 354.

the law is based upon precedents, so long as judges multiply them, and so long as printing presses issue them," he argued, lawyers could not help but be case lawyers, especially because their competitors were case lawyers too. "The process goes after this fashion," he jested:

> Jones, who has been a man of small beginnings, broadens out into federal practice and buys the Supreme Court Reports. Smith, his rival, immediately does the same, adding the Federal Reporter. Jones retaliates with a series or two of selected cases; whereupon Smith mortgages his home and installs the whole Reporter system. At the end of the war both are on a paper basis. Jones cites 10 cases in his support; Smith counters with 20; and nothing but the limits of time and energy will debar Jones from evening up the score.

But Davis was making a serious point. The case lawyer "is not wholly a self-made man," he concluded. "His weakness is not entirely of his own deliberate choosing. He is rather the product of an environment and of circumstances which he is powerless of his own motion to change or greatly modify." Even a lawyer with a philosophical preference for principles over precedents had to become a case lawyer if he hoped to earn a living.[88]

The growing legal research industry was eager to convert any holdouts. The Edward Thompson Company of Northport, New York, published digests and encyclopedias to help lawyers find the cases they needed. In 1897, the company also began publishing a magazine for the bar called *Law Notes*. In the very first volume, the company assured lawyers that there was nothing wrong with being a case lawyer. "We sometimes hear a lawyer spoken of disparagingly as a mere 'case lawyer,'" the company observed. "But we think every lawyer, no matter how familiar he may be with the general principles applicable to his case, is glad to find his opinion confirmed by a case exactly in point."[89] John Glover, a member of Congress from St. Louis, founded a mail-order legal research firm. "The practitioner states his point in writing and receives in reply, cases which decide the point," an approving attorney explained. "Judges depend more and more upon exact precedents, and the chief drudgery of the legal profession consists in the harassing search for them. The practitioner who could meet every formidable point with one more decision precisely in point may through this agency obtain them at the expense of a merely nominal charge."[90] Glover urged potential

[88] John W. Davis, "The Case for the Case Lawyer," *Massachusetts Law Quarterly* 2 (1918): 103, 104, 101.

[89] Untitled editorial, *Law Notes* 1 (1897): 46.

[90] "The Littleton Law Library," *Central Law Journal* 22 (1886): 337.

customers to become case lawyers. "There are those who will say to the seeker after light: 'Depend upon *principle*, upon *the reason of the thing.* . . . Do not be a *case lawyer*,'" Glover mocked. He thought there was but "a half, or rather a quarter of truth in this advice; but in its whole effect it is misleading and dangerous." In fact, he asserted, "Familiarity with the actual course of judicial decisions is absolutely necessary to the successful practice of the law."[91]

Lawyers understood the profession to have changed. When case reports were few, lawyers built arguments on reason and principle, but now that case reports were everywhere, legal arguments were based on cases. "With each court there is connected a pipe promptly to convey its product to the great centre of distribution," lamented the law professor John Bassett Moore, "and from this centre, day by day, month by month, year by year, there is poured out, as through a great main, upon a gasping, sputtering Bar, a turgid stream of judicial decisions." The lawyers were simultaneously beneficiaries and victims of the flood of cases. "This system is supported by the Bar, with mingled feelings of gratitude and despair," Moore continued, "for the Bar is conscious of the fact that while it is in a sense served by the system, it is also enslaved and debauched by it. The very multiplicity of cases, and the consequent impossibility of dealing with them scientifically, reduces practitioners to a reliance upon particular decisions rather than upon general principles."[92] "Case lawyer" was no longer an insult, when a lawyer could not be any other kind.

If judges had an infinite amount of time and lawyers had an infinite number of pages, perhaps the growing use of published precedents would not have affected the use of natural law. But in the resource-constrained world of litigation, the growth of law publishing meant the decline of natural law. As lawyers relied more on published opinions, they relied less on broad principles of natural law. If the judge wanted the most apposite precedents, and if one's opponent had a well-stocked library of case reports, it was professional suicide to rely on natural principles rather than on the text of court opinions. As the volume of case reports swelled, the role of natural law correspondingly diminished.

[91] John M. Glover, "How to Find the Law," *Counsellor* 1 (1892): 129.

[92] John Bassett Moore, *The Passion for Uniformity* (Philadelphia: University of Pennsylvania, 1914), 14.

6

The Two-Sidedness of Natural Law

In the 19th-century United States, politically contested issues often worked their way into litigation. As Tocqueville famously observed, with some exaggeration, "There is almost no political question in the United States that is not resolved sooner or later into a judicial question."[1] Natural law played an important role in litigation, so some of these controversies were litigated in the language of natural law. This chapter will focus on four areas of dispute—the death penalty, property, the role of women, and race relations.

In political argument and litigated cases involving these topics, opponents took contrary positions on what the law of nature required. For every argument that natural law said one thing, there was a standard response that natural law said the opposite. Eventually, lawyers and judges began to display some impatience with the use of natural law in legal argument. If the law of nature was capacious enough to include both sides of disputed questions, lawyers began to suggest, perhaps it was too ambiguous and too subjective to be of practical use within the legal system.

The Death Penalty

Capital punishment first became a subject of controversy in the United States in the late 18th and early 19th centuries.[2] Opponents made several arguments, including that prison would be more effective in deterring crime, that death was

---

[1] Alexis de Tocqueville, *Democracy in America*, ed. Harvey C. Mansfield and Delba Winthrop (Chicago: Univ. of Chicago Press, 2000), 257. On the extent of Tocqueville's exaggeration, see Mark A. Graber, "Resolving Political Questions into Judicial Questions: Tocqueville's Thesis Revisited," *Constitutional Commentary* 21 (2004): 485–545.

[2] Stuart Banner, *The Death Penalty: An American History* (Cambridge: Harvard Univ. Press, 2002), 88–143.

The Decline of Natural Law. Stuart Banner, Oxford University Press (2021). © Oxford University Press.
DOI: 10.1093/oso/9780197556498.003.0007

a disproportionate punishment, and that the justice system should shift its emphasis from punishing criminals to rehabilitating them. But much of the critique of the death penalty was couched in terms of natural law. Capital punishment, critics argued, was contrary to the law of nature.

"The sixth commandment, 'Thou shalt not kill,' is in perfect accord with the law of nature founded on the fitness of things," insisted the Philadelphia physician John Elkington. "What language is more peremptory, decisive, universal, unconditional? It does not say thou shalt not kill, *except it be one who hath killed another*."[3] Edward Coles, the governor of Illinois, expressed his hope that the state would one day abolish the death penalty "and conform to the great fundamental laws of nature, and of nature's God, as to no longer sanction by law the taking of human life."[4] The Massachusetts senator Charles Sumner agreed that "if the individual man can defend himself without taking life, he is bound to do so; and this is the limitation imposed by natural law and reason upon the State."[5] Such arguments drew on the long tradition of considering natural law as superior to positive law. The law of nature provided a basis for urging reform.

Opponents of the death penalty often reasoned from the natural rights of the individual to the power of the government formed by an association of individuals. Each man has a "right to self existence," one pamphleteer argued, and "*no man can surrender or transfer it,* consistently with the mandates of Nature, consequently Society cannot *receive it, nor does it exist* in any assembly of men whatever."[6] The New Hampshire minister Arthur Caverno sermonized on a point frequently made when attacking the death penalty—that society possessed only those powers delegated to it by individuals, but the law of nature gives no individual the right to kill, so such a right could never have been delegated.[7] When Maine considered abolishing the death penalty in the 1830s, State Senator Tobias Purrington made a more refined version of the argument. "All men have the right of self-defence by the natural law," he acknowledged, "and if absolutely necessary, to take the life of an enemy to preserve our own." This right could be delegated from individuals to the state. But when a state executed a prisoner, the necessity for self-defense did not exist, because the prisoner was no longer an immediate threat. "Having overcome our enemy," Purrington

[3] John A. Elkinton, *Lecture on Capital Punishment* (Philadelphia: J. Van Court, 1841), 23.

[4] Clarence Walworth Alvord, ed., *Governor Edward Coles* (Springfield: Illinois State Historical Library, 1920), 281.

[5] Marvin H. Bovee, *Christ and the Gallows; or, Reasons for the Abolition of Capital Punishment* (New York: Masonic Publishing, 1869), 56.

[6] M. E., *Essays on the Injustice and Impolicy of Inflicting Capital Punishment* (Philadelphia: Democratic Press, 1800), 17.

[7] Arthur Caverno, *A Sermon Delivered at Great-Falls, N.H., Aug. 9, 1835, on the Subject of Abolishing Capital Punishment* (Portsmouth: Miller and Brewster, 1836), 11–12.

continued, "and bound or confined him securely, we should not be justified, in the opinion of any civilized community, in taking his life, because the necessity which justified the other case, is absent in this."[8]

Supporters of the death penalty responded in kind, by arguing that capital punishment was consistent with or even required by natural law. "The universality of the sentiment in the soul of man respecting the justice and necessity of the punishment of death for murder is such, that we might well regard it as a part of the Law of God written on the heart," declared the minister George Cheever. "The common thoughts and usages of nations, even in the light of nature merely, would go far to corroborate this opinion."[9] When the physician Benjamin Rush published an essay urging the abolition of the death penalty, one critic suggested that Rush had let his intellect outrun his natural sense of justice. "Our author, I suppose, has never had a father, a brother, a wife, or a child murdered by the cruel hands of any ruffian," he observed. "It is all theory with him. But if ever it be his lot (which may providence prevent) to have a beloved son violently murdered, he will feel otherwise than he does now; his fictitious humanity will evaporate before the strong and irresistible feelings of nature, and perceptions of justice and equity."[10]

Supporters of capital punishment could point to several passages in the Bible that seemed to indicate that "capital punishment is, in our view, a divine institution."[11] "The death penalty for murder occupies a remarkable place in the Scriptures," explained the minister Edward Kirk. "It is almost, if not the only, command addressed by Jehovah to human societies as such."[12] In the Bible, agreed Jonathan Cogswell, "God has given us the interpretation of his own law, in language too plain to be misunderstood."[13] But natural law could be discerned by reason as well as revelation. Supporters of the death penalty identified a universal human instinct in favor of punishing murderers with death. When a committee of the Pennsylvania legislature rejected a proposal to abolish capital punishment, the committee explained that the death penalty "is so clearly a law of nature" that abolition would be futile. "The mob finding the law impotent, would take its execution in their own hands," the committee reasoned. "This

---

[8] T. Purrington, *Report on Capital Punishment, Made to the Maine Legislature in 1836* (Washington, ME: Gideon, 1852), 31.

[9] George B. Cheever, *Punishment by Death: Its Authority and Expediency* (New York: M.W. Dodd, 1842), 84.

[10] "Observations on Capital Punishments," *American Museum* 4 (1788): 450.

[11] "Capital Punishment," *New Englander* 1 (1843): 30.

[12] Edward N. Kirk, *The Murderer: A Discourse Occasioned by the Trial and Execution of John W. Webster* (Boston: Tappan, Whittemore & Mason, 1850), 6.

[13] Jonathan Cogswell, *A Treatise on the Necessity of Capital Punishment* (Hartford: Elihu Geer, 1843), 23.

cannot be looked upon as the feeling of revenge, but the voice of nature within us."[14] As those favoring retention of the death penalty saw it, those favoring abolishing capital punishment were seeking a reform "contrary to the dictates of human nature."[15]

Where supporters of the death penalty saw scriptural warrant, opponents saw only blind adherence to tradition. "It is as absurd to tolerate capital punishments merely because Moses ordained them," one critic complained, "as it would be to wear the garments of that day because they were then found convenient."[16] "Universal consent proves nothing," insisted another critic. "Mankind are influenced, whether wandering in the forest or inhabiting the populous city, by the same motives of interest, and the same instigations of passion." The law of nature, in his view, what not what people had always done, but what they ought to do. "That man, in an uncivilized state, so far from adhering to the dictates of the law of nature, contravenes them in his relations both as a friend and enemy, is proved by the whole current of history," he argued. "The law of nature is the rule of moral action, deducible by the exercise of right reason, from the visible works of God. That they therefore who are actuated by passion, and not by reason, should deviate from this law, would seem inevitable."[17]

This political debate about whether to abolish the death penalty was reproduced inside the courtroom, in the arguments of lawyers in capital trials. The lawyers knew that some jurors were likely to harbor doubts about capital punishment, which might make them reluctant to convict defendants of capital crimes. Defense lawyers played on these doubts, by offering arguments against the death penalty. Prosecutors responded with arguments in favor. On both sides, as in the world outside the courtroom, these arguments were often expressed in the language of natural law.

For example, when Thomas Gayner was tried in South Carolina for killing his wife, his lawyer acknowledged to the jury that murder was "justly deserving the severest and most effectual punishment." But he expressed doubt "whether justice, humanly so called . . . can ever sanction its punishment by death."[18] At a murder trial in New Hampshire, the defendant's lawyer argued that because "religion imposes upon us obligations above the force of human law," jurors need not follow the state law imposing the death penalty for murder. "Whatever,

---

[14] *Report of the Majority and Minority of the Committee on the Judiciary System, Relative to Capital Punishment* (Harrisburg: M'Kinley & Lescure, 1843), 21.

[15] William I. Budington, *Capital Punishment: A Discourse, Occasioned by the Murder of the Late Warden of the Mass. State Prison* (Boston: T.R. Marvin, 1843), 5.

[16] "Peter Peaceable," *Philadelphia Repertory* 2 (1812): 316.

[17] *Remarks on Capital Punishments*, 2nd ed. (Utica: William Williams, 1821), 8.

[18] *A Report (in Part) of the Trial of Thomas Gayner, for the Alleged Murder of His Wife* (Charleston, SC: W.P. Young, 1810), 22.

then, may be found in any human code," he declared, "if the law of the Ruler of the Universe, if the christian religion does not sanction the taking of life by human tribunals, then as you hope for future salvation, lift not in supplication to Heaven, your hands stained with the blood of your fellow man."[19] Defense lawyers reminded jurors that positive law was inferior to "higher and more solemn considerations," as one put it.[20] "Are we to be told, that the legislature have enacted that murder shall be punished with death, and that *there* you must stop your inquiries?" asked one defense lawyer. "Religion imposes upon us obligations above the power of human law, and for the violation of which no human law can give us dispensation."[21]

Prosecutors fought back by arguing to juries that the death penalty was consistent with the law of nature. "Some had doubted, whether one man, or one community of men, could have a right to take the life of an individual," admitted the prosecutor in Ebenezer Mason's trial. But he insisted that such doubts were misplaced. The death penalty "seemed to be the dictate of nature, read by the candle of conscience lighted in the breast of man," he argued, "and, when promulgated to the Hebrews, by the Author of Nature, was only an awful repetition of what was then acknowledged to be law by all the nations on the earth."[22] At the trial of Dominic Daley and James Halligan, the prosecutor likewise declared that capital punishment had been ordained by God, "resulting by nature from the transaction by which human life was destroyed."[23] Jurors should have no "doubt of the right, or the justice, of punishing murder, by taking away the life of the offender," affirmed the prosecutor in another case, "since our law, which requires this punishment, is clearly founded on the divine command."[24] As Perez Morton, the attorney general of Massachusetts, suggested to the jury in one capital case, the death penalty was a "law, which nature, as well as the institutions of society, proclaims and sanctions."[25] Pronouncing the guilt of a murderer was "a duty to perform to your God," one New York prosecutor argued.[26]

---

[19] *Report of the Trial of Abraham Prescott, on an Indictment for the Murder of Mrs. Sally Cochran* (Concord, NH: M.G. Atwood and Currier & Hall, 1834), 90.

[20] *Trial of Daniel Davis Farmer, for the Murder of the Widow Anna Ayer* (Concord, NH: Hill and Moore, 1821), 40.

[21] C. E. Potter, *Report of the Trial of Bradbury Ferguson, on an Indictment for the Murder of Mrs. Eliza Ann Ferguson* (Concord, NH: Morrill, Silsby, 1841), 43–44.

[22] *Impartial Account of the Trial of Ebenezer Mason, on an Indictment for the Murder of William Pitt Allen* (Dedham, MA: H. Mann, 1802), 8.

[23] *Report of the Trial of Dominic Daley and James Halligan, for the Murder of Marcus Lyon* (Northampton, MA: S. & E. Butler, 1806), 68.

[24] *Report of the Trial of Henry Phillips for the Murder of Gaspard Denegri* (Boston: s.n., 1817), 6.

[25] *Report of the Trials of Stephen Murphy and John Doyle* (Boston: Chester Stebbins, 1817), 3.

[26] *Report of the Trial of Barent Becker* (New York: s.n., 1815), 5.

As opposition to the death penalty grew at mid-century, prosecutors adopted a second strategy. Rather than contending that capital punishment was required by natural law, they began to argue that natural law should play no role in the legal system. "What is the law?" asked one Ohio prosecutor. "It is that which has been established by legislative enactment, and judicial decision. The human heart has nothing to do with it."[27] In New York, a prosecutor argued similarly that "whatever sentiments the Court or you or I entertain on these questions they are to have no weight in dealing with a matter of this kind."[28] The prosecutor at the murder trial of Reuben Dunbar insisted that the jury had to follow the statutes and nothing else. "Believe me, gentlemen," the prosecutor concluded, "he is but a poor casuist, who would look to some 'higher law' for a justification for the commission of moral perjury."[29] In an effort to obtain convictions, prosecutors made some of the earliest arguments in favor of a position that would become common only later in the century, that cases should be decided solely according to positive law, with no contribution from natural law.

By the middle of the 19th century, death penalty cases featured natural law arguments on both sides, arguments that drew upon decades of policy debates about the justice of capital punishment. Defense lawyers made the standard arguments that the death penalty was contrary to the law of nature. Prosecutors provided the standard rejoinders, that capital punishment was consistent with natural law, and that the question was in any event not one for jurors to consider. A neutral observer might have been forgiven for wondering whether, at least in this area, nature was ceasing to be a useful source of law.

Property

When natural law was an unquestioned part of the legal system, property was virtually always classified as a natural right.[30] "We do not derive our property from the State, or from the laws," insisted one late 18th-century resident of Massachusetts. "Property is our natural right, and government is intended to support and protect us in the use and enjoyment of it. The dollar I earn is mine, independent of the power of the State, and they can have no right to take it away

---

[27] *Trial, Commonwealth, vs. Henry Daniel: Indictment for Murder* (Cincinnati: Brough & Robinson, 1845), 20.

[28] *Trial of William Miller for the Murder of George West* (Troy, NY: Daily Budget Office, 1844), 24.

[29] S. H. Hammond, *The Closing Argument in the Case of the People vs. Reuben Dunbar, for Murder* (Albany: Joel Munsell, 1851), 30.

[30] Wilson, *Works of Honourable James Wilson*, 2:467; "Restrictions Upon State Power in Relation to Private Property," *Law Intelligencer* 1 (1829): 59.

from me, and give it to you."[31] In his introductory law lectures at the University of Virginia, Henry St. George Tucker remarked that the existence of property among disparate peoples all over the world suggested that there must be a "natural law of property," the principles of which "are planted in the heart" and "obligatory upon the conscience."[32] The conventional view was that property was part of human nature, in that God had designed human beings to acquire and own property.[33] The Bible seemed to suggest that property originated when God gave mankind dominion over the world. "To take, own, use, and enjoy the things of this earth became thus early the birthright of man and woman," concluded James Schouler, whose treatise on the law of personal property became a standard reference work. "The right to acquire and exercise dominion over these things—to 'subdue' the earth, as it is said—is universally felt to be a natural right."[34]

But the natural law of property became another area of contestation in the middle of the 19th century, with the emergence of a competing egalitarian version of natural law in which private ownership was a *departure* from the natural state, in which property was shared by the community. "We know, as a matter of history, that in the beginning God gave to man a general dominion over the earth and all things appertaining thereto," reasoned the law professor Timothy Walker, "but this would only make the first inhabitants *owners in common* of the whole, and not exclusive owners of any specific part." Walker drew the conclusion that "the right of exclusive ownership is conventional, and not divine or natural."[35] Some of the advocates of this view expressed it in a distinctly religious idiom.[36] The minister Charles Henry Parkhurst, for example, delineated what he called "the Christian conception of property," according to which "the proprietary rights of the individual are to be arbitrated from the stand-point of the State, and not the rights of the State from the stand-point of the individual." Parkhurst provided a clear example of what he had in mind. "Suppose that I am hungry and can obtain nothing to eat, and have no means of earning it," he imagined. "What

---

[31] "On Publick and Private Credit," *Worcester Magazine* 3 (1787): 135.

[32] Henry St. George Tucker, *A Few Lectures on Natural Law* (Charlottesville: James Alexander, 1844), 12.

[33] E. P. Hurlbut, *Essays on Human Rights and Their Political Guarantees* (New York: Greeley & McElrath, 1845), 178.

[34] James Schouler, "Property and Its Origin," *United States Jurist* 2 (1872): 317. This essay would later appear as the introductory chapter of James Schouler, *A Treatise on the Law of Personal Property* (Boston: Little, Brown, 1873).

[35] Timothy Walker, *Introduction to American Law* (Philadelphia: P.H. Nicklin & T. Johnson, 1837), 257.

[36] "How Exclusive Ownership in Property First Originated: Communism," *American Catholic Quarterly Review* 3 (1878): 13; James A. Cain, "The Origin of Private Property," *Catholic World* 47 (1888): 547.

am I to do? Starve? I cannot of course state what my reader would do; but I can vouch for myself that I should not perish of inanition so long as I had the power to beg bread or steal it. The loaf on my neighbor's shelf is, in a sense, not mine; but at the same time, in a sense it is mine, because it belongs in a truer sense to God than it does to my neighbor, and I call God Father."[37] But there was nothing inherently religious about the view that natural law required a more egalitarian distribution of property, a view that was congenial to those who urged greater taxation and regulation of the wealthy. "There is a natural right of property," declared one proponent of redistribution. "Every man must have a right to an equal portion of the earth, or an equivalent, for his subsistence and use." The existing regime of private property "deprives a large part of mankind of this natural right," by giving much of the earth "to some few in exclusive and indefensible appropriation."[38]

This egalitarian version of the natural law of property received a boost from the early anthropologists of law, who inferred the origins of property in ancient times by studying existing societies they deemed primitive. These studies suggested that property did not originate in individual claims of exclusive rights over particular territories, as earlier philosophers had speculated, but rather in *group* claims of *collective* rights. The most well known of these anthropologists in the United States was the English law professor Henry Sumner Maine, whose research in India persuaded him that the earliest forms of property belonged to entire villages, not to individuals.[39] After examining property arrangements in Indonesia and Malaysia, the French anthropologist Charles Letourneau likewise concluded that "the genesis of the right of private property in land has been much the same in all parts of the world. If it be not a natural law, it is at all events a very general fact, that the soil has at first been everywhere in common, in joint ownership."[40] Such reports, from a new type of expert widely understood to be studying humanity from a more scientific standpoint than before, lent support to the view that collective property, not private property, was consistent with the law of nature.

By the later 19th century, property was one more contested topic on which both sides claimed the authority of natural law. On one hand, the economist Richard Ely noted, natural law was invoked to defend existing rights of property, but at the same time "the socialists attempt to show that the present theory of

[37] C. H. Parkhurst, "The Christian Conception of Property," *New Princeton Review* 1 (1886): 37, 35.

[38] "What is the Reason?," *United States Magazine and Democratic Review* 16 (1845): 19.

[39] Henry Sumner Maine, *Ancient Law* (1861) (Boston: Beacon Press, 1963), 253–64.

[40] Charles Letourneau, *Property: Its Origin and Development* (New York: Charles Scribner's Sons, 1907), 115.

property is untenable, because it violates what they consider natural rights."[41] The New York lawyer Samuel Belcher Clarke voiced his exasperation with the indeterminacy of this debate. "Has ever human being, as against others, a natural right to land? and if so, is there any limit to such right except that prescribed by the equal rights of other human beings?" Clarke wondered. "Pretty much all that one man can do for another towards solving" such questions, he concluded, "is to present them clearly and ask 'What do you think?'"[42] When arguments over property were conducted in the language of natural law, natural law was coming to seem less and less useful.

The Role of Women

By "the laws of Nature, and of God," John Quincy Adams declared, "in the formation of the Social Compact, the will or vote of every family must be given by its head, the husband and father." Adams was speaking in 1842 to the Franklin Lyceum, a learned society in Providence, on the nature of government. The body politic, he explained, is not an association of *individuals*. Rather, "The union of the sexes, founded in the law of nature, necessarily precedes the social compact which constitutes the body politic, which is *an association of families*." Women, Adams continued, thus had no role to play in political life. "By the law of nature, the physical effect and the moral obligations of the two parties to the covenant of union, are widely different," he suggested. "The woman therefore can have no direct agency in the social compact which constitutes the body politic." What this meant in practice, he concluded, was that women should not be allowed to vote. "The vote, by the law of nature and of God, must be confined to the male sex," Adams asserted, "because the contract, embracing the whole family, one member of the family must pledge the faith, and stipulate for the rights of the whole. That member is the husband and father. The wife is not qualified to vote, because, by the nuptial tie and the law of God, her will has been subjected to that of her husband."[43]

Adams was elaborating upon what had long been the conventional wisdom— that according to natural law, women were subservient to men and were thus unsuited for much of public life. This subservience has "at least some countenance

---

[41] Richard T. Ely, *Property and Contract in Their Relations to the Distribution of Wealth* (New York: Macmillan, 1914), 2:534.

[42] Samuel B. Clarke, "Criticisms Upon Henry George, Reviewed from the Stand-Point of Justice," *Harvard Law Review* 1 (1888): 271–72.

[43] John Quincy Adams, *The Social Compact, Exemplified in the Constitution of the Commonwealth of Massachusetts* (Providence: Knowles and Vose, 1842), preface, 7–8, 13.

in the law of nature," observed Joel Bishop in his 1873 treatise *The Law of Married Women*. Nature "gave strength to the man and feebleness and dependence to the woman; putting into his hands the weapons of war, and building in her heart the golden throne before which the victor and the vanquished alike bow." Bishop jested that if the natural allocation of roles were ever to switch—an event he clearly considered unlikely—the positive law might adjust accordingly. "Should times change," he suggested, "and the same law of nature draw the women into the field of battle and into the harvest fields, and array the men in kitchens and nurseries with the dishcloths and the other cloths; and should the golden throne pass to the hearts of the men, and the rod of iron to the hands of the women; with this change of Nature's law, and the consequent change of manners, the law of the land ought also to change, and undoubtedly it would." By the time Bishop wrote, reformers had been urging for decades that women should be allowed to vote, to hold public office, and to enter professions. He cited natural law as a reason for limiting women to their traditional roles.[44]

When the women's movement gained substantial force in the mid-19th century, advocates for women's equality also used the language of natural law. Sometimes natural law was invoked in an affirmative way, as providing support for women's claims to participate in political life. One conspicuous example was the Seneca Falls Declaration of 1848, which deliberately mimicked the Declaration of Independence in its reliance on natural law. "All laws which prevent woman from occupying such a station in society as her conscience shall dictate, or which place her in a position inferior to that of man, are contrary to the great precept of nature, and therefore of no force or authority," the Seneca Falls Declaration asserted. "We hold these truths to be self-evident: that all men and women are created equal; that they are endowed by their Creator with certain inalienable rights; that among these are life, liberty, and the pursuit of happiness."[45]

Advocates for women's equality also took care to rebut the natural law arguments in favor of women's traditional roles. As one anonymous reviewer of Bishop's treatise put it, "This talk about the law of nature, &c., is all balderdash." Natural law could be invoked to support any traditional practice, but whether a practice was traditional, and whether it was required by the law of nature, were two different inquiries. "The argument (what there is of it) is the same which from time immemorial has been used to justify cruelty, extortion, robbery, the Inquisition, slavery, and every oppression which has at any time been practiced by the strong upon the weak," the reviewer insisted. "The law of the status of

---

[44] Joel Prentiss Bishop, *Commentaries on the Law of Married Women* (Boston: Little, Brown, 1873), 1:27–28.

[45] The Seneca Falls Declaration can be found in many places, including the Elizabeth Cady Stanton & Susan B. Anthony Papers Project, at http://ecssba.rutgers.edu/docs/Seneca.html.

women is the last vestige of slavery," the reviewer concluded, but one that "will sooner or later be broken to pieces."[46]

This argument over the content of natural law moved into the courtroom in the later part of the 19th century, in litigation over whether women could vote, practice law, and engage in other aspects of public life. When Myra Bradwell sought to practice law, US Supreme Court justice Joseph Bradley rejected her claim that the Constitution guaranteed her that right. "The civil law, as well as nature itself, has always recognized a wide difference in the respective spheres and destinies of man and woman," Bradley declared. "Man is, or should be, woman's protector and defender. The natural and proper timidity and delicacy which belongs to the female sex evidently unfits it for many of the occupations of civil life. The constitution of the family organization, which is founded in the divine ordinance, as well as in the nature of things, indicates the domestic sphere as that which properly belongs to the domain and functions of womanhood." Bradley drew on the long tradition of evaluating positive law for consistency with natural law to conclude that the Constitution did not, and indeed should not, provide women with a right to practice law. "The paramount destiny and mission of woman are to fulfil the noble and benign offices of wife and mother," he held. "This is the law of the Creator. And the rules of civil society must be adapted to the general constitution of things."[47]

Joseph Bradley was hardly alone. Judges often resorted to natural law to reject arguments for gender equality made in the course of litigation. When Lavinia Goodell sought admission to the Wisconsin bar, the state supreme court acknowledged that nothing in the state's statutes or the court's rules excluded women from becoming lawyers. But the court nevertheless held that Goodell could not practice law. "The law of nature destines and qualifies the female sex for the bearing and nurture of the children of our race and for the custody of the homes of the world and their maintenance in love and honor," Chief Justice Edward Ryan reasoned. "Nature has tempered woman as little for the juridical conflicts of the court room, as for the physical conflicts of the battle field. Womanhood is moulded for gentler and better things." He shuddered at the prospect "that woman should be permitted to mix professionally in all the nastiness of the world which finds its way into courts of justice." One function of the law of nature was to fill in the gaps where no positive law directed an outcome. Because Wisconsin's positive law neither required nor prohibited the admission of women as lawyers, natural law supplied the answer.[48]

---

[46] "Married Women," *American Law Review* 6 (1871): 61, 73 (reviewing an earlier edition of Bishop's treatise).

[47] *Bradwell v. Illinois*, 83 U.S. 130, 141–42 (1872) (Bradley, J., concurring in the judgment).

[48] *In re Goodell*, 39 Wis. 232, 234, 245–46 (1875).

Natural law played the same role when Mary Phelps left her husband in Pennsylvania and moved to New York, on her own, without obtaining a divorce or the consent of her husband. When Phelps died, it became important to the administration of her estate to know whether she had lawfully established residence in New York or whether the law deemed her a resident of Pennsylvania. New York had no positive law addressing whether Phelps could change her residence, the court recognized. "But there is still an excellent reason why a woman should not be allowed to choose her own residence in another state or county from that of her husband," the court continued. Under "the laws of nature," the court reasoned, "man, by reason of his superior physical strength and the fact that he does not bear the children, must ever be one to bear arms in war, and upon him must always fall the responsibility of providing for the family. The burden of his responsibility is the secret of his authority." While still married, "Either the husband or the wife must have the final say in the matter of where their home is to be," and because the law of nature gave authority over such matters to the husband, Phelps could not change her state of residence without her husband's consent.[49]

Litigants seeking gender equality fought back with natural law arguments of their own. As in the world outside the courtroom, sometimes natural law was invoked to support equality. When the Kansas Supreme Court had to decide whether women could vote in school district elections, the relevant statutes did not provide a clear answer. The court held that women could vote, on a ground directly contrary to the one taken by John Quincy Adams a few decades before. "There is nothing in the nature of things, or in the nature of government, which would prevent it," Justice Daniel Valentine explained. "Women are members of society—members of the great body politic, citizens—as much as men, with the same natural rights."[50] And as in the world outside the courtroom, litigants favoring equality took care to counter natural law arguments supporting tradition. "We shall not indulge in speculation concerning the natural aptitude and physical ability of women to perform the duties of the profession," declared the Colorado Supreme Court in the course of admitting Mary Thomas to the state bar. Other courts had discussed "questions of impropriety and inexpediency based upon the laws of nature," the court acknowledged, but "these are matters as to which differences of opinion exist, and we conceive that they have little, if any, bearing upon" whether women could practice law. In Colorado, women were already ministers, physicians, and teachers, and the court had little trouble in concluding that they could be lawyers as well.[51]

---

[49] *In re Bushbey*, 112 N.Y.S. 262, 263–64 (N.Y. Surr. Ct. 1908).
[50] *Wheeler v. Brady*, 15 Kan. 26, 33 (1875).
[51] *In re Thomas*, 27 P. 707, 707 (Colo. 1891).

Gender equality was thus another subject of litigation that featured natural law arguments on both sides, litigating strategies that drew upon decades of policy debate from the political world outside the courtroom. By the end of the 19th century there were standard natural law arguments on both sides. Like capital punishment, gender equality was a field in which natural law's value in the courtroom was coming to seem dubious.

Slavery and Race Relations

As the movement to abolish slavery gained force in the early 19th century, one of the movement's primary arguments was that slavery was contrary to natural law.[52] "It is impossible that one man should be the property of another," reasoned one advocate for the abolition of slavery in Virginia. "The master cannot derive his claim of property, from the laws of nature; because, by that law, all men are equally free and independent."[53] The abolitionist Lysander Spooner began his book about slavery with an entire chapter on natural law, which he argued invalidated the state statutes ostensibly permitting slavery in the South. "Whatever else it might spare," Spooner said of the law of nature, "it would spare no vestige of that system of human slavery, which now claims to exist by authority of law."[54] This argument became a staple of antislavery books and speeches. "Legislatures can pass no laws, that will chattleize man because no one can confer upon them such authority," insisted the lawyer Joel Tiffany. "The law of nature . . . is superior in obligation to every other law."[55] In urging the repeal of the Fugitive Slave Act, the Massachusetts senator Charles Sumner likewise emphasized slavery's inconsistency with natural law. Slavery, Sumner argued, was "repugnant to the law of nature and the inborn Rights of Man."[56] As the New York senator William Seward put it, in a well-publicized antislavery speech on the floor of the Senate, "there is a higher law than the Constitution."[57] In a

[52] Justin Buckley Dyer, *Natural Law and the Antislavery Constitutional Tradition* (New York: Cambridge Univ. Press, 2012). For an example, see "Inconsistency of Slavery with the Law of Nature," *Christian Philanthropist*, 4 June 1822, 14.

[53] E. B., *Moral and Political Observations, Addressed to the Enlightened Citizens of Virginia* (Richmond: John Warrock, 1817), 7.

[54] Lysander Spooner, *The Unconstitutionality of Slavery* (Boston: Bela Marsh, 1845), 5–17 (quotation at 17).

[55] Joel Tiffany, *A Treatise on the Unconstitutionality of American Slavery* (Cleveland: J. Calyer, 1849), 26.

[56] Charles Sumner, *Freedom National; Slavery Sectional: Speech of Hon. Charles Sumner, of Massachusetts, on his Motion to Repeal the Fugitive Slave Bill* (Boston: Ticknor, Reed, and Fields, 1852), 15.

[57] *Congressional Globe*, 31st Cong., 1st Sess., App. 265.

political culture in which liberty was often said to be a natural right, slavery was an obvious issue for the invocation of natural law arguments.

Supporters of slavery professed astonishment at the use of natural law to attack the institution. "A divine law, a natural law?" asked Henry Clay. "And who are they that venture to tell us what is divine and what is natural law? Where are their credentials of prophecy?"[58] Abolitionists supposed that the laws enforcing slavery "are contrary to what they are pleased to style an *anterior* or a *higher* law of paramount obligation, by which they mean, I presume, the natural law," observed the Louisiana law professor Christian Roselius. "The absurdity of such a position must strike the mind of every reflecting person at once."[59] In fact, remarked one New Orleans lawyer, "Mr. Seward and his compeers will find arrayed against them, the ablest expounders of reason and revelation."[60] Justice William Littleton Harris of the Mississippi Supreme Court mocked "the unmeaning twaddle, in which some humane judges and law writers have indulged, as to the influence of the 'natural law.' "[61]

Defenders of slavery insisted that it was consistent with natural law.[62] "Man is a social and gregarious animal, and all such animals hold property in each other," reasoned George Fitzhugh, who was perhaps the leading proslavery intellectual of the 1850s. "Nature imposes upon them slavery as a law and necessity of their existence." Fitzhugh concluded that "slavery arises under the higher law, and is, and ever must be, coeval and coextensive with human nature."[63] When the law professor and future Confederate congressman James Holcombe addressed the Virginia State Agricultural Society, he entitled his speech "Is Slavery Consistent with Natural Law?" His answer was yes. "When two distinct races are collected upon the same territory," Holcombe suggested, "the one being as much superior to the other in strength and intelligence as the man to the child, there the rightful relation between them is that of authority upon the one side, and subordination in some form, upon the other."[64] The Georgia lawyer Thomas Cobb began his treatise on slavery with a mirror image of Lysander Spooner's first chapter, an

---

[58] *The Life and Speeches of the Hon. Henry Clay* (Hartford: Silas Andrus & Son, 1853), 2:630.

[59] Roselius, *Introductory Lecture*, 6.

[60] James McConnell, *The Ethic Elements in the Character and Laws of Nations* (New Orleans: Office of the "Creole," 1855), 20.

[61] *George v. State*, 37 Miss. 316, 320 (1859).

[62] Elizabeth Fox-Genovese and Eugene D. Genovese, *The Mind of the Master Class: History and Faith in the Southern Slaveholders' Worldview* (New York: Cambridge Univ. Press, 2005), 613–35; Alfred L. Brophy, *University, Court, and Slave: Pro-slavery Thought in Southern Colleges and Courts and the Coming of the Civil War* (New York: Oxford Univ. Press, 2016), 67–71, 248–49.

[63] George Fitzhugh, *Cannibals All! Or, Slaves Without Masters* (Richmond: A. Morris, 1857), 341.

[64] James P. Holcombe, "Is Slavery Consistent with Natural Law?," *Southern Literary Messenger* 27 (1858): 407.

extended exploration of slavery's consistency with natural law. Cobb concluded that in light of "the negro character, . . . a state of bondage, so far from doing violence to the law of his nature, develops and perfects it; and that, in that state, he enjoys the greatest amount of happiness, and arrives at the greatest degree of perfection of which his nature is capable."[65]

In response to such arguments, opponents of slavery characterized nature as a condition to be transcended rather than mimicked, just as opponents of capital punishment did in response to the natural law arguments for preserving the death penalty. "Oppression, and cruelty, and all unkindness, uniformly and universally characterize the works of nature in all her departments," insisted one abolitionist. "Can it be regarded as necessarily right to act in harmony with nature, or necessarily wrong vehemently to oppose her?"[66] Nature was so violent, another critic suggested, "that every species of violence among men may be justified by the law of nature!" A true Christian, he concluded, would "learn his duty from the precepts of his religion and the example of the Prince of peace, and not from the examples of carnivorous animals, or from birds and beasts of prey."[67]

This political dispute over the consistency of slavery with natural law was often reproduced in the courtroom, because natural law could be a useful tool for both sides in slavery-related litigation. One recurring question was whether a slave who was taken to a jurisdiction where slavery was unlawful thereby became free, even after her owner brought her back home. In 1799, for example, the Maryland General Court considered a freedom suit filed by an enslaved man whose mother had been taken to England for a period before he was born, which, he contended, made him free, as the child of a free person. "Slavery is incompatible with every principle of religion and morality," his lawyer argued. "It is unnatural, and contrary to the maxims of political law, more especially in this country, where 'we hold these truths to be self-evident, that all men are created equal,' and that liberty is an 'unalienable right.' These doctrines are supported by the writers on natural law." The lawyer on the other side responded that the courts had always affirmed the lawfulness of transactions in slaves, which meant that slavery "is not against the law of nature and of God. Every case which has been cited maintains this position, that the master has an interest in the negro, and is entitled to his services; that property once acquired cannot be divested unless by the misconduct of the owner." The court rejected the slave's claim to freedom.[68]

---

[65] Thomas R. R. Cobb, *An Inquiry into the Law of Negro Slavery in the United States of America* (Philadelphia: T. & J.W. Johnson, 1858), 1:3–52 (quotation at 1:51).

[66] "Moral and Natural Law Contradistinguished," *DeBow's Review*, 1 Mar. 1862, at 287.

[67] "Self-Defence a Law of Nature," *Friend of Peace* 3 (1824): 79–80.

[68] *Mahoney v. Ashton*, 4 H. & McH. 295, 297, 319, 325 (Md. 1799).

The line between slavery and freedom could raise all kinds of questions for which natural law could provide arguments. Where a slaveowner's will provided for the manumission of a slave when she reached the age of thirty, what was the status of her children who were born while she was in her twenties? Were they slaves or were they free? "Slavery is contrary to reason, and the principles of natural law," declared Justice Samuel Harrington of the Delaware Supreme Court, who thought the children must therefore be free. "It is going too far to say that this kind of property in slaves is precisely like every other species of property." But Harrington was outvoted by his colleagues, who held that the children were slaves.[69]

Judicial thought regarding slavery soon coalesced in an uneasy compromise, under which slavery was contrary to natural law but was nevertheless lawful where it was established by positive law. For American lawyers, the first well-known expression of this view was the 1772 English case *Somerset v. Stewart*, in which the King's Bench, the highest court in England, held that a slave brought to England became free and could not be forced to return to North America. "The state of slavery is of such a nature," Lord Mansfield explained, "that it is incapable of being introduced on any reasons, moral or political; but only positive law, which preserves its force long after the reasons, occasion, and time itself from whence it was created, is erased from memory: it's so odious, that nothing can be suffered to support it, but positive law."[70] On this view, the lawfulness of slavery depended entirely on the positive law in force in a particular location. Because there was no positive law authorizing slavery in England, a slave ceased to be a slave once in England.

It took a little time for American law to follow. In 1786, for example, the Pennsylvania Supreme Court determined that slavery "is in itself so consistent with the precepts of nature, that we must now consider it as the law of the land," despite the absence of any positive law allowing slavery in Pennsylvania. The court accordingly held that a slave brought from Maryland into Pennsylvania did not become free.[71] By the early 1820s, however, even southern state supreme courts had determined that slavery was contrary to natural law. "Slavery is condemned by reason and the laws of nature," the Mississippi Supreme Court affirmed in 1818. "It exists, and can only exist, through municipal regulations."[72] The Kentucky Supreme Court agreed that the ownership of slaves was "a right existing by positive law of a municipal character, without foundation in the law of nature."[73] "No man can, by the laws of nature, have dominion over his

---

[69] *Jones v. Wootten*, 1 Harr. 77, 85 (Del. 1832).

[70] *Somerset v. Stewart*, 98 Eng. Rep. 499, 510 (K.B. 1772).

[71] *Pirate v. Dalby*, 1 U.S. 167, 169 (Pa. 1786).

[72] *Harry v. Decker*, 1 Miss. 36, 42 (1818).

[73] *Rankin v. Lydia*, 9 Ky. 467, 470 (1820).

fellow-man," the court explained, "and property in slaves, therefore, can only exist where the necessary means is afforded by law to enforce the right of the master."[74]

The US Supreme Court soon took the same view. That slavery "is contrary to the law of nature will scarcely be denied," Chief Justice John Marshall declared. "That every man has a natural right to the fruits of his own labour, is generally admitted; and that no other person can rightfully deprive him of those fruits, and appropriate them against his will, seems to be the necessary result of this admission." But slavery nevertheless flourished in much of the United States, and Marshall acknowledged that a court had to respect the positive law of the community. "Whatever might be the answer of a moralist to this question," he concluded, "a jurist must search for its legal solution, in those principles of action which are sanctioned by the usages, the national acts, and the general assent, of that portion of the world of which he considers himself a part, and to whose law the appeal is made." Because the positive law of the southern states permitted slavery, slavery was lawful there despite its inconsistency with natural law.[75]

As Robert Cover has suggested, natural law's subordinate status where slavery was concerned no doubt owed much to the inner tension experienced by the judges, many of whom considered slavery an obvious evil but who were committed to a professional role that required them to suppress their own personal opinions on controversial questions.[76] "It is only our province to construe and apply the existing law," the California Supreme Court insisted in 1858. "It is not necessary therefore to inquire whether slavery is or is not contrary to the law of nature. Our individual opinions on this question are of no importance in this case. The institution exists by positive law, and that positive law is paramount, and must be enforced."[77] Judge Thomas Clerke of the New York Court of Appeals provided the same disclaimer. "Whether slavery is agreeable or in opposition to the law of nature; whether it is morally right or wrong," he noted, "are questions very interesting within the domain of theology, or ethics, or political economy, but totally inappropriate to the discussion of the purely legal questions now presented for our consideration."[78]

Antebellum judges were not nearly as eager to dismiss the importance of natural law when cases involved issues other than slavery. In ordinary cases, judges

---

[74] *Stanley v. Earl*, 15 Ky. 281, 185 (1824).

[75] *The Antelope*, 23 U.S. 66, 120–21 (1825). See John T. Noonan Jr., *The Antelope: The Ordeal of the Recaptured Africans in the Administrations of James Monroe and John Quincy Adams* (Berkeley: Univ. of California Press, 1977).

[76] Robert M. Cover, *Justice Accused: Antislavery and the Judicial Process* (New Haven: Yale Univ. Press, 1975).

[77] *In re Archy*, 9 Cal. 147, 162 (1858).

[78] *Lemmon v. People*, 20 N.Y. 562, 632–33 (1860).

understood their role to encompass the interpretation, and normally the har-
monization, of both natural and positive law. But when cases involved slavery,
judges tended to describe their role as more circumscribed. "With the abstract
principles of slavery, courts called to administer this law have nothing to do,"
said the US Supreme Court justice John McLean, in a case involving the Fugitive
Slave Act. "It is for the people, who are sovereign, and their representatives, in
making constitutions, and in the enactment of laws, to consider the laws of nature, and the immutable principles of right. This is a field which judges can not
explore. Their action is limited to conventional rights. They look to the law, and
to the law only."[79]

For many judges, slavery must have been an issue on which there was an
exceptionally sharp divergence between natural and positive law. Few people
would have become lawyers, and even fewer lawyers would have become
judges, without a sense that that the rules of the legal system by and large
comported with justice. Except for slavery, natural and positive law would
have seemed generally in tune, requiring only occasional tinkering with positive law to bring the two into alignment. But slavery was different. To bring
the positive law of the slave states into alignment with natural law would have
required a complete overhaul of the southern economy and the southern legal
system. Such an overhaul would have been nearly universally perceived, by
lawyers at least, as far beyond the proper role of a judge. Justice Clark Bissell
of the Connecticut Supreme Court summed up the dilemma. "It has been
urged," Bissell remarked,

> that slavery is opposed to the laws of nature and of God; that its exist-
> ence among us is forbidden, by our obligation to these laws; and that
> they are paramount to the law of the domicil. I may be permitted to
> enquire here, what is the precise meaning of this argument, and how
> far is it intended to be carried? Is it meant, that the whole law of slavery
> is absolutely void? And that no obligation whatever can grow out of it?
> Is it to be seriously urged, that no obligation, no contract, bottomed on
> slavery, as a system, can be enforced in our courts of justice? Unless the
> argument is to be carried this length, it is difficult to see its application
> to the case: and before we can be called upon to take this ground, we
> must be asked to denounce a system, which has prevailed among us for
> more than a century.[80]

[79] *Miller v. McQuerry*, 17 F. Cas. 335, 339 (C.C.D. Ohio 1853). McLean made similar remarks in
Jones v. Vanzandt, 13 F. Cas. 1040, 1045–46 (C.C.D. Ohio 1843), another slavery case.

[80] *Jackson v. Bulloch*, 12 Conn. 38, 57 (1837).

Rather than undertaking this impossible task, northern judges retreated into a slavery-specific positivism, by rejecting the relevance of natural law in slavery cases.

US Supreme Court justice Joseph Story voiced the same reluctance to invoke natural law where slavery was involved, for the same reason. "It cannot admit of serious question," Story noted, that slavery "is founded in a violation of some of the first principles, which ought to govern nations. It is repugnant to the great principles of Christian duty, the dictates of natural religion, the obligations of good faith and morality, and the eternal maxims of social justice." But Story was equally certain that a judge had no authority grounded in natural law to find slavery unlawful in states that allowed it. "I shall take up no time in the examination of the history of slavery, or of the question, how far it is consistent with the natural rights of mankind," he explained. "That it has interwoven itself into the municipal institutions of some countries, and forms the foundation of large masses of property in a portion of our own country, is known to all of us. Sitting, therefore, in an American court of judicature, I am not permitted to deny, that under some circumstances it may have a lawful existence."[81]

Until the Civil War, northern state supreme courts would continue to assert that slavery was contrary to natural law but was nevertheless lawful where it was authorized by positive law. "Though slavery is contrary to natural right," explained Massachusetts chief justice Lemuel Shaw, and although slavery had long been abolished in his own state, "if any other state or community see fit to establish and continue slavery by law, so far as the legislative power of that country extends, we are bound to take notice of the existence of those laws, and we are not at liberty to declare and hold an act done within those limits, unlawful and void, upon our own views of morality."[82] As Justice Thomas Bartley of the Ohio Supreme Court put it, "We do not sit here to administer the divine law." He agreed with those who condemned "slavery as repugnant to reason and the principles of natural law," but he recognized the right of Kentucky to permit slavery.[83]

Southern courts, by contrast, began shortly before the Civil War to assert that slavery was consistent with natural law. "Slavery in this country is derived from the pure and absolute slavery existing among the tribes of Africa," the Mississippi Supreme Court reasoned in 1859. "It is in no wise opposed to the law of nature."[84] The following year, a South Carolina court affirmed that "slavery is not contrary to the divine law promulgated in the Holy Scriptures." Indeed, the court noted, "It must be consistent with nature, for in some form or other it

---

[81] *United States v. La Jeune Eugenie*, 26 F. Cas. 832, 845–46 (C.C.D. Mass. 1822).

[82] *Commonwealth v. Aves*, 35 Mass. 193, 215 (1836).

[83] *Anderson v. Poindexter*, 6 Ohio St. 622, 724 (1856).

[84] *Mitchell v. Wells*, 37 Miss. 235, 258–59 (1859).

is inevitable; and, in fact, prevails universally."[85] Slavery *was* the natural status of black people, the Georgia Supreme Court insisted in 1857. "To be the 'servant of servants' is the judicial curse pronounced upon their race," the court declared. "And this Divine decree is unreversible. It will run on parallel with time itself. And heaven and earth shall sooner pass away, than one jot or tittle of it shall abate. Under the superior race and no where else, do they attain to the highest degree of civilization."[86] Northern and southern courts were reproducing both sides of the political debate as to whether slavery was contrary to or consistent with natural law.

During the Civil War, whether slavery was consistent with natural law continued to be an important question, because it played a part in emancipation.[87] Ordinarily, a victorious army could not confiscate the property of the enemy. On what ground, then, could the Union claim the power to free the slaves? What distinguished slaves from other forms of property? One answer was that slavery, unlike other kinds of property ownership, was contrary to natural law. "Ordinary goods," explained the New York lawyer Grosvenor Lowrey, "are property by the law of nature." But slaves were different, because "the slave whom we capture as property, is, after his capture and the transfer to himself of all the captured title of his master, no longer a chattel, but a man, insusceptible of recapture."[88] Francis Lieber, the German-born lawyer who shaped the legal framework for the Union's conduct of the Civil War, authored an order directing armies in the field that any slaves coming under their protection were immediately entitled to freedom. He explained that "slavery, complicating and confounding the ideas of property, (that is of a *thing*,) and of personality, (that is of *humanity*,) exists according to municipal law or local law only. The law of nature and nations has never acknowledged it."[89] When the war ended, the widespread belief in the North that slavery was contrary to natural law facilitated the enactment of the Thirteenth Amendment.[90] In abolishing slavery, the amendment deprived many white southerners of vast amounts of their property, an outcome that would have been hard to imagine with any kind of property other than slaves.

---

[85] *Willis v. Jolliffee*, 32 S.C. Eq. 447, 463 (1860).

[86] *American Colonization Society v. Gartrell*, 23 Ga. 448, 464 (1857).

[87] Stephen C. Neff, *Justice in Blue and Gray: A Legal History of the Civil War* (Cambridge: Harvard Univ. Press, 2010), 128–49; John Fabian Witt, *Lincoln's Code: The Laws of War in American History* (New York: Free Press, 2012), 199–219.

[88] Grosvenor P. Lowrey, *The Commander-in Chief; A Defence Upon Legal Grounds of the Proclamation of Emancipation* (New York: G.P. Putnam, 1863), 24.

[89] Francis Lieber, *General Order No.100—Adjutant General's Office: Instructions for the Government of Armies of the United States in the Field* (New York: D. Van Nostrand, 1863), 13.

[90] Alexander Tsesis, *The Thirteenth Amendment and American Freedom: A Legal History* (New York: New York Univ. Press, 2004), 101–04.

Even after slavery had been abolished, the question of its consistency with natural law lingered on. There were still many people who owed money on pre-abolition contracts for the sale of slaves. Did they have to pay? The federal judge Henry Clay Caldwell held that they did not, because a contract for the sale of a slave was inconsistent with natural law. The law could not uphold "contracts which are against good morals, religion, and natural right," Caldwell reasoned. "Under what law can the slave dealer assert his right of action? Not under the laws that sanctioned the right, for they are abolished. He must then seek it under the common law. But the common law brands all such contracts as vicious, immoral, contrary to the law of nature, and void."[91] When the issue reached the US Supreme Court, however, a majority took the opposite view. "It has been earnestly insisted that contracts for the purchase and sale of slaves are contrary to natural justice and right," the Court observed. But selling slaves had been lawful at the time these contracts had been entered into, the Court concluded, and the validity of a contract had to be assessed as of the time it was made, not at some later time when the law had changed. Whether slavery was contrary to natural law was simply not a relevant consideration. "Whatever we may think of the institution of slavery viewed in the light of religion, morals, humanity, or a sound political economy," the Court explained, "as the obligation here was valid when executed, sitting as a court of justice, we have no choice but to give it effect." Chief Justice Salmon Chase dissented. Before the war, Chase had been a prominent abolitionist and one of the founders of the antislavery Free Soil Party. He argued that "contracts for the purchase and sale of slaves were and are against sound morals and natural justice," and for that reason could no longer be enforced in the absence of positive law authorizing slavery.[92] The controversy over slavery's status under natural law outlived slavery itself.

In the late 19th and early 20th centuries, when slavery had ceased to exist but segregation and other forms of discrimination were routine, the debate shifted to whether these practices were consistent with natural law. Proponents of segregation insisted that the law of nature required separating the races. "Miscegenation and amalgamation" were "equal folly," declared the Kentucky judge Samuel Nicholas. "The law of nature against the propagation of hybrids vindicates its supremacy by a visible deterioration from both races."[93] The Alabama lawyer D. D. Shelby agreed that "God has made the races dissimilar. The instincts with which he has endowed them indicates that they should not overstep the line that he has drawn between them." Shelby argued that the Equal Protection Clause of the recently ratified Fourteenth Amendment thus did not require the southern

[91] *Buckner v. Street*, 4 F. Cas. 578, 580, 583 (C.C.E.D. Ark. 1871).
[92] *Osborn v. Nicholson*, 80 U.S. 654, 660–61, 663 (1871).
[93] S. S. Nicholas, *Conservative Essays Legal and Political* (Philadelphia: J.B. Lippincott, 1865), 30.

states to allow racial intermarriage. "The natural separation of the races is an un-deniable fact," he asserted, "and all social organization that leads to their amalga-mation or intermarriage, is repugnant to the law of nature."[94]

The view that natural law required segregation was often expressed in lit-igation, even by judges in the northern states. In 1867, for example, the Pennsylvania Supreme Court considered a challenge to a railroad's policy of op-erating segregated train cars. The court held that segregation was lawful because it was consistent with the law of nature. "Why the Creator made one black and the other white, we know not," the court reasoned, "but the fact is apparent, and the races distinct, each producing its own kind and following the peculiar law of its own constitution." The court explained that "the natural law which forbids their intermarriage and their social amalgamation" applied with full force on a train, because "all social organizations which lead to their amalgamation are re-pugnant to the law of nature."[95] In New York, the state's highest court approved the statutory requirement of segregated schools for much the same reason. "In the nature of things there must be many social distinctions and privileges," the court suggested. Whether the races would ever be integrated depended "upon the operation of natural laws," not on positive laws "which conflict with the ge-neral sentiment of the community."[96]

Courts in all parts of the country grounded segregation on natural law. Could a theater reserve the orchestra seats for whites and require black patrons to sit in the balcony? Yes, said the Missouri Supreme Court; the theater's seating policy "does no more than work out natural laws and race peculiarities."[97] Could a state require segregated schools? Yes, said a Kentucky court. "The separation of the human family into races, distinguished no less by color than by temperament and other qualities, is as certain as anything in nature." The sentiment that "some call race prejudice" was in fact "nature's guard to prevent the amalgamation of the races."[98] A subtler but much better-known example was *Plessy v. Ferguson*, the 1896 case in which the US Supreme Court upheld the constitutionality of state laws requiring segregated railroad cars. The Equal Protection Clause of the Fourteenth Amendment "was undoubtedly to enforce the absolute equality of the two races before the law," the Court held, "but, in the nature of things, it could not have been intended to abolish distinctions based upon color." The

[94] D. D. Shelby, "The Thirteenth and Fourteenth Amendments," *Southern Law Review* 3 (1874): 531.

[95] *West Chester and Philadelphia Railroad Co. v. Miles*, 55 Pa. 209, 213 (1867).

[96] *People ex rel. King v. Gallagher*, 93 N.Y. 438, 448 (1883).

[97] *Younger v. Judah*, 19 S.W. 1109, 1111 (Mo. 1892).

[98] *Berea College v. Commonwealth*, 94 S.W. 623, 626 (Ky. Ct. App. 1906). This decision was affirmed by the US Supreme Court without any discussion of natural law. *Berea College v. Kentucky*, 211 U.S. 45 (1908).

Court considered race discrimination to be part of the "nature of things." The Court added that "if the two races are to meet upon terms of social equality, it must be the result of natural affinities" rather than any human-made law.[99] If segregation was understood to be natural, a feature of human nature, then enacting legislation to prevent it would be futile, so it was hard to conceive that any rational legislator would have intended to do so.

The presumed naturalness of segregation would last a long time. "It seems that segregation is not only recognized in constitutional law and judicial decision," the federal judge Robert Wilkin remarked in 1952, shortly before constitutional law would change dramatically in *Brown v. Board of Education* and related decisions, "but that it is also supported by general principles of natural law. As nature has produced different species, so it has produced different races of men. Distinguishing racial features have not been produced by man, or man-made laws. They are the result of processes of evolution and it seems natural and customary for different species and different races to recognize and prefer as intimate associates their own kind."[100]

Opponents of segregation argued that it was contrary to natural law. "The doctrines of natural law and of christianity forbid that rights be denied on the ground of race or color," the Iowa Supreme Court declared, in the course of requiring a steamboat company to allow African American passengers to eat at the same table as white passengers.[101] Even some who found integration unpleasant contended that it was consistent with natural law. "Men of refined instincts will doubtless agree that it is shocking bad taste for a white man to intermarry with an African, or a Mongolian, or an Indian," the lawyer William Snyder supposed. "Nevertheless it may be pertinent to inquire whence society derives the moral right at least to punish a man because of his taste." Snyder pointed out that there was nothing unnatural about intermarriage. "The human family descends from common parents, and constitutes but one species," he observed. "Members of diverse races have intermarried from the earliest times."[102]

Slavery and race relations were among the most politically salient topics to which natural law was applied in the 19th century, and they were also among the most contested. Americans argued constantly, both in political debate and in litigation, over whether slavery and segregation were consistent with natural law. After a century of debate, the issue remained as divisive as ever. Each side was certain that its view of natural law was the right one. The stalemate raised

---

[99] *Plessy v. Ferguson*, 163 U.S. 537, 544, 551 (1896).

[100] *Hayes v. Crutcher*, 108 F. Supp. 582, 585 (M.D. Tenn. 1952).

[101] *Coger v. Northwestern Union Packet Co.*, 37 Iowa 145, 154 (1873).

[102] William L. Snyder, *The Geography of Marriage or Legal Perplexities of Wedlock in the United States* (New York: G.P. Putnam's Sons, 1889), 65–67.

questions about the usefulness of natural law in the legal system. Natural law appeared to be ambiguous enough to support the argument that slavery was forbidden *and* the argument that slavery was compelled. Natural law seemed such a matter of personal opinion that it could lead to the conclusion that segregation was required *and* the conclusion that segregation was prohibited. If everyone had his own version of natural law, what good was it?

Disenchantment with Natural Law

Of course, thoughtful lawyers had always realized that there were difficult questions of natural law on which reasonable people might disagree. "Questions of natural right are triable by their conformity with the moral sense," Thomas Jefferson observed. "Those who write treatises of natural law, can only declare what their own moral sense and reason dictate." When such authors differed, "and they often differ, we must appeal to our own feelings and reason to decide between them."[103] And lawyers had always realized that introspection was sometimes an unreliable guide. "As the law of nature and reason is the oldest, and enacted by the Deity himself, and so the most obligatory, it is the true foundation of all law," explained the Massachusetts lawyer Nathan Dane. "But then men ought to be constantly aware, that they are too apt to think *their own* notions, his will and his law; or as one's own mind approves or condemns, so does he too often mistake its own for His decisions, as to what is right and what is wrong."[104] Natural law had been created by God, but it had to be discerned by fallible human beings who had trouble looking past their own self-interest. Sometimes the most earnest declarations of what natural law required were simply wrong. "What we want is, some test by which to distinguish, in cases of dispute, what is Right, and what is Wrong," the lawyer Richard Hildreth acknowledged. "But so long as each man appeals to his own particular reason, his own particular conscience, his own particular moral sentiment, as the ultimate and infallible tribunal, just as he appeals to his eye in matters of color, to his sight and touch upon questions of form, and to his ear upon questions of sound, no such test does, or can, exist."[105]

Before the middle of the 19th century, disagreement over the content of natural law tended not to be cited as a reason for rejecting the use of natural law altogether. It was a reason to be cautious in accepting the views published in a treatise.

---

[103] Thomas Jefferson, "Opinion on the Treaties with France, 28 April 1793," in John Catanzariti et al., eds., *The Papers of Thomas Jefferson* (Princeton: Princeton Univ. Press, 1950–), 25:613.

[104] Nathan Dane, *A General Abridgment and Digest of American Law* (Boston: Cummings, Hilliard, 1823–29), 6:626.

[105] Richard Hildreth, *Theory of Morals* (Boston: Charles C. Little and James Brown, 1844), 3.

It served as a reminder to have some skepticism about one's own instincts. But it was not a reason to doubt that natural law should play a fundamental role in the legal system. Jefferson, after noting that authors often disagreed as to the content of natural law, proceeded to consult several books on natural law to determine whether treaties made with France before the French Revolution remained binding afterward. When Dane observed that people sometimes mistook their own ideas for God's, he meant only to reject poorly reasoned human efforts to discern natural law, not to reject natural law itself.

In the mid-19th century, however, lawyers began to cite pervasive disagreement over the content of natural law as a reason for declining to use natural law at all. The Ohio judge Simeon Nash was exasperated by litigants who claimed a natural right to property. "Where can be found *any book of authority* upon that branch of the law of nature, which regulates the acquisition, the possession, and the protection of property?" he lamented. "Nay, is it not notorious, that scarce any two agree[?]" A judge knew better than anyone that using natural law in litigation required reposing considerable trust in the wisdom and conscience of judges, "a conscience which may be right, or which may be wrong." It was "to avoid the confiding of any such unbounded discretion in man," he concluded, "why civil laws are as minute and numerous as they are, and why we have resorted to written constitutions, bills of rights, and fixed laws."[106]

In the 1860s, the Pennsylvania Supreme Court declared that "the vague generalities of natural law" were of little use in deciding cases.[107] "It is true that written law depends itself on ulterior principles of natural law," the court acknowledged, "but those principles are subject to very great diversities of application, and lack entirely their definiteness, which is an essential quality of law as a rule of common or social conduct." The very purpose of positive law, the court suggested, was to make natural principles more concrete, and thus more practical for deciding who should win a case. "Law is intended to be a definition of those principles in such a form as to fit them for a ready and ordinary use," the court explained, "and to avoid the disputes that necessarily grow out of more general principles."[108] Daniel Agnew, one of the justices on the Pennsylvania Supreme Court, expounded on this view in a speech at Union College in Ohio. "Conclusions drawn from the light of nature alone are obscure, uncertain, and variable," he insisted. "The reason is obvious, as they depend upon individual judgment." Principles of natural law were of little use to a judge, because "it is of the very essence of law that it should be a standard of authority, binding on every

---

[106] Simeon Nash, "Reply to the Review of *Good v. Zercher*, in the January Number of this Journal," *Western Law Journal* 2 (1845): 264–65.

[107] *Sutter v. The Trustees of the First Reformed Dutch Church*, 42 Pa. 503, 509 (1862).

[108] *Commonwealth v. Meeser*, 44 Pa. 341, 343–44 (1863).

conscience, admitting of no dispute." Positive law met this description, but natural law did not. A system in which judges resorted to natural law, "the product of human judgment only, would not be law, but opinion."[109]

Assertions like these became more common toward the end of the century. Legal education had customarily begun with natural law, but in his introductory lecture at the City University of New York, Judge Isaac Franklin Russell explained that "the law of nature presents a mass of muddy speculation" he would not even discuss.[110] At the University of Michigan, students learned that natural law "fluctuates as public opinion changes," and that it "is enforced by indeterminate and uncertain authority. There are no tribunals in which it may be administered."[111] After decades of debate, in political fora and in the courts, over the implications of natural law for some high-profile questions, there was a growing sense among lawyers and judges that natural law was simply too uncertain to be of much practical use.

Meanwhile, conventional attitudes on some of these questions had transformed so much over the century as to call into doubt the notion that there was even such a thing as an eternal, unchanging natural law. Slavery had been passionately defended as consistent with or even required by natural law, but slavery existed no more. Many had argued that natural law denied political and legal equality to women, but by the end of the century women were allowed to own property on terms equal to men, to practice professions, and in some jurisdictions to vote. These developments did not *necessarily* require rethinking the status of natural law. One could conclude instead, for example, that defenders of slavery and the traditional role of women had simply misperceived the content of natural law, and that natural law, correctly understood, required equality between races and genders. But these changes were enough to cause some observers, at least, to doubt the very existence of natural law. The law professor Christopher Tiedeman, for example, was a conservative critic of late 19th-century social and economic developments who favored a strong role for the judiciary in curbing what he saw as legislative excesses.[112] His views, in the first half of the century, would very likely have been expressed in the language of natural law. But Tiedeman did not think that natural law gave courts any ground to intervene. After surveying some of the social changes of the preceding century, particularly involving the rights of women, Tiedeman had become convinced that natural law did not exist. "There

---

[109] Daniel Agnew, *The Spirit and Poetry of Law* (Philadelphia: Sherman, 1866), 10.

[110] Isaac Franklin Russell, *Lectures on Law for Women* (New York: New York Economical Printing, 1893), 3.

[111] Walter Denton Smith, *A Manual of Elementary Law* (St. Paul, MN: West Publishing, 1896), 4.

[112] David N. Mayer, "The Jurisprudence of Christopher G. Tiedeman: A Study in the Failure of Laissez-Faire Constitutionalism," *Missouri Law Review* 55 (1990): 93–161.

is," he asserted, "no such thing, even in ethics, as an absolute, inalienable, natural right." The changes he described demonstrated that "the so-called natural rights depend upon, and vary with, the legal and ethical conceptions of the people."[113] Lawyers had once agreed that natural law occupied a central position in the legal system. Now they were starting to have some doubts.

---

[113] Christopher G. Tiedeman, *The Unwritten Constitution of the United States* (New York: G.P. Putnam's Sons, 1890), 76.

PART III

THE TRANSITION AND AFTER

7

The Decline of Natural Law and Custom

The late 19th century was the first period in which American lawyers in significant numbers began to doubt whether natural law should play any role in the legal system. There had always been occasional critics of the use of natural law in litigation, but this criticism had little effect until the 1870s. It had a big effect thereafter. Natural law was almost universally accepted in the legal system in 1870, but it was almost completely gone by the early 20th century.

A second big change in legal thought also took place during the same period. Lawyers had understood the common law to be based in part on custom, but this belief likewise went into decline in the late 19th century. By the early 20th century, custom had largely lost its status as a grounding for the common law.

These were important changes, because they knocked out the common law's two traditional foundations. Lawyers had understood the common law as a mixture of reason and custom. To the extent the common law was based on reason, it was a form of applied natural law—universal principles, discernable by reason, applied to the specific circumstances of American life. To the extent the common law was based on custom, it was a distillation of the conventional practices and beliefs of Anglo-Americans over the course of centuries. If neither natural law nor custom were to play a role in the legal system, lawyers would have to rethink the grounding of the common law and the nature of common law decision-making.

Natural law's disappearance from the legal system also posed a question for the interpretation of statutes. Natural law had been a guide for judges in ascertaining the meaning of statutes and sometimes even in striking them down. What were judges supposed to do when natural law was no longer available?

This chapter will focus on the decline of natural law and custom. Chapter 8 will examine the ways in which these developments forced the profession to rethink the process of judging.

The Decline of Natural Law. Stuart Banner, Oxford University Press (2021). © Oxford University Press.
DOI: 10.1093/oso/9780197556498.003.0008

The Decline of Natural Law

Criticism of natural law was nothing new. For American lawyers, the first prominent critic was the English philosopher Jeremy Bentham. Bentham's name was often mentioned in American court opinions.[1] In the 1840s, the Georgia Supreme Court even referred to him as "Jeremy Bentham, who, with all his eccentricities, is undoubtedly the Father of modern law reform."[2] Bentham's voluminous writings included some well-known passages criticizing the concept of natural law.[3] In the American edition of his *Principles of Legislation*, published in Boston in 1830, he complained of the "multitude of professors, of jurists, of magistrates, of philosophers, who make your ears ring with the *Law of Nature*." Each one, Bentham scoffed, "favours you with his opinions as so many chapters of the *Law of Nature*."[4] Bentham could not have been any clearer about his own view. "There are no such things as natural rights," he insisted, "no such things as rights anterior to the establishment of government." Rather, "The expression is merely figurative," a mere "error that leads to mischief" if taken literally.[5]

Bentham's skepticism about natural law did not have any immediate effect on the American legal system, however. Nor did the similar view of John Austin, the other major early 19th-century English critic of natural law.[6] Austin argued that the conventional conception of natural law was "misleading and pernicious jargon" that inhibited clear thinking about the law.[7] But Austin's works did not become well known in the United States until they were republished in the later part of the century, when the intellectual climate had already changed enough to give them a favorable reception.[8]

Before the late 19th century, American lawyers only occasionally expressed doubts about the existence of natural law. Abel Upshur, a Virginia judge who would soon become secretary of state for a brief period, sounded a bit like

---

[1] See, e.g., *Dunham v. Gould*, 16 Johns. 367, 380 (N.Y. Sup. Ct. 1819); *Cram v. Hendricks*, 7 Wend. 569, 662 (N.Y. Sup. Ct. 1831); *Rost v. Henderson*, 4 Rob. 468, 474 n.* (La. 1843); *Bacon v. County of Wayne*, 1 Mich. 461, 462 (1850); *Hopkins v. Hopkins*, 23 S.C. Eq. 207, 211 (1850).

[2] *Flint River Steamboat Co. v. Foster*, 5 Ga. 194, 207 (1848).

[3] Lieberman, *Province of Legislation Determined*, 222–40.

[4] Jeremy Bentham, *Principles of Legislation* (Boston: Wells and Lilly, 1830), 204.

[5] Bentham, *Works*, 2:500.

[6] On the influence of Bentham and Austin on other aspects of American legal thought, see Peter J. King, *Utilitarian Jurisprudence in America: The Influence of Bentham and Austin on American Legal Thought in the Nineteenth Century* (New York: Garland Publishing, 1986).

[7] John Austin, *The Province of Jurisprudence Determined* (London: John Murray, 1832), 191. See also John Austin, *Lectures on Jurisprudence* (London: John Murray, 1869), 2:585–90.

[8] John C. Gray, "Some Definitions and Questions in Jurisprudence," *Harvard Law Review* 6 (1892): 21–22; Richard A. Cosgrove, *Our Lady the Common Law: An Anglo-American Legal Community, 1870–1930* (New York: New York Univ. Press, 1987), 113.

Bentham in a speech at William and Mary in 1841. "What are our natural rights?" Upshur asked. "Have we any?" He did not think so. "The only law of nature is brute force," he concluded. "If there be any *right* of nature, it is a right which nature herself does not respect."[9] Caleb Cushing, the former attorney general, voiced similar skepticism while arguing on behalf of a client in 1866. Cushing had been influenced by Henry Sumner Maine's recent book *Ancient Law*, which traced the history of the concept of natural law to its Greek and Roman roots.[10] After mentioning "ethical rules," Cushing paused to clarify his choice of terms. "I will not say the natural law," he explained. "After reading Maine's admirable Treatise on Ancient Law, and seeing how thoroughly the illusions and delusions of natural law are there exploded, I am ashamed to use the phrase."[11] An anonymous lawyer complained in 1868 that despite the work of Austin and Maine, legal education still began with the study of natural law. "The crude and obsolete speculations of the commentator of the last century," he lamented, referring to Blackstone's discussion of natural law, "are still taught as the undeniable conclusions of legal and historical science."[12] Before the 1870s, however, such assertions do not seem to have been very common. Few American lawyers doubted that natural law should play an important role in the legal system.

But this near-consensus on the appropriateness of using natural law rested on a foundation that had slowly been cracking for much of the century, in the ways we have seen in the preceding chapters.

First, the adoption of written constitutions made lawyers doubt whether judges even had the authority to employ natural law in one especially salient group of cases—those challenging the validity of a statute. The arguments they made against natural law in these cases, particularly that it was too subjective and uncertain to be entrusted to the handling of judges, etched away lawyers' confidence that natural law belonged in the legal system at all. After all, if natural law was subject to multiple interpretations when the validity of a statute was at issue, it was just as uncertain in every other kind of case.

Second, the gradual separation of law and religion into distinct spheres made lawyers doubt whether principles grounded in religious belief should be enforceable in court. When Christianity was considered to be part of the common law, there was nothing anomalous about judges employing conventional Christian doctrines to decide cases. But as religion was redefined as a private pursuit,

---

[9] Abel Upshur, *Address to the Literary Societies of William and Mary College, Va.* (Philadelphia: A. Waldie, 1841), 10–11.

[10] Henry Sumner Maine, *Ancient Law* (1861) (Boston: Beacon Press, 1963), 42–108.

[11] Caleb Cushing, *Arguments for the Plaintiff in the Case of Charles T. James vs. Atlantic Delaine Co.* (Washington, DC: McGill & Withrerow, 1867), 14.

[12] "The Law of Nature," *Every Saturday* 6 (1868): 378.

separate from the public, governmental realm of law, the use of natural law in secular courts came to seem more and more anomalous.

Third, the explosion in law publishing made natural law seem less necessary to practicing lawyers. In a world with few published court opinions, legal argument had to rest in large part on broad principles, including principles drawn from natural law. As court opinions became more available, they began to push the broad principles aside. Judges increasingly expected lawyers to cite specific cases directly on point. Lawyers increasingly realized that citing published opinions was the best strategy for winning cases. Natural law became less useful in court.

Finally, after decades of litigation over controversial issues like slavery and segregation, gender roles, property, and the death penalty, litigation in which natural law was deployed on both sides of many cases, lawyers were coming to have doubts about the usefulness of natural law in court.

Because of these developments, arguments against the use of natural law that had not seemed plausible in the early part of the 19th century began to attract adherents toward the end of the century. The first hint of this change in attitude could be seen in the 1870s, when American law journals began reprinting articles originally published in England that denied the existence of natural law. Jurisprudence "has undergone an intellectual transmutation," argued W. A. Hunter of University College London, in a lecture reprinted in the *American Law Record*. "It dwelt for ages in the cloud-land of metaphysics; it has now been brought to the earth and planted on a solid foundation by Jeremy Bentham." Bentham's advance, Hunter explained, was to dispense with natural law. "If we ask what this law of nature is," Hunter continued, "it is an empty name. Nothing can be taken out of it, but what is first put into it." He wondered how "an abstraction so barren as the law of nature" could have "retained its sway for ages."[13] The English lawyer Henry Raymond Fink, in another article republished in the United States, insisted that "there is no analogy between the laws of the material world and the laws of nature in the sense of the jurist." The laws that governed human affairs had no natural existence but were based on people's sense "of justice and injustice, sound policy and expediency."[14]

American lawyers made similar arguments against the existence of natural law in the 1880s and 1890s. "There is no such thing as a prohibition of natural law," declared the New York lawyer Hugh Weightman. He was writing about the rule barring the marriage of close relatives, one of the doctrines conventionally said to rest on natural law, but Weightman insisted that the rule was based

---

[13] W. A. Hunter, "The Metaphysical and Positive Methods in Jurisprudence," *American Law Record* 1 (1873): 450.

[14] Henry Raymond Fink, "Law—Philosophy: The Rival Schools," *American Law Record* 2 (1873): 84–85.

entirely on positive law.[15] J. Bleecker Miller, another lawyer in New York, rejected Blackstone's canonical discussion of the law of nature, which Miller suggested showed "the usual confusion of ideas of writers of that period," and deserved the criticism leveled by Bentham.[16] William Gardiner Hammond, dean of the St. Louis Law School, lamented "the confusion of law and ethics under the name of the Law of Nature."[17]

By 1895, the *Yale Law Journal* could publish an article titled "Survival of the Theory of Natural Rights in Judicial Decisions," as if such rights were merely a vestige of an earlier era.[18] A few years later, readers of the *Columbia Law Review* were apprised that the law of nature was never "anything but an empty abstraction or even hallucination."[19] "There has developed in our day a very general disposition to deny the existence of the absolute jural order, the *jus naturae,*" explained one observer.[20] "The law of nature, so called," noted another, "has ceased to have any practical interest."[21] A third observer summed up the trend more emphatically. "Modern jurisprudence and modern political philosophy," he declared, "have incontestably proved the mistake underlying this assumption of natural law or natural rights. They have shown that natural law is simply the idea of particular thinkers of a particular age of what ought to be the law."[22] The concept of natural law was coming to be understood as an error that modern thinkers had corrected.

This denial of natural law's existence was more pronounced in universities than among practicing lawyers and judges. Abbot Lawrence Lowell, the former lawyer who served as president of Harvard for much of the early 20th century, classified natural law as "a confusion between what is and what ought to be, between law and ethics, between facts and aspirations, between the real and the imaginary."[23] The historian Albert Bushnell Hart, author of a biography of Chief Justice Salmon Chase, among many other books, thought the law of nature "is after all simply what men now living suppose was believed by ancestors long since dead."[24] Edward Elliott, a political scientist at Princeton, reported that "the

---

[15] Hugh Weightman, "Marriage and Its Prohibitions," *American Law Review* 17 (1883): 166.

[16] J. Bleecker Miller, *Trade Organizations in Politics* (New York: Baker & Taylor, 1887), 87.

[17] William Gardiner Hammond, *Public Education* (Iowa City: Republican, 1890), 6.

[18] John E. Keeler, "Survival of the Theory of Natural Rights in Judicial Decisions," *Yale Law Journal* 5 (1895): 24.

[19] John S. Ewart, "What is the Law Merchant?," *Columbia Law Review* 3 (1903): 142.

[20] F. M. Taylor, *The Right of the State to Be* (Ann Arbor: Univ. of Michigan, 1891), 12.

[21] Emlin McClain, *Our Common Humanity and the Common Law* (Chicago: Univ. of Chicago Press, 1909), 8.

[22] Edwin R. A. Seligman, *Essays in Taxation* (New York: Macmillan, 1895), 68.

[23] A. Lawrence Lowell, *The Government of England* (New York: Macmillan, 1912), 2:477.

[24] Albert Bushnell Hart, "A Government of Men," *American Political Science Review* 7 (1913): 6.

law of nature and natural rights are no longer seriously regarded in the world of political thought."[25] Isaac Franklin Russell of New York University's law school disparaged it as the "so-called law of nature."[26] "The old conception of a law certain and final is gradually being challenged," explained E. F. Albertsworth, a law professor at Cleveland's Western Reserve University. "That law is in itself inherently just or right," he advised, "is believed by some jurists and philosophers to be untenable."[27]

These academic critics were likely influenced by contemporary philosophical discussions of natural law, which placed a new emphasis on the difference between natural laws in the physical world, which were now said to be empirical descriptions with no moral content, and the natural laws conventionally thought to govern human affairs, which were now considered normative moral injunctions with no empirical content outside human preferences. Discussions of natural law had previously tended to ignore or dismiss the importance of this difference, but in the late 19th century writers began to find the difference significant. Perhaps the best-known example was John Stuart Mill, whose essay "Nature," first published in 1874, included an extended discussion of these two very different senses of natural law. "No word is more commonly associated with the word Nature, than Law," Mill explained, "and this last word has distinctly two meanings, in one of which it denotes some definite portion of what is, in the other, of what ought to be." In the first category were the law of gravity, the laws of motion, and so on, which were "neither more nor less than the observed uniformities in the occurrence of phenomena." In the second category were the natural laws in the lawyer's sense, "all of which are portions of what ought to be, or of somebody's suppositions, feelings, or commands respecting what ought to be." Mill lamented "the liability of these two meanings of the word to be confounded," as if they were a single concept.[28]

American intellectuals soon began emphasizing this difference between the scientific and legal senses of natural law.[29] Woodrow Wilson was a young political scientist (and a former lawyer) when he published his textbook *The State*

[25] Edward Elliott, *American Government and Majority Rule* (Princeton: Princeton Univ. Press, 1916), 124.

[26] Isaac Franklin Russell, "Thoughts on the Study of Law," *Intercollegiate Law Journal* 1 (1892): 219.

[27] E. F. Albertsworth, "The Changing Conception of Law," *American Bar Association Journal* 8 (1922): 675.

[28] John Stuart Mill, *Nature, the Utility of Religion, and Theism*, 3rd ed. (London: Longmans, Green, 1885), 14.

[29] See, e.g., "The Genesis of Rights in Natural Law," *New Englander* 34 (1875): 152–53; Westel Woodbury Willoughby, *An Examination of the Nature of the State* (New York: Macmillan, 1896), 91–105.

in 1889. It included a section on "laws of nature and laws of the state," which Wilson insisted were two very different things. Drawing heavily on the work of the English biologist Thomas Huxley, Wilson observed that the laws of the state are commands that can be obeyed or disobeyed, while natural laws are not commands but descriptions, which are not capable of being disobeyed. "In brief," Wilson concluded, "human choice enters into the laws of the state, whereas from natural laws that choice is altogether excluded: they are dominated by fixed necessity."[30]

Among American law professors, the most enthusiastic natural law-basher in the early 20th century was Roscoe Pound, who was still near the beginning of a career that would make him one of the best-known law professors of the era.[31] Pound relentlessly attacked the concept of natural law, or "Cloudcuckoo-town law," as he referred to it.[32] He called it a "fiction" and defined it as "the law which should in theory, but does not in fact, exist."[33] He argued that natural law was nothing but lawyers' conviction "that conformity to their individual conscience is a criterion of the validity of a law."[34] He castigated it as "a system of enforcing magisterial caprice."[35] He lamented that students were still "trained to accept the eighteenth-century theory of natural law."[36] He despaired that "after philosophical, political, economic and sociological thought have given up the eighteenth-century law of nature, it is still the premise of the American lawyer."[37] Pound rarely missed an occasion to say something derogatory about natural law.

Over time, skepticism about natural law's existence spread from academic circles to the bench and bar. "It is clear, I think, that the old idea of a natural law was a misapprehension," reflected the Pittsburgh lawyer Edwin Smith, who was president of the Pennsylvania Bar Association.[38] Frank Johnston, a judge in Chicago, agreed that "the whole subject was wrapped up in speculation, resting merely on a priori reasoning and not on an actual investigation of the facts." Johnston contrasted the old reliance on natural law with, as he titled his book,

---

[30] Woodrow Wilson, *The State* (Boston: D.C. Heath, 1889), 630–31. Wilson was drawing upon Thomas Huxley, *Science Primer: Introductory* (1882) (New York: American Book, 1890), 12–14.

[31] N. E. H. Hull, *Roscoe Pound and Karl Llewellyn: Searching for an American Jurisprudence* (Chicago: Univ. of Chicago Press, 1997); David Wigdor, *Roscoe Pound: Philosopher of Law* (Westport, CT: Greenwood Press, 1974).

[32] Roscoe Pound, "Uniformity of Commercial Law on the American Continent," *Michigan Law Review* 8 (1909): 92.

[33] Roscoe Pound, "Spurious Interpretation," *Columbia Law Review* 7 (1907): 383, 379.

[34] Roscoe Pound, "Inherent and Acquired Difficulties in the Administration of Punitive Justice," *Proceedings of the American Political Science Association* 4 (1907): 225.

[35] Roscoe Pound, "Mechanical Jurisprudence," *Columbia Law Review* 8 (1908): 605.

[36] Roscoe Pound, *The Law and the People* (Chicago: Univ. of Chicago Press, 1910), 10.

[37] Roscoe Pound, "Law in Books and Law in Action," *American Law Review* 44 (1910): 25.

[38] Edwin W. Smith, "Law and the Function of Legislation," *American Law Review* 46 (1912): 167.

the *Modern Conception of Law*. As he recalled with disapproval, "the 'law of nature' was imagined to be a true law towards which all human law conformed."[39] The New York lawyer Theodore Demarest declared that natural law was "supernatural" and "quite above the province of the understanding."[40] A lawyer in Philadelphia reported that belief in natural law had "been abandoned by thoughtful men."[41] "I wasted considerable time worrying through treatises on jurisprudential subjects on a hunt for a *statement* of that basic 'natural law' with which most of the writers seemed to be so familiar," joked one St. Louis lawyer. "Of course my research was resultless."[42] The New Hampshire Supreme Court declared forthrightly that "there is no such thing as natural law."[43]

Indeed, the most famous of the early critics of natural law was a sitting judge, although one with an unusual interest in philosophical matters.[44] Oliver Wendell Holmes Jr. had been a judge for more than thirty years, first on the Massachusetts Supreme Court and then on the US Supreme Court, when he published a short article entitled "Natural Law" in 1918. "The jurists who believe in natural law," Holmes declared, "seem to me to be in that naïve state of mind that accepts what has been familiar and accepted by them and their neighbors as something that must be accepted by all men everywhere." In fact, Holmes suggested, virtually all of the social arrangements said to be based on natural law were better understood as mere traditions or conventions with no grounding in any higher law. A right was not something found in nature, but "only the hypostasis of a prophecy—the imagination of a substance supporting the fact that the public force will be brought to bear upon those who do things said to contravene it." All that lay behind so-called natural rights was "the fighting will of the subject to maintain them, and the spread of his emotions to the general rules by which they are maintained; but that does not seem to me the same thing as the supposed a priori discernment of a duty or the assertion of a preexisting right."[45]

---

[39] Frank Johnston Jr., *Modern Conception of Law* (Chicago: T.H. Flood, 1925), 6.

[40] Theodore F. C. Demarest, *Studies in American Jurisprudence* (New York: Banks Law Publishing, 1906), 349.

[41] Robert P. Reeder, *The Validity of Rate Regulations* (Philadelphia: T. & J.W. Johnson, 1914), 203.

[42] S. M. Doan, "Correspondence," *American Law Review* 39 (1905): 791.

[43] *Carter v. Craig*, 90 A. 598, 599 (N.H. 1914).

[44] G. Edward White, *Justice Oliver Wendell Holmes: Law and the Inner Self* (New York: Oxford Univ. Press, 1993); Louis Menand, *The Metaphysical Club: A Story of Ideas in America* (New York: Farrar, Straus and Giroux, 2001).

[45] Oliver Wendell Holmes Jr., "Natural Law," *Harvard Law Review* 32 (1918): 41–42. Holmes later made this point more clearly in private correspondence, in a fascinating passage suggesting that he had a similar understanding of natural law in the nonhuman realm. "So we prophesy that the earth and sun will act toward each other in a certain way," Holmes noted. "Then as we pretend to account for that mode of action by the hypothetical cause, the force of gravitation, which is merely the hypostasis of the prophesied fact and an empty phrase. So we get up the empty substratum, a *right*, to

But while legal intellectuals like Pound and Holmes doubted whether natural law even existed, practicing lawyers and judges tended to take a smaller step. They were not in the habit of debating philosophical questions. For them, the practical question was not about the *existence* of natural law but about its *use* within the legal system. Even if human affairs were governed by natural law in a moral sense, did the law of nature have any force in the courts? Lawyers and judges increasingly began to assert that it did not. "It must be kept in mind," a Kentucky court held regarding the duties of contracting parties, "that we are now speaking of the *legal* right, and not the *moral* obligation. Both may exist, the one being based upon civil and the other upon natural law."[46] The Rhode Island Supreme Court agreed that "natural justice is not law. To make it law is therefore a legislative act, forbidden by the Constitution to the courts of this state." The existence of a *natural* right of privacy thus did not imply the existence of a *legal* right of privacy, because "there is no room in our constitutional theory for any transcendent right or instinct of nature."[47] As one lawyer concluded, "Natural law is not a subject with which the lawyer deals."[48]

By the turn of the century it was already conventional to assert that while natural law existed in the realm of morality, it played no role in the legal system. "Natural law is not itself legally authoritative," the Columbia law professor John Ordronaux instructed. "In order to be judicially operative, it must first be incorporated with positive law."[49] Students at the University of Cincinnati Law School were taught that while natural law was "the standard of conduct by which men ought as a matter of conscience to govern themselves," natural laws "are not laws in our sense of the term," because "for an infraction of such a law one is answerable only in the forum of conscience," not in a court.[50] An Indianapolis bankruptcy lawyer acknowledged that "the rights of men have their foundation or root in human nature itself," but he insisted that this was not a matter of much practical professional interest. "The law of nature is not a law in the sense that it is administered by legal tribunals," he explained.[51] Frederick Judson, a lawyer in St. Louis, declared that "the English and American conception of law is a body

pretend to account for the fact that the courts will act in a certain way." Holmes to Frederick Pollock, 19 Jan. 1928, in Mark De Wolfe Howe, ed., *Holmes-Pollock Letters* (Cambridge: Harvard Univ. Press, 1946), 2:212.

[46] *McCracken v. Mercantile Trust Co.,* 1 S.W. 585, 586 (Ky. Ct. App. 1886).

[47] *Henry v. Cherry & Webb,* 73 A. 97, 106, 104 (R.I. 1909).

[48] W. D. L., "Book Review," *American Law Register* 42 (1894): 409.

[49] John Ordronaux, *Constitutional Legislation in the United States* (Philadelphia: T. & J.W. Johnson, 1891), 605.

[50] Gustavus H. Wald, *A Lecture Introductory to the Study of the Law of Contract* (Cincinnati: s.n., 1896), 2.

[51] Noble C. Butler, "Natural Rights," *American Law Review* 36 (1902): 484, 486.

of rules enforced by the courts and is therefore distinguished from the so-called natural law."[52] Lawyers and judges were coming to understand natural law as a subject for philosophers and ministers, but not for the legal system.

There were still many lawyers, judges, and law professors who believed in natural law's traditional role within the legal system. They realized that the tide of opinion within the profession was turning, and they worried about the consequences. "The old conception of the law, to which it owes its scientific development, and to which in former times it owed also the success of its administration, has with modern lawyers died away," complained the Los Angeles lawyer George Smith. Under the new conception, he acknowledged, "The courts have nothing to do with *justice, common sense, right* and *wrong,* or *rights,* in the familiar and proper sense of these terms, or with other similar misleading notions; but their function is simply to administer the law as prescribed by statutes and judicial decisions." Smith considered the change disastrous. "Such views cannot but affect the moral nature both of lawyers and judges," he warned. When judges were willing to "stifle the natural instincts of conscience" and merely follow the letter of the law, they were likely to reach unjust decisions. "Nor is the effect of this theory upon the intellect of the profession less disastrous," Smith continued. "The distinction between reasoning from principle and from authority, once well known to lawyers, has been almost lost." He argued that by giving up natural law, the bench and bar had untethered the legal system from its grounding in the universal sense of justice. "Such is the natural and inevitable effect of seeking for the law in statutes and precedents, and not in its reason and principles," he concluded, "and hence the degeneration of a once noble profession that can now hardly be regarded as a respectable trade."[53]

Such laments became commonplace at the turn of the century. Some had an explicitly political cast, as lawyers worried that a disregard for natural law would free legislatures to curtail property rights or even bring about socialism. "This theory, knowing no higher criterion than 'might is right,' practically foments the struggles of capital and labor for power," contended the Texas judge Hans Teichmueller. He preferred the older view, which he believed to be a protection against redistribution. "The opposite theory, recognizing *property* as an *institution of nature,* as much so as man himself, insists upon *its inherent natural law,* to which the rules of positive law must conform."[54] Allen Ripley Foote, the founder of the National Tax Association, worried that advocates of labor reform were "preparing the way for a widespread destruction of property through the

[52] Frederick N. Judson, *The Judiciary and the People* (New Haven: Yale Univ. Press, 1913), 60.

[53] George H. Smith, "Of the Certainty of the Law and the Uncertainty of Judicial Decisions," *American Law Review* 23 (1889): 715–16.

[54] Hans Teichmueller, "Economic Freedom," *American Law Review* 29 (1895): 375.

dissemination of false conceptions of the principles of justice." Property would be secure only when workers were made to realize that "the natural law of justice is superior to all constitutions, all enacted laws, all court decisions."[55] The Minnesota lawyer W. W. Billson despaired at "the desuetude, if not discredit, which in both popular and philosophic circles has overtaken the theories of natural law." In Billson's view, principles of natural law were the "floodgates, the crumbling of which below a certain point, would mean a socialistic deluge."[56]

But many who were concerned about the decline of natural law had no overt political agenda. They simply believed that natural law existed and undergirded the legal system, just as most Americans had believed since the 18th century, and that it was foolish to ignore this basic fact.[57] "Natural law may have been neglected, but it has not ceased to be necessary," explained René Holaind, whose very job title— Lecturer on Natural and Canon Law at Georgetown University—presupposed the value of attending to natural law. "A *pettifogger* may, perhaps, do very well with positive law alone, so long as he confines himself to legal technicalities; but a *constitutional lawyer* is often obliged to refer to those high maxims of individual and social morality which are axioms of natural law, or evident deductions from these axioms."[58] The Chicago lawyer William Addison Blakely acknowledged that "law, by some, has been regarded as a bundle of previous decisions, rather than as a science founded, like other sciences, on the immutable law of nature." Blakely thought this was a fundamental mistake. "The erroneousness of such a view," he charged, "must be obvious to all who have given it a reflection."[59]

Others suggested that the legal system should continue to employ natural law because of the respect it still commanded among nonlawyers. If the lay public realized that law was based entirely on the will of fallible humans, without any grounding in eternal justice, would the public lose respect for the legal system? Lucilius Emery, a former judge on the Maine Supreme Court, noted the growing divergence between lawyers and nonlawyers on this topic. While lawyers were giving up on using natural law, Emery cautioned, nonlawyers still had faith that "there is some law of nature or in nature, some criterion, which if ascertained and obeyed would be perfect justice."[60] Arthur Twining Hadley, the president

---

[55] Allen Ripley Foote, *The Right to Property in an Idea* (Philadelphia: Franklin Institute, 1898), 13–14.

[56] W. W. Billson, *Legal Outlook* (Duluth: Christie Lithograph & Printing, 1909), 12.

[57] John J. Sullivan, "The Study of the Natural Law," *American Law Register* 48 (1900): 522–42; Edward Lindsey, "The Development of a Scientific View of Law," *American Law Review* 45 (1911): 513–33.

[58] René Holaind, *Natural Law and Legal Practice* (New York: Benziger Brothers, 1899), 40.

[59] William Addison Blakely, comp., *American State Papers Bearing on Sunday Legislation* (Washington, DC: Religious Liberty Association, 1911), 27–28.

[60] Lucilius A. Emery, *Concerning Justice* (New Haven: Yale Univ. Press, 1914), 24.

of Yale University, thought that one benefit of removing natural law from litigation was that "the courts have been estopped from talking no small amount of nonsense." But that gain came at a cost, he continued, because "it may at times menace the general respect for the judiciary and general authority of the law as a whole."[61] Julius Goebel of Columbia Law School considered natural law to be no more than the ideals in which people believed, but he thought Oliver Wendell Holmes had gone too far in belittling the older view. "There is no need to jeer at persons who believe in natural law," Goebel admonished. "Indeed it seems not only proper but practical that a belief in natural law should be fostered," because regardless of what lawyers wrote about it, "the conviction in a natural law which seems to be general among human beings will persist."[62]

Despite such defenses, natural law began to disappear from the courtroom. We can chart this development, very roughly, by counting references in published court opinions to some of the leading treatises on natural law. Thomas Rutherforth's *Institutes of Natural Law* was cited in twenty-seven cases between 1840 and 1859, but only thirteen cases in the next twenty years, and only ten in the twenty years after that, despite the rapid increase in the annual number of reported cases. Rutherforth dwindled to irrelevance in the early 20th century, when he was cited once per decade between 1900 and 1929 and then not at all in the 1930s. Jean-Jacques Burlamaqui's *Principles of Natural and Politic Law* followed the same path. It was cited in twenty-nine cases between 1840 and 1869, but in only eight cases between 1870 and 1899, and in only six between 1900 and 1929. In the 1930s, Burlamaqui wasn't cited at all.[63] These works were of course more than a century old by then, but they were not replaced in court opinions by newer treatises on natural law. Judges stopped referring to *any* natural law treatises.

By the middle of the 20th century, natural law no longer played a significant role in published judicial opinions. Natural law did not disappear from the case reports completely, but it became a rarity rather than the ordinary part of the lawyer's toolkit it had once been. When a judge did invoke natural law, it tended to be in contexts where the judge felt so strongly about the matter that he was willing to use unconventional methods of argument. In 1945, for example, a judge in New York had to decide whether a man had been validly married in Arkansas. The man was already married to someone else in New York, and New York law clearly prohibited being married to two people at once. "The marriage in question is contrary to the natural law and to the express provisions

[61] Arthur T. Hadley, "The Relation Between Economics and Politics," *Yale Law Journal* 8 (1899): 201.

[62] Julius Goebel Jr., Book review, *Virginia Law Review* 7 (1921): 494–95.

[63] This count comes from the Westlaw database.

of the New York statute," the judge declared. Then he quickly backtracked. "The court realizes that a discussion of the natural law or a finding of it is not necessary for a determination of this case," he conceded. The judge nevertheless spent a few paragraphs quoting Cicero and the Ten Commandments to establish that polygamy was contrary to natural law.[64] A few years later, in a Georgia case in which the court allowed a child to be placed in the custody of his aunt and uncle rather than his parents, the dissenting judge expressed his outrage by insisting that state law could "not repeal the natural law," under which "it is the duty and the right of parents to have the custody of their children."[65] Natural law had once been a thoroughly normal part of litigation, but by the mid-20th century it had become a fringe rhetorical technique, to be used only sparingly.

When litigants tried to invoke natural law, judges cautioned that natural law was not a legitimate ground on which to decide cases. In older cases, the Virginia Supreme Court acknowledged in 1932, "Language is used which seems to imply that there is a body of natural laws, superior to any laws which the state might make, which the courts of the state must recognize and enforce." But the court made clear that times had changed. "Upon reason and principle," the court declared, "there are no so-called natural laws which a court may recognize and enforce." If natural law "has any existence, it is enforceable only by force of arms, or by the forces of nature, or by divine power."[66] The California Supreme Court agreed that "the realm of statecraft includes no such thing as a 'natural law.'"[67] When a lawyer in New York tried to base his argument on natural law, the judge would have none of it. "It is not my function as a judge to determine whether natural law requires" a particular outcome, the judge insisted. "Nor need I concern myself with age old theological disputations over which view represents the true natural law and the claim of the supremacy of the latter over positive law. The sworn duty of a judge in such matters is to adhere to the law of the land."[68] Natural law had once been one of the conventional components of litigation, but no longer.

Two related aspects of this change bear emphasizing.

First, the change was primarily within the legal system rather than in the wider culture. It was more a change in lawyers' beliefs about the sources of law that judges should use to resolve cases than it was a change in beliefs about whether natural law or God exists. The decline of natural law within the legal system does not appear to have been caused by any decline in the religiosity of lawyers and

---

[64] *Sodero v. Sodero*, 56 N.Y.S.2d 823, 827 (N.Y. Sup. Ct. 1945).

[65] *Hedquist v.Gottke*, 75 S.E.2d 18, 20 (Ga. 1953) (Head, J., dissenting).

[66] *Commonwealth v. City of Newport News*, 164 S.E. 689, 695 (Va. 1932).

[67] *People v. Gallardo*, 243 P.2d 532, 535 (Cal. 1952).

[68] *Attar v. Attar*, 181 N.Y.S.2d 265, 267 (N.Y. Sup. Ct. 1958).

judges, but rather by a growing belief that positive law and natural law belonged in separate realms.

Second, for this reason, it would be a mistake to assign much causal weight to broader intellectual changes during the period that weakened belief in religion. This was a period in which evolution and other new ideas struck blows at conventional religious beliefs, but conventional religious beliefs were (and still are) entirely compatible with the view that in the courtroom the only law that counts is human-made. So far as religion is concerned, the more important causal factor was the partitioning of law into two spheres, a realm of positive law within the legal system and a realm of natural law in the world outside.

As natural law's role in litigation diminished, the use of natural law began to take on a distinctly political cast, as a rhetorical technique used on the conservative side of an argument. This was something new. When natural law was a conventional part of the legal system, it had no political slant. Natural law was invoked on both sides of arguments—by supporters and opponents of slavery, by supporters and opponents of capital punishment, by supporters and opponents of traditional roles for women, and so on. In litigation, citing natural law was a politically neutral act, like citing statutes or citing common law. Until the late 19th century, there was nothing conservative about natural law.

But when the prominence of natural law receded, it receded more slowly on the conservative side of arguments, where natural law continued to be invoked to support traditional arrangements against disruption by legal change. The clearest example was in the field of property. In the late 19th and early 20th centuries, states and the federal government enacted new kinds of regulatory programs, many of which impinged on traditional uses of property.[69] Natural law became a weapon used in an effort to fend off such attacks on existing patterns of wealth.

The idea that property is not a natural right was most forcefully and famously stated by Bentham, who insisted that "there is no natural property—that property is entirely the creature of law." Bentham argued that no one had any property in a lawless state of nature, and that law thus had to precede property. "The idea of property consists in an established expectation—in the persuasion of power to derive certain advantages from the object," he contended. "But this expectation, this persuasion, can only be the work of the law. I can reckon upon the enjoyment of that which I regard as my own, only according to the promise of the law, which guarantees it to me."[70] Bentham's view was heretical when he wrote it, but it came close to orthodoxy among American lawyers by the early

---

[69] Morton Keller, *Regulating a New Economy: Public Policy and Economic Change in America, 1900–1933* (Cambridge: Harvard Univ. Press, 1990).

[70] Bentham, *Works*, 1:308.

20th century, as the use of natural law declined. The lawyer Amasa Redfield, for example, attacked "the mistaken notion that the beneficent institution of property rests on any natural right of man."[71] The older view that property was a natural right, averred the law professor Orrin McMurray, was "a theory so out of keeping with modern conceptions of the relation of the community to the individual, with social and economic needs," that it "must seriously confuse legal thinking."[72] Property, as one lawyer put it, had lost much of its sanctity.[73]

As a strictly logical matter, there need not have been any connection between the diminishing naturalness of property and the willingness to accept economic regulation. A person who accepted Bentham's view that property was not founded on natural law might nevertheless have instrumental reasons for protecting property against the effects of regulation, while a belief that property was a natural right was not necessarily incompatible with an acceptance of regulation and even redistribution. As a practical matter, however, attitudes toward property's naturalness tended to be associated with attitudes toward regulation and redistribution. When an author denied that property was a natural right, it was often to assert that the government could, or should, limit it in some way. When property was cited as a natural right, by contrast, it was often to argue that the government lacked the power to regulate it or redistribute it to others.

For example, one proponent of regulation insisted that "at every step, the right of property is a creation by the social body. What it gave, it can take away."[74] Because property had been created by law, not by nature, property rights could be limited by new law. On the other side of the debate, US Supreme Court justice Henry Billings Brown was concerned about socialism, the prospect of which he considered calamitous. Brown accordingly argued that "man has a natural right to the fruits of his own toil," a right the state could not abridge.[75] "To deny the natural right of property," declared one correspondent to the *New York Times*, "is to throw down the defences against the most odious communism."[76] The Iowa judge John Forrest Dillon, who likewise decried "socialistic attacks on private property," argued at length against the growing view "that there is no such thing as a natural right of inheritance, or natural right to dispose of property by will."

[71] Amasa A Redfield, "The Liberty of Testamentary Bequests," *American Law Review* 23 (1889): 15.

[72] Orrin K. McMurray, "Liberty of Testation and Some Modern Limitations Thereon," in *Celebration Legal Essays by Various Authors to Mark the Twenty-fifth Year of Service of John H. Wigmore as Professor of Law in Northwestern University* (Chicago: Northwestern Univ. Press, 1919), 539.

[73] "The Right of Property vs. the Right of Self-Preservation," *American Lawyer* 11 (1903): 1.

[74] "Property: Its Origin and Development," *Literary World* 23 (1892): 290.

[75] Henry B. Brown, "The Distribution of Property," *Annual Report of the American Bar Association* 16 (1893): 226, 231.

[76] *New York Times*, 17 Aug. 1902, 8.

Writers who adopted that view, he maintained, "take a position in conflict with the universal sentiments and convictions of mankind."[77]

To the extent natural law survived into the 20th century as part of legal argument, it was thus increasingly put to conservative purposes. Natural law became something one turned to in defense of tradition, against proposed novelties one wished to avoid. Natural law had no such political slant in earlier periods, when advocates of all stripes invoked it to support their desired ends.

The Decline of Custom

Just as lawyers were moving away from using natural law in court, they were rejecting the traditional idea that the common law was based on custom.

For most of the 19th century, lawyers understood the common law to be based largely on custom. Customary practices, when identified by judges and applied to resolve disputes, became doctrines of the common law. On this understanding, judges did not *make* the common law. Rather, they *found* it, either in present-day customs or in reports of older cases identifying the customs of the past.

This traditional understanding of the common law began to be seriously questioned toward the end of the 19th century. "Blackstone bases the common law upon established customs," William Hornblower observed in an 1892 address to the students of Columbia Law School. Hornblower was an alumnus of the school and a prominent local lawyer. He advised the students that the traditional view, as exemplified by Blackstone, "is very pretty theory, but wholly at variance with the facts." When judges ostensibly "found" the common law, "The new rules laid down are nothing more nor less than judicial legislation."[78]

Some suggested that even if "customs in early times made the law," as one Missouri court put it, custom had long since ceased to be a basis of the common law.[79] "In the more advanced stages of a nation," explained the New York lawyer Robert Ludlow Fowler, "the importance of custom declines until at last there comes a period when all law is written law. It is either written case law or written statute law." Fowler insisted that "custom has never, in this State, been in any way a fertile source of law."[80] The Cornell law professor Edwin Woodruff agreed that regardless of how the common law had originated centuries ago, "at the present

---

[77] John F. Dillon, "Property—Its Rights and Duties in our Legal and Social Systems," *American Law Review* 29 (1895): 163, 179, 181.

[78] William B. Hornblower, "Appellate Courts," *Columbia Law Times* 5 (1892): 151–52.

[79] *Johnston v. Parrott*, 92 Mo. App. 199, 203 (1902).

[80] Robert Ludlow Fowler, *Codification in the State of New York* (Albany: Weed, Parsons, 1884), 9.

day we do not conceive of the Common law as being custom."[81] The indefatigable Roscoe Pound was of the same opinion. "Formerly it was argued that common law was superior to legislation because it was customary and rested upon the consent of the governed," he recalled. "Today we recognize that the so-called custom is a custom of judicial decision, not a custom of popular action."[82]

Others doubted whether custom had *ever* played the role that lawyers traditionally assigned it. "It has often been assumed, almost as a matter of course, that legal customs preceded judicial decisions, and that the latter have but served to give expression to the former, but of this there appears to be little proof," noted John Chipman Gray, a Harvard law professor and Boston lawyer. "It seems at least as probable that customs arose from judicial decisions." If one looked closely at the origins of familiar common law doctrines, Gray suggested, the likeliest conclusion was that the doctrines "originated in the courts, and that the bulk of the community had nothing to do with them and knew nothing about them." Gray specialized in the law of property, so he chose two common law rules familiar to property lawyers as his examples. "How can we believe," he asked, "that the Rule in Shelley's Case, for instance, had its origin in popular custom? Indeed, with many rules, such as the Rule against Perpetuities, we know the history of their origin and development and that they were the creatures of the judges." Gray concluded that judges had adopted such doctrines, not because they were customs, "but because they commended themselves to the judges' own sense of right or policy."[83]

John Dickinson, a law professor at the University of Pennsylvania, found it implausible that *any* common law rules could have originated in custom. Every society had its customs, he acknowledged. "Thus in modern occidental communities custom publishes such rules as that shoes or other covering for the feet must be worn in public, that men must wear trousers and not skirts and must cut their hair short, that food must be transferred to the mouth with a fork or spoon and not with a knife." But how could there ever be occasions for any such customs to become doctrines of the common law? "Practically none of the customs just instanced is, however, in any way fit for a rule of decision applicable to a legal controversy." Dickinson then approached the problem from the other direction. If one looked at the common law rules actually applied in litigation, it was hard to see how any of them could ever have been popular customs. "Thus take the conflicting rules applied in different states to the effect that a third party beneficiary of a contract (exclusive of an

[81] Edwin H. Woodruff, *Introduction to the Study of Law* (New York: Baker, Voorhis, 1898), 60.

[82] Roscoe Pound, "Common Law and Legislation," *Harvard Law Review* 21 (1908): 406.

[83] John Chipman Gray, *The Nature and Sources of the Law* (New York: Columbia Univ. Press, 1909), 280–81, 277–78, 284.

insurance contract) can or cannot maintain an action. Can it possibly be said that in one group of states it is customary, and in the others not customary, for people to make such contracts, and that this custom antedated and dictated the rule of law?" Most common law rules, Dickinson continued, affected only a small number of people. The rules regarding third-party beneficiaries of contracts were good examples. Could rules affecting so few people properly be called customs? "Indeed," he observed, "probably a larger number of persons will always use narcotic drugs than will make contracts (other than insurance contracts) for the benefit of third persons. Does this mean that the use of narcotic drugs is a custom which the law ought to recognize as legal, or that contracts for the benefit of third parties are not customary and therefore ought not to be held legally valid?"[84]

The traditional view of custom still had its defenders, the most prominent of whom was James Coolidge Carter, one of the most distinguished lawyers of the era.[85] Carter argued many cases in the US Supreme Court on behalf of business clients, including *Pollock v. Farmers' Loan and Trust Company*, in which the Court held the federal income tax unconstitutional. He was president of the American Bar Association and the New York City Bar Association, and he was active in the movement to reform city government. Carter may be best remembered today for leading the successful opposition to efforts to replace much of New York's common law with a civil code. It was in this last capacity that he wrote at length in praise of the common law, which he considered far superior to legislation.

Carter contended that the common law's foundation in custom was one of the principal points in its favor. When a case came before a judge for decision, he argued, "The true rule must be somehow *found*. Judges and advocates—all together—engage in the *search*. Cases more or less nearly approaching the one in controversy are adduced. Analogies are referred to. The customs and habits of men are appealed to." When judges and lawyers searched for the true rule, "The field of search is the habits, customs, business and manners of the people, and those previously declared rules which have sprung out of previous similar inquiries into habits, customs, business and manners." The product of the search was not a new rule, but one already observed in practice even if it had not previously been recognized by a judge. In this sense, Carter concluded, the common law "is not a command, or a body of commands, but consists of rules springing

---

[84] John Dickinson, "The Law Behind Law," *Columbia Law Review* 29 (1929): 129.

[85] Lewis A. Grossman, "James Coolidge Carter and Mugwump Jurisprudence," *Law and History Review* 20 (2002): 577–629; Lewis A. Grossman, "Langdell Upside-Down: James Coolidge Carter and the Anticlassical Jurisprudence of Anticodification," *Yale Journal of Law & the Humanities* 19 (2007): 149–219.

from the social standard of justice, or from the habits and customs from which that standard has itself been derived."[86]

Carter provided an extended example of how this process of discovering custom worked in practice. "I may take the homely instance of a milkman suing for milk which he has furnished. The defendant pleads and proves, as a complete, or, at least, a partial defense, that the milk was watered, and the plaintiff seeks to avoid the effect of the evidence by proving that milkmen generally thus adulterate their milk." At a trial, in arguing to the judge, the lawyers would "talk of principles and rules. But these are nothing but customs. The plaintiff tacitly relies upon the rule or principle that purchasers must pay for the goods they buy. Without this he would have no *prima facie* case even. But why is this a principle? Plainly, for no other reason than that it is the universal custom. If such were not the custom, there would be no such principle." The defendant would counter that watering milk was not a custom. He would argue "that the selling of milk is but an instance of the larger custom of selling goods generally, and that the sellers of goods generally do not adulterate their wares; and finally, he shows that the adulteration of milk, so far as it is a custom at all, is the custom of those who are denominated in society as rogues." In short, "The whole argument of the parties, although they are constantly speaking of rules and principles, really turns upon what the customs are." The judge would rule in favor of the defendant, "And his decision consists simply in affirming that the transaction, instead of coming under a custom which society approves, falls under one which it condemns."[87]

Carter then discussed how customs were applied to novel fact situations, in which one could plausibly argue that no custom had yet developed. "When the first action was brought against a telegraph company to recover damages sustained by an error in sending a dispatch," he recalled, "the real dispute turned instantly upon whether there was a custom to pay such losses. The defendant asserted there was none, and could be none, for the reason that the case was the first instance of such a claim. The plaintiff asserted that there was a custom where one party undertook to perform a service for another for a reward, and performed it negligently and imperfectly, to pay the loss, and that the example in controversy was an instance of that custom." Thus even entirely new circumstances could be governed by a common law founded in custom.[88] "Habit and custom," Carter concluded, "furnish the rules which govern human conduct," and "they still exert over enlightened man the same imperious dominion

---

[86] James Coolidge Carter, *The Ideal and the Actual in the Law* (Philadelphia: Dando Printing and Publishing, 1890), 10–11.

[87] *Id.* at 15–16.

[88] *Id.* at 16.

that they did among the primeval hordes which peopled the world before the dawn of civilization."[89]

But this was a conception of the common law that was on the decline at the turn of the 20th century. Carter provided the most thorough defense of the common law's foundation in custom ever offered by an American lawyer, precisely because in earlier eras there had been no occasion to defend the proposition, as no one was attacking it. In 1800, most of what Carter said about custom and the common law would have seemed self-evident to American lawyers. In Carter's own time, much of what he said seemed absurd. Critics took evident glee in picking Carter's argument apart. "Mr. Carter's view seems to amount to this," John Chipman Gray sneered: "There are two or three general notions of popular positive morality with which the rules laid down by the judges (and legislators) are usually not inconsistent. His conclusion is that all Law (statutory as well as non-statutory) is custom. I submit that his conclusion is not justified by his premise."[90] Thomas Ewing, the former chief justice of the Kansas Supreme Court, thought Carter's account of common law development was "purely fanciful."[91] The view expressed by Gray and Ewing would come to be the new orthodoxy by the middle of the 20th century.

The idea that custom is a source of the common law never died out completely. There would always be lawyers and judges who asserted, as did the Maine judge Clarence Hale, that "common custom makes common law."[92] Like reliance on natural law, however, explicit reliance on custom would wane in the 20th century, until it became an unusual occurrence. "Undoubtedly the creative energy of custom in the development of common law is less today than it was in bygone times," observed Benjamin Cardozo, a judge on New York's highest court (and later on the US Supreme Court), in his 1922 book *The Nature of the Judicial Process*. Cardozo himself thought that custom was still a legitimate, if rarely used, source of common law. "The telegraph and the telephone," he recalled, "have built up new customs and new law. Already there is a body of legal literature that deals with the legal problems of the air," which he implied would be resolved by giving legal sanction to the customs of aviators. But he acknowledged that the use of custom was on the decline. "Judges do not feel the same need of putting

---

[89] James Coolidge Carter, *Law: Its Origin, Growth, and Function* (New York: G.P. Putnam's Sons, 1907), 119.

[90] Gray, *Nature and Sources*, 274.

[91] Ewing, "Codification," 440.

[92] Clarence Hale, "Common Custom Makes Common Law," *Maine Law Review* 9 (1916): 57. See, e.g., A. A. Graham, "The Law is Custom, Not Reason," *Central Law Journal* 82 (1916): 46; *Interstate Co. v. Jolly*, 125 So. 838 (Miss. 1930).

the *imprimatur* of law upon customs of recent growth, knocking for entrance into the legal system," he recognized.[93]

In an earlier era, the rejection of custom as a source of the common law would have left the law of nature as an alternative source. As we saw in chapter 2, the common law was understood as the application of general principles of natural law to the specific circumstances of a given time and place. It was "the application of the dictates of natural justice, and of cultivated reason, to particular cases," James Kent had explained.[94] But as American lawyers turned away from custom, they were simultaneously rejecting the use of natural law. Without natural law to fall back on, lawyers had given up both of the common law's traditional sources. Natural law and custom were what allowed judges to *find* the common law, because natural law and custom existed before the judge ever had to decide a case. When both were gone, what was left for a judge to find? If nothing was left to find, how should a judge discern the common law?

[93] Benjamin N. Cardozo, *The Nature of the Judicial Process* (New Haven: Yale Univ. Press, 1922), 59–62.

[94] Kent, *Commentaries on American Law*, 1:439.

8

Substitutes for Natural Law

As natural law began to drop out of the legal system, lawyers were left with a dilemma. Natural law had performed several functions. It had guided the interpretation of statutes and had sometimes even rendered them void. It had provided judges with a reservoir of principles to use when positive law ran out. It had served, alongside custom, as the grounding for common law decision-making. Without natural law, how would these functions be performed? Could they be performed at all? In the absence of natural law, was a judge's opinion a correct statement of the law by definition, or was there some other reference point one could use to evaluate it? Without natural law, was the Constitution the only limit on legislative power? Or was there some other yardstick one could use to interpret and to evaluate the validity of statutes? Natural law had occupied a significant place in the legal system. As it slipped away, it left a big hole.

The decline of natural law took place at the same time as the emergence of "classical legal thought," an umbrella term encompassing a few distinct modes of thought characteristic of the legal profession in the late 19th and early 20th centuries. This chapter argues that the rise of classical legal thought is best understood as an effort to find a substitute for natural law, either by replicating the method of natural law with principles found elsewhere than in nature or by bringing natural law into the courtroom indirectly through positive law. Classical legal thought pictured the judge as a finder of preexisting principles, just as natural law had done. The innovation of classical legal thought was to relocate these principles to sources other than nature, now that nature was ceasing to be an acceptable source of law.

The decline of natural law also took place at the same time as the emergence of the view that judges are law-*makers* rather than law-*finders*. Here too there was a causal connection. Many lawyers responded to the decline of natural law, not by seeking to replace principles of natural law with principles found elsewhere, but rather by rejecting the picture of the judge as a finder of preexisting principles. They began instead to describe judges as makers of law who choose among competing rules on grounds of policy rather than consistency with preexisting

The Decline of Natural Law. Stuart Banner, Oxford University Press (2021). © Oxford University Press.
DOI: 10.1093/oso/9780197556498.003.0009

principle. Today we tend to associate this view with the legal realists of the 1920s and 1930s and a few of their predecessors, and for that reason we tend to think of this view as having emerged in opposition to classical legal thought, but in fact it emerged simultaneously with classical legal thought, because both were responses to the decline of natural law.

The rise of these would-be substitutes for natural law hastened natural law's decline, because they provided alternative methods of performing the tasks that natural law had performed. To the extent they succeeded, they reduced the need to retain natural law's role within the legal system.

This chapter describes five developments in legal thought that began in the late 19th century. They took place simultaneously, not sequentially. Two were short-lived and are thus no longer well known today. Two were more successful; they lasted for decades and proved enormously influential. The fifth was the most successful of all, in the sense that we are still living with it today.

One of the short-lived developments, known as "historical jurisprudence," was an effort to ground decisions in the history of common law doctrines. This school of thought produced perhaps the most famous book in American jurisprudence, Oliver Wendell Holmes's *The Common Law*, along with many other works in a similar vein. The idea was for historical research to serve the function once served by the law of nature, as a guide for judges in common law cases. Historical jurisprudence never made the jump from the academy into practice. It largely died out in the early 20th century.

The second development, one that also faded soon after it began, was an effort to establish the principles of economics as a new kind of natural law, one with a social-scientific rather than a religious or philosophical grounding. Proponents understood economic laws as found in nature, not created by humans. To some lawyers, economic principles seemed well suited to evaluate the validity of human laws. This effort, like historical jurisprudence, faltered quickly.

Third, this period saw the growth within elite law schools of a way of thinking about the common law that historians call "classical orthodoxy." Law professors began to think of the common law as a self-contained system in which the general principles once found in nature were now inferred from the decided cases themselves. These principles could then be used the way natural law had been, to evaluate the correctness of later-decided cases. This understanding of the common law would become the standard way law was taught for decades.

The fourth development was the rise of the constitutional doctrine that would come to be called "substantive due process," under which the due process clauses of state and federal constitutions came to be understood as conduits for importing into positive law some of the limits on legislative power that had previously been found in natural law, most importantly the ban on "class legislation," legislation that favored one group over another. The due process clauses provided a positivist hook allowing judges to use natural law principles, now that natural law in its own right was losing its authority. Substantive due process would be a key component of constitutional law until the 1930s.

The four modes of thought listed so far—historical jurisprudence, natural principles of economics, classical orthodoxy, and substantive due process— were substitutes for natural law in the sense that they aimed to give judges something else to *find* when they decided hard cases, now that natural law, of its own force, was no longer considered an appropriate source of law for judges to use. In each mode of thought, the judge was understood to be finding preexisting principles, not making new ones. These principles might be found in history, or in economics, or in the cases themselves, or they might be natural law principles brought into positive law through a due process clause, but whatever their source, they were understood to have an existence prior to and independent of the judge's decision. These four modes of thought thus retained the traditional conception of the judge as a finder, not a maker, of law.

The fifth response to the decline of natural law, by contrast, was to deny that there were any preexisting principles to be found. On this view, the judge in hard cases was not a finder of law at all. The judge was a maker of law. The judge's work could not be evaluated by whether he accurately ascertained preexisting principles, because those principles did not exist. Positive law was all there was. When positive law did not provide a clear answer, there was nothing out there that constrained the judge's decision. The only way to evaluate the judge's work was as a policymaker. This view was the sharpest break with natural law, in that the gap left by natural law was not filled by some other source of principles. Rather, the role of the judge was reconceptualized so that the gap no longer mattered. This response would eventually become the conventional way lawyers think about the legal system.

These are all rich subjects on which a great deal has been written.[1] There is much more to be said about them than can be said here. The purpose of this chapter is not to describe or analyze them at any length, but rather to offer a fresh

---

[1] See, e.g., William M. Wiecek, *The Lost World of Classical Legal Thought: Law and Ideology in America, 1886–1937* (New York: Oxford Univ. Press, 1998); Duncan Kennedy, *The Rise and Fall of Classical Legal Thought* (Washington, DC: Beard Books, 2006); Neil Duxbury, *Patterns of American Jurisprudence* (Oxford: Clarendon Press, 1995); Morton J. Horwitz, *The Transformation of American Law, 1870–1960: The Crisis of Legal Orthodoxy* (New York: Oxford Univ. Press, 1992); Laura Kalman, *Legal Realism at Yale, 1927–1960* (Chapel Hill: Univ. of North Carolina Press, 1986); John Henry Schlegel, *American Legal Realism and Empirical Social Science* (Chapel Hill: Univ. of North Carolina Press, 1995); William W. Fisher III, Morton J. Horwitz, and Thomas A. Reed, eds., *American Legal Realism* (New York: Oxford Univ. Press, 1993); James E. Herget, *American Jurisprudence, 1870–1970: A History* (Houston: Rice Univ. Press, 1990).

perspective on them by showing their connection to the decline of natural law, a connection that was understood at the time but has since been largely forgotten.

Historical Jurisprudence

One would-be substitute for natural law was the study of history. American legal thinkers of the late 19th century became very interested in the history of the Anglo-American legal system. Legal scholars devoted an enormous amount of attention—far more than they ever had before—to excavating the origins of common law doctrines.[2] This effort was understood as having immediate practical relevance for lawyers. It was not the pursuit of knowledge for its own sake. Nor was the goal to understand the social, cultural, or political context in which the law is embedded. Rather, the purpose of studying history was to help resolve legal questions in the present and to identify appropriate reforms for the future. This goal was reflected in the name that was given to this field of study. It was not called "legal history," but rather "historical jurisprudence." Practitioners of historical jurisprudence believed that history could take the place once occupied by natural law as a guide to the proper development of the law.

In turning to history, Americans were taking a cue from Germany, where this way of thinking had been prominent for some time. American legal intellectuals were familiar with German historical jurisprudence.[3] Several of the historical works of Friedrich Karl von Savigny, the leading German law professor of the first half of the 19th century, existed in English translation. Books written by Savigny's successor, Rudolf von Jhering, were likewise published in English translation toward the end of the century. American scholars often acknowledged the influence of these authors, especially Savigny.[4] For example, the first American book of legal history—*Essays in Anglo-Saxon Law*, written collectively by Henry Adams and his students—begins by praising "the long and patient labors of German scholars" in tracing the ostensibly German origins of

---

[2] David M. Rabban, *Law's History: American Legal Thought and the Transatlantic Turn to History* (New York: Cambridge Univ. Press, 2013); Stephen A. Siegel, "Historism in Late Nineteenth-Century Constitutional Thought," *Wisconsin Law Review* 1990 (1990): 1431–1547.

[3] "The German Historical School of Jurisprudence," *American Jurist* 14 (1835): 43–62; Rudolph Leonhard, "Methods Followed in Germany by the Historical School of Law," *Columbia Law Review* 7 (1907): 573–81 (Leonhard was a German scholar who had been invited to speak at Columbia).

[4] Mathias Reimann, "The Historical School against Codification: Savigny, Carter, and the Defeat of the New York Civil Code," *American Journal of Comparative Law* 37 (1989): 95–119. As Reimann notes, "It seems clear that there was a full-fledged American 'historical school' in the closing decades of the 19th and the opening decades of the 20th century and that Savigny was widely admired by American academics as a model scholar and father of modern legal science." *Id.* at 95 n. 2.

what would become English legal institutions.[5] A small group of American law professors eagerly adopted this mode of scholarship in the late 19th century. The new school of thought is revealed in the titles of their books, such as Melville Bigelow's *History of Procedure in England*, or James Barr Ames's *Lectures on Legal History*.[6]

Such works had the explicit goal of making sense of present-day legal doctrine. As Bigelow explained, legal history was "the true and main source of our present law." For that reason, he suggested, "History which throws light on the law as actually administered by our courts is a necessary part of a sound education for the bar."[7] The law of the United States, agreed Francis Wharton, "is not a scheme invented by statesmen at a particular crisis, but is the silent and spontaneous evolution of the nation, past as well as present, adapting itself to the conditions in which in each epoch it is placed."[8] Historical study would thus illuminate the law of the present. It could also provide guidance for the law of the future. "Those who attentively consider the long and strange story of the development of the English jury," James Bradley Thayer insisted in his book on the history of the jury, "will find here a basis for conclusions as to the scope and direction of certain much-needed reforms in the whole law of evidence and procedure."[9]

In the best-remembered work in this vein, Oliver Wendell Holmes's *The Common Law*, Holmes left no doubt that in his view the purpose of studying legal history was to inform the development of the law in the present. His famous aphorism—"The life of the law has not been logic: it has been experience"— expressed precisely this point. "The law embodies the story of a nation's development through many centuries, and it cannot be dealt with as if it contained only the axioms and corollaries of a book of mathematics," Holmes argued. "In order to know what it is, we must know what it has been, and what it tends to become." As Holmes put it, in another passage still familiar to American lawyers, "In Massachusetts to-day, while, on the one hand, there are a great many rules which are quite sufficiently accounted for by their manifest good sense, on the other, there are some which can only be understood by reference to the infancy of procedure among the German tribes, or to the social condition of Rome

[5] *Essays in Anglo-Saxon Law* (Boston: Little, Brown, 1876), 1.

[6] Melville Madison Bigelow, *History of Procedure in England* (London: Macmillan, 1880); James Barr Ames, *Lectures on Legal History* (Cambridge: Harvard Univ. Press, 1913).

[7] Melville M. Bigelow, "A Scientific School of Legal Thought," *Green Bag* 17 (1905): 1.

[8] Francis Wharton, *Commentaries on Law* (Philadelphia: Kay & Brother, 1884), iv. On Wharton's historical jurisprudence, see Stephen A. Siegel, "Francis Wharton's Orthodoxy: God, Historical Jurisprudence, and Classical Legal Thought," *American Journal of Legal History* 46 (2004): 422–46.

[9] James Bradley Thayer, *A Preliminary Treatise on Evidence at the Common Law: Part I, Development of Trial by Jury* (Boston: Little, Brown, 1896), 3.

under the Decemvirs."[10] One purpose of attending to early German or Roman legal doctrines was to better comprehend the law of the United States.

Another purpose of studying legal history, Holmes believed, was to guide the future development of the law. "The study upon which we have been engaged is necessary both for the knowledge and for the revision of the law," he explained. "However much we may codify the law into a series of seemingly self-sufficient propositions, those propositions will be but a phase in a continuous growth. To understand their scope fully, to know how they will be dealt with by judges trained in the past which the law embodies, we must ourselves know something of that past."[11] Holmes, well known for his skepticism about natural law, looked to history to do much of the work that natural law had once done.

The historical school was attractive to those who rejected both the untethered speculation they found in natural law and the anything-goes vision of government power that seemed to be entailed by positivism. James Coolidge Carter, the New York lawyer who was historical jurisprudence's best-known adherent among the bar, insisted that natural law "can scarcely be regarded as scientific. If there were no other objection to it, it would be enough that we know of no certain means whereby we can pronounce what the law of nature is." But he had no greater love for positivism, under which "everything which the so-called supreme power of the State commands, whatever its character in point of right, is law." Carter believed both views were equally misguided, in that "while the one tendency would enthrone Right, the other would erect Force, as the arbiter of human conduct."[12] Historical jurisprudence was supposed to be a middle ground between these two pitfalls.

The law professor William Gardner Hammond agreed in his new American edition of Blackstone's *Commentaries*. Blackstone, he noted, had been roundly criticized by Bentham, Austin, and their followers, whose writing was often referred to as "analytical" jurisprudence. Hammond shared their skepticism about natural law, but he also thought that "much of the work done by the so-called school of analytic jurists in England I believe to have been in the wrong direction, leading farther away from the true sense of law, as we now understand it, than Blackstone's own view." Like Carter, Hammond saw historical jurisprudence as a better replacement for natural law than positivism could ever be. "The change made by what is known as the historical theory of law is fundamental," he declared, "and must be understood by any one who would know

---

[10] Oliver Wendell Holmes Jr., *The Common Law* (Boston: Little, Brown, 1881), 1–2.

[11] *Id.* at 36–37.

[12] James Coolidge Carter, *Law: Its Origin, Growth and Function* (New York: G.P. Putnam's Sons, 1907), 11–12.

the common law as it is now administered in America, to say nothing of its past development."[13]

While historical jurisprudence had its day among legal academics, it never really caught on among judges or practicing lawyers. There are no court decisions one could cite as exemplars of historical jurisprudence. Within the academy, the movement largely died out soon after the turn of the century. Even Oliver Wendell Holmes, the most acclaimed American practitioner of historical jurisprudence, came to doubt its worth after many years on the bench. "The tendency of professors is to overvalue antiquarianism," he complained in 1908. History was "valuable and delightful" for its own sake, Holmes concluded, "but its bearing on the law of to-day as a speculative force is mainly, to my mind, in the tendency to produce a wide scepticism about the worth of various doctrines by showing how they arose. That again is a very limited sphere."[14] Lawyers and historians continued to investigate the law's past, but they lost the faith that the knowledge so obtained would guide the law's future.

The reason for the quick demise of historical jurisprudence may simply be that the study of legal history seemed to offer little of use to the working legal system. Knowledge of what the law had once been, a long time ago, was of dubious relevance for deciding what the law ought to be today, when conditions had become very different. By 1908, Roscoe Pound already included the historical school and natural law as two branches of what he derided as outdated "mechanical jurisprudence."[15] Historical jurists had tried to overthrow natural law, he suggested, but instead they had "preserved the method of their predecessors, merely substituting new premises." Rather than seeking the true nature of law in philosophical speculation, "They sought the nature of right and of law in historical deduction from the Roman sources, from Germanic legal institutions, and from the juristic development based thereon."[16] But the study of history proved no more fruitful.

Today, barely anyone reads the leading works of historical jurisprudence that once seemed to offer such promise. Even *The Common Law* is, one suspects, cited far more often than it is actually read. Once lawyers gave up the belief that ancient legal doctrines illuminate the law of the present and the future, these books came to seem like pointless, tedious slogs through ancient cases.

[13] William Blackstone, *Commentaries on the Laws of England*, ed. William G. Hammond (San Francisco: Bancroft-Whitney, 1890), 1:xviii.

[14] Holmes to Lewis Einstein, 22 Mar. 1908, in James Bishop Peabody, ed., *The Holmes-Einstein Letters* (New York: St. Martin's Press, 1964), 37.

[15] Pound, "Mechanical Jurisprudence," 610.

[16] Roscoe Pound, "The Scope and Purpose of Sociological Jurisprudence," *Harvard Law Review* 24 (1911): 600.

The Natural Laws of Economics

If history could not serve as a yardstick for evaluating the output of courts and legislatures, how about economics? To some lawyers, economics seemed a promising foundation for a new kind of natural law, one based not on religion or tradition but on science.

This idea has been almost entirely forgotten, and so have the broader possibilities to which it briefly pointed. Natural law need not have any connection to God or religion. Nonreligious people believe in the existence of natural laws in the nonhuman realm, or "scientific" laws as we call them today. One can imagine an alternative history in which the separation of Christianity from law and government led to the reconceptualization of natural law as a wholly secular enterprise. On this path not taken (or at least not taken very far), lawyers would have continued to understand natural law to govern human affairs, but it would have been a natural law with no religious origin or content, one that lost its Christian grounding but acquired a secular, social-scientific grounding instead.

In the late 19th and early 20th centuries, some believed that economic laws could serve this purpose. "The great laws which govern the industrial growth, are laws of nature," reasoned Robert Thompson of the University of Pennsylvania. "The business of the economist is to discover its laws, and that of the statesman to remove all hindrance to their free operation. It never can be the business of either to set them aside." Like the older natural principles of justice, these economic laws constrained human lawmaking, because "it is impossible to improve upon them, and nothing but harm will come from trying."[17] A New York lawyer referred to "the natural law of free exchange and competition," while a lawyer in Indiana likewise declared that "these economic principles, within their field, are parts of what we call natural law; that is, they are expressions of established consequences existing in the nature of things."[18] Lawyers and judges, accustomed to speaking in terms of natural law, easily adopted the vocabulary of natural law when discussing economic matters. The legislature "cannot change the laws of nature," insisted a Pennsylvania judge, in refusing to enforce a statute setting the capitalization of a surety at a level the court believed was too low. "Water will not boil at 110° nor freeze at 52°; twelve times twelve will always be one hundred and forty-four; *insufficient* cannot be made the equivalent of *sufficient*," the judge explained. "No legislation can make $100,000 or $250,000 sufficient security, as

---

[17] Robert Ellis Thompson, *Protection to Home Industry* (New York: D. Appleton, 1886), 3.

[18] Franklin Pierce, *The Tariff and the Trusts* (New York: Macmillan, 1907), 167; Merritt Starr, *Legislative and Judicial Development of the Law Concerning Competition Contrasted* (s.l.: s.n., 1907), 29.

in the case of the city treasurer or of the register of wills or of a tenant for life of personal estate, for the custody of $300,000, $500,000, or $1,000,000."[19]

The "natural law of supply and demand," as the West Virginia Supreme Court called it, was often said to override conflicting human laws, just as natural law had once been understood to supersede human law to the contrary.[20] "The law of supply and demand is perhaps the most general and fundamental of all the brotherhood of natural laws," Henry Wood argued in a book called *Natural Law in the Business World*. He gave as an example legislation setting maximum interest rates, which in Wood's view "not only did not accomplish the purpose intended, but actually made interest dearer, by obstructing supplies [and] injuring confidence."[21] Minimum wage laws would be fruitless, some critics contended, because the price of labor would inevitably be set by its supply and demand. "There are certain rules of economics which, when formally expressed, are merely the statement of certain natural laws," suggested the Minneapolis lawyer Rome G. Brown, who opposed Minnesota's recent minimum wage statute. "Such economic laws are controlling in the same way, even if not to the same extent, as natural laws of physics."[22] New York's highest court took this view in an 1884 decision holding that a statute could not be construed to regulate the wages paid by employers. "Experience has shown that legislation on the subject must always be futile and ineffectual," the court reflected, "for the reason that it is controlled by the natural laws determining the value of labor and property, and which are as much beyond the power of statutes to affect as they are above the control of the wishes of the parties interested therein."[23]

Other economic questions also seemed, at least to some lawyers, to be governed by natural laws. The New Hampshire Supreme Court determined that "by natural law," a sales tax would be borne by the purchaser, not the seller. "Legislative power may reenact the law of nature by assessing the taxes of manufactured and imported goods upon the consumer, and the land-tax upon the tenant," the court reasoned, "or assess the former upon the manufacturer and importer and the latter upon the owner, and leave the law of nature, without reenactment, to employ the manufacturer, importer, and landlord as tax-collectors."[24] Cartels were contrary to "the general and natural laws of business," the Massachusetts Supreme Court held, and were unlawful for that reason, despite the apparent absence of any positive law forbidding them.[25]

[19] *In re American Banking and Trust Co.*, 17 Pa. D. 757, 761 (Pa. Orphans' Court 1895).
[20] *State v. Goodwill*, 10 S.E. 285, 287 (W. Va. 1889).
[21] Henry Wood, *Natural Law in the Business World* (Boston: Lee & Shepard, 1887), 23, 27.
[22] Rome G. Brown, *The Minimum Wage* (Minneapolis: Review Publishing, 1914), 11.
[23] *McCarthy v. City of New York*, 96 N.Y. 1, 5 (1884).
[24] *Morrison v. Manchester*, 58 N.H. 538, 554–55 (1879).
[25] *Martell v. White*, 69 N.E. 1085, 1087 (Mass. 1904).

Although lawyers would continue to use the tools of economics for a long time—indeed, they still do today—the effort to use economics within the legal system as an updated form of natural law faltered soon after it began. When a statute rubbed up against an economic principle, economically minded lawyers began to say that the law was merely unwise, not that it was invalid. A lawyer who reviewed Henry Wood's book on *Natural Law in the Business World* called it "the worst of a very bad lot," largely because "natural law is not a subject with which the lawyer deals."[26] Skepticism about the role of natural law within the legal system had grown deep enough to encompass even a very different kind of natural law, one based on economics rather than morality or religion.

Classical Orthodoxy

History and economics faded away quickly as potential alternatives to natural law in the search for a standpoint from which to evaluate court decisions and legislation. Other efforts were much more successful.

One was the method of analyzing common law cases developed by law professors at elite law schools, most conspicuously at Harvard under the deanship of Christopher Langdell. Their method addressed a pressing question: once natural law was no longer available to serve as the standard for evaluating the correctness of a common law decision, how could one tell whether a decision was right or wrong? Without any such standard, whatever the court decided would be, by definition, the law. But this was an unsatisfying outcome for many lawyers, especially those who taught in the university-based law schools that were on the verge of assuming a dominant position in American legal education. These law professors believed law to be an academic subject, not merely a field of practice. They considered their role to involve assisting judges in identifying the common law correctly. Earlier in the 19th century, in the heyday of natural law, university-based law professors like Henry St. George Tucker and David Hoffman had taught their students the law of nature as the foundation of the common law and the ultimate yardstick for measuring whether a judge had gone astray. At the end of the century, as natural law was slipping out of the legal system, law professors needed a different approach.

The method they adopted was to conceive of the common law as a closed system, one without any grounding in natural law. On this view, general legal principles could be ascertained purely by induction from examining court opinions. These principles—not the court opinions themselves—were the law.

---

[26] Book reviews, *American Law Register and Review* 42 (1894): 409.

Once the principles had been identified, they could then be used to evaluate whether any specific case was decided correctly. "Law, considered as a science, consists of certain principles or doctrines," explained Langdell, the dean at Harvard Law School from 1870 to 1895. Each doctrine was found "by studying the cases in which it is embodied."[27] But the cases themselves were not the law. "The adjudicated cases constitute nothing more than materials out of which the scientific jurist is to construct a science of jurisprudence," the law professor Christopher Tiedeman insisted. "They are not law in themselves, they are but applications of the law to particular cases. Law is not *made* by the courts, at the most only promulgated by them."[28] The law consisted of the general principles, not the specific cases in which the principles were applied.

This self-contained way of thinking about law has retrospectively been called "classical orthodoxy." Those who participated in this mode of thinking seem not to have given it any name at all, perhaps because they did not think of themselves as constituting a new jurisprudential movement. Their explanations of how they understood law were found mostly in teaching materials or discussions of pedagogy rather than in self-consciously theoretical writing. Nevertheless, they did develop a new approach to understanding the legal system, one that grounded common law principles in the cases themselves rather than in natural law.

The law professors who pursued this approach often analogized their work to that of natural scientists, who likewise studied individual phenomena for the purpose of discerning the broader regularities that were the principles of their respective sciences. Their work was "what scientific men call original investigation," Langdell declared. "The Library is to us what a laboratory is to the chemist or the physicist, and what a museum is to the naturalist."[29] William Keener, who taught at Harvard in the 1880s before becoming the dean of Columbia Law School in the 1890s, described the task of a legal scholar as seeking the "principles to be found in the adjudged cases, the cases being to him what the specimen is to the geologist."[30] On another occasion, Keener used physics as his analogy. "If I may borrow a simile," he explained, "the facts of the case correspond to the apple which suggested to Sir Isaac Newton the law of gravitation."[31] Cases were

[27] C. C. Langdell, *A Selection of Cases on the Law of Contracts* (1871), 2nd ed. (Boston: Little, Brown, 1879), viii.

[28] Christopher G. Tiedeman, untitled section of Edward J. Phelps et al., "Methods of Legal Education," *Yale Law Journal* 1 (1892): 153–54.

[29] *Forty-Ninth Annual Report of the President of Harvard College, 1873–74* (Cambridge: Press of John Wilson and Son, 1875), 67.

[30] William A. Keener, *A Selection of Cases on the Law of Quasi-Contracts* (Cambridge: Charles W. Sever, 1888), 1:vi.

[31] William A. Keener, "The Inductive Method in Legal Education," *Annual Report of the American Bar Association* 17 (1894): 477.

like experiments, in that they provided data points that could be assembled, through a process of induction, into general rules.

Continuing this analogy, the library, where the books containing all the court opinions were kept, was the laboratory where professors and students did their work. "Reported cases must be analyzed, compared, and combined in substantial accordance with the methods of experiment and observation and inductive reasoning which are pursued in a laboratory," insisted Eugene Wambaugh of the University of Iowa's law school. "The work of the law student is like much of the experimenting and testing performed in a laboratory."[32] The law professor H. L. Wilgus noted that a law school needed "no laboratory but the library."[33] Even Frederick Cheever Shattuck of Harvard's medical school accepted the analogy. "A law school is not necessarily costly to maintain," he remarked. "It has only one laboratory, its library."[34] By the 1890s it was conventional to refer to the law library as a laboratory.[35]

In repeatedly analogizing their work to that of scientists, the law professors were no doubt attempting to appropriate some of the ever-increasing prestige of the natural sciences, but they genuinely believed that law was a science like the natural sciences they were emulating. Langdell was especially insistent on this point. "That law is not only a science, but one of the greatest and noblest of sciences, there is and can be no dispute," he thundered. "A law school which does not profess and endeavor to teach law as a science has no reason for existence."[36] Speaking to alumni, Langdell declared: "If law be not a science, a university will consult its own dignity in declining to teach it. If it be not a science, it is a species of handicraft, and may best be learned by serving an apprenticeship to one who practices it."[37] Charles Thaddeus Terry of Columbia Law School called law "a science based on logic. Its principles are reached by process in induction and deduction."[38] It was a commonplace among judges of the era that law was "a science

[32] Eugene Wambaugh, *The Best Education for a Lawyer* (Iowa City: Published by the University, 1892), 12.

[33] H. L. Wilgus, "Legal Education in the United States," *Michigan Law Review* 6 (1908): 658.

[34] Frederick Cheever Shattuck, "Address to the Candidates for Degrees," *University of Cincinnati Record* 4 (1908): 69.

[35] Anson Bingham, *A Treatise on the Law of Real Property* (Albany, NY: Weare C. Little, 1880), 24; Melville M. Bigelow, *Elements of the Law of Torts* (Boston: Little, Brown, 1891), v; Austin Abbott, "Existing Questions on Legal Education," *Yale Law Journal* 1 (1893): 11–12; George Wharton Pepper, *Legal Education and Admission to the Bar* (Philadelphia: s.n., 1895), 13.

[36] *Annual Reports of the President and Treasurer of Harvard College, 1880–81* (Cambridge: University Press, 1882), 83–84.

[37] C. C. Langdell, "Teaching Law as a Science," *American Law Review* 21 (1887): 123.

[38] Charles Thaddeus Terry, "Law as an Education Study," *Columbia University Quarterly* 12 (1909): 30.

of principles" that transcended the individual cases from which the principles were drawn.[39]

Lawyers had long claimed that law was a science. "Common law," the Supreme Court justice James Wilson had declared a century before, "when properly studied, is a science founded on experiment."[40] Indeed, Thomas Cooper, who taught law and chemistry in the early 19th century, when one person could still be expert in both disciplines, had drawn the same analogy between his two subjects as Langdell did. "Cases serve, like the experiments in Chemistry," Cooper told his law students. "They are multiplied, till, by careful analysis and comparison of each with the others, we discover the general law that pervades and explains them all." He concluded: "It is thus that law assumes the dignity of science."[41]

But such earlier claims of law's scientific status rested on an older and broader conception of science than the one advanced by Langdell and his colleagues.[42] In the first half of the century, when lawyers asserted that law was a science, they normally meant that it was an organized body of knowledge, as opposed to a haphazard assortment of rules. "Science, Gentlemen, in the sense in which I propose to speak of it, is a lofty word," declared the lawyer Henry Whiting Warner in an 1832 address to the New York Law Institute. "It is knowledge—and more, it is knowledge reduced to order; knowledge classified into results; knowledge arranged and generalized according to the natural properties, actions and relations of things." It was in this sense, Warner explained, that he spoke "of nothing less than *the science of the laws*."[43]

This earlier conception of science rested on the belief that the law of nature was the ultimate source of human law. After defining law as a science, Warner went on to insist that "the law, Gentlemen, is a branch of general ethics; a middle branch between theological divinity on the one hand, and the moralities of mere

---

[39] *Paul v. Davis*, 100 Ind. 422, 427 (Ind. 1885); see also *Wabash Western Railway Co. v. Friedman*, 34 N.E. 1111, 1111 (Ill. 1893) (Magruder, J., dissenting); *Read v. Reynolds*, 59 A. 669, 669 (Md. 1905); *Astin v. Chicago, Milwaukee & St. Paul Railway Co.*, 128 N.W. 265, 268 (Wis. 1910).

[40] Wilson, *Works of James Wilson*, 1:458.

[41] Cooper, *Introductory Lecture*, 24.

[42] Robert W. Gordon, "Legal Thought and Legal Practice in the Age of American Enterprise, 1870–1920," in Gerald L. Geison, ed., *Professions and Professional Ideologies in America* (Chapel Hill: Univ. of North Carolina Press, 1983), 70–110; Howard Schweber, "The 'Science' of Legal Science: The Model of the Natural Sciences in Nineteenth-Century American Legal Education," *Law and History Review* 17 (1999): 421–66; M. H. Hoeflich, "Law & Geometry: Legal Science from Leibniz to Langdell," *American Journal of Legal History* 30 (1986): 95–121; Charles L. Barzun, "Common Sense and Legal Science," *Virginia Law Review* 90 (2004): 1051–92; Steven J. Macias, *Legal Science in the Early Republic: The Origins of American Legal Thought and Education* (Lanham, MD: Lexington Books, 2016).

[43] H. W. Warner, *A Discourse on Legal Science* (New York: G. & C. & H. Carvill, 1833), 5–6.

conscience on the other." Warner's view of the law was thoroughly conventional for the era. "The law," he explained, "consists substantially of principles that are founded in moral reason, and accessible to the light of moral evidence." The work of the legal scientist was to understand the true nature of things, and to derive human law from the unwritten principles of the law of nature. "Science follows nature," he reasoned. "It is the business of juridical science to find reasons of law in the nature of things, and then to carry out those reasons, either for support or reform, into the positive arrangements of civil government."[44] A reviewer of James Kent's *Commentaries* agreed that "the whole law is a science so far, and so far only, as it agrees with natural justice."[45] What made this effort scientific was not that it involved experiments or induction from individual instances, but rather that it involved rationally organized information about the actual nature of the world.

Another good example of this older conception of legal science can be found in an anonymous article entitled "Whether Law Is a Science?" published in the *American Jurist* in 1833. "When we say that a branch of human knowledge is a science," the author explained, "we mean, in general, that it is founded on principles inherent in the subjects to which it relates. We mean also that those principles serve as a basis whereon we may classify the subjects of that particular branch of knowledge." On this definition, the author continued, law was indeed a science. It was a science precisely *because* it was founded on the law of nature. "When we teach and learn the law, if we teach and learn it aright," he concluded, "we investigate the rights of man as they are manifested in the *nature* which has been impressed upon him, and his *state* of being." There were true legal principles capable of discernment because humanity had a true nature. These principles existed in nature, regardless of what human law had to say. "His nature is ever the same, and therefore the rights which belong to him by nature are unchangeable, and the laws which secure those rights are unalterable," the author noted. "Without any Roman statute against rape, the insult and violence offered to Lucretia, would have been an offense against that eternal and immutable law which must apply to every intelligence."[46]

Law professors of the late 19th century, by contrast, believed they were pursuing a science in which the law of nature played no part. The general principles they sought to discern from the cases were not principles of natural law, capable of being identified through philosophical thought. Rather, they were distinctly legal principles, doctrines that could be found only by reading

---

[44] *Id.* at 13, 17, 23–24.

[45] Review of James Kent, *Commentaries on American Law* (10th ed.), *North American Review* 93 (1861): 337.

[46] "Whether Law is a Science?," *American Jurist* 9 (1833): 349–50.

court opinions and that had no purchase outside the court system. They were replacements for the principles that lawyers had once found in nature.[47]

These law professors rejected the use of natural law within the legal system. "No principle of natural law can be regarded as law," insisted Joseph Henry Beale of Harvard Law School. Such natural principles "are addressed to the individual conscience rather than to magistrates and jurists."[48] Langdell agreed that "all duties originate in commands of the State."[49] "As commonly used by lawyers," he explained on another occasion, the word *law* merely "means law as administered by courts of justice in suits between litigating parties."[50] John Chipman Gray, also of Harvard, found it "extremely doubtful whether there are any principles of Law which are so ingrained in human nature as to be immutable and necessary." As Gray saw it, the era of natural law was over. "The possibility of General Jurisprudence as a science of *necessary* principles rests on a theory of the universe which has, in these last days, been badly shaken," Gray argued. Natural law was "a theory which supposes a permanence in social relations the existence of which is very uncertain."[51] John Henry Wigmore, the dean of Northwestern Law School, shared this opinion. "A hundred years ago, and more," he noted, there were many "treatises on the law of Nature," he noted. But "that philosophy has been discarded."[52]

Law was thus, as Beale put it, "a homogenous, scientific, and all-embracing body of principle," just as natural law had once been, but this was a body of principle shorn of any connection to God or nature. Nevertheless, these principles served the same function that natural law had once served, as the means by which the output of the courts could be evaluated. Applying the principles to cases "is

---

[47] Thomas Grey and William LaPiana both make a similar point, although they characterize the thing being replaced as religion generally rather than natural law specifically. Thomas C. Grey, "Langdell's Orthodoxy," *University of Pittsburgh Law Review* 45 (1983): 36; William P. LaPiana, *Logic and Experience: The Origin of Modern American Legal Education* (New York: Oxford Univ. Press, 1994), 70.

[48] Joseph Henry Beale, *A Treatise on the Conflict of Laws* (Cambridge: Harvard Univ. Press, 1916), 143.

[49] C. C. Langdell, "Classification of Rights and Wrongs," *Harvard Law Review* 13 (1900): 540.

[50] C. C. Langdell, "Dominant Opinions in England During the Nineteenth Century in Relation to Legislation as Illustrated by English Legislation, or the Absence of It, During That Period," *Harvard Law Review* 19 (1906): 151. On the other hand, Langdell seems to have accepted that authors and inventors had a natural right to the use of their creations, so perhaps he was not as determinedly positivist as the quotations in the text suggest. See C. C. Langdell, "Patent Rights and Copy Rights," *Harvard Law Review* 12 (1899): 553.

[51] Gray, *Nature and Sources*, 132. On the similarities and differences between Gray's views and those of his Harvard colleagues, see Stephen A. Siegel, "John Chipman Gray and the Moral Basis of Classical Legal Thought," *Iowa Law Review* 86 (2001): 1513–99.

[52] John H. Wigmore, "The Terminology of Legal Science (With a Plea for the Science of Nomothetics)," *Harvard Law Review* 28 (1914): 7.

the work of a tribunal which, being human, may err," Beale explained. When a court erred, "The positive law of the state becomes different from the basic system." But when a court strayed from these principles of law, the court did not *change* the law, a task that Beale considered impossible. The court merely got the law wrong. "It must be obvious," Beale concluded, "that neither by legislative nor by judicial legislation can the basic system of law be changed."[53] Beale, Langdell, and their contemporaries developed, in effect, a natural law without nature, in which the cases themselves yielded the general principles that constituted the true law, the law by which subsequent cases could be evaluated.

This vision of the legal system encompassed only the private law fields in which the main sources of law were court decisions, such as the topics in which Langdell specialized, contracts and equity. It excluded the vast swaths of public law governed by statutes or constitutional provisions—constitutional law, administrative law, labor law, taxation, and the like. Langdell and his colleagues did not teach or write about such subjects, which they classified as something other than law in the strict sense. "We have no such subjects in our curriculum," Beale proudly declared. James Barr Ames likewise reported that the Harvard faculty was "unanimously opposed to the teaching of anything but pure law in our department."[54]

The understanding of the legal system represented by Langdell and his colleagues has been roundly criticized ever since the late 19th century on two grounds, one of which is not entirely accurate. The partly inaccurate basis for criticism is that these law professors treated the law as an entirely logical system in which "policy" concerns—that is, attention to the desirability or undesirability of the real-world consequences of decisions—had no role. This line of criticism began with Oliver Wendell Holmes's 1880 review of Langdell's contracts casebook, in which Holmes sarcastically called Langdell "the greatest living legal theologian," because he read Langdell as someone concerned only with "the *logical* integrity of the system as a system," not with the "justice and reasonableness of a decision."[55] Holmes said privately of Langdell that "to my mind he represents the powers of darkness. He is all for logic and hates any reference to anything outside of it."[56] This critique would often be repeated in subsequent years, directed not just at Langdell but at the school of thought he represented.

---

[53] Beale, *Conflict of Laws*, 136, 145.

[54] Quoted in Robert Stevens, *Law School: Legal Education in America from the 1850s to the 1980s* (Chapel Hill: Univ. of North Carolina Press, 1983), 40.

[55] Oliver Wendell Holmes Jr., "Book Notices," *American Law Review* 14 (1880): 234.

[56] Holmes to Frederick Pollock, 10 Apr. 1881, in Howe, *Holmes-Pollock Letters*, 1:17. Even after Langdell's death, Holmes was still complaining of "the narrow side of his mind, his feebleness in philosophising, and . . . his rudimentary historical knowledge." Holmes to Pollock, 6 July 1908, in *id.*, 1:140.

But the claim that Langdell and similar thinkers cared only about logic was not completely true. As his biographer has shown, Langdell *did* consider the policy implications of legal doctrines.[57] So did the contemporaries who shared Langdell's understanding of the nature of the legal system. Beale, for example, insisted, in an article on liability for various kinds of activities, that "when carriers undertake to convey persons by the powerful but dangerous agency of steam, public policy and safety require that they be held to the greatest possible care and diligence."[58] Such policy concerns could help explain the content of the principles discernable from the cases, even if they were not invoked in reasoning from the principles down to the results of cases.

The more accurate ground for criticism is not that this way of thinking was completely divorced from policy considerations, but rather that it was circular.[59] On one hand, general principles were identified by a process of induction from decided cases. On the other, these same general principles were used to evaluate the correctness of the individual cases. But when a case and a principle were in conflict, how was one to know whether the case was wrongly decided or whether the principle had been erroneously inferred? The natural sciences did not suffer from the same circularity, because the physical world provided the definitive reference point against which both the experimental result and the putative general principle could be checked to see which was in error. There was no such external reference point for late 19th-century legal science. The law of nature had once been considered to be that external reference point, but the law professors of the late 19th century were trying to construct a system that had no need for natural law.

Despite such criticism, this understanding of common law decision-making became the conventional way law was taught in university-based law schools. It was part of a package of teaching methods that originated at Harvard and spread to other schools, often when Harvard graduates became professors themselves. The package included several other innovations that have remained standard to this day, including the reading of court opinions rather than treatises summarizing the law, the employment of full-time faculty rather than practicing

---

[57] Bruce A. Kimball, *The Inception of Modern Professional Education: C.C. Langdell, 1826–1906* (Chapel Hill: Univ. of North Carolina Press, 2009), 108–29.

[58] Joseph H. Beale Jr., "Gratuitous Undertakings," *Harvard Law Review* 5 (1891): 230. As David Rabban and Brian Tamanaha have shown, even the most supposedly formalist judges and scholars of the era do not look particularly formalist when their work is examined closely. Rabban, *Law's History*; Brian Z. Tamanaha, *Beyond the Formalist-Realist Divide: The Role of Politics in Judging* (Princeton: Princeton Univ. Press, 2010).

[59] The best discussion of this criticism is in Grey, "Langdell's Orthodoxy," 20–32.

lawyers or judges, and the use of the "Socratic" method in the classroom.[60] The idea that correct answers to common law questions can be found by extracting general principles from the mass of decided cases has likewise remained the tacit theory underlying much of what is taught in law school, especially during the first year. It is a theory that is more often implicitly modeled by teachers in their classroom dialogues with students than explicitly elaborated in print, but it has nevertheless influenced generations of lawyers, who have been educated to find legal principles in the cases themselves rather than in the law of nature.

Substantive Due Process

Langdell and his colleagues believed they had found a replacement for natural law as a reference point for evaluating common law decision-making. But natural law had also been used to interpret, and sometimes even to invalidate, legislation. Langdell's method was of no use here, because legislators, unlike judges, were deliberately creating new law rather than interpreting precedent. Some other reference point was needed if one wished to evaluate legislation in a manner analogous to the way the law professors were evaluating common law decisions. Lawyers would find that reference point in the due process clauses of state and federal constitutions, which they would interpret to incorporate many of the same limits on legislation that had once been found in natural law.

The era of "substantive due process" would last around sixty years, from the 1870s through the 1930s. While courts' aggressiveness in striking down legislation should not be overstated—much more economic regulation was upheld than was invalidated[61]—the period nevertheless saw the rise of a distinctive mode of constitutional thought. Its roots lay in the natural law of the first half of the 19th century.

When natural law was a working part of the American legal system, as we saw in chapter 3, it was understood to proscribe "class legislation"—that is, statutes that granted special privileges to particular groups, or that transferred wealth from one group to another. "It is manifestly contrary to the first principles of civil liberty and natural justice," the Massachusetts Supreme Court declared in 1814, "that any one citizen should enjoy privileges and advantages which are

---

[60] On the curricular innovations at Harvard during this period, see Daniel R. Coquillette and Bruce A. Kimball, *On the Battlefield of Merit: Harvard Law School, The First Century* (Cambridge: Harvard Univ. Press, 2015), 304–520.

[61] Roman J. Hoyos, "Beyond Classical Legal Thought: Law and Governance in Postbellum America, 1865–1920," in Sally E. Hadden and Alfred L. Brophy, eds., *A Companion to American Legal History* (Chichester, UK: Wiley-Blackwell, 2013), 96–97.

denied to all others in like circumstances."[62] The Georgia Supreme Court likewise castigated "class legislation" as contrary to "the great fundamental principles of human rights."[63] Supreme Court Justice Samuel Chase famously imagined, as an example of a legislative act that would be void as contrary to natural justice, "a law that takes property from A. and gives it to B."[64]

As we also saw in chapter 3, natural law was also understood to proscribe abridgments of property rights, even in ways that were not expressly forbidden by a provision of the constitution. Property was a quintessential natural right, one that early American lawyers understood as preexisting the positive laws that had been enacted to protect it. The security of one's property "is a right inalienable," the Iowa Supreme Court noted, "a right which a written constitution may recognize or declare, but which existed independently of and before such recognition, and which no government can destroy."[65]

In the latter part of the 19th century, as the use of natural law waned, courts began to invoke the due process clauses of the state and federal constitutions to accomplish these same purposes. The Fifth Amendment of the federal Constitution, ratified in 1791, forbade the federal government from depriving anyone of life, liberty, or property, without due process of law. State constitutions included similar restrictions on state governments. In 1868, the ratification of the Fourteenth Amendment added a second Due Process Clause to the Constitution, this one applicable to the states but otherwise worded identically. When natural law was no longer available as a barrier to class legislation and incursions on property rights, due process took its place.[66]

The Michigan judge Thomas Cooley was among the first to discuss at length the possibility of using due process in this way, in his widely read treatise on constitutional law. The due process clauses did not just require that government follow certain processes, Cooley insisted. They also imposed substantive limits on what the government could do. "When the government, through its established agencies, interferes with the title to one's property, or with his independent enjoyment of it," he reasoned, "we are to test its validity by those principles of civil liberty and constitutional defence which have become established in our system of law, and not by any rules that pertain to forms of procedure

---

[62] *Holden v. James*, 11 Mass. 396, 405–06 (1814).

[63] *Bethune v. Hughes*, 28 Ga. 560, 565 (1859).

[64] *Calder v. Bull*, 3 U.S. 386, 388 (1798).

[65] *Henry v. Dubuque & Pacific Railroad Co.*, 10 Iowa 540, 544 (1860).

[66] Here I follow Howard Gillman in finding the roots of substantive due process in early 19th-century thought regarding class legislation: Howard Gillman, *The Constitution Besieged: The Rise and Demise of Lochner-Era Police Powers Jurisprudence* (Durham: Duke Univ. Press, 1993). But I supplement his account by showing that the key move in the later part of the century was transferring the source of the ban on class legislation from natural law to the due process clauses.

merely." His primary example of a statute that would be contrary to due process was precisely the example Samuel Chase had cited as a statute that would be contrary to natural law—a redistribution of property from one person or group to another. "There is no rule or principle known to our system under which private property can be taken from one man and transferred to another for the private use and benefit of such other person," Cooley explained. "The purpose must be public, and must have reference to the needs of the government. No reason of general public policy will be sufficient to protect such transfers where they operate upon existing vested rights."[67]

Just as redistribution would deprive owners of their *property* without due process, Cooley continued, any sort of class legislation would deprive individuals of their *liberty* without due process. Cooley understood liberty in its broadest sense, to encompass not just freedom from physical restraint but also a person's "capacity to make contracts, or to receive conveyances," or to build a house, or to follow "a lawful trade or employment," or to undertake just about any kind of remunerative activity. "The man or the class forbidden the acquisition or enjoyment of property in the manner permitted to the community at large would be deprived of *liberty* in particulars of primary importance," he argued. In setting forth this capacious understanding of liberty, Cooley drew upon earlier natural law theorists such as Blackstone and Burlamaqui, who, as Cooley acknowledged, were defining "natural liberty" rather than a clause in written constitutions that did not yet exist when they wrote.[68]

In subsequent years, many other judges followed Cooley in shifting the basis for the proscriptions against class legislation and incursions on property and contract rights from the law of nature to the due process clauses of state and federal constitutions. In this sense, the due process clauses were understood to incorporate natural law. They provided a textual hook that brought natural law into the courtroom. Four years after the Fourteenth Amendment's Due Process Clause was ratified, Supreme Court justice Stephen Field argued in the *Slaughter-House Cases* that the Due Process Clause was "intended to give practical effect to the declaration of 1776 of inalienable rights, rights which are the gift of the Creator, which the law does not confer, but only recognizes."[69] Field was dissenting, but the view he and Cooley expressed soon became the law. In an 1877 case, the Supreme Court declared that a law redistributing property from one person to another, an earlier generation's paradigmatic example of a law contrary to natural justice, would be a deprivation of property without due process

---

[67] Cooley, *Constitutional Limitations*, 356–57.

[68] *Id.* at 393.

[69] *Slaughter-House Cases*, 83 U.S. 36, 105 (1872) (Field, J., dissenting).

under the Fourteenth Amendment.[70] Lower courts quickly followed in shifting the standard against which economic regulation would be evaluated from natural law to due process. Unjust statutes could not be invalidated as contrary to the law of nature, the New York Court of Appeals acknowledged. Rather, "The main guaranty of private rights against unjust legislation is found in that memorable clause in the bill of rights, that no person shall 'be deprived of life, liberty or property without due process of law.' "[71]

In several of these cases, judges explicitly stated that they were using the Due Process Clause as a textual hook to bring natural law into the courtroom. Natural law, of its own force, was no longer an acceptable reference point for evaluating the validity of legislation. But the written Constitution certainly was. If the Due Process Clause instructed judges to look to natural law in evaluating the validity of legislation, then judges were merely doing their duty by evaluating statutes for consistency with natural law. In one 1898 case, for example, the US Supreme Court explained that the Due Process Clause declared no new rights but merely articulated "certain immutable principles of justice, which inhere in the very idea of free government." The words "due process of law," the Court observed, "imply a conformity with natural and inherent principles of justice, and forbid that one man's property, or right to property, shall be taken for the benefit of another."[72] The government has "no right to prevent the lawful owner of property from exercising over it all the lawful rights of ownership," one lower court judge suggested. "Older than the Constitution, older than Magna Charta, older than the Ten Tables, as old as civilization and coeval with the first organization of human society, is the provision of the law of nature that no one should be deprived of life, liberty, or property without due process of law."[73] The arguments that had once appeared in judicial opinions expounding the law of nature now reappeared in opinions interpreting the requirements of due process.

Indeed, it became common for courts to treat the requirements of natural law and the requirements of due process as synonymous. "It is a fundamental rule of our law, founded in the plainest principles of natural justice, that no man shall be deprived of his life, liberty, or property without due process of law," declared the Missouri Supreme Court in 1899.[74] A few years later, in upholding the constitutionality of tax sales (that is, the practice of seizing and selling real estate when the owner had not paid the property tax), the US Supreme Court observed that "the 14th Amendment would be satisfied by showing that" state law "was

---

[70] *Davidson v. City of New Orleans*, 96 U.S. 97, 102 (1877).

[71] *Bertholf v. O'Reilly*, 74 N.Y. 509, 514–15 (1878).

[72] *Holden v. Hardy*, 169 U.S. 366, 389–90 (1898).

[73] *Fulton v. District of Columbia*, 2 App. D.C. 431, 437 (1894).

[74] *Turner v. Gregory*, 52 S.W. 234, 235 (Mo. 1899).

in conformity with natural justice."[75] The Wisconsin Supreme Court referred to "those principles of natural justice which afford due process of law."[76]

When natural law was an accepted part of litigation, there had always been some uncertainty about whether it was a proper ground for invalidating statutes, because of the debate over whether constitutions provided the exclusive grounds for doing so. This uncertainty evaporated once due process provided natural law's textual hook, because there was no doubt that courts were authorized to interpret the constitution. The shift from a freestanding natural law to a natural law incorporated through due process thus removed what once had been a major inhibitor of the invalidation of statutes.

This shift also reoriented the way judges conceived of their task. In its heyday, as we saw in chapters 1 and 3, natural law had been used much more often to interpret statutes than to invalidate them. Courts tended to stretch the language of statutes to bring them into compliance with natural law, on the assumption that the legislature could not have meant to enact a provision contrary to the law of nature. This was no longer the case when due process replaced the freestanding law of nature as the yardstick. When a court determined that a statute was contrary to due process, the court typically did not labor to interpret the statute in a nonliteral way so as to render it constitutional. Rather, the court simply declared the statute void.

For example, in *Lochner v. New York*, the 1905 case that became a synecdoche for this era of due process jurisprudence, the Supreme Court confronted a statute that barred bakery employees from working more than ten hours a day or sixty hours a week. The Court held the statute unconstitutional on the ground that "the right to purchase or to sell labor is part of the liberty protected by" the Due Process Clause, and the Court did not believe the state's claim that the statute would protect the health of bakery employees.[77] In the early part of the century, when courts looked to natural law directly rather than through the conduit of due process, a court would likely have strained to interpret the statute in some way that would have saved its validity—perhaps by construing it to apply only to bakers in poor health, or only to bakeries with especially unsanitary working conditions. Not any longer. The solicitude for the legislature that had been characteristic of the natural law era was replaced by a harder judicial attitude. Now, if a statute was contrary to natural law as incorporated through the Due Process Clause, the statute was simply invalid.

Contemporaries recognized that due process had taken the place once occupied by natural law. Some, like the law professor Christopher Tiedeman,

---

[75] *Turpin v. Lemon*, 187 U.S. 51, 57 (1903).

[76] *Ekern v. McGovern*, 142 N.W. 595, 619 (Wis. 1913).

[77] *Lochner v. New York*, 198 U.S. 45, 53 (1905).

approved of this development. "Fundamental principles of natural right and justice cannot, in themselves, furnish any legal restrictions upon the governmental exercise of police power," he recognized. "Yet they play an important part in determining the exact scope and extent of the constitutional limitations." The entry point for natural law was the Due Process Clause, which authorized a court "to avoid an unrighteous exercise of the police power," even where "the strict letter of the constitution does not prohibit the exercise of such a power." For example, if a legislature enacted a law "which prohibited the prosecution of some employment which did not involve the infliction of injury upon others, or which restricts the liberty of the citizen unnecessarily, and in such a manner that it did not violate any specific provision of the constitution, it may be held invalid, because in the one case it interfered with the inalienable right of property, and in the other case it infringed upon the natural right to life and liberty." Judges could implement natural law through the medium of due process, now that natural law, by itself, was no longer an acceptable vehicle.[78]

Critics of this use of due process, by contrast, considered it an illegitimate way of smuggling natural law back into the process of deciding cases, after it had ostensibly been cast aside. Judges were reading into the Due Process Clause their "own ideas as to what the absolute, eternal, and immutable principles of law ought to be with reference to the case in question," charged the political scientist Robert Cushman. They were returning to the "juridical philosophy which had served the vastly simpler speculative needs of the pioneer society of the forties and fifties."[79] The *Lochner*-style due process cases "represent the application of old theories of natural law," agreed Benjamin Wright, another political scientist. "For all the differences in terminology," he observed, "the basic idea is identical with the philosophy underlying many of the decisions and much of the juristic writing of the period of Marshall, Kent, and Story."[80] Roscoe Pound blamed "the training of lawyers and judges in eighteenth-century theories of natural law." As a result, he argued, "constitutional law is full of natural notions."[81]

Much of the legislation found contrary to this view of due process was intended to strengthen the position of workers with respect to their employers.

---

[78] Tiedeman, *Limitations of Police Power*, 10–11. See also Henry C. Clark, "Jus Gentium—Its Origin and History," *Illinois Law Review* 14 (1919): 354; Elmer Hugo Grimm, "Administrative Determinations," *St. Louis Law Review* 3 (1919): 142.

[79] Robert Eugene Cushman, "The Social and Economic Interpretation of the Fourteenth Amendment," *Michigan Law Review* 20 (1922): 745.

[80] B. F. Wright Jr., "American Interpretations of Natural Law," *American Political Science Review* 20 (1926): 540. Wright would later publish an expanded version of this article as Benjamin Fletcher Wright Jr., *American Interpretations of Natural Law: A Study in the History of Political Thought* (Cambridge: Harvard Univ. Press, 1931).

[81] Roscoe Pound, "Liberty of Contract," *Yale Law Journal* 18 (1909): 464, 465.

These were measures that mid-19th-century economic thought—which was simple common sense to late-century judges—condemned as doomed to fail at best and disastrous at worst.[82] Examples include a federal statute prohibiting employers from barring their employees from joining labor unions (struck down by the US Supreme Court in 1908),[83] a West Virginia law requiring mining companies to pay miners in real money rather than scrip (struck down by the West Virginia Supreme Court in 1889),[84] and a Los Angeles ordinance establishing an eight-hour workday under contracts with the city (struck down by the California Supreme Court in 1890).[85] Critics of such decisions contended that judges were mistaking their own laissez-faire policy preferences for fundamental principles. Dissenting in *Lochner*, Oliver Wendell Holmes charged: "This case is decided upon an economic theory which a large part of the country does not entertain."[86] Grumbling in private about a later decision, he complained that it was "another case of treating the XIV Amendment as prohibiting what 5 out of 9 old gentlemen don't think about right."[87] As this sort of criticism suggested, the expansive view of due process that supplanted natural law suffered from the same indeterminacy that had come to seem so troubling about natural law. Different people could have different views about what due process required, just as they had different views about what natural law required, and those views were likely to coincide with their instinctive beliefs about what was right.

Over time, as substantive due process became an established doctrine, it lost much of its explicit grounding in natural law, because it acquired a grounding in precedent instead. Courts could limit their consideration to the body of earlier cases evaluating similar legislation, without having to look through those cases back to the natural principles on which the earliest judges in the chain had relied. The language of natural law gradually dropped out of the substantive due process cases. For instance, the Supreme Court's famous early 20th-century cases in this genre, such as *Lochner v. New York* and *Adair v. United States*, do not mention natural law at all. They refer only to prior cases. Substantive due process's origin as a replacement for natural law thus gradually became effaced.

---

[82] Herbert Hovenkamp, "The Political Economy of Substantive Due Process," *Stanford Law Review* 40 (1988): 379–447.

[83] *Adair v. United States*, 208 U.S. 161 (1908).

[84] *State v. Goodwill*, 10 S.E. 285 (W. Va. 1889).

[85] *Ex parte Kubach*, 24 P. 737 (Cal. 1890).

[86] *Lochner*, 198 U.S. at 75 (Holmes, J., dissenting).

[87] Holmes to Harold Laski, 18 Dec. 1929, in Mark De Wolfe Howe, ed., *Holmes-Laski Letters* (New York: Atheneum, 1963), 2:299.

Contemporaries with long memories, however, recognized that the Due Process Clause was serving as a conduit for the law of nature.[88] When natural law no longer played a role in its own right in the working legal system, a capacious interpretation of due process took its place as a way of evaluating the validity of legislation.

From Law-Finder to Lawmaker

Historical jurisprudence, natural economic principles, classical orthodoxy, and substantive due process were attempts to identify preexisting principles that could perform the functions that natural law had once performed. Meanwhile, other lawyers argued that no replacement for natural law was necessary or even possible because there were no preexisting principles for judges to find. Judges, they contended, did not *find* the law. Judges *made* it.

This view already had a long history in the late 19th century. Reformers from Bentham onward had argued that judges make the law, but typically as criticism rather than as a neutral statement of fact. In the 1830s, for example, the Massachusetts lawyer Robert Rantoul was a proponent of replacing much of the common law with statutes, as had recently been done in France and much of continental Europe. The common law was in fact *"judicial legislation,"* Rantoul argued. "No one knows what the law is, *before* [the judge] lays it down; for it does not exist even in the breast of the judge." The common law did not exist out there in the world, waiting to be found. Rather, "The Judge makes law, by extorting from precedents, something which they do not contain. He extends his precedents, which were themselves the extension of others, till, by this accommodating principle a whole system of law is built up without the authority or interference or the Legislator."[89] One of Rantoul's contemporaries similarly declared that "the supposition of an ancient and forgotten custom is, as every one knows, a mere fiction." Judges did not find the common law in custom, he insisted. Rather, "The courts in point of fact make the law."[90] David Dudley Field, another ardent codifier, likewise argued that the common law's supposed flexibility, one of the points often cited in its defense, was proof that judges were

---

[88] Charles Grove Haines, *The Revival of Natural Law Concepts* (Cambridge: Harvard Univ. Press, 1930); J. A. C. Grant, "The Natural Law Background of Due Process," *Columbia Law Review* 56 (1931): 56–81; Edward S. Corwin, "The 'Higher Law' Background of American Constitutional Law," *Harvard Law Review* 42 (1928): 149–85, and 42 (1929): 365–409; Fowler Vincent Harper, "Natural Law in American Constitutional Theory," *Michigan Law Review* 26 (1927): 62–82.

[89] Robert Rantoul, *An Oration Delivered Before the Democrats and Antimasons, of the County of Plymouth; at Scituate* (Boston: Seals & Greene, 1836), 36, 38.

[90] "Written and Unwritten Systems of Laws," *American Jurist & Law Magazine* 9 (1833): 11.

making it rather than finding it. After all, Field pointed out, "If it be an exposition of existing law, then it is not alterable by the judges, and, of course, is no more flexible in their hands than a statute would be."[91] Contemporaries recognized that such comments were meant to be insults. As Pennsylvania's chief justice John Bannister Gibson observed, the common law "has been contemptuously called judge-made law."[92]

In the late 19th century, by contrast, many lawyers began asserting straight-forwardly, without any hint of opprobrium, that the law was made, not found, by judges. Lawyers "habitually employ a double language," Henry Sumner Maine suggested in his widely read *Ancient Law*. Before a case was decided, lawyers spoke as if the court would merely be ascertaining law that already existed, but once the court's opinion had been published, "we now admit that the new deci-sion *has* modified the law."[93] One of the earliest sustained American expressions of this view can be found in John Norton Pomeroy's 1864 textbook for students. "It is an entire misconception of the functions of the judicial tribunals, to de-scribe them as wanting the legislative power, but as possessing only the capacity to declare the law to exist, as though from time immemorial a legal principle or rule had lain hidden and unnoticed, awaiting a discoverer," Pomeroy instructed. "It is folly, a mere perversion of language to support a theory, to say that the tribunals have not legislated as really and as effectively" as the legislature. The true difference between the two was that while legislators were aware of what they were doing, judges were not. "The legislation of the one is conscious," Pomeroy concluded, "that of the other unconscious."[94]

Oliver Wendell Holmes provided a better-known version of this point a few years later. When judges decided a case according to the common law, "The official theory is that each new decision follows syllogistically from existing precedents," Holmes noted. "On the other hand, in substance the growth of the law is legislative." Despite their claims to find the common law, judges actu-ally made it, by considering "what is expedient for the community concerned. Every important principle which is developed by litigation is in fact and at bottom the result of more or less definitely understood views of public policy." The judges themselves might not realize it. "Under our practices and traditions," Holmes observed, judges' decisions were likely to be "the unconscious result of

---

[91] David Dudley Field, *Legal Reform: An Address to the Graduating Class of the Law School of the University of Albany* (Albany: W.C. Little, 1855), 28.

[92] *McClure v. Foreman*, 4 Watts & Serg. 278, 280 (Pa. 1842).

[93] Maine, *Ancient Law*, 30.

[94] John Norton Pomeroy, *An Introduction to Municipal Law* (New York: D. Appleton, 1864), 176–77. See also "Judicial Legislation," *Albany Law Journal* 1 (1870): 105; Albert J. Chapman, "Judicial Legislation," *Western Jurist* 6 (1872): 204.

instinctive preferences and inarticulate convictions" rather than self-conscious acts of policymaking. Nevertheless, he concluded, common law decisions were "traceable to public policy in the last analysis."[95]

By the 1890s, as natural law slipped out of the legal system, both the older and newer views of the judge were in wide circulation. "Here arises a question as to which there is a great difference of opinion," advised Eugene Wambaugh of the University of Iowa in his 1891 guide for beginning law students. "Do judges make law; or do they simply declare it?" Wambaugh explained that "the view long held by all lawyers, and still held by the vast majority of them, is that decisions merely illustrate law and that judges simply declare law." But the "modern" view, he continued, was "that the common law, or case law, is a creation of the courts, and that it is as truly the result of judicial legislation as statutes are the result of ordinary legislation." Wambaugh saw no need to choose sides, because on either view, "One who is searching for the common law must study the decisions," and Wambaugh's purpose was to teach students how to do that.[96] But by the last decade of the 19th century, even beginning law students knew that the view of judges as law-finders was weaker than it had once been.

Wambaugh may have overestimated the tenacity with which lawyers clung to the older view of the common law, because some of his contemporaries thought that most of the profession had already abandoned it. "We were all taught that it was the duty of judges to declare but not to make the law," said a speaker at the American Bar Association's 1883 annual meeting. "We all know that this is one of the resplendent fictions."[97] Edgar Kinkead, a law professor at Ohio State, summarized professional opinion in his textbook on jurisprudence. "Whatever may have been the fact in the earlier history of the common law," Kinkead explained, "there is now no doubt that the modern view is, that the judges make the law."[98] Judges themselves tended to be more circumspect about claiming lawmaking power, but every so often even judges admitted that they were lawmakers. "There was once a theory," a Kentucky judge recalled in 1885, "that the law, when declared by the court, was supposed to have been always theretofore known." But the judge no longer believed it. He called it "a theory which seems to have been designed as an anticipation and avoidance of Bentham's stricture on judge-made law."[99]

---

[95] Oliver Wendell Holmes Jr., "Common Carriers and the Common Law," *American Law Review* 13 (1879): 630–31.

[96] Eugene Wambaugh, *The Study of Cases* (Boston: Little, Brown, 1891), 33–35.

[97] John M. Shirley, *The Future of Our Profession: A Paper Read Before the American Bar Association* (Philadelphia: George S. Harris & Sons, 1883), 19.

[98] Edgar B. Kinkead, *Jurisprudence: Law and Ethics* (New York: Banks Law Publishing, 1905), 201.

[99] *McMurty v. Vowells*, 6 Ky. L. Rep. 719, 722 (Super. Ct. 1885).

By the turn of the century it was common for lawyers to speak of judges as lawmakers.[100] For example, Ezra Thayer, who would go on to become the dean of Harvard Law School, observed that the phrase "judicial legislation" was once a term of reproach. But Thayer insisted that judicial legislation "is a desirable, and indeed a necessary, feature of our system," because judges legislated whenever they adapted the law to meet new circumstances.[101] "Do judges make law?" asked the Boston lawyer William Webster. "In theory they never do." In practice, however, the law was often "made, declared and applied simultaneously, which proves that it is in fact 'judge-made.'"[102] Because "life is continually developing new and unforeseeable situations," noted the legal philosopher Morris Cohen, "and judges are obliged to decide every case before them (these decisions serving as binding precedents) it follows that they must in the course of their work develop new rules."[103] As the law professor Frederick deSloovere concluded, "every student of the law now realizes that the courts are not finding but making law in most cases."[104]

The older view that judges found the law was increasingly described as a fiction.[105] "The idea of judges laboriously delving into nothing, nowhere, and pretending that they are unearthing primeval aphorisms, axioms and principles," one lawyer remarked—"I don't believe it."[106] The older view lingered on in the official discourse of the legal system, but increasingly as a figure of speech rather than a sincere belief. "Judicial legislation is hampered by the fiction that the courts do not make law, but only find it," argued the Columbia law professor Munroe Smith in 1887. "Nobody really believes in the fiction, but few judges have been bold enough to defy it openly."[107]

Benjamin Cardozo, one of those few bold judges, provided a revealing account of how lawmaking felt from a judge's perspective. Cardozo had gone to law school and had begun his legal career during the midst of this change in the conventional view of the judge's role. When he became a judge he felt lost

---

[100] Emlin McClain, "The Evolution of the Judicial Opinion," *Annual Report of the American Bar Association* 25 (1902): 383–84; LeBaron B. Colt, "Law and Reasonableness," *Annual Report of the American Bar Association* 26 (1903): 359; A. M. Mackey, "Judge-Made Law," *Oklahoma Law Journal* 2 (1903): 197.

[101] Ezra Thayer, "Judicial Legislation: Its Legitimation in the Development of the Common Law," *Harvard Law Review* 5 (1891): 172.

[102] William Webster, "Do Judges Make Law," *The Advocate* 2 (1890): 33.

[103] Morris Cohen, "The Process of Judicial Legislation," *American Law Review* 48 (1914): 169.

[104] Frederick deSloovere, book review, *Georgetown Law Journal* 13 (1925): 281.

[105] "Codification," *Western Jurist* 5 (1871): 289–90; "Current Topics," *Albany Law Journal* 29 (1884): 481; Harris Taylor, "Legitimate Functions of Judge-Made Law," *Green Bag* 17 (1905): 562.

[106] John S. Ewart, "What is the Common Law?", *Columbia Law Review* 4 (1904): 125.

[107] Munroe Smith, "State Statute and Common Law," *Political Science Quarterly* 2 (1887): 121.

when positive law did not dictate an outcome. "I was much troubled in spirit, in my first years on the bench, to find how trackless was the ocean on which I had embarked," Cardozo recalled. "I sought for certainty. I was oppressed and disheartened when I found that the quest for it was futile." But he eventually realized that there would always be cases in which "the judge assumes the function of a lawgiver." As the years went by, "and as I have reflected more and more upon the nature of the judicial process, I have become reconciled to the uncertainty, because I have grown to see it as inevitable. I have grown to see that the process in its highest reaches is not discovery, but creation."[108]

As lawyers began to reconceive judging as lawmaking, the older view of the law as something preexisting the judge's decision came to seem more and more absurd. "What was the Law in the time of Richard Coeur de Lion on the liability of a telegraph company to the persons to whom a message was sent?" wondered John Chipman Gray. How could there have *been* any law governing telegraphs before the telegraph was invented? When courts changed the law, Gray continued, the concept of preexisting law became even stranger. "In Massachusetts," he recalled, "it was held in 1849, by the Supreme Judicial Court, that if a man hired a horse in Boston on a Sunday to drive to Nahant, and drove instead to Nantasket, the keeper of the livery stable had no right to sue him in trover for the conversion of the horse. But in 1871 this decision was overruled, and the right was given to the stable-keeper. Now, did stable-keepers have such rights, say, in 1845? If they did, then the court in 1849 did not discover the Law. If they did not, then the court in 1871 did not discover the Law."[109]

If the older conception of judging was so implausible, why would lawyers have subscribed to it? One possibility was that they had never actually believed judges were law-finders, but merely said so to hoodwink nonlawyers. Perhaps "the judges adopted this device in order to lend a fictitious authority to their judgments," speculated the Massachusetts lawyer Jabez Fox. "We can well imagine that it was easier for a judge to dispose of a disappointed suitor by saying: 'Thus saith the Law,' than by saying: 'I have decided against you because that is my opinion of the merits of your case.' "[110] John Chipman Gray thought it more likely that the lawyers had deceived themselves as well, because of their "unwillingness to face the certain fact that courts are constantly making ex post facto Law," law that did not exist until after the occurrence of the events it regulated. "The unwillingness is natural," Gray reasoned, "particularly on the part of the courts, who do not

---

[108] Cardozo, *Nature of Judicial Process*, 166.
[109] Gray, *Nature and Sources*, 96–97.
[110] Jabez Fox, "Law and Fact," *Harvard Law Review* 12 (1899): 547.

desire to call attention to the fact that they are exercising a power which bears so unpopular a name, but it is not reasonable."[111]

The older conception of judging as law-finding always had defenders. "There is in some minds a feeling that inasmuch as unwritten law in new and doubtful cases is not known until it is declared by the courts, the office really performed by the courts is in truth that of *making* the law, and that the notion that they only *declare* pre-existing law is a pretence," James Coolidge Carter acknowledged. But he was certain that this view was "quite erroneous." The task of a judge, he argued, was "simply *to examine the transaction*; that is, to scrutinize closely all the facts of which it is made up." The judge would then compare the facts of the present case with the facts of past cases, and determine which category of cases the present one belonged in. The judge's role "consists simply in the examination, arrangement, and classification of human actions according to the legal characteristics which they exhibit." Carter's judge did not invent new rules; he merely sorted cases into preexisting categories.[112]

But Carter was fighting a losing battle. The change in the profession's conventional conception of judging was cleverly summarized in 1910 by Harry Randolph Blythe, a student at Harvard Law School. Blythe was a regular contributor to *The Green Bag*, a Boston monthly that billed itself as "an entertaining magazine for lawyers." As he neared graduation, Blythe published a brief poem in *The Green Bag* called "A Theory":

> When judges pass on pretty points
>   Not passed upon before,
> Do they declare what is the law
>   Or what it was of yore?
>
> I know a man who often says
>   (It may be legal sin)
> That brand new cases but declare
>   What law has always been.
>
> The court but simply calls to work
>   The living legal word,
> Whose force has ruled the race of man
>   Since Eve in Eden erred.

---

[111] Gray, *Nature and Sources*, 97.

[112] James Coolidge Carter, *The Provinces of the Written and the Unwritten Law* (New York: Banks & Bros., 1889), 41–42, 28.

> This logic, therefore, would conclude
>   (Though I confess it jars)
> That there prevailed in Babylon
>   The law of motor cars.

> The theory may be beautiful,
>   But its results—Gee Whiz!
> For one, I'm quite content to say
>   Courts make the law that is.[113]

As Blythe's poem demonstrated, lawyers were increasingly thinking of judges as makers, not finders, of the law.

This conception of judges as lawmakers is often associated with the legal realists, an eclectic group of law professors in the 1920s and the 1930s (although there was much more to realism than this), and with a few of the realists' intellectual predecessors such as Oliver Wendell Holmes and Roscoe Pound. This conception of judges is often remembered as a reaction to classical legal thought, because classical legal thought was the primary target of the realists' critiques. The realists expressed disagreement with their own contemporaries, not with the legal thinkers of previous generations. As we have seen, however, the conception of judges as lawmakers already pervaded the legal profession by the turn of the century, decades before realism, while classical legal thought was at its peak. The conception of judges as lawmakers arose at the same time as classical legal thought and coexisted with classical legal thought for decades, even though they were inconsistent with each other, because they were both reactions to the decline of natural law. Schools of thought don't usually succeed one another in neat stages. Usually they coexist for some time, held by people of heterogenous views, until one triumphs over the other. Holmes, Pound, and the realists were giving voice to a conception of judging that was already widely shared among lawyers. The realists may have nudged it across the finish line in its contest with classical legal thought, but most of the race had already been run.

By the middle of the 20th century, the race was over. The Supreme Court formally abandoned substantive due process in the 1930s.[114] Christopher Langdell's successors, the professors at elite law schools, had mostly stopped believing that the common law consists of true principles inferable from decided

---

[113] Harry R. Blythe, "A Theory," *Green Bag* 22 (1910): 193.

[114] Barry Cushman, *Rethinking the New Deal Court: The Structure of a Constitutional Revolution* (New York: Oxford Univ. Press, 1998).

cases. Virtually all lawyers agreed that judges make law. "The concept that courts only find law, judges and justices do not make law, has been demythologized," the Pennsylvania Supreme Court explained.[115] In their opinions, judges often continued to write *as if* they were finding the law rather than making it, but lawyers generally recognized that this was a fiction. "I am not so naïve," Justice Antonin Scalia noted in an unusually candid aside, "as to be unaware that judges in a real sense 'make' law. But they make it as judges make it, which is to say as though they were 'finding' it—discerning what the law is, rather than decreeing what it is today changed to, or what it will tomorrow be."[116] In the late 19th and early 20th centuries, judges had been transformed in conventional professional thought from law-finders to lawmakers.

This transformation produced a corresponding change in the profession's understanding of court opinions. When the common law was something judges discovered, court opinions had been considered *evidence of* the common law, which had an existence independent of what any given judge thought it might be. Court opinions were literally the judges' opinions of the common law; they were not the common law itself. By contrast, as the common law came to be understood as something judges made, the conventional understanding of court opinions underwent a parallel transformation. When the common law had no existence independent of judges' opinions, the opinions themselves became the common law. "The notion that cases are the original sources of the law is one of very recent importation into our law," George Smith recognized in 1890. "The old doctrine is that they are merely evidence, of more or less weight, of what the law is."[117] As John Chipman Gray put it, court decisions were "not the expression of preexisting Law, but the Law itself," created by the judges.[118]

One well-known marker of this change was a series of Supreme Court cases addressing a basic question of how litigation would be conducted in the federal courts. The Judiciary Act of 1789 instructed that where no federal statute or constitutional provision was applicable, "the laws of the several states" would apply. That phrase obviously included state statutes. But did it include the decisions of the state courts? Were they "laws"? In an 1842 case called *Swift v. Tyson*, the Supreme Court held that they were not. "In the ordinary use of language," Justice

---

[115] *Speck v. Finegold*, 439 A.2d 110, 120 n. 4 (Pa. 1981).

[116] *James B. Beam Distilling Co. v. Georgia*, 501 U.S. 529, 549 (1991) (Scalia, J., concurring in the judgment).

[117] George H. Smith, "The True Method of Legal Education," *American Law Review* 24 (1890): 215.

[118] Gray, *Nature and Sources*, 93.

Joseph Story reasoned, "it will hardly be contended that the decisions of courts constitute laws. They are, at most, only evidence of what the laws are, and are not, of themselves, laws."[119] Story expressed the then-conventional view that judges were not *making* the common law when they wrote opinions but were merely recording their conclusions as to what it was.

At the Supreme Court this view came under sharp attack in the early 20th century, at first in several dissenting opinions by Oliver Wendell Holmes. "The common law is not a brooding omnipresence in the sky," Holmes insisted, "but the articulate voice of some sovereign." The sovereign—the state—spoke through its judges, who made the common law. "I recognize without hesitation," he declared, "that judges do and must legislate."[120] In another dissent, Holmes rejected what he called the "subtle fallacy" that the common law was a single body of law, which judges in various states were all searching for when they decided cases. "There is no such body of law," he affirmed. "The common law so far as it is enforced in a State, whether called common law or not, is not the common law generally but the law of that State," as made by the state's judges. "In my opinion," Holmes concluded, "the authority and only authority is the State, and if that be so, the voice adopted by the State as its own should utter the last word."[121] In private correspondence, Holmes expressed his frustration with his colleagues' "tendency to think of judges as if they were independent mouthpieces of the infinite," whose job it was "to speculate about *the* Common Law *in abstracto*."[122] Holmes's view was eventually embraced by the Court shortly after his death, in an opinion that quoted liberally from his dissents. State court decisions were now considered "laws" to be applied in the federal courts, just as much as state statutes. The opinions of judges had come to be understood as the common law itself, made by the judges, rather than as evidence of a preexisting common law.[123]

---

[119] *Swift v. Tyson*, 41 U.S. 1, 18 (1842). The practical effect of *Swift* was to authorize federal courts to develop a nationally uniform common law to govern interstate commercial transactions, a goal that no doubt contributed to the Court's willingness to say that court decisions were not the law itself. See Tony Freyer, *Harmony & Dissonance: The Swift & Erie Cases in American Federalism* (New York: New York Univ. Press, 1981).

[120] *Southern Pacific Co. v. Jensen*, 244 U.S. 205, 222, 221 (1917) (Holmes, J., dissenting).

[121] *Black & White Taxicab & Transfer Co. v. Brown & Yellow Taxicab & Transfer Co.*, 276 U.S. 518, 533, 535 (1928) (Holmes, J., dissenting).

[122] Holmes to Harold Laski, 29 Jan. 1926, in Howe, *Holmes-Laski Letters*, 2:75.

[123] *Erie Railroad Co. v. Tompkins*, 304 U.S. 64 (1938). This account greatly simplifies a long and complex story. See Edward A. Purcell Jr., *Litigation and Inequality: Federal Diversity Jurisdiction in Industrial America, 1870–1958* (New York: Oxford Univ. Press, 1992); Edward A. Purcell Jr., *Brandeis and the Progressive Constitution: Erie, the Judicial Power, and the Politics of the Federal Courts in Twentieth-Century America* (New Haven: Yale Univ. Press, 2000).

As judges were reconceived as lawmakers, the vocabulary they used in writing opinions also changed. If judges were making the law rather than finding it, their task was not to find the *correct* rule, as measured by its consistency with preexisting principles, but rather the *best* one, as measured by its consequences. A lawmaking judge was necessarily a policymaker. "I think the judges themselves have failed adequately to recognize their duty of weighing considerations of social advantage," Holmes remarked in 1897. "The duty is inevitable, and the result of the often proclaimed judicial aversion to deal with such considerations is simply to leave the very ground and foundation of judgments inarticulate, and often unconscious."[124] Roscoe Pound's call for a "sociological jurisprudence" was likewise a plea for lawyers to focus on the practical, empirical effects of legal rules. "We must seek the basis of doctrines, not in Blackstone's wisdom," Pound suggested, "but in a scientific apprehension of the relations of law to society and of the needs and interests and opinions of society of today."[125] This call for judges to speak in the vocabulary of policy was taken up by the legal realists in the 1920s and 1930s. Karl Llewellyn reported that among realists "there is very general agreement on the need for courts to face squarely the policy questions in their cases," and "fairly general agreement that effects of rules, so far as known, should be taken account of in making or remaking the rules."[126] By explicitly acknowledging that they were policymakers, Jerome Frank argued, judges would "deal realistically with their materials and their technique." The result would be "frequent adaption of the legal rules so as to relate them to the realities of contemporary social, industrial and political conditions."[127] As judges came to think of themselves as lawmakers, they adopted a lawmaker's writing style, and they began to speak in terms of policy.

The decline of natural law thus led to a reconceptualization of judging. After decades of controversy in which lawyers proposed various replacements for natural law as sources of principles for judges to find, the profession eventually rejected all of them in favor of rethinking the judge's role. Thereafter, the judge would be a maker of law, not a finder of law. The judge's opinions would *be* the law, not merely evidence of the law. In deciding hard cases, the judge would weigh the available policy options rather than searching for preexisting principles. With the judge's role reimagined in this way, natural law's absence from the legal system no longer left a gap to fill.

[124] Oliver Wendell Holmes Jr., "The Path of the Law," *Harvard Law Review* 10 (1897): 467.

[125] Roscoe Pound, "The Need of a Sociological Jurisprudence," *Annual Report of the American Bar Association* 30 (1907): 918.

[126] Karl N. Llewellyn, "Some Realism About Realism—Responding to Dean Pound," *Harvard Law Review* 44 (1931): 1254.

[127] Jerome Frank, *Law and the Modern Mind* (1930) (New York: Coward-McCann, 1949), 243.

9

Echoes of Natural Law

For more than a century now, natural law has not been a significant part of the working legal system. Lawyers do not normally rely on it in their arguments. Judges only rarely discuss it in their opinions. It is not usually taught in law schools, except in courses like Jurisprudence or Legal History that are not billed as having any immediate relevance for practicing lawyers. If my experience is typical, most lawyers know very little about natural law other than that there was once a time, long ago, when lawyers considered it important.

But natural law is not completely gone. It survives as a subject of academic inquiry (although in the academic world the term "natural law" means something a bit different today from what it meant to 19th-century lawyers). And in some respects, the working legal system still feels the influence of natural law.

Academic Interest in Natural Law

Natural law never disappeared for long in academic circles. "A few years ago, nothing seemed to be so dead as 'natural law,'" Roscoe Pound observed in 1913. But Pound noted that law professors in France and Germany were once again writing about natural law.[1] A year later Pound told a group of lawyers that a similar interest in natural law had taken hold among law professors in the United States.[2] In his 1922 *Introduction to the Philosophy of Law*, Pound pronounced: "Today . . . we hear of a revival of natural law."[3] Pound had done more than any American law professor to slay the beast of natural law, but it kept coming back to life.

---

[1] Roscoe Pound, book review, *Harvard Law Review* 27 (1913): 191.

[2] Roscoe Pound, *The Judicial Office in the United States* (s.l.: s.n., 1914), 16.

[3] Roscoe Pound, *An Introduction to the Philosophy of Law* (New Haven: Yale Univ. Press, 1922), 56.

The Decline of Natural Law. Stuart Banner, Oxford University Press (2021). © Oxford University Press.
DOI: 10.1093/oso/9780197556498.003.0010

Pound was not the only one to notice that natural law seemed to be constantly reviving among American legal intellectuals familiar with trends in Europe. "Now and then we are told that a revival of the Law of Nature is in process or impending," remarked the Massachusetts lawyer Arthur Spencer, who chalked the development up to "European speculation."[4] The legal philosopher Morris Cohen, who had little patience for theorists of natural law, lamented that "while in this country only old judges and hopelessly antiquated text-book writers still cling to this supposedly eighteenth century doctrine, on the Continent the doctrine of natural law has been revived by advanced jurists of diverse schools, in France, Germany, Belgium, and Italy, and stands forth unabashed and in militant attire."[5] The historian Carl Becker recalled: "Many years ago, when I was still a student, I learned to associate the phrase Natural Law . . . with the eighteenth century." Becker had been taught that "the myth had of course been long since exploded" by scholars who recognized that there was no such thing as natural law. "Having got the subject so conveniently arranged and filed away for ready reference," he joked, "what a nuisance it was years later, to learn that respectable savants were once more dallying with the old heresy, to learn, from so eminent an authority as Dean Pound, that 'a resurrection of the Natural Law is going on the world over.'"[6] Among a relatively small group of American academics and theoretically minded lawyers, interest in natural law persisted.

In the United States, in the first few decades of the 20th century, the study of natural law was kept alive primarily at the law schools affiliated with the Roman Catholic Church, such as Notre Dame, Georgetown, and Fordham.[7] There was a long Catholic natural law tradition going back to Thomas Aquinas. To the extent this tradition was distinctly Catholic, it had not been a significant part of the American legal system in the 18th and 19th centuries, when there was still considerable prejudice against Catholics and few Catholics were among the leaders of the bar. Faculty members at the church-affiliated law schools were nevertheless conscious that by studying natural law, in any form, they were preserving a tradition that had largely disappeared from the legal system. "Only in the Catholic law schools is *natural law*, the basis of all law, properly taught," argued Herbert Noonan of Creighton. William Clarke, the dean of DePaul's law school, agreed that in the legal system, "little short of a repudiation of the natural law is

---

[4] A. W. Spencer, "The Revival of Natural Law," *Central Law Journal* 80 (1915): 346–47.

[5] Morris Cohen, "Jus Naturale Redivivum," *The Philosophical Review* 25 (1916): 761.

[6] Carl Becker, book review, *Yale Law Journal* 41 (1931): 152–53.

[7] See, e.g., Owen A. Hill, "The Natural Law," *Georgetown Law Journal* 13 (1925): 367–72; Charles C. Miltner, "The Progressiveness of Law," *Notre Dame Lawyer* 7 (1932): 421–32; Brendan F. Brown, "Natural Law and the Law-Making Function in American Jurisprudence," *Notre Dame Lawyer* 15 (1939): 9–25.

to be found," and that a Catholic law school was uniquely suited for teaching and writing about natural law.[8] In the prestigious secular law schools like Harvard and Yale, by contrast, natural law was only a tiny part of the intellectual landscape, and among practicing lawyers it was barely noticeable at all.

That changed in the 1930s, when the rise of totalitarian governments in Europe created a sudden burst of interest in natural law among American lawyers and law professors.[9] If there were no natural principles or natural rights, some wondered, on what grounds could the repellent laws of Nazi Germany be criticized? Had the American legal system gone too far in rejecting natural law? "If one asks why, at bottom, retroactivity of penal laws is objectionable," the law professor Jerome Hall suggested, or why "unequal sentences are unjust if applied to like offenders in like circumstances, the answers will inevitably take the form of certain 'first principles.' Once these 'fundamental' values are rejected, no amount of argument carries the slightest weight."[10] After all, another law professor noted during the war, in Poland "It is the jural right of Aryan citizens to heap untold indignities upon those of Polish blood." That was the positive law. And "were an order to be promulgated in Berlin, making citizenship depend upon the killing of a Jew, that, too, would be the law." These shocking results, he concluded, "follow irresistibly from a denial of natural law."[11] Friedrich Kessler, who fled Germany in 1934 and became a law professor at Yale and the University of Chicago, recognized that in trying to understand precisely what was wrong with fascism, "many in their bewilderment turn to natural law in order to find an answer."[12]

Some critics even argued that the rejection of natural law (for which they sometimes mistakenly faulted the legal realists) had contributed to the rise of totalitarianism, by removing one of the main obstacles to its acceptance. This critique was first leveled by Catholic natural law theorists. Francis Lucey of Georgetown Law School insisted that "Realism is being tried out today in Germany and Russia. The Jurisprudence of these countries is the 'Is' Instrumentalism or Pragmatism of the Realist. What works is good. They exclude principles and morals and God from the picture of law." As Lucey saw it, "There is not a single tenet of Realism that these dictatorships do not cherish, adhere to, and try to apply. On the other

[8] William F. Clarke, "The Problem of the Catholic Law School," *University of Detroit Law Journal* 2 (1940): 170–71.

[9] Edward A. Purcell Jr., *The Crisis of Democratic Theory: Scientific Naturalism and the Problem of Value* (Lexington: Univ. Press of Kentucky, 1973), 159–78.

[10] Jerome Hall, "Nulla Poena Sine Lege," *Yale Law Journal* 47 (1937): 192.

[11] Leroy Marceau, "The Relation of Natural to Positive Law," *Notre Dame Lawyer* 18 (1942): 31–32.

[12] Friedrich Kessler, "Natural Law, Justice and Democracy—Some Reflections on Three Types of Thinking About Law and Justice," *Tulane Law Review* 19 (1944): 33.

hand, there is one Jurisprudence they denounce and detest. That Jurisprudence is Natural Law."[13]

The critique soon reached the much larger audience of practicing lawyers. In 1945, the *American Bar Association Journal* published an article with the provocative title "Hobbes, Holmes and Hitler," in which a Minneapolis attorney called Oliver Wendell Holmes a "totalitarian." "If totalitarianism comes to America," he warned, "it will not come with saluting, 'heiling,' marching uniformed men." Rather, it would "come through dominance in the judiciary of men who have accepted a philosophy of law that has its roots in Hobbes and its fruition in implications from the philosophy of Holmes." The positivism of Holmes would lead "straight to the abasement of man before the absolutist state."[14] Fortunately, he concluded, there was an "antidote to totalitarianism. . . . That antidote is to be found, in the judgment of many scholars, in a revival of natural law concepts."[15] Another attorney responded with an article called "Justice Holmes Was Not on a Ladder to Hitler," in which he argued that natural law was so indeterminate that totalitarians could invoke it as plausibly as anyone else.[16] That this debate could take place in the pages of a magazine mailed to all ABA members suggests that many lawyers saw a connection between Nazism and the rejection of natural law. As one of the justices of the Texas Supreme Court observed a few years later, quoting with approval the words of a German author, "Totalitarian regimes are in their very nature the ultimate consequences of the positivist denial of natural law."[17]

Some of the leading realists hastened to defend themselves against the charge that they had abetted the rise of fascism by denigrating natural law. They argued that realism was in fact a partial *return* to natural law, in the sense that realism, like natural law, freed judges from an excessive rule-boundedness and invested them with the authority to reach reasonable outcomes by considering the policy effects of their decisions.[18] Jerome Frank, who had become a federal judge and

---

[13] Francis E. Lucey, "Natural Law and American Legal Realism: Their Respective Contributions to a Theory of Law in a Democratic Society," *Georgetown Law Journal* 30 (1942): 523–24.

[14] Ben W. Palmer, "Hobbes, Holmes and Hitler," *American Bar Association Journal* 31 (1945): 572–73.

[15] Ben W. Palmer, "Defense Against Leviathan," *American Bar Association Journal* 32 (1946): 328.

[16] Charles W. Briggs, "Justice Holmes Was Not on a Ladder to Hitler," *American Bar Association Journal* 32 (1946): 631. Francis Biddle, Holmes's law clerk in 1911–12 and attorney general in the Roosevelt administration, discussed this debate over Holmes in Francis Biddle, *Justice Holmes, Natural Law, and the Supreme Court* (New York: Macmillan, 1961).

[17] Graham B. Smedley, book review, *Texas Law Review* 26 (1948): 836.

[18] Dan Priel and Charles Barzun, "Legal Realism and Natural Law," in Maksymilian Del Mar and Michael Lobban, eds., *Law in Theory and History: New Essays on a Neglected Dialogue* (Oxford: Hart Publishing, 2016), 167–87; Harry W. Jones, "Law and Morality in the Perspective of Legal Realism," *Columbia Law Review* 61 (1961): 799–809; Malcolm P. Sharp, "Realism and Natural Law," *University of Chicago Law Review* 24 (1957): 648–60. For a description of the realist Thurman Arnold as an

thus had an additional reason to temper his former iconoclasm, added a new preface to the reprinting of his realist manifesto *Law and the Modern Mind*. Frank declared: "I do not understand how any decent man today can refuse to adopt, as the basis of modern civilization, the fundamental principles of Natural Law."[19] Soon after becoming a judge, Frank suggested that the "reasonable man" standard used in many legal contexts "was the common law way of taking over the 'Natural Law' concepts of the Roman Law and of Scholastic Jurisprudence." Under either name, he explained, judges could take "policy considerations" into account in ascertaining the law, considerations that "are not static, but grow or decline with shifts in judicial views as to what is socially desirable."[20] During natural law's heyday, as we saw in chapter 1, lawyers equated natural law with reasonableness and common sense. In Frank's view, realist judges did the same.

Karl Llewellyn likewise expressed "wonderment to find any Natural Law man and any so-called realist engaged in pegging brickbats at each other." He thought the two schools had much in common. "Each sees the positive rules and concepts of here and now as present and potent. Each regards them as requiring examination in terms of their effective going value. Each sees one major guide to their evaluation in the service which they prove on examination either to render or not to render to the society which brought them forth." Llewellyn concluded: "It is difficult for me to conceive of the ultimate legal ideals of any of the writers who have been called realists in terms which do not resemble amazingly the type and even the content of the principles of a philosopher's Natural Law."[21] Toward the end of his career, Llewellyn summed up his view of natural law in a way that made it sound quite like his account of realism. Natural law was "the sustained quest for and accounting to the best reason a court can find," he argued. It required "careful and conscious responsibility to the going legal heritage of the society around him, and to its reckonable future ordering." It involved "working out grounds for tomorrow as well as today." It was not "an armchair technique or an arrogant one," but one that "answers instead to current life."[22] If natural law was no more than a policy-sensitive reasonableness, natural law could be understood as an early form of realism.

exponent of natural law, see Edward H. Levi, "The Natural Law, Precedent, and Thurman Arnold," *Virginia Law Review* 24 (1938): 587–612.

[19] Frank, *Law and the Modern Mind*, xvii. Frank was much more skeptical of natural law in Jerome Frank, *Courts on Trial* (1949) (New York: Atheneum, 1963), 346–73.

[20] *Beidler & Bookmyer, Inc. v. Universal Insurance Co.*, 134 F.2d 828, 830 & n.7 (2d Cir. 1943).

[21] Karl N. Llewellyn, "One 'Realist's' View of Natural Law for Judges," *Notre Dame Lawyer* 15 (1939): 7–8.

[22] Karl N. Llewellyn, *The Common Law Tradition: Deciding Appeals* (Boston: Little, Brown, 1960), 422–23.

But there was much more to natural law than just a policy-sensitive reasonableness. In their eagerness to find a similarity between natural law and realism, Frank and Llewellyn were overlooking the differences. Realists did not believe that there were fundamental principles in nature that regulated human affairs, that were placed there by God, and that applied to all people at all times. But the mere fact that some of the realists sought to align themselves with natural law suggests how acutely they felt the criticism that they had contributed in some way to the rise of totalitarianism in Europe.

This renewed interest in natural law lasted for several years after the war ended. There were many articles in law journals seeking to explain the idea of natural law to a legal community that had largely forgotten it.[23] "What is the doctrine of natural law?" asked a New York attorney, introducing one typical effort. "What are its implications for American law and lawyers?"[24] The *American Bar Association Journal* continued to present discussions of natural law to a wide readership of practicing lawyers, in articles with titles like "The Natural Law: Scientific or Supernatural," and "Natural Law: Sense and Nonsense."[25] Scholars in the Catholic natural law tradition wrote pieces for nonspecialists in an effort to dispel what one called "a lot of gobbledygook written about the natural law."[26] This flurry of mainstream interest in natural law eventually petered out by the end of the 1950s, once the need for an intellectual resource to combat Nazism no longer felt so pressing.

The Catholic tradition of natural law scholarship continued throughout the 20th century and into the 21st. In 1949, Notre Dame Law School established a Natural Law Institute, "to explain the meaning of the natural law in terms of actual statutes, actual court decisions, and actual legal principles in our

[23] See, e.g., Robert N. Wilkin, "Status of Natural Law in American Jurisprudence," *Notre Dame Lawyer* 24 (1949): 343–63; Max Radin, "Natural Law and Natural Rights," *Yale Law Journal* 59 (1950): 214–37; Howard I. Forman, "Survey of Natural Law: A Modern Doctrine of Ancient Origin," *Dickinson Law Review* 56 (1951): 100–106; William H. Rose, "The Law of Nature: An Introduction to American Legal Philosophy," *Ohio State Law Journal* 13 (1952): 121–59; Note, "Natural Law for Today's Lawyer," *Stanford Law Review* 9 (1957): 455–514.

[24] Eugene C. Gerhart, "The Doctrine of Natural Law," *N.Y.U. Law Review* 26 (1951): 76–119.

[25] Lawrence S. Apsey, "The Natural Law: Scientific or Supernatural," *American Bar Association Journal* 37 (1951): 35–38; Max C. Peterson, "Natural Law: Sense and Nonsense," *American Bar Association Journal* 37 (1951): 38–39, 68–69; Clarence Manion, "The Founding Fathers and the Natural Law: A Study of the Source of Our Legal Institutions," *American Bar Association Journal* 35 (1949): 461–64, 529–30.

[26] Miriam Theresa Rooney, "Natural Law Gobbledygook," *Loyola Law Review* 5 (1949): 16; David C. Bayne, "The Supreme Court and the Natural Law," *DePaul Law Review* 1 (1952): 216–42; Edward F. Barrett, "The Natural Law and the Lawyer's Search for a Philosophy of Law," *Buffalo Law Review* 4 (1954): 1–19; David C. Bayne, "The Natural Law for Lawyers—a Primer," *DePaul Law Review* 5 (1956): 159–215.

American system," the university's president announced. "It is here fundamentally postulated," he continued, "that the law is not merely what a court says it is; nor that the principles of law must change with changing times. It is here postulated that the controlling principles of law never change."[27] The Natural Law Institute published an annual journal for a few years. After a brief hiatus, the journal was reborn in 1956 as the *Natural Law Forum*. (The journal was renamed in 1968 to widen its coverage. It became the *American Journal of Jurisprudence*.) The Catholic natural law tradition remains as lively as ever.[28]

The term "natural law" also acquired a second meaning in the mid-20th century, one that became the primary sense of the phrase for American philosophers of law outside the Catholic tradition. Under this new definition, "natural law" has come to mean a view of law in which there is no sharp separation between what the law is and what it ought to be, or to put it another way, no sharp separation between law and morality.

This modified definition of natural law seems to have been introduced by the Harvard law professor Lon Fuller in his 1940 book *The Law in Quest of Itself*, which originated as a series of lectures Fuller delivered at Northwestern Law School. His first lecture began by setting out the opposition between positivism and natural law. "By legal positivism," Fuller explained, "I mean that direction of legal thought which insists on drawing a sharp distinction between the law *that is* and the law *that ought to be*." Positivism, Fuller continued, "is associated with a degree of ethical skepticism," in the sense that what the law should be was considered just a matter of personal preference, about which nothing definitive could be said. "Natural law, on the other hand," he asserted, "is the view which denies the possibility of a rigid separation of the *is* and the *ought*, and which tolerates a confusion of them in legal discussion." A proponent of natural law in this sense "draws no hard and fast line between law and ethics." A judge's effort to discern what the law *is* inevitably involves consideration of what the law should be.[29]

Fuller's definition of natural law included some aspects that would have been familiar to American lawyers during the period when natural law was part of the legal system. 19th-century lawyers would have agreed that natural law incorporates ethical considerations. They would have agreed there are times when a judge properly considers what the law should be in determining what it actually is. But Fuller's definition lacked several aspects of natural law that would have been important to 19th-century lawyers. Such lawyers believed that

---

[27] John J. Cavanaugh, "Introduction," *Natural Law Institute Proceedings* 1 (1949): 2.

[28] Prominent examples include John Finnis, *Natural Law and Natural Rights* (Oxford: Clarendon Press, 1980); and Robert P. George, *In Defense of Natural Law* (Oxford: Clarendon Press, 1999).

[29] Lon L. Fuller, *The Law in Quest of Itself* (1940) (Boston: Beacon Press, 1966), 5–6.

the principles governing human affairs were "natural" because they inhered in the nature of human beings, just as the natural laws governing inanimate objects were inherent in the nature of those objects. Fuller's definition was missing this sense that "natural" law was found in nature. Fuller's definition was also missing a set of beliefs common to 19th-century lawyers—most importantly that natural law had been created by God and that natural law was the same at all times and places. From the perspective of an American lawyer circa 1840, Fuller's definition of natural law would only have been half-recognizable.

From the perspective of an American law professor in 1940, by contrast, Fuller's definition was readily understandable. When early 20th-century law professors—including Fuller's predecessors and colleagues at Harvard Law School—criticized natural law, they often argued that the error committed by proponents of natural law was to conflate what the law is with what it ought to be. The law "is not that which is in accordance with religion, or nature, or morality," John Chipman Gray had insisted. "It is not that which ought to be, but that which is."[30] Roscoe Pound had made this point over and over again.[31] By the time Fuller delivered his lectures, perhaps the most common critique of natural law among American lawyers rested on its "confusion of moral and legal rights, a failure to observe the boundary between the field of ethics and the field of political science," as one lawyer put it. Natural law, in this view, was "confusion between the actual law and the law as it ought to be."[32] When Fuller sought to combat what he saw as the errors of positivism, it thus made perfect sense that he would call his position "natural law."

Reviewers of *The Law in Quest of Itself* were nevertheless quite critical of Fuller's redefinition of natural law. Morris Cohen complained of "Professor Fuller's strange definition of positivism and natural law," which he suggested "does violence to the historic meaning of those terms."[33] Huntington Cairns likewise observed that Fuller's "conception of natural law may do some violence, chiefly by way of omission, to certain traditional assertions of its meaning."[34] One law professor noted that Fuller "uses the term in a non-traditional sense," while another thought his argument would have been more persuasive had he

---

[30] Gray, *Nature and Sources*, 92.

[31] Pound, "Scope and Purpose," 605 n. 50; Roscoe Pound, "Interests of Personality," *Harvard Law Review* 28 (1915): 346; Roscoe Pound, "The Theory of Judicial Decision," *Harvard Law Review* 36 (1923): 658.

[32] Edward Clark Lukens, "Prohibition and Nullification," *American Bar Association Journal* 14 (1928): 551.

[33] Morris Cohen, "Should Legal Thought Abandon Clear Distinctions?," *Illinois Law Review* 36 (1941): 244.

[34] Huntington Cairns, book review, *Harvard Law Review* 54 (1940): 158.

avoided the term altogether.[35] Even Fuller eventually conceded that "it is difficult to achieve effective communication in any discussion of a term that bears as
many meanings as does 'natural law.' "[36]

Despite its novelty, however, Fuller's conception of natural law had an enormous influence among American philosophers of law. *The Law in Quest of Itself*
was read and reviewed unusually widely for a book of its kind.[37] Fuller returned
to the topic in a celebrated exchange in the *Harvard Law Review* with the English
legal philosopher H. L. A. Hart, whose riposte to Fuller was titled "Positivism
and the Separation of Law and Morals," a title that further cemented the idea
that "natural law" meant primarily a rejection of the separation of law and
morals.[38] By the 1950s, among American scholars outside the Catholic tradition, and among the small number of lawyers and judges who kept abreast of
academic developments, the phrase "natural law" had become a shorthand for
a particular view about the relationship between law and morality, without the
other attributes of natural law in earlier periods.[39]

That remains true today. As one introduction to natural law explains, according to the "standard account" of the difference between natural law and
positivism, "The two approaches disagree on whether there is a necessary connection between law and morality. Natural law theorists, it is said, argue that
there is a necessary or conceptual connection, while legal positivists deny this
claim."[40] Ronald Dworkin, perhaps the best-known natural law theorist of the
late 20th century in this sense, would not have been considered a natural law
theorist in the 19th century, because his work exhibits few of the characteristics
of 19th-century natural law apart from the view that what the law is depends in
part on what it should be. But as Dworkin acknowledged with evident exasperation, if "any theory which makes the content of law sometimes depend on the

---

[35] Jacob D. Hyman, book review, *Journal of Legal Education* 1 (1948): 316; Edwin W. Patterson,
book review, *Iowa Law Review* 26 (1940): 171.

[36] Lon L. Fuller, "Human Purpose and Natural Law," *Natural Law Forum* 3 (1958): 68.

[37] Robert S. Summers, *Lon L. Fuller* (Stanford: Stanford Univ. Press, 1984), 6.

[38] H. L. A. Hart, "Positivism and the Separation of Law and Morals," *Harvard Law Review* 71
(1958): 593–629; Lon L. Fuller, "Positivism and Fidelity to Law—a Reply to Professor Hart,"
Harvard Law Review 71 (1958): 630–72.

[39] John J. Parker, "Liberty and Law: The Role of Law in a Free Society," *American Bar Association
Journal* 36 (1950): 525; Mark De Wolfe Howe, "The Positivism of Mr. Justice Holmes," *Harvard Law
Review* 64 (1951): 531–32; Helmut Coing, "Tendencies in Modern American Legal Philosophy—a
Survey," *Georgetown Law Journal* 40 (1952): 554.

[40] George Duke and Robert P. George, "Introduction," in George Duke and Robert P. George,
eds., *The Cambridge Companion to Natural Law Jurisprudence* (Cambridge: Cambridge Univ.
Press, 2017), 1. Duke and George go on to criticize this standard account. For another example
stating and criticizing the conventional account, see Lloyd L. Weinreb, *Natural Law and Justice*
(Cambridge: Harvard Univ. Press, 1987), 2–3.

correct answer to some moral question is a natural law theory, then I am guilty of natural law."[41] Some commentators have tried to bring clarity to the term by suggesting that "natural law" refers to both a *legal* theory and a *moral* theory, and that the two theories have no necessary connection with each other. Using this taxonomy, the newer definition popularized by Fuller is natural law as a legal theory, while the older definition that survives primarily in its Catholic variant is the moral theory.[42] But American lawyers who used natural law when it was part of the working legal system would surely have objected to this way of describing natural law. Their understanding of natural law, they would no doubt have said, was different from both.

The Profession's Disregard of Natural Law

These academic discussions of natural law have had few discernable effects on the working legal system. Judges, with but very rare exceptions, have insisted that their role is to consider only positive law, not the law of nature. "Natural law exists outside the constructs of government," explained a Kansas judge in 2016, in a typical expression of this view. "Courts, as creatures of the government, are empowered to construe and apply the rules of the government as expressed in an organic document, legislative enactments, and judicial precedent. They have no license to reach beyond those rules."[43]

For some time now, when litigants have ventured arguments based on natural law, judges have nearly always rejected them. When an Alaskan contended that the state's courts should not follow *Roe v. Wade*, on the ground that "preborn children have natural rights" superior to the constitutional right to abortion recognized in *Roe*, the Alaska Supreme Court had little patience for the argument. "We are bound to follow the text, structure, and binding interpretations of the Constitution," the court briskly held. A court could not "invalidate a recognized constitutional right, regardless of whether that right purportedly conflicts with natural law."[44] In New York, when protesters who blocked access to an abortion clinic claimed that the statute prohibiting their conduct was void because it conflicted with natural law, the judge gave them a stern lecture. "I don't recognize my authority to refuse to issue an injunction under natural law,"

---

[41] Ronald A. Dworkin, "'Natural' Law Revisited," *University of Florida Law Review* 34 (1982): 165.

[42] See, e.g., Philip Soper, "Some Natural Confusions about Natural Law," *University of Michigan Law Review* 90 (1992): 2394–403.

[43] *Hodes & Nauser v. Schmidt*, 368 P.3d 667, 690 (Kans. Ct. App. 2016) (Atcheson, J., concurring).

[44] *DesJarlais v. Office of the Lieutenant Governor*, 300 P.3d 900, 903, 906 (Alaska 2013).

he declared. "This is not a church, this is not a temple, this is not a mosque. And we don't live in a theocracy. This is a court of law."[45]

Indeed, at the US Supreme Court, the primary use of the term "natural law" since the 1940s has been as an insult leveled by dissenters at majority opinions they believed strayed too far from the text of the Constitution. This was a pet rhetorical strategy of Justice Hugo Black. In 1945, for example, the Court held that a state court could exercise jurisdiction over an out-of-state defendant only in circumstances consistent with "traditional notions of fair play and substantial justice." In dissent, Black accused the majority of "superimposing the natural justice concept on the Constitution's specific prohibitions." He complained that "this natural law concept" would make "judges the supreme arbiters of the country's laws and practices."[46] Black repeated the accusation two decades later, when the Court struck down a state law banning the use of contraceptives, in a decision that Black alleged rested on the discredited "natural law due process philosophy" of the *Lochner* era.[47] In another case, Black was so vexed by what he saw as the illicit use of natural law that he added an "Addendum" to his dissenting opinion for the sole purpose of complaining about it. The doctrines elaborated by the Court "represent nothing more or less than an implicit adoption of a Natural Law concept which under our system leaves to judges alone the power to decide what the Natural Law means," he argued. "If the judges, in deciding whether laws are constitutional, are to be left only to the admonitions of their own consciences, why was it that the Founders gave us a written Constitution at all?"[48] On yet another occasion, Black accused the Court of trying "to improve on the Bill of Rights by substituting natural law concepts."[49] Black's colleagues denied these charges. In determining the content of "due process," Justice Felix Frankfurter explained, some consideration of fairness and justice was inevitable. "Due process of law thus conceived is not to be derided as resort to a revival of 'natural law,' " he protested.[50]

Black was not the only Supreme Court justice to use "natural law" as an epithet. In 1999, when the Court held that Congress could not subject states to suits in their own courts, Justice David Souter accused the majority of basing the decision on "natural law, a universally applicable proposition discoverable by reason." Justice Anthony Kennedy defended the Court against this grave

---

[45] Quoted in *United States v. Lynch*, 104 F.3d 357, *2 (2d Cir. 1996).

[46] *International Shoe Co. v. Washington*, 326 U.S. 310, 325–26 (1945) (separate opinion of Black, J.).

[47] *Griswold v. Connecticut*, 381 U.S. 479, 515 (1965) (Black, J., dissenting).

[48] *Sniadach v. Family Finance Corp.*, 395 U.S. 337, 350–51 (1969) (Black, J., dissenting).

[49] *Adamson v. California*, 332 U.S. 46, 90 (1947) (Black, J., dissenting).

[50] *Rochin v. California*, 342 U.S. 165, 171 (1952).

insult. "The dissent attributes our reasoning to natural law," he complained. "We seek to discover, however, only what the Framers and those who ratified the Constitution sought to accomplish when they created a federal system. We appeal to no higher authority than the Charter which they wrote and adopted."[51] The following year, when the Court held that the Due Process Clause includes a "fundamental right of parents to make decisions concerning the care, custody, and control of their children," Justice Antonin Scalia criticized the majority for arriving at a conclusion reachable only via natural law, which was no business for judges. "In my view," he explained, "a right of parents to direct the upbringing of their children is among the 'unalienable Rights' with which the Declaration of Independence proclaims 'all men . . . are endowed by their Creator.'" But the Declaration of Independence conferred no authority on the courts to enforce natural law, he continued. Judges could enforce only the rights enumerated in the Constitution. "Consequently, while I would think it entirely compatible with the commitment to representative democracy set forth in the founding documents to argue, in legislative chambers or in electoral campaigns, that the State has *no power* to interfere with parents' authority over the rearing of their children," he concluded, "I do not believe that the power which the Constitution confers upon me *as a judge* entitles me to deny legal effect to laws that (in my view) infringe upon what is (in my view) that unenumerated right."[52] The justices in the majority did not respond directly to Scalia's critique, but it is clear that they did not believe themselves to be relying on natural law.

Were Justice Black and like-minded critics correct when they accused the Court of surreptitiously relying on natural law? If one means natural law as it was used in the 18th and 19th centuries, the critics were not correct. To pick just one example from the cases discussed above, when the Court held in *Griswold v. Connecticut* that the Constitution bars a state from prohibiting the use of contraceptives by married couples, the Court did not assert that a right to use contraceptives exists in nature, or that such a right was created by God, or that the right exists at all times and places. The notion of unchanging rights inherent in the very nature of human beings would have been hard to reconcile with the view that constitutional rights should evolve to keep up with changing social conditions, which was the constitutional philosophy underlying the Court's famous mid-century law-changing cases, such as *Griswold*, *Brown v. Board of Education*, *Miranda v. Arizona*, and *Roe v. Wade*.[53] The concept

---

[51] *Alden v. Maine*, 527 U.S. 706, 762, 758 (1999).

[52] *Troxel v. Granville*, 530 U.S. 57, 66, 91–92 (2000).

[53] Hard to reconcile, but not impossible. If a natural right were pitched at a sufficiently high level of generality—as "liberty," for example, rather than marital privacy—it would have been possible to argue that the right itself was unchanging even if particular instances of the right changed to keep up with social conditions. But this was not the strategy chosen in *Griswold* and similar cases.

of a "living Constitution" was, in this respect, the very opposite of natural law. In *Griswold*, the Court thus did not look to nature for any eternal world-wide principles. Rather, the Court looked to the text of several constitutional provisions, from which it inferred a right of marital privacy, the substance of which depended heavily on the living arrangements of middle-class married couples in the contemporary United States. If the justices in the *Griswold* majority were asked whether there had been an identical right of marital privacy five thousand years earlier, or whether such a right existed in a country with a differently worded and differently interpreted constitution, the answer would surely have been no.

On the other hand, Black was not entirely wrong in hearing echoes of natural law in the style in which *Griswold* and similar opinions were written. Black and like-minded critics objected to what they perceived as the subjectivity of these decisions. If judges were unconstrained by the text of the Constitution, they worried, judges could adopt whatever view of the law best suited their own personal senses of justice. This had also been one of the main criticisms of natural law in the late 19th century—that the use of natural law gave too much policymaking discretion to judges, whose understanding of natural law would mirror their own preferences. In *Griswold*, when Justice William Douglas's opinion for the Court predicted that a law forbidding the use of contraceptives would have "a maximum destructive impact" upon marital relationships, and when Douglas warned that barring contraceptives would "allow the police to search the sacred precincts of marital bedrooms," Black bristled at what sounded like more like political argument than legal reasoning.[54] His concern was not really that Douglas was invoking natural law, but rather that Douglas was engaging in the style of policy-based argument that had sometimes accompanied the use of natural law in an earlier era.

More recent critics of so-called "natural law" have followed Black in using the phrase to attack a reasoning style they believe gives judges too much power to make policy. Robert Bork, for example, praised Black for repeatedly dissenting from this "natural law method of making up rights." But Bork was not concerned with natural law. He was concerned with constraining liberal judges. "I want judges to be confined by the law, not make it up," he declared. "I believe in interpreting it, not creating it."[55] The use of "natural law" as a pejorative term in constitutional argument has really been a shorthand way of objecting to interpretive methods that the critic believes gives judges too much leeway. It has little

---

[54] *Griswold*, 381 U.S. at 485–86.

[55] *Nomination of Robert H. Bork to be Associate Justice of the Supreme Court of the United States: Hearings Before the U.S. Senate Committee on the Judiciary* (Washington, DC: Government Printing Office, 1989), 820.

to do with natural law in the sense in which the term was used in the 18th and 19th centuries.

To be sure, judges of our own era do sometimes write opinions in a broad first-principles style reminiscent of that used by judges centuries ago who were relying on natural law. Consider this passage from an opinion of the US Supreme Court: "At the heart of liberty is the right to define one's own concept of existence, of meaning, of the universe, and of the mystery of human life." Or this one, describing pregnancy and childbirth: "These sacrifices have from the beginning of the human race been endured by woman with a pride that ennobles her in the eyes of others and gives to the infant a bond of love." This sort of reasoning about the nature of liberty and childbirth would not have been out of place in a 19th-century opinion discussing natural law. But these passages are from *Planned Parenthood v. Casey*, the 1992 case in which the Supreme Court reaffirmed that in certain circumstances the "liberty" mentioned in the Fourteenth Amendment's Due Process Clause includes a right to have an abortion.[56] In dissent, Justice Antonin Scalia was sharply critical of this type of first-principles reasoning. The issue in the case, he insisted, was "not whether the power of a woman to abort her unborn child is a 'liberty' in the absolute sense." Scalia conceded that the freedom to have an abortion was part of liberty in the abstract. Rather, "The issue is whether it is a liberty protected by the Constitution," and Scalia was certain that it was not, because "longstanding traditions of American society have permitted it to be legally proscribed."[57] As Scalia seems to have recognized, if there was a fault in the majority opinion, it was not that the majority was relying on natural law, but rather that the majority had adopted a faulty method of interpreting positive law—in this case, the word "liberty" in the Due Process Clause.

A similar debate took place in *Obergefell v. Hodges*, the 2015 case in which the Court held that the Fourteenth Amendment's guarantee of "liberty" likewise encompasses same-sex marriage. Throughout his majority opinion, Justice Anthony Kennedy expounded on the nature of marriage. "The lifelong union of a man and a woman always has promised nobility and dignity to all persons," he averred. "Marriage is sacred to those who live by their religions and offers unique fulfillment to those who find meaning in the secular realm. Its dynamic allows two people to find a life that could not be found alone, for a marriage becomes greater than just the two persons. Rising from the most basic human needs, marriage is essential to our most profound hopes and aspirations." Interpreting the Constitution to require states to allow same-sex marriage,

---

[56] *Planned Parenthood v. Casey*, 505 U.S. 833, 851–52 (1992).

[57] *Id.* at 980 (Scalia, J., concurring in the judgment in part and dissenting in part).

Kennedy concluded, "furthers our understanding of what freedom is and must become."[58] Although the outcome of the case would have astonished lawyers of the 19th century, the opinion's reasoning style would not have struck them as unusual. In using natural law to fill gaps in the positive law, a judge was supposed to draw conclusions from human nature.

In its own era, however, Kennedy's reasoning did strike many lawyers as unusual. One of them was Chief Justice John Roberts, who chided the majority for confusing its "own preferences with the requirements of the law," by resolving the case "based not on neutral principles of constitutional law, but on its own 'understanding of what freedom is and must become.'" Roberts accused Kennedy of treating the case "as a matter of moral philosophy" rather than of law.[59] Scalia offered similar criticism, more sharply. Kennedy's "opinion is couched in a style that is as pretentious as its content is egotistic," Scalia complained. "The Supreme Court of the United States has descended from the disciplined legal reasoning of John Marshall and Joseph Story to the mystical aphorisms of the fortune cookie." If he even had to join such an opinion, Scalia smirked, "I would hide my head in a bag."[60] Scalia was in part complaining about Kennedy's writing style, not without cause, but his objection was broader than that. He was also objecting to Kennedy's adoption of a style of reasoning that allowed him to engage in these philosophical discussions about the nature of human relationships.

When the Court decided *Obergefell*, and then again three years later when Kennedy retired, lawyers often remarked on the opinion's unusual style. Many suggested that in discussing at length the nature and importance of marriage, without reference to positive law, Kennedy seemed to have intended the opinion to be read and understood by nonlawyers. But Kennedy was also a man keenly aware of his place in the history of the Supreme Court. In major cases like *Obergefell*, Kennedy sometimes adopted a judicial voice more characteristic of earlier eras than of his own, perhaps in an effort to live up to what he considered the high standards of his predecessors. For a reader familiar with the use of natural law in the 18th and 19th centuries, the style of *Obergefell* felt less like an attempt to communicate with nonlawyers than like an attempt to imitate the great judges of the past, judges for whom natural law reasoning was part of the job.

Casey and *Obergefell* are examples in which this style was used to support arguments more welcome to the Left than to the Right, but there is no inherent political slant to the use of a reasoning style reminiscent of the era of natural law. The style has been used by judges of both political parties, to reach outcomes amenable to both sides of the aisle. In a 1976 Supreme Court opinion written

---

[58] *Obergefell v. Hodges*, 135 S. Ct. 2584, 2594, 2603 (2015).

[59] *Id.* at 2612, 2621 (Roberts, C.J., dissenting).

[60] *Id.* at 2630 & n.22 (Scalia, J., dissenting).

by Justice William Rehnquist, for example, the Court decided that Congress lacks the power to regulate the wages and hours of state government employees. Rehnquist did not reach this conclusion by a close reading of the text of the Constitution, which authorizes Congress to regulate interstate commerce but says nothing about whether state employees are exempt. Instead, Rehnquist reasoned from the nature of state sovereignty. "There are attributes of sovereignty attaching to every state government," he posited. "One undoubted attribute of state sovereignty is the States' power to determine the wages which shall be paid to those whom they employ in order to carry out their governmental functions, what hours those persons will work, and what compensation will be provided where these employees may be called upon to work overtime."[61] In dissent, Justice William Brennan criticized Rehnquist for having "manufactured an abstraction without substance, founded neither in the words of the Constitution nor on precedent."[62] The harder it is to support a decision based on the strict text of the positive law, the more likely a judge—of any political stripe—is to engage in a reasoning style reminiscent of an earlier era in which judges were supposed to consider natural law.

But the use of a broad policy-based mode of reasoning is not the same as reliance on natural law. Judges like Kennedy and Rehnquist understood their task as limited to the interpretation of positive law. They would no doubt have recoiled from the suggestion that they should look to nature for universal principles and use such principles to interpret positive law.

In recent decades, the term *natural law* has played an explicit role in court decisions in only one narrow circumstance, and even here the relevant consideration is what lawyers of the 18th century thought was natural law, not what anyone today thinks it is. As we saw in chapter 3, several constitutional provisions were understood, at the time of their ratification, to declare preexisting natural rights rather than to create new rights. This fact can be important for judges who employ the originalist method of interpreting the Constitution, because in determining the meaning of such provisions, one might need to know the contours of these preexisting natural rights. In the 2008 case *District of Columbia v. Heller*, for example, the Supreme Court had to decide whether the Second Amendment protects an individual's right to bear arms, without any connection to a militia. Justice Scalia's opinion for the Court surveyed some 18th-century sources and concluded that the Second Amendment, when ratified, was understood to codify a preexisting natural right to bear arms for self-defense, not just for militia

---

[61] *National League of Cities v. Usery*, 426 U.S. 833, 845 (1976).
[62] *Id.* at 860 (Brennan, J., dissenting).

service.[63] But this originalist use of *18th-century* natural law is far removed from the claim that *present-day* natural law has any relevance for judges.

The consensus of lawyers and judges that natural law should play no role in the legal system was on vivid display at the 1991 confirmation hearings of Clarence Thomas to be a justice of the US Supreme Court. In the 1980s, while he was chair of the Equal Employment Opportunity Commission, Thomas had given speeches and written articles advocating the use of natural law. "Natural rights and higher law arguments are the best defense of liberty and of limited government," he wrote in 1989. "Higher law is the only alternative to the willfulness of both run-amok majorities and run-amok judges." He suggested that the Court's opinion in *Brown v. Board of Education* would have been stronger had it relied on natural law.[64] In another article, Thomas discussed "the 'higher-law' background of the Constitution" and criticized "the cynical rejection of 'the laws of nature and of nature's God' from jurisprudence."[65] In a speech at the Heritage Foundation, Thomas urged a reinvigoration of the use of natural law. He praised a recent article by Lewis Lehrman arguing that abortion and slavery were both contrary to natural law.[66] It had been a very long time since a nominee for the Supreme Court had expressed such positive views about natural law.

It is often said that judicial confirmation hearings are a form of theater. If so, one of the things being performed is the legal profession's sense of what is inside, and what is outside, the boundaries of permissible legal argument. At Thomas's hearings, several Democratic senators objected to what seemed like his view that natural law should play an explicit role in judicial decisions. "You come before this committee," Joseph Biden observed, "with a philosophy different from that which we have seen in any Supreme Court nominee in the 19 years since I have been in the Senate. For as has been widely discussed and debated in the press, you are an adherent to the view that natural law philosophy should inform the Constitution." Patrick Leahy complained that "natural law, we all know, is an elastic concept. It can be used to defend but also to deny basic rights." Herbert Kohl worried that Thomas might "overturn rulings which you believe conflict

[63] *District of Columbia v. Heller*, 554 U.S. 570, 592–95 (2008).

[64] Clarence Thomas, "The Higher Law Background of the Privileges or Immunities Clause of the Fourteenth Amendment," *Harvard Journal of Law & Public Policy* 12 (1989): 63–64, 68.

[65] Clarence Thomas, "Toward a 'Plain Reading' of the Constitution—the Declaration of Independence in Constitutional Interpretation," *Howard Law Journal* 30 (1987): 993, 995.

[66] Clarence Thomas, "Why Black Americans Should Look to Conservative Policies" (1987), https://www.heritage.org/political-process/report/why-black-americans-should-look-conservative-policies; Lewis E. Lehrman, "The Right to Life and the Restoration of the American Republic" (1986), https://www.crisismagazine.com/1986/the-right-to-life-and-the-restoration-of-the-american-republic.

with natural law principles."[67] Members of the Senate Judiciary Committee were likely concerned less with the use of natural law in the abstract than with the results they expected Thomas to reach by applying natural law in particular cases, especially abortion cases. And their views of natural law were not well informed. "One of the more curious displays of cultural illiteracy has been the consternation and bafflement created by Judge Clarence Thomas's expressions of esteem for 'natural law,'" noted the *New York Times*. "For some of the critics of the nominee to the Supreme Court, it was as though the man had let slip a reference to torture by thumbscrews. Others squinted as though Judge Thomas had discussed an obscure and probably sinister belief in alchemy."[68] The *Chicago Tribune* agreed that "from their reaction you would think they had found him at the airport in a Hare Krishna robe."[69] It was nevertheless understandable that people familiar with the legal system would be unfamiliar with the concept of natural law, because nearly a century had passed since judges discussed natural law while deciding cases.

Clarence Thomas played his assigned role in the ritual delineation of the bounds of acceptable legal discourse. He agreed with his critics that natural law formed no part of the work of a judge, and he denied any intention to use natural law on the Supreme Court. "I don't see a role for the use of natural law in constitutional adjudication," Thomas explained. "My interest in exploring natural law and natural rights was purely in the context of political theory." He had discussed natural law "as a part-time political theorist," not as a judge. "The Constitution is our law," Thomas assured the Senate. "My job is to uphold the Constitution of the United States, not personal philosophy or political theories."[70] Whether or not Thomas was accurately reporting his past views, the episode underscored the prevailing sense of the legal profession that judges had no business relying on natural law. Everyone understood that if one hoped to become a Supreme Court justice, it was prudent to disclaim any practical interest in natural law. In his long tenure on the Court, Justice Thomas has been true to his word. As promised, he has not invoked natural law as the basis for any of his opinions.

A mirror image of this colloquy, but one with a similar endpoint, took place during Elena Kagan's confirmation hearings in 2010. Kagan had not written about natural law at any point during her career. Natural law was nevertheless on the mind of Republican senator Tom Coburn, a proponent of gun rights, because of the *Heller* decision two years earlier. Kagan was nominated to replace

---

[67] *Nomination of Judge Clarence Thomas to be Associate Justice of the Supreme Court of the United States* (Washington, DC: Government Printing Office, 1994), 2, 54, 81.

[68] *New York Times*, 17 Aug. 1991, 9.

[69] *Chicago Tribune*, 18 July 1991, 27.

[70] *Nomination of Judge Clarence Thomas*, 112, 116, 171.

Justice John Paul Stevens, who had dissented in *Heller*, so the Court's broad interpretation of the Second Amendment was not at immediate risk, but Coburn was sufficiently concerned to ask Kagan whether she believed that "it is a fundamental preexisting right to have an arm to defend yourself." When Kagan responded by explaining, "I accept *Heller*," Coburn persisted. "I'm not asking you about your judicial—I'm asking you, Elena Kagan, do you personally believe there is a fundamental right in this area?" he sputtered. "Do you agree with Blackstone that the natural right of resistance and self-preservation, the right of having and using arms for self-preservation and defense?" Kagan responded just as Clarence Thomas had two decades earlier, by affirming the conventional professional view that natural law was irrelevant to the work of a judge. "Senator Coburn, to be honest with you," she said, "I don't have a view of what are natural rights, independent of the Constitution. And my job as a justice will be to enforce and defend the Constitution and other laws of the United States." When Coburn asked yet another version of his question, Kagan gave another version of her answer. "I'm not saying I do not believe that there are rights preexisting the Constitution and the laws," she explained, "but my job as a justice is to enforce the Constitution and the laws."[71]

For Kagan, as for Thomas, natural law could be part of a judge's personal beliefs, but it could not be part of a judge's professional role. On neither end of the political spectrum was there much support for reintroducing natural law into the working legal system. As the federal judge Diarmuid O'Scannlain recognized, Kagan's "agnosticism about natural rights reflects the mainstream of contemporary legal thinking."[72]

In light of this professional consensus against the use of natural law in the legal system, in modern times it has taken an unusual judge to embrace natural law as a basis for a court's decision. One such judge was Roy Moore, the chief justice of the Alabama Supreme Court for two brief periods in the early 21st century. In 2002, Moore wrote an opinion arguing that gay parents should never have custody of their own children, because "homosexual conduct is, and has been, considered abhorrent, immoral, detestable, a crime against nature, and a violation of the laws of nature and of nature's God upon which this Nation and our laws are predicated."[73] None of Moore's colleagues joined his opinion. He was removed from office the following year for refusing to comply with a federal court order to relocate a marble monument of the Ten Commandments he

---

[71] *The Nomination of Elena Kagan to be an Associate Justice of the Supreme Court of the United States: Hearing Before the Committee on the Judiciary, U.S. Senate,* 111th Cong., 2d Sess. (2010), 284.

[72] Diarmuid F. O'Scannlain, "The Natural Law in the American Tradition," *Fordham Law Review* 79 (2011): 1514.

[73] Ex parte *H.H.,* 830 So. 2d 21, 26 (Ala. 2002) (Moore, C.J., concurring specially).

had installed in the courthouse. Moore was removed from the chief justiceship a second time in 2017, after he persisted in directing state employees to deny marriage licenses to same-sex couples in defiance of the US Supreme Court's decision in *Obergefell v. Hodges*. He would not follow *Obergefell*, Moore explained, because it was contrary to "the natural order God has created," an order that included "the institution of marriage as the union of a man and a woman."[74]

Moore asserted that these decisions were supported by natural law. "Natural law forms the basis of the common law," he reasoned. "Natural law is the law of nature and of nature's God as understood by men through reason, but aided by direct revelation found in the Holy Scriptures."[75] General statements like these had been commonplace two centuries earlier, although they were vanishingly rare among judges of Moore's own era. But Moore advanced a decidedly nontraditional view of how natural law worked within the legal system. His 19th-century predecessors would hardly have agreed that a judge's view of natural law authorized him to flout the rulings of a higher court. When natural law was part of the working legal system, no judge understood it as a license to privilege his own moral views over the positive law. Moore was an unorthodox judge for his era simply in claiming that a judge should take natural law into account, but his understanding of natural law would have been unorthodox in any era.

Echoes of Natural Law

Despite the expulsion of natural law from the explicit discourse of the American legal system, natural law has continued to exert some influence. American lawyers and judges do not expressly rely on natural law by name, but in some areas they still make arguments reminiscent of natural law arguments, because of the position natural law once occupied within American legal thought.

The international law concept of "human rights," for example, which rose to prominence in the second half of the 20th century, has strong echoes of the natural law tradition.[76] Human rights are often understood as rights that exist simply by virtue of being human, even where they are not conferred by, or indeed are contrary to, the positive law of the nation in which the person claiming the right lives. Human rights need not be grounded on natural law. They can be found in international agreements or in the customary practices of nations. But

---

[74] Ex parte *State ex rel. Alabama Policy Institute*, 200 So. 3d 495, 569 (2016) (Moore, C.J., concurring specially).

[75] Ex parte *H.H.*, 830 So. 2d at 32.

[76] Samuel Moyn, *The Last Utopia: Human Rights in History* (Cambridge: Harvard Univ. Press, 2010).

the very idea of a *human* right, as distinct from a treaty-based or customary right, carries a strong flavor of natural law.

That flavor comes from the history of international law, which was always the area in which natural law was most prominent, because of the absence of international legislatures capable of generating positive law. Indeed, the decline of natural law caused some early 20th-century lawyers to wonder whether international law could survive without it. International law "is based upon a political theory which has long been discarded by political scientists," worried the eminent law librarian Frederick Charles Hicks. "There is no such thing as a law of nature which may be treated as a positive code."[77] The German-born English law professor Lassa Oppenheim agreed that "we are now-a-days no longer justified in teaching a law of nature and a 'natural' law of nations."[78] When the law of nature was discarded, what was left of international law? "We very much wish that some one would inform us what international law is anyway," one lawyer joked. "The very term is misleading."[79] Specialists hastened to explain that there *was* still something to international law.[80] But some lawyers would continue to harbor doubts, right up through the present, about whether international law was really *law*, once its natural law basis had been replaced by the positivist sensibility that permeates the profession.[81]

The constitutional protection of property rights also continues to be influenced by the former status of natural law within the legal system. Property was once understood as a paradigmatic natural right. The state and federal constitutions protected property, but they did not create it; property was understood to exist anterior to, and independent of, the constitutional provisions that shielded it from government encroachment. Property was found in nature, not created by law. When lawyers stopped using natural law, they were left with a puzzle. If natural rights were no longer cognizable in court, and if property was therefore entirely a creature of positive law, how could any particular positive law infringe the right of property? A property owner's rights would always be defined by the positive law in effect at any given time. To base property rights entirely on positive law thus threatened to nullify the constitutional provisions that protected property. But could that prospect be averted by any means other than

[77] Frederick Charles Hicks, "The Equality of States and the Hague Conferences," *American Journal of International Law* 2 (1908): 532.

[78] L. Oppenheim, "The Science of International Law: Its Task and Method," *American Journal of International Law* 2 (1908): 328.

[79] "International Law?," *American Lawyer* 8 (1900): 389.

[80] Stephen C. Neff, *Justice Among Nations: A History of International Law* (Cambridge: Harvard Univ. Press, 2014), 221–59.

[81] Anthony D'Amato, "Is International Law Really 'Law'?," *Northwestern University Law Review* 79 (1985): 1293–1314.

reviving the view that property is a natural right? The courts have never been able to develop a satisfying answer to this dilemma, because it is a genuine dilemma.[82] Instead, they have swept the problem under the carpet, by identifying assets as "property" based on their own intuitions as to what property looks like, regardless of the content of positive law. For example, when Florida law defined the interest on certain court-managed bank accounts as owned by the state rather than by the owners of the principal, the US Supreme Court rejected that characterization. The Court insisted that "a State, by *ipse dixit*, may not transform private property into public property."[83] In cases like these, courts do not use the term "natural law," but they use the method of reasoning that courts used in the era when they applied natural law. In the Florida case, for instance, the Court decided that the owner of principal owns the interest, although there was no positive law requiring that outcome. The decision was based on the nature—or less charitably, on the justices' perception of the nature—of interest on bank accounts.

A similar dilemma arose in the 2017 case *Nelson v. Colorado*, when the Supreme Court confronted a Colorado statute that in most circumstances prevented criminal defendants whose convictions had been reversed from recovering the fines and fees they had paid to the state. Colorado argued, with some justification, that under the state's positive law, the money belonged to the state, not to the defendant. But the Court rejected the argument. Once a conviction had been reversed, the Court held, the fines and fees were once more the property of the defendant, so the state had to provide an adequate procedure for refunding them. This conclusion certainly made intuitive sense, but there was no positive law that said this money belonged to the defendant. In the 19th century, a court might have determined that under natural law, money paid as a fine reverts to the defendant when a conviction is reversed. But that method of resolving the case is no longer available. All the Court could do was to assert that the money belonged to the defendant despite state law to the contrary.[84]

Further echoes of natural law can be heard when courts interpret statutes. Lawyers are familiar with "canons of construction," rules of thumb to apply when the meaning of a statute is not clear.[85] Where do these canons come from? Today they are found in prior court opinions, which are cited as precedent to support the canons' existence, but where did the judges who wrote these prior

---

[82] Thomas W. Merrill, "The Landscape of Constitutional Property," *Virginia Law Review* 86 (2000): 885–999.

[83] *Webb's Fabulous Pharmacies v. Beckwith*, 449 U.S. 155, 164 (1980).

[84] *Nelson v. Colorado*, 137 S. Ct. 1249 (2017). I was Nelson's counsel.

[85] Amy Coney Barrett, "Substantive Canons and Faithful Agency," *Boston University Law Review* 90 (2010): 109–82.

court opinions find them? In the past, what we now call canons of construction were often said to be principles of natural law.

For example, statutes are presumed not to apply retroactively to conduct that antedated the statutes' enactment, while the common law *is* presumed to apply retroactively to conduct that antedated the common law's declaration by a court, including the conduct of the parties before the court. That statutes should not apply retroactively was once an often-cited principle of natural law.[86] It was a "principle of natural justice," the New York Supreme Court noted in 1851, "that a statute shall not have a retrospective effect."[87] As a Massachusetts lawyer put it, "Retrospective laws are repugnant to natural justice."[88] Today, the presumed nonretroactivity of statutes is accepted as a background principle of the legal system, but it is no longer said to be a *natural* principle.

The presumed retroactivity of the common law is likewise a holdover from the era of natural law. Today, when we believe that judges make and even change the common law in their decisions, applying a court decision retroactively seems just as unfair as applying a statute retroactively. In either case, one might wonder, how are people supposed to conform their conduct to a rule that does not yet exist? The answer is that in the official discourse of the legal system judges are still said to find the law rather than to make it. "Judicial declaration of the law," one judge has explained, is treated as "merely a statement of what the law has always been."[89] This view is now understood as a fiction, but two centuries ago it was understood as a fact. When lawyers believed that the common law was based on natural law, it made sense for common law to apply retroactively. The law of nature certainly antedated the conduct of the parties before the court. It had always existed. And the law of nature could be discerned by any reasoning human being. No specialized knowledge was required. There was thus nothing unfair about applying the common law retroactively.

Another canon of construction presumes that a person cannot be convicted of a crime unless he has an evil intent. This presumption also began as a principle of natural law. One Missouri court, for instance, referred to "the universality of the natural law which deems no one to merit punishment unless he intended evil."[90] Courts still invoke this principle to read a requirement of intent into criminal statutes that do not expressly mention intent. For instance, the Supreme Court recently considered a statute that made it a crime to transmit a threat to

[86] R. H. Helmholz, *Natural Law in Court: A History of Legal Theory in Practice* (Cambridge: Harvard Univ. Press, 2015), 144.

[87] *Wilson v. Baptist Education Society of New York*, 10 Barb. 308, 312 (N.Y. Sup. Ct. 1851).

[88] *Foster v. Essex Bank*, 16 Mass. 245, 252 (1819).

[89] *Cash v. Califano*, 621 F.2d 626, 628 (4th Cir. 1980).

[90] *State v. Reilly*, 4 Mo. App. 392, 397 (Mo. Ct. App. 1877).

injure another person. The defendant argued that despite the menacing tone of his words, he had not intended to threaten anyone—he was merely an aspiring rap artist who intended his violent lyrics as art. The statute did not say that the defendant had to intend his words to be a threat. The statute included no requirement of a mental state at all. The Court nevertheless concluded that some culpable mental state was a requirement, based not on the text of the statute but on the background principle that "wrongdoing must be conscious to be criminal."[91] To show that this truly was a background principle undergirding the criminal law, the Court cited several of its prior opinions applying the principle. Two centuries ago, the Court would likely have discussed it as a principle found in nature. But lawyers no longer think of this presumption as a doctrine of natural law. It is just another of those background principles, to be found in musty old cases.

The origin of these canons of construction is no longer an important practical question for lawyers, who, to the extent they think about the matter at all, can assume that statutes are drafted by people who are aware that their words will be interpreted in light of the canons, and thus that by invoking the canons they are implementing the legislature's intent.[92] But in using the canons, today's lawyers are unwittingly following presumptions that were once considered natural principles.

We can also find a lingering influence of natural law in the many substantive doctrines of American law that, although now existing by virtue of positive law, were once understood as natural principles. The right to use force in self-defense when one is attacked, for example, is part of the positive law of every state. Washington, for example, has a statute declaring that is lawful to use force against another person "by a party about to be injured . . . in preventing or attempting to prevent an offense against his or her person."[93] Two centuries ago, lawyers called self-defense a natural right that would exist even in the absence of any positive law authorizing it.[94] The positive law of every state likewise requires parents to support their young children. This too was once considered a principle of natural law.[95] Our law today includes many rules that lawyers once

---

[91] *Elonis v. United States*, 135 S. Ct. 2001, 2009 (2015) (quoting *Morissette v. United States*, 342 U.S. 246, 252 (1952)).

[92] On the doubtfulness of this assumption, see Abbe R. Gluck and Lisa Schultz Bressman, "Statutory Interpretation from the Inside: An Empirical Study of Congressional Drafting, Delegation, and the Canons," *Stanford Law Review* 65 (2013): 901–1025; *Stanford Law Review* 66 (2014): 725–801.

[93] Wash. Rev. Code § 9A.16.020(3).

[94] *Gray v. Combs*, 30 Ky. 478, 481 (1832); *Russell v. Barrow*, 7 Port. 106, 109 (Ala. 1838); *McPherson v. State*, 29 Ark. 225, 233–34 (1874).

[95] *Stanton v. Willson*, 3 Day 37, 41, 51 (Conn. 1808).

classified as rules of natural law, but we no longer think of them that way. The substance of the law has not changed, but our perception of the source of the law is completely different.

Finally, and perhaps most fundamentally, natural law lingers on in the voice lawyers and judges adopt in their professional lives. While making arguments or writing opinions, they speak as if judges find the law, while in their hearts they believe that judges make it. (There are some law professors who still defend the view that judges find the law, but, as one of their number acknowledges, "Suffice it to say that this view is not in vogue.")[96] This is an aspect of lawyers' daily existence that is both familiar and exceedingly strange. In their public-facing professional discourse, when addressing courts or deciding cases, lawyers and judges speak as if judges merely apply preexisting law to decide cases, as if judging involved nothing more than looking up the appropriate rule in a book. By contrast, when talking candidly among themselves, lawyers say that judges often make law where none existed before. This tension is one of the lessons absorbed by law students, who learn very quickly that there can be a big difference between what a judge *says* and what a judge *does*. The divergence between these two accounts of judging is on stark display every time the Senate considers the appointment of a new Supreme Court justice, when all concerned will piously declare that a judge should never make law while they work furiously to ensure that the appointee is someone who will make law to their liking. Justice Antonin Scalia described this odd situation particularly well, in an unusually candid opinion that I have already quoted but which deserves a reprise. He acknowledged that "judges in a real sense 'make' law. But they make it *as judges make it*, which is to say *as though* they were 'finding' it—discerning what the law *is*, rather than decreeing what it is today *changed to*, or what it will *tomorrow* be."[97] This difference between what lawyers say and what they think is a holdover from an era in which lawyers really did believe that judges found the law. They would gradually stop believing this, but the official discourse of the legal system did not change accordingly.

A Different Route to the Same End

As these examples suggest, the shift away from natural law was one of method rather than results. Any substantive rule that could be reached via natural law could also be reached without it. The substance of the law of course changed considerably between 1800 and 1950, but it would be wrong to attribute any

---

[96] Stephen E. Sachs, "Finding Law," *California Law Review* 107 (2019): 529.

[97] *James B. Beam Distilling Co. v. Georgia*, 501 U.S. 529, 549 (1991) (Scalia, J., concurring in the judgment).

of these substantive changes to the abandonment of natural law. They would almost certainly have taken place even if natural law had continued to play a role in the working legal system.

An extended example may help to illustrate this point. Two centuries ago, perhaps the most common use of natural law in the course of deciding cases was to fill in the gaps where positive law ran out. When no statutes or precedents applied, natural law provided a reservoir of principles. It was often said, as the North Carolina Supreme Court put it in 1823, that "where the positive laws are silent, all Courts must determine on maxims of natural justice, dictated by reason; that is, according to the law of nature."[98]

Today there are still cases where positive law runs out—probably a smaller percentage, because there is so much more positive law, but still some. Judges must still reach a decision in these cases. Today we describe what judges do in such cases as interstitial lawmaking, in the gaps where no law yet exists. We say that judges reach the result that represents the most reasonable policy. But if one ignores the label and looks closely at what judges are doing, their method of deciding these cases is not all that different from the method that was once called natural law, and they reach substantive results they could easily reach with natural law.

In the 1990 case *Moore v. Regents of the University of California*, for instance, doctors used blood cells removed from a patient to develop a lucrative cell line. The patient, who learned about the doctors' commercial purpose only after the cells had been taken from his body, argued that the cells were his property and that he was thus entitled to a share of the doctors' revenue. The California Supreme Court was confronted with a question that had never arisen before: does a person own cells that have been removed from his body? No statutes or previous court decisions addressed this question. Technological change had generated a new issue that was not governed by any positive law.[99]

If this question could have arisen in the early 19th century, judges would almost certainly have described their decision-making process as one that relied on natural law. Perhaps they would have identified as a natural principle the doctrine that every person (or, in an age when slavery still existed, every free person) is the owner of his or her own body. They might then have reasoned that a person either does or does not continue to exercise property rights over body parts that have been removed. Judges might have cited examples of conventional ownership practices regarding removed body parts in other contexts, such as organ donation or the disposal of medical waste, as evidence of how ordinary

[98] *Hargrave v. Dusenberry*, 9 N.C. 326, 328 (1823).
[99] *Moore v. Regents of the University of California*, 793 P.2d 479 (Cal. 1990).

people exercising an innate moral faculty instinctively resolved the question. They might have considered the practical consequences of recognizing or not recognizing a patient's property right in these circumstances—whether, for example, recognizing a property right would chill or encourage medical research. All of these considerations would have been understood as part of the process of discerning how the law of nature applied to this particular factual situation.

In 1990, the judges of the California Supreme Court did not conceive their role as involving natural law. Rather, the judges described their decision-making process as involving two kinds of inquiries.

First, they claimed to be discerning the will of the legislature in an indirect fashion, by drawing inferences from statutes that governed other aspects of medical or scientific practice. In his majority opinion, Justice Edward Panelli discussed a state statute addressing the disposal of anatomical waste and the federal statute governing patents. Justice Allen Broussard countered in his dissenting opinion by discussing a state statute regulating organ donations. Both sides agreed that none of these statutes resolved the case, but both sides implied that the statutes offered clues as to what Congress or the California legislature would have wanted the outcome of the case to be. Neither side examined the contemporary practices of ordinary people regarding excised body parts, because the community's intuitive sense of justice had long ago ceased to be an appropriate input for a judge to consider explicitly. But the examination of these statutes was a close substitute. If one assumed that the statutes had been enacted because they reflected community preferences in these matters (or that Californians followed the law, even if grudgingly, when they donated organs and disposed of anatomical waste), the statutes served the same purpose custom once had, as a barometer of the community's innate sense of what was right.

Second, the judges engaged in a debate over which outcome would be better policy. As Panelli noted, "When the proposed application of a very general theory of liability in a new context raises important policy concerns, it is especially important to face those concerns and address them openly."[100] Panelli identified two competing policy concerns: on one side, the importance of allowing patients to make their own medical decisions, and on the other, the fear that imposing liability on the doctors would deter socially useful scientific research. He determined that the latter outweighed the former. "The theory of liability that Moore urges us to endorse threatens to destroy the economic incentive to conduct important medical research," he worried. "If the use of cells in research is a conversion [that is, an unlawful taking of property], then with every cell sample a researcher purchases a ticket in a litigation lottery."[101] Broussard

---

[100] *Id.* at 488.
[101] *Id.* at 496.

retorted that no research would be deterred because liability would be extraordinarily rare. This kind of frank policy discussion had also been part of natural law reasoning in the 19th century. Modern courts still discuss policy, but now they think of it as an end in itself rather than as means of discerning the law of nature. Policy discussion was once said to be part of law-*finding*; now it is said to be part of law-*making*.

Moore is a good example of a recurring phenomenon. To a great extent, courts are still doing what they always did when positive law offers little guidance. Courts try to discern conventional practices, and they try to assess the policy implications of the decision. Ultimately they reach the result they find most reasonable. We no longer use the term "natural law" to describe this process, but it is similar to the process that judges used when natural law was part of the legal system.

That said, there are some differences between the way judges think about such cases today and the way they thought about them in the heyday of natural law. A 19th-century judge who understood himself to be finding the law of nature would be inclined to think in terms of timeless principles, while a 21st-century judge who considers herself an interstitial policymaker would emphasize present-day circumstances. The 19th-century judge in search of natural principles would have recourse to philosophical treatises, some written long before his own era, while the 21st-century judge would be more interested in up-to-date empirical accounts. Most fundamentally, the 19th-century judge thought he was finding the law; the 21st-century judge thinks she is making it.

The consequence of abandoning natural law was thus not any change in the *content* of the law. It was a change in the way judges understood their method of discerning the law. When natural law was a component of the legal system, judges believed that they were finders of law, even in hard cases where the positive law did not yield a certain answer. Today, by contrast, judges in such cases think of themselves as makers of law.

INDEX

For the benefit of digital users, indexed terms that span two pages (e.g., 52–53) may, on occasion, appear on only one of those pages.

Adair v. United States, 211
Adams, Henry, 191–92
Adams, John, 37, 60–61, 109, 119–20
Adams, John Quincy, 145–46, 148
Adams, Thomas, 60–61
Agnew, Daniel, 161–62
Albertsworth, E.F., 171–72
American Indians, 20, 44–45
Ames, James Barr, 191–92, 203
Anthon, John, 53
Aquinas, Thomas, 223–24
Austin, Benjamin, 55–56
Austin, John, 168–69, 193–94

Baldwin, Henry, 11, 88–89
Barber, Arthur, 97
Barculo, Seward, 85
Bartley, Thomas, 155
Bayard, Thomas, 14
Beale, Joseph Henry, 202–3, 204
Becker, Carl, 223
Bennett v. Boggs, 88–89
Bentham, Jeremy, 16, 193–94, 212–13, 214
    influence in United States, 168
    skepticism about natural law, 78, 168–69,
        170–71, 180–81
Berlin, Isaiah, 35–36
Biden, Joseph, 238–39
Bigelow, Melville, 191–92
Billson, W.W., 176–77
Bishop, Joel, 56, 94–95, 129–30, 145–47
Bissell, Clark, 154
Black, Hugo, 232–35
Black, Jeremiah, 91
Blackstone, William, 60–61, 193–94, 207,
    221, 239–40

on common law, 48–49, 98
on custom, 47–48, 56, 182
on judicial review, 72–73, 77–78
on natural law, 12–13, 15–16, 17–19, 24
view of natural law rejected, 168–69, 170–71
Blakeley, William Addison, 177
Bledsoe, Jesse, 128–29
Blythe, Harry Randolph, 217, 218
Bork, Robert, 234–35
Boyle, Robert, 35–36
Brackenridge, Hugh Henry, 52–53
Bradley, Joseph, 14, 147
Bradwell, Myra, 147
Brennan, William, 236–37
Brewer, David, 108
Broussard, Allen, 248–49
Brown, Henry Billings, 181–82
Brown, Rome G., 196
Brown v. Board of Education, 233–34, 238
Burlamaqui, Jean-Jacques, 32–33, 37, 207
    on natural law, 13–14, 15, 178
Butler, Benjamin, 39–40

Cairns, Huntington, 229–30
Calder v. Bull, 74–78, 79, 83–85, 87–88
Caldwell, Henry, 121–22, 157
Campbell, John Wilson, 24
canons of construction, 243–45
capital punishment, 6–7, 137–42, 180
Cardozo, Benjamin, 186–87, 215–16
Carter, James Coolidge, 184–86, 193–94, 217
Cartwright, John, 109
Caverno, Arthur, 138–39
Chase, Salmon, 157, 171–72
Chase, Samuel, 75–76, 77–78, 79, 80, 83–85,
    87–88, 205–7

Cheever, George, 139
Cheves, Langdon, 59
Chipman, Daniel, 44–45
Chipman, Nathaniel, 36, 59
Choate, Rufus, 23
Christiancy, Isaac, 129–30
Christianity
    relation with common law, 6, 97–110, 113–18
    relation with natural law, 3–4, 6, 12–14, 17–18,
        29–30, 96, 118, 169–70, 195, 240–41
    separation from legal system, 96, 110–18
Clarke, Samuel Belcher, 144–45
Clarke, William, 223–24
classical legal thought, 7, 188–89, 218
classical orthodoxy, 189, 190, 197–205, 212
Clay, Henry, 150
Clerke, Thomas, 153
Clifford, Nathan, 86–87
Cobb, Thomas, 150–51
Coburn, Tom, 239–40
codification, 126–27, 212–13
Cogswell, Jonathan, 139–40
Cohen, Morris, 215, 223, 229–30
Coke, Edward, 12–13, 49, 123
Coles, Edward, 138
common law
    American adoption of, 49–51, 59–63
    basis in custom, 46–58
    basis in reason, 46–51, 58–63
    relation with natural law, 4, 63–68
    whether made or found by judges, 4, 46, 63–68,
        188–89, 190, 212–21, 246, 248–49
Conkling, Alfred, 128–29
constitutions, relation with natural law, 6, 19, 21–
        22, 72–95, 169
Cooley, Roger, 121–22
Cooley, Thomas, 92, 104, 206–8
Cooper, Thomas, 39, 113–14, 200
Cover, Robert, 153
Cowell, John, 46–47
Cushing, Caleb, 168–69
Cushing, Luther, 27–28
Cushman, Robert, 210
custom, as basis of common law, 7, 51–58, 182–87

Dane, Nathan, 97, 160–61
Davis, David, 131–32
Davis, John W., 134–35
death penalty. See capital punishment
Declaration of Independence, 7–8, 146, 232–33
Demarest, Theodore, 173–74
Dent, Marmaduke, 113
deSloovere, Frederick, 215
Dickinson, John, 183–84
Dillon, John Forrest, 128, 132–33, 181–82
District of Columbia v. Heller, 237–38, 239–40
Dixon, Luther, 84–85

Doe, Charles, 89–90, 115
Dos Passos, John, 134
Douglas, William, 234
Drake, Charles, 131
Du Ponceau, Peter, 53, 120–21
Duncan, Thomas, 103
Dwight, Theodore, 39–40
Dworkin, Ronald, 230–31

Earl, Robert, 126
economics, 189, 190, 195–97
Elkington, John, 138
Elliott, Edward, 171–72
Ellsworth, Oliver, 74–75
Ely, Richard, 144–45
Emery, Lucilius, 177–78
Ewing, Thomas, 125, 186

Field, David Dudley, 126–27, 212–13
Field, Stephen, 207–8
Fink, Henry Raymond, 170
Fitzhugh, George, 150–51
Fletcher v. Peck, 79–80
Foote, Allen Ripley, 176–77
Fowler, Robert Ludlow, 182–83
Fox, Jabez, 216–17
Frank, Jerome, 221, 225–26, 227
Frankfurter, Felix, 232
Friese, Philip, 23
Fuller, Lon, 228–31

Gardner v. Village of Newburgh, 93–94
Gibson, John Bannister, 26–27, 57–58,
        107, 212–13
Gilbert, Hiram, 121–22
Gilbert, Sylvester, 39
Glover, John, 135–36
Goebel, Julius, 177–78
Goodell, Lavinia, 147
Goodenow, John, 13–14
Gray, John Chipman, 183, 186, 202, 216–17,
        219, 229
Green, Nathan, 81–82
Greenleaf, Simon, 96
Gridley, Jeremiah, 37
Grimké, Thomas, 33
Griswold v. Connecticut, 233–34

Hadley, Arthur Twining, 177–78
Hale, Clarence, 186–87
Hale, Matthew, 97–98, 113–14
Hall, Jerome, 224
Halleck, Henry, 41
Hammond, William Gardiner, 170–71, 193–94
Harrington, Samuel, 152
Harris, William Littleton, 150
Hart, Albert Bushnell, 171–72

Hart, H.L.A., 230
Hicks, Frederick Charles, 242
Hildreth, Richard, 160
Hill, Jeremiah, 64–65
Hilliard, Francis, 22
historical jurisprudence, 189, 190, 191–94, 212
Hoffman, David, 11, 16, 38, 120–21, 197
Holaind, René, 177
Holcombe, James, 150–51
Holdsworth, William, 98
Holmes, Oliver Wendell, Jr., 218, 225
    on classical orthodoxy, 203
    on historical jurisprudence, 189, 192–93, 194
    on judges as makers of law, 213–14, 220–21
    on natural law, 174–75, 177–78
    on substantive due process, 210–11
Hopkins, John Henry, 112
Hopkinson, Joseph, 58–59
Hornblower, William, 182
Hosmer, Stephen, 83–84
Hosmer, William, 13
Hume, David, 16
Humphries, Charles, 60–61
Hunter, W.A., 170
Hurlbut, E.P., 16
Huxley, Thomas, 172–73

Ingersoll, Charles, 124–25
international law, 41, 241–42
Iredell, James, 76–79, 80, 83–84, 88–89, 131–32

Jefferson, Thomas, 37, 109–10, 113–14, 160–61
Jhering, Rudolf von, 191–92
Johnson, William, 79–80
Johnson v. M'Intosh, 20
Johnston, Frank, 173–74
judges, as finders or makers of law, 1–2, 3, 63–68, 188–89, 190, 212–21, 246, 248–49
Judson, Frederick, 175–76

Kagan, Elena, 239–40
Kames, Lord, 15, 31
Keener, William, 198–99
Kellogg, George, 33–34
Kennedy, Anthony, 232–33, 235–36, 237
Kent, James
    on Christianity, 98–102, 108, 109, 115
    on common law, 51, 52–53, 64–65, 187
    on natural law, 14–15, 22–23, 24–25, 93–94, 200–201
    on published case reports, 119–20, 125–26
    reputation of, 126
Kessler, Friedrich, 224
King, Martin Luther, 7–8
Kinkead, Edgar, 214
Kirk, Edward, 139–40
Kohl, Herbert, 238–39

Langdell, Christopher, 197–200, 202–4, 205, 218–19
law publishing
    growth of, 6, 119–28
    relation with natural law, 6, 128–36, 170
Lawson, John, 56, 59, 121–22
Leahy, Patrick, 238–39
legal education
    classical orthodoxy in, 198, 204–5
    natural law in, 7, 37–41, 162, 223–24
legal realism, 188–89, 218, 221, 224–27
Lehrman, Lewis, 238
Letourneau, Charles, 144
Lieber, Francis, 13, 63–64, 156
Livingston, Henry Brockholst, 29
Livingston v. Moore, 89
Llewellyn, Karl, 221, 226–27
Lochner v. New York, 209, 210–11, 232
Locke, John, 33–34
Lowber v. Wells, 62
Lowell, Abbot Lawrence, 171–72
Lowrey, Grosvenor, 156
Lucey, Francis, 224–25
Lumpkin, Joseph Henry, 67, 94, 103–4

Mackintosh, James, 32–33
Maine, Henry Sumner, 144, 168–69, 213
Mansfield, Lord, 37, 152
Marshall, John, 20, 79–80, 153
Mason, George, 18–19
McLean, John, 153–54
McMurray, Orin, 180–81
Mill, John Stuart, 172
Miller, J. Bleecker, 170–71
Miller, Samuel, 133
Minge v. Gilmour, 76–78
Miranda v. Arizona, 233–34
Montesquieu, Baron de, 13–14, 31, 38–39
Moore, Alfred, 131–32
Moore, John Bassett, 136
Moore, Roy, 240–41
Moore v. Regents of the University of California, 247–49
Morton, Perez, 141
Moulton, Joseph, 17–18
Murphy, J.H., 33–34
Murray, Hugh, 82–83

Nash, Simeon, 161
National Rifle Association, 7–8
Natural Law Forum, 227–28
Natural Law Institute, 227–28
natural rights, 4
Nicholas, Samuel, 157–58
Ninth Amendment, 74
Noonan, Herbert, 223–24

Obergefell v. Hodges, 235–37, 240–41
Oliver, Benjamin, 12–13
O'Neall, John Belton, 103–4
Oppenheim, Lassa, 242
Ordronaux, John, 175–76
originalism, 237–38
O'Scannlain, Diarmuid, 240

Page, Henry Folsom, 43–44
Paige, Alonzo, 40–41
Panelli, Edward, 248–49
Parker, Joel, 131
Parkhurst, Charles Henry, 143–44
Paterson, William, 79
Pierson v. Post, 29
Planned Parenthood v. Casey, 235, 236–37
Platt, W.H., 106–7
Plessy v. Ferguson, 158–59
Pomeroy, John Norton, 213
Porter, William, 22–23
positive law, relation with natural law, 12, 18–31
Positivism, 4, 193–94, 228–31
Pound, Roscoe, 218, 221
    on custom, 182–83
    on historical jurisprudence, 194
    on natural law, 173, 175, 194, 210, 222–23, 229
Proctor, Lucius, 129–30
Proffatt, John, 33–34
property, 6–7, 44–45, 142–45, 170,
    180–82, 242–43
Purrington, Tobias, 138–39

Quincy, Josiah, 38–39

Rantoul, Robert, 212–13
Rawle, William, 17, 20–21
Redfield, Amasa, 180–81
Rehnquist, William, 236–37
religion. *See* Christianity
Republican Party, 7–8
Richardson, James, 14–15
Richmond, H.L., 88
Ritter, George, 104
Roane, Spencer, 61
Roberts, John, 236
Robeson, George, 88
Roe v. Wade, 231–32, 233–34
Roosevelt, James, 62
Root, Erastus, 100–1
Root, Jesse, 57–58, 64–65
Rose, Uriah, 134
Roselius, Christian, 150
Ross, John, 58–59
Rush, Benjamin, 139
Rush, Jacob, 12
Rush, Richard, 61
Russell, Isaac Franklin, 162, 171–72

Rutherforth, Thomas, 16, 87–88, 178
Ryan, Edward, 40–41, 147

Sampson, William, 122–23
Savigny, Friedrich Karl von, 191–92
Scalia, Antonin, 218–19, 232–33, 235, 236,
    237–38, 246
Schouler, James, 43–44, 142–43
science, law as a, 198–202
Sedgwick, Theodore, 83–84, 106
Segregation, 157–60, 170
Seneca Falls Declaration, 146
Seward, William, 149–50
Sharswood, George, 39
Shattuck, Frederick Cheever, 199
Shaw, Lemuel, 21–22, 25–26, 49–50, 111–12,
    126, 155
Shelby, D.D., 157–58
Shewalter, J.D., 131
Slaughter-House Cases, 207–8
Slavery, 6–7, 20, 149–58, 159–60, 162–63, 170
Smith, Adam, 15
Smith, Edwin, 173–74
Smith, George, 125–26, 176, 219
Smith, Munroe, 215
Snyder, William, 159
Somerset v. Stewart, 152
Souter, David, 232–33
Southmayd, Charles, 131–32
Spencer, Arthur, 223
Spooner, Lysander, 149–51
    statutes, relation to natural law, 22–23, 93–95,
        209, 243–44
Stevens, John Paul, 239–40
Story, Joseph
    on Christianity, 101–2, 109–10, 115
    on common law, 52, 61–62, 219–20
    on constitutional rights, 21–22, 80
    on equity, 30
    law lectures of, 38–39, 101–2
    on natural law, 11, 24–25, 80
    on published case reports, 120–21
    on slavery, 155
Strong, William, 116
substantive due process, 189–90, 205–12
    natural law origin of, 84–85, 206–9
Sullivan, James, 57–58
Sumner, Charles, 138, 149–50
Swift, Zephaniah, 33, 60–61
Swift v. Tyson, 219–20

Tappan, Benjamin, 65–66
Teichmueller, Hans, 176–77
Terrett v. Taylor, 80
Terry, Charles Thaddeus, 199–200
Terry, David, 83
Thayer, Ezra, 215

Thayer, James Bradley, 115–16, 192
Thomas, Clarence, 238–40
Thomas, Mary, 148
Thompson, Robert, 195–96
Thompson, Seymour, 132–33
Tiedeman, Christopher, 102, 162–63, 197–98, 209–10
Tiffany, Joel, 22, 149–50
Tocqueville, Alexis de, 137
Tompkins, Daniel, 101
Trimble, Robert, 91
Tucker, Henry St. George, 31–32, 39, 142–43, 197

Upshur, Abel, 168–69

Valentine, Daniel, 148
Van Ness v. Pacard, 61–62
Verplanck, Gulian, 90

Waite, Morrison, 131–32
Walker, James, 22
Walker, Timothy, 121, 122–23, 143–44
Wambaugh, Eugene, 199, 214
Wanamaker, Reuben, 133
Ware, Ashur, 22

Warner, Henry Whiting, 200–1
Warren, Charles, 121–22
Webster, Daniel, 105–6
Webster, William, 215
Weightman, Hugh, 170–71
West, John, 127–28
Wharton, Francis, 73–74, 115–16, 192
Wheaton, Henry, 41
Whyte, Robert, 112
Wigmore, John Henry, 202
Wilgus, H.L., 199
Wilkin, Robert, 159
Willett, J.J., 133–34
Wilson, James
    on common law, 52–53, 58–59, 66–67, 97, 200
    death of, 74–75
    on international law, 41
    on natural law, 31–32, 33
Wilson, Woodrow, 172–73
Women, role of, 6–7, 145–49, 162–63, 180
Wood, Henry, 196, 197
Wood, Thomas, 46–47, 49
Woodruff, Edwin, 182–83
Wright, Benjamin, 210
Wythe, George, 51, 67–68